Sociological Paradigms and Organisational Analysis

Elements of the Sociology of Corporate Life

Gibson Burrell
Lecturer in the Department of Behaviour in Organisations,
University of Lancaster, England

Gareth Morgan
Associate Professor of Organisational Behaviour and
Industrial Relations, York University, Toronto

ASHGATE

First published in 1979 by Heinemann Educational Books
Reprinted 1980, 1982

Reprinted 1985, 1987, 1988 by Gower Publishing Company Limited
Reprinted 1992 by Ashgate Publishing Limited

Reprinted 1993, 1994 by Arena

Published by
Ashgate Publishing Limited
Wey Court East
Union Road
Farnham, Surrey
GU9 7PT England

Ashgate Publishing Company
Suite 420
101 Cherry Street
Burlington, VT 05401-4405
USA

Ashgate website: http://www.ashgate.com

Reprinted 1998, 2000, 2001, 2003, 2005, 2006, 2008, 2009, 2011 (twice)

British Library Cataloguing in Publication Data
Burrell, Gibson
      Sociological paradigms and organisational
      analysis : elements of the sociology of corporate
      life.
      1. Organisation
      I. Title II. Morgan, Gareth
      302.3'5   HM131

ISBN 978 0 566 05148 7 (HBK)
      978 1 85742 114 9 (PBK)

#7829654

MIX
Paper from
responsible sources
FSC FSC® C018575
www.fsc.org

Printed and bound in Great Britain by
the MPG Books Group, UK

Contents

List of Figures

List of Tables

Acknowledgements

We have worked on this book at a pace which has varied from the intense to the intolerable, and as a consequence we have asked and received a great deal of our families and friends. We owe to them all a great debt of thanks. In particular we wish to thank Christine Burrell for her considerable patience, help and encouragement, which were stretched up to and sometimes beyond the limits. Our work owes much to our colleagues and students at Lancaster, particularly those in the Department of Behaviour in Organisations, where the stimulating and convivial combination of critical enquiry, friendship and debate has been a major feature of our enterprise.

The ideas expressed in the book are the product of extensive discussion and as such are to be seen as shared. However, the responsibility for the production of the manuscript in its present form has fallen largely upon Gareth Morgan, who has undertaken the task of converting early drafts into a finished text and of imposing stylistic unity on the work as a whole. Needless to say, in the spirit of our endeavour, responsibility, credit and blame are jointly assumed.

Thanks are due to Jean Atkinson, Janet Fisher, Joy Howson, Sue Lawrence and Lynne Rymarz for typing various sections of the manuscript. The assistance of the Social Science Research Council, in sponsoring field research which contributed to many of the ideas presented here, is gratefully acknowledged.

Gibson Burrell would like to register his gratitude to his mother and family, especially to Christine who, while the book was being written, carried twins *in* and *ex utero* while he merely carried books *in* and *ex libris*.

Gareth Morgan wishes to extend special thanks and appreciation to his parents, Idris and Rachel Morgan, for all that they have given.

We also wish to thank the following publishers for permission to reproduce extracts from their books on the pages indicated:

Harvard University Press: F.J. Roethlisberger and W.J. Dickson, *Management and the Worker* (1939), on pp. 134,

136−7, 137−8, and Figs. 5.3 and 5.4 on pp. 135 and 137.

Houghton Mifflin Company: A. Rose, *Human Behavior and Social Processes* (1962), on pp. 79−80.

John Wiley & Sons, Inc.: P.M. Blau, *Exchange and Power in Social Life* (1964), on pp. 89, 90.

Merlin Press Ltd.: P. Thévenaz, *What is Phenomenology?* (1962), on p. 241.

Methuen and Co Ltd.: Jean-Paul Sartre, *Being and Nothingness* (1966), on p. 305.

Penguin Books Ltd.: Steven Lukes, *Emile Durkheim: His Life and Work: A Historical and Critical Study* (1973), on pp. 45−6.

Prentice-Hall, Inc.: L.A. Coser, *Georg Simmel* (1965), on pp. 70, 71, 72.

Routledge and Kegan Paul Ltd.: John Rex, *Key Problems in Sociological Theory* (1961), on pp. 353−4.

University of Chicago Press: H. Blumer, *The Sociological Implications of the Thought of G.H. Mead* (1966), on pp. 78, 81.

Gibson Burrell, Gareth Morgan
Lancaster, December 1978

Introduction

This book, which has devoured the last two years of our lives, is the product of a friendship and intellectual partnership. It began as an innocuous idea which grew with such strength that it developed into a 'way of seeing'. It has changed the ways in which we think about social theory, and we hope that it will do the same for others.

The book is intended to clarify and help overcome what seem to be some of the major sources of confusion within the social sciences at the present time. Initially it had a fairly specific objective: to attempt to relate theories of organisation to their wider sociological context. In the course of development, however, this endeavour widened in scope and evolved into an enterprise embracing many aspects of philosophy and social theory in general. As such it now stands as a discourse in social theory of relevance to many social science disciplines, of which those in the general area of organisation studies – industrial sociology, organisation theory, organisational psychology and industrial relations – are but special cases by which we illustrate our general themes.

Our proposition is that social theory can usefully be conceived in terms of four key paradigms based upon different sets of metatheoretical assumptions about the nature of social science and the nature of society. The four paradigms are founded upon mutually exclusive views of the social world. Each stands in its own right and generates its own distinctive analyses of social life. With regard to the study of organisations, for example, each paradigm generates theories and perspectives which are in fundamental opposition to those generated in other paradigms.

Such an analysis of social theory brings us face to face with the nature of the assumptions which underwrite different approaches to social science. It cuts through the surface detail which dresses many social theories to what is fundamental in determining the way in which we see the world which we are purporting to analyse. It stresses the crucial role played by the scientist's frame of reference in the generation of social theory and research.

The situation with regard to the field of organisation studies at the present time, as in other social science disciplines, is that a vast proportion of theory and research is located within the bounds of just one of the four paradigms to be considered here. Indeed, the bulk of it is located within the context of a relatively narrow range of theoretical possibilities which define that one paradigm. It is no exaggeration, therefore, to suggest that the social-scientific enterprise in general is built upon an extremely narrow set of metatheoretical assumptions. This concentration of effort in a relatively narrow area defines what is usually regarded as the dominant orthodoxy within a subject. Because this orthodoxy is so dominant and strong, its adherents often take it for granted as right and self-evident. Rival perspectives within the same paradigm or outside its bounds appear as satellites defining alternative points of view. Their impact upon the orthodoxy, however, is rarely very significant. They are seldom strong enough to establish themselves as anything more than a somewhat deviant set of approaches. As a result the possibilities which they offer are rarely explored, let alone understood.

In order to understand alternative points of view it is important that a theorist be fully aware of the assumptions upon which his own perspective is based. Such an appreciation involves an intellectual journey which takes him outside the realm of his own familiar domain. It requires that he become aware of the boundaries which define his perspective. It requires that he journey into the unexplored. It requires that he become familiar with paradigms which are not his own. Only then can he look back and appreciate in full measure the precise nature of his starting point.

The work presented here is an attempt to take the student of organisations into realms which he has probably not explored before. It is a journey upon which we, the authors, unwittingly embarked as a result of certain nagging doubts and uncertainties about the utility and validity of much contemporary theory and research in our subject. We were concerned about the way in which studies of organisational activities had generated mountains of theory and research which seemed to have no obvious links outside narrow discipline areas. We were concerned about the essentially ephemeral nature of our subject. We were concerned about the academic sectarianism reflected at various times in open hostility, ostrich-like indifference and generally poor-quality dialogue and debate between essentially related schools of thought. In short, we felt that our subject area called for a close examination of the assumptions upon which it is based with a view to seeing it in a new, and hopefully refreshing, light. Our book in essence presents an account of our journey and a record of the conclusions and insights which have emerged.

We began our enterprise by considering how we could distinguish between different approaches to the study of organisations. The view that 'all theories of organisation are based upon a philosophy of science and a theory of society' seemed to recur time and again in our conversations and we soon found it defining two major dimensions of analysis. Although organisation theorists are not always very explicit about the basic assumptions which inform their point of view, it is clear that they all take a stand on each of these issues. Whether they are aware of it or not, they bring to their subject of study a frame of reference which reflects a whole series of assumptions about the nature of the social world and the way in which it might be investigated.

Our attempt to explore these assumptions led us into the realm of social philosophy. We were confronted with problems of ontology and epistemology and other issues which rarely receive consideration within the field of organisation studies. As we investigated these issues we found that they underpinned the great philosophical debates between social theorists from rival intellectual traditions. We realised that the orthodoxy in our subject was based in essence upon just one of these traditions, and that the satellite perspectives which we had observed as surrounding the orthodoxy were, in fact, derived from quite a separate intellectual source. We realised that they were attempting to articulate points of view which derived from diametrically opposed assumptions about the basic nature of the social world; accordingly they subscribed to quite different assumptions about the very nature of the social-scientific enterprise itself.

In investigating assumptions with regard to the nature of society we were, at first, able to operate on firmer ground. The sociology of the 1960s had focused upon the 'order-conflict debate' — whether sociology emphasises the 'problem of order' or the 'problem of conflict and change'. By the late 1960s the debate had been pronounced dead, and these two views of society were seen merely as two aspects of the same problematic. In reviewing the literature relevant to this debate we became increasingly convinced that it had met a premature death. Whilst it was clear that academic sociologists had convinced themselves that the 'problem of conflict' could be subsumed under the 'problem of order', theorists outside this tradition, particularly those interested in Marxist theory, were actively engaged in the development of social theories which placed the problems of conflict and change at the forefront of their analysis. Although academic sociologists and

Marxist social theorists appeared content to work in isolation, ignoring the contradictory perspectives which they presented, it seemed that any adequate analysis of theories of society must take these rival perspectives into account.

Our journey into Marxist literature took us into yet another new realm as far as our initial interests were concerned. We were surprised to find striking parallels between intellectual developments within Marxist theory and academic sociology. We found that the assumptions about the nature of social science which had divided academic sociologists into different schools of thought also divided Marxist theorists. In that realm, too, the dominant theoretical framework was surrounded by satellite schools of thought offering rival explanations. Pursuing these traditions to their source, we found that they emerged from precisely the same bounds of social philosophy which had underwritten divergent elements within sociology itself. It became clear that the rival traditions emphasising 'order' as opposed to 'conflict' shared the same pedigree as far as their roots in social philosophy were concerned. Deriving from similar assumptions about the ontological and epistemological status of social science, they had been wedded to fundamentally different frames of reference with regard to the nature of society.

Given these cross linkages between rival intellectual traditions, it became clear to us that our two sets of assumptions could be counter-posed to produce an analytical scheme for studying social theories in general: the two sets of assumptions defined four basic paradigms reflecting quite separate views of social reality. On attempting to relate this scheme to the social science literature we found that we possessed an extremely powerful tool for negotiating our way through different subject areas, and one which made sense of a great deal of the confusion which characterises much contemporary debate within the social sciences. The scheme offered itself as a form of intellectual map upon which social theories could be located according to their source and tradition. Theories rarely if ever appear out of thin air; they usually have a well established history behind them. We found that our intellectual map allowed us to trace their evolution. Theories fell into place according to their origins. Where rival intellectual traditions had been fused, distinctive hybrid versions seemed to appear. What had first offered itself as a simple classificatory device for organising the literature now presented itself as an analytical tool. It pointed us towards new areas of investigation. It allowed us to appraise and evaluate theories against the backcloth of the intellectual tradition which they sought to emulate. It allowed us to identify embryonic theories and anticipate potential lines of development. It allowed us to write this book.

In the following chapters we seek to present our analytical scheme and to use it to negotiate a way through the literature on social theory and organisational analysis. We have aimed to present it as clearly and directly as we can whilst avoiding the pitfalls of oversimplification. But the concepts of one paradigm cannot easily be interpreted in terms of those of another. To understand a new paradigm one has to explore it from the inside, in terms of its own distinctive problematic. Thus, whilst we have made every effort to present our account as plainly as possible as far as the use of the English language is concerned, we have necessarily had to draw upon concepts which may at times be unfamiliar.

The remaining chapters in Part I define the nature of our two key dimensions of analysis and the paradigms which arise within their bounds. In this analysis we polarise a number of issues and make much use of rough dichotomisations as a means of presenting our case. We do so not merely for the purposes of classification, but to forge a working tool. We advocate our scheme as a heuristic device rather than as a set of rigid definitions.

In Part II we put our analytical framework into operation. For each of our four paradigms we conduct an analysis of relevant social theory and then proceed to relate theories of organisation to this wider background. Each of the paradigms is treated in terms consistent with its own distinctive frame of reference. No attempt is made to criticise and evaluate from a perspective *outside* the paradigm. Such criticism is all too easy but self-defeating, since it is usually directed at the foundations of the paradigm itself. All four paradigms can successfully be demolished in these terms. What we seek to do is to develop the perspective characteristic of the paradigm and draw out some of its implications for social analysis. In so doing we have found that we are frequently able to strengthen the conceptualisations which each paradigm generates as far as the study of organisations is concerned. Our guiding rule has been to seek to offer something to each paradigm within the terms of its own problematic. The chapters in Part II, therefore, are essentially expository in nature. They seek to provide a detailed framework upon which future debate might fruitfully be based.

Part III presents a short conclusion which focuses upon some of the principal issues which emerge from our analysis.

1. Assumptions about the Nature of Social Science

Central to our thesis is the idea that 'all theories of organisation are based upon a philosophy of science and a theory of society'. In this chapter we wish to address ourselves to the first aspect of this thesis and to examine some of the philosophical assumptions which underwrite different approaches to social science. We shall argue that it is convenient to conceptualise social science in terms of four sets of assumptions related to ontology, epistemology, human nature and methodology.

All social scientists approach their subject via explicit or implicit assumptions about the nature of the social world and the way in which it may be investigated. First, there are assumptions of an *ontological* nature – assumptions which concern the very essence of the phenomena under investigation. Social scientists, for example, are faced with a basic ontological question: whether the 'reality' to be investigated is external to the individual – imposing itself on individual consciousness from without – or the product of individual consciousness; whether 'reality' is of an 'objective' nature, or the product of individual cognition; whether 'reality' is a given 'out there' in the world, or the product of one's mind.

Associated with this ontological issue, is a second set of assumptions of an *epistemological* nature. These are assumptions about the grounds of knowledge – about how one might begin to understand the world and communicate this as knowledge to fellow human beings. These assumptions entail ideas, for example, about what forms of knowledge can be obtained, and how one can sort out what is to be regarded as 'true' from what is to be regarded as 'false'. Indeed, this dichotomy of 'true' and 'false' itself pre-supposes a certain epistemological stance. It is predicated upon a view of the nature of knowledge itself: whether, for example, it is possible to identify and communicate the nature of knowledge as being hard, real and capable of being transmitted in tangible form, or whether 'knowledge' is of a softer, more subjective, spiritual or even transcendental kind, based on experience and insight of a unique and essentially personal nature. The epistemological assumptions in these instances determine extreme positions on the issue of whether knowledge is something which can be acquired on the one hand, or is something which has to be personally experienced on the other.

Associated with the ontological and epistemological issues, but conceptually separate from them, is a third set of assumptions concerning *human nature* and, in particular, the relationship between human beings and their environment. All social science, clearly, must be predicated upon this type of assumption, since human life is essentially the subject and object of enquiry. Thus, we can identify perspectives in social science which entail a view of human beings responding in a mechanistic or even deterministic fashion to the situations encountered in their external world. This view tends to be one in which human beings and their experiences are regarded as products of the environment; one in which humans are conditioned by their external circumstances. This extreme perspective can be contrasted with one which attributes to human beings a much more creative role: with a perspective where 'free will' occupies the centre of the stage; where man is regarded as the creator of his environment, the controller as opposed to the controlled, the master rather than the marionette. In these two extreme views of the relationship between human beings and their environment we are identifying a great philosophical debate between the advocates of determinism on the one hand and voluntarism on the other. Whilst there are social theories which adhere to each of these extremes, as we shall see, the assumptions of many social scientists are pitched somewhere in the range between.

The three sets of assumptions outlined above have direct implications of a *methodological* nature. Each one has important consequences for the way in which one attempts to investigate and obtain 'knowledge' about the social world. Different ontologies, epistemologies and models of human nature are likely to incline social scientists towards different methodologies. The possible range of choice is indeed so large that what is regarded as science by the traditional 'natural scientist' covers but a small range of options. It is possible, for example, to identify methodologies employed in social science research which treat the social world like the natural world, as being hard, real and external to the individual, and others which view it as being of a much softer, personal and more subjective quality.

If one subscribes to a view of the former kind, which treats the social world as if it were a hard, external, objective reality, then the scientific endeavour is likely to focus upon an analysis of relationships and regularities between the various elements which it comprises. The concern, therefore, is with the identification and definition of these elements and with the discovery of ways in which these relationships can be expressed. The methodological issues of importance are thus the concepts themselves, their measurement and the identification of underlying themes. This perspective expresses itself most forcefully in a search for universal laws which explain and govern the reality which is being observed.

If one subscribes to the alternative view of social reality, which stresses the importance of the subjective experience of individuals in the creation of the social world, then the search for understanding focuses upon different issues and approaches them in different ways. The principal concern is with an understanding of the way in which the individual creates, modifies and interprets the world in which he or she finds himself. The emphasis in extreme cases tends to be placed upon the explanation and understanding of what is unique and particular to the individual rather than of what is general and universal. This approach questions whether there exists an external reality worthy of study. In methodological terms it is an approach which emphasises the relativistic nature of the social world to such an extent that it may be perceived as 'anti-scientific' by reference to the ground rules commonly applied in the natural sciences.

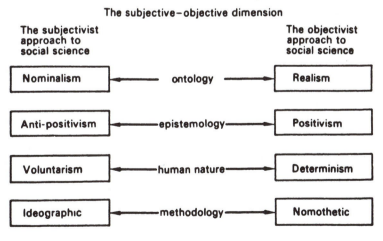

Figure 1.1   A scheme for analysing assumptions about the nature of social science

In this brief sketch of various ontological, epistemological, human and methodological standpoints which characterise approaches to social sciences, we have sought to illustrate two broad and somewhat polarised perspectives. Figure 1.1 seeks to depict these in a more rigorous fashion in terms of what we shall describe as the subjective—objective dimension. It identifies the four sets of assumptions relevant to our understanding of social science, characterising each by the descriptive labels under which they have been debated in the literature on social philosophy. In the following section of this chapter we will review each of the four debates in necessarily brief but more systematic terms.

The Strands of Debate
Nominalism–realism: the ontological debate[1]

These terms have been the subject of much discussion in the literature and there are great areas of controversy surrounding them. The nominalist position revolves around the assumption that the social world external to individual cognition is made up of nothing more than names, concepts and labels which are used to structure reality. The nominalist does not admit to there being any 'real' structure to the world which these concepts are used to describe. The 'names' used are regarded as artificial creations whose utility is based upon their convenience as tools for describing, making sense of and negotiating the external world. Nominalism is often equated with conventionalism, and we will make no distinction between them.[2]

Realism, on the other hand, postulates that the social world external to individual cognition is a real world made up of hard, tangible and relatively immutable structures. Whether or not we label and perceive these structures, the realists maintain, they still exist as empirical entities. We may not even be aware of the existence of certain crucial structures and therefore have no 'names' or concepts to articulate them. For the realist, the social world exists independently of an individual's appreciation of it. The individual is seen as being born into and living within a social world which has a reality of its own. It is not something which the individual creates—it exists 'out there'; ontologically it is prior to the existence and consciousness of any single human being. For the realist, the social world has an existence which is as hard and concrete as the natural world.[3]

Anti-positivism–positivism: the epistemological debate[4]

It has been maintained that 'the word "positivist" like the word "bourgeois" has become more of a derogatory epithet than a useful descriptive concept'.[5] We intend to use it here in the latter sense, as a descriptive concept which can be used to characterise a particular type of epistemology. Most of the descriptions of positivism in current usage refer to one or more of the ontological, epistemological and methodological dimensions of our scheme for analysing assumptions with regard to social science. It is also sometimes mistakenly equated with empiricism. Such conflations cloud basic issues and contribute to the use of the term in a derogatory sense.

We use 'positivist' here to characterise epistemologies which seek to explain and predict what happens in the social world by searching for regularities and causal relationships between its constituent elements. Positivist epistemology is in essence based upon the traditional approaches which dominate the natural sciences. Positivists may differ in terms of detailed approach. Some would claim, for example, that hypothesised regularities can be verified by an adequate experimental research programme. Others would maintain that hypotheses can only be falsified and never demonstrated to be 'true'.[6] However, both 'verificationists' and 'falsificationists' would accept that the growth of knowledge is essentially a cumulative process in which new insights are added to the existing stock of knowledge and false hypotheses eliminated.

The epistemology of anti-positivism may take various forms but is firmly set against the utility of a search for laws or underlying regularities in the world of social affairs. For the anti-positivist, the social world is essentially relativistic and can only be understood from the point of view of the individuals who are directly involved in the activities which are to be studied. Anti-positivists reject the standpoint of the 'observer', which characterises positivist epistemology, as a valid vantage point for understanding human activities. They maintain that one can only 'understand' by occupying the frame of reference of the participant in action. One has to understand from the inside rather than the outside. From this point of view social science is seen as being essentially a subjective rather than an objective enterprise. Anti-positivists tend to reject the notion that science can generate objective knowledge of any kind.[7]

Voluntarism–determinism: the 'human nature' debate

This debate revolves around the issue of what model of man is reflected in any given social-scientific theory. At one extreme we can identify a determinist view which regards man and his activities as being completely determined by the situation or 'environment' in which he is located. At another extreme we can identify the voluntarist view that man is completely autonomous and free-willed. Insofar as social science theories are concerned to understand human activities, they must incline implicitly or explicitly to one or other of these points of view, or adopt an intermediate standpoint which allows for the influence of both situational and voluntary factors in accounting for the activities of human beings. Such assumptions are essential elements in social-scientific theories, since they define in broad terms the nature of the relationships between man and the society in which he lives.[8]

Ideographic–nomothetic theory: the methodological debate

The ideographic approach to social science is based on the view that one can only understand the social world by obtaining first-hand knowledge of the subject under investigation. It thus places considerable stress upon getting close to one's subject and exploring its detailed background and life history. The ideographic approach emphasises the analysis of the subjective accounts which one generates by 'getting inside' situations and involving oneself in the everyday flow of life – the detailed analysis of the insights generated by such encounters with one's subject and the insights revealed in impressionistic accounts found in diaries, biographies and journalistic records. The ideographic method stresses the importance of letting one's subject unfold its nature and characteristics during the process of investigation.[9]

The nomothetic approach to social science lays emphasis on the importance of basing research upon systematic protocol and technique. It is epitomised in the approach and methods employed in the natural sciences, which focus upon the process of testing hypotheses in accordance with the canons of scientific rigour. It is preoccupied with the construction of scientific tests and the use of quantitative techniques for the analysis of data. Surveys, questionnaires, personality tests and standardised research instruments of all kinds are prominent among the tools which comprise nomothetic methodology.[10]

Analysing Assumptions about the Nature of Social Science

These four sets of assumptions with regard to the nature of social science provide an extremely powerful tool for the analysis of social theory. In much of the literature there is a tendency to conflate the issues which are involved. We wish to argue here that considerable advantages accrue from treating these four strands of social-scientific debate as analytically distinct. While in practice there is often a strong relationship between the positions adopted on each of the four strands, assumptions about each can in fact vary quite considerably. It is worth examining this point in more detail.

The extreme positions on each of the four strands are reflected in the two major intellectual traditions which have dominated social science over the last two hundred years. The first of these is usually described as 'sociological positivism'. In essence this reflects the attempt to apply models and methods derived from the natural sciences to the study of human affairs. It treats the social world as if it were the natural world, adopting a 'realist' approach to ontology. This is backed up by a 'positivist' epistemology, relatively 'deterministic' views of human nature and the use of 'nomothetic' methodologies. The second intellectual tradition, that of 'German idealism', stands in complete opposition to this. In essence it is based upon the premise that the ultimate reality of the universe lies in 'spirit' or 'idea' rather than in the data of sense perception. It is essentially 'nominalist' in its approach to social reality. In contrast to the natural sciences, it stresses the essentially subjective nature of human affairs, denying the utility and relevance of the models and methods of natural science to studies in this realm. It is 'anti-positivist' in epistemology, 'voluntarist' with regard to human nature and it favours ideographic methods as a foundation for social analysis. Sociological positivism and German idealism thus define the objective and subjective extremes of our model.

Many sociologists and organisation theorists have been brought up within the tradition of sociological positivism, without exposure to the basic tenets of German idealism. Social science for them is seen as consonant with the configuration of assumptions which characterise the objective extreme of our model. However, over the last seventy years or so there has been an increasing interaction between these two traditions, particularly at a socio-philosophical level. As a result intermediate points of view have emerged, each with its own distinctive configuration of assumptions about the nature of social science. They have all spawned theories, ideas and approaches characteristic of their intermediate position. As we shall argue in later chapters, developments in phenomenology, ethnomethodology and the action frame of reference are to be understood in these terms. These perspectives, whilst offering their own special brand of insight, have also often been used as launching pads for attacks on sociological positivism and have generated a considerable amount of debate between rival schools of thought. The nature of this debate can only be fully understood by grasping and appreciating the different assumptions which underwrite the competing points of view.

It is our contention that the analytical scheme offered here enables one to do precisely this. It is offered not as a mere classificatory device, but as an important tool for negotiating social theory. It draws attention to key assumptions. It allows one to focus on precise issues which differentiate socio-scientific approaches. It draws attention to the degree of congruency between the four sets of assumptions about social science which characterise any given theorist's point of view. We offer it here as the first principal dimension of our theoretical scheme for analysing theory in general and organisational theory in particular. For the sake of convenience we shall normally refer to it as the 'subjective—objective' dimension, two descriptive labels which perhaps capture the points of commonality between the four analytical strands.

Notes and References

1. For a further discussion of the nominalism—realism debate, see Kolakowski (1972), pp. 15–16.
2. Kolakowski (1972), pp. 158–9. In its most extreme form nominalism does not recognise the existence of any world outside the realm of individual consciousness. This is the solipsist position, which we discuss in more detail in Chapter 6.

3. For a comprehensive review of 'realism', see Keat and Urry (1975), pp. 27–45. They make much of the distinction between 'positivism' and 'realism' but, as they admit, these terms are used in a somewhat unconventional way.
4. For a further discussion of the positivism—anti-positivism debate, see, for example, Giddens (1974) and Walsh (1972).
5. Giddens (1974), p. 1.
6. See, for example, Popper (1963).
7. For a good illustration of an anti-positivist view of science, see Douglas (1970b), pp. 3–44.
8. The human nature debate in its widest sense involves many other issues which we have not referred to here. The precise model of man to be employed in any analytical scheme, however, is underwritten by assumptions which reflect the voluntarism-determinism issue in one way or another. We have isolated this element of the debate here as a way of treating at its most basic level a necessary assumption of all social-scientific theories which purport to account for human activities. Detailed propositions with regard to the precise explanation of human activities elaborate in one way or another this basic theme.
9. For an excellent discussion of the nature of the ideographic approach to social science, see Blumer (1969), ch. 1.
10. It is important to emphasise here that both nomothetic and ideographic methodologies can be employed in a deductive and inductive sense. Whilst the inductive—deductive debate in science is a subject of considerable interest and importance, we do not see it as being central to the four dimensions suggested here as a means of distinguishing between the *nature* of social science theories. That notwithstanding, it remains an important methodological issue, of relevance to both sociology and organisational analysis, *within* the context of the assumptions explored here.

2. Assumptions about the Nature of Society

All approaches to the study of society are located in a frame of reference of one kind or another. Different theories tend to reflect different perspectives, issues and problems worthy of study, and are generally based upon a whole set of assumptions which reflect a particular view of the nature of the subject under investigation. The last twenty years or so have witnessed a number of attempts on the part of sociologists to delineate the differences which separate various schools of thought and the meta-sociological assumptions which they reflect.

The Order—Conflict Debate

Dahrendorf (1959) and Lockwood (1956), for example, have sought to distinguish between those approaches to sociology which concentrated upon explaining the nature of social order and equilibrium on the one hand, and those which were more concerned with problems of change, conflict and coercion in social structures on the other. This distinction has received a great deal of attention and has come to be known as the 'order—conflict debate'. The 'order theorists' have greatly outnumbered the 'conflict theorists', and as Dawe has observed, 'the thesis that sociology is centrally concerned with the problem of social order has become one of the discipline's few orthodoxies. It is common as a basic premise to many accounts of sociological theory which otherwise differ considerably in purpose and perspective' (Dawe, 1970, p. 207).[1]

Many sociologists now regard this debate as dead or as having been a somewhat spurious non-debate in the first place (Cohen, 1968; Silverman, 1970; van den Berghe, 1969). Influenced by the work of writers such as Coser (1956), who pointed to the functional aspects of social conflict, sociologists have been able to incorporate conflict as a variable within the bounds of theories which are primarily geared towards an explanation of social order. The approach advocated by Cohen, for example, clearly illustrates this. He takes his point of departure from the work of Dahrendorf and elaborates some of the central ideas in the order—conflict debate to present two models of society, which are characterised in terms of competing sets of assumptions which attribute to social systems the characteristics of *commitment, cohesion, solidarity, consensus, reciprocity, co-operation, integration, stability* and *persistence* on the one hand, and the characteristics of *coercion, division, hostility, dissensus, conflict, malintegration* and *change* on the other (Cohen, 1968, pp. 166-7).

Cohen's central criticism is that Dahrendorf is mistaken in treating the order and conflict models as being entirely separate. He in effect suggests that it is possible for theories to involve elements of both models and that one need not necessarily incline to one or the other. From this point of view, the order and conflict views of society are but two sides of the same coin; they are not mutually exclusive and thus do not need to be reconciled. The force of this sort of argument has been very powerful in diverting attention away from the order—conflict debate. In the wake of the so-called counter-culture movement of the late 1960s and the failure of the 1968 revolution in France, orthodox sociologists have become much more interested in and concerned with the problems of the 'individual' as opposed to those of the 'structure' of society in general. The influence of 'subjectivist' movements such as phenomenology, ethnomethodology and action theory, which we referred to in passing in the previous chapter, have tended to become much more attractive and more worthy of attention. As a result, interest in continuing the conflict—order debate has subsided under the influence of issues relating to the philosophy and methods of social science.

Our contention here is that if one reviews the intellectual source and foundations of the order—conflict debate, one is forced to conclude that it has met a premature death. Dahrendorf and Lockwood sought to revitalise the work of Marx through their writings and to restore it to a central place in sociological theory. For the most part Marx had been largely ignored by leading sociologists, the influence of theorists such as Durkheim, Weber and Pareto having been paramount. Interestingly enough, these latter three sociologists are all very much concerned with the problem of social order; it is Marx who is preoccupied with the role of conflict as the driving force behind social change. Stated in this way, therefore, the order—conflict debate is underwritten by a difference between the perspectives and concerns of leading social theorists of the nineteenth and early twentieth centuries. Modern sociology has done little more than articulate and develop the basic themes initiated by these pioneers of social analysis. To state that the order—conflict debate is 'dead' or a 'non-debate' is thus to underplay, if not ignore, substantial differences between the work of Marx and, for example, Durkheim, Weber and Pareto. Anyone familiar with the work of these theorists and aware of the deep division which exists between Marxism and sociology is forced to admit that there are fundamental differences, which are far from being reconciled.[2] In this chapter therefore, we wish to re-evaluate the order—conflict issue with a view to identifying a key dimension for analysing the assumptions about the nature of society reflected in different social theories. In order to do so, let us return to the work of Dahrendorf, who seeks to set out the opposing issues in the following terms:

> The integration theory of society, as displayed by the work of Parsons and other structural-functionalists, is founded on a number of assumptions of the following type:
> (1) Every society is a relatively persistent, stable structure of elements.
> (2) Every society is a well integrated structure of elements.
> (3) Every element in a society has a function, i.e., renders a contribution to its maintenance as a system.
> (4) Every functioning social structure is based on a consensus of values among its members . . . .
> . . . What I have called the coercion theory of society can also be reduced to a small number of basic tenets, although here again these assumptions oversimplify and overstate the case:
> (1) Every society is at every point subject to processes of change; social change is ubiquitous.
> (2) Every society displays at every point dissensus and conflict; social conflict is ubiquitous.
> (3) Every element in a society renders a contribution to its disintegration and change.
> (4) Every society is based on the coercion of some of its members by others. (Dahrendorf, 1959, pp. 160–2)

The opposing adjectives which Dahrendorf's schema suggests for distinguishing approaches to the study of society can be conveniently brought together in the form of a table, as follows:

Table 2.1

Two theories of society: 'order' and 'conflict'

The 'order' or 'integrationist' view of society emphasises:	The 'conflict' or 'coercion' view of society emphasises:
Stability	Change
Integration	Conflict
Functional co-ordination	Disintegration
Consensus	Coercion

As Dahrendorf admits, this conceptualisation is something of an oversimplification, and whilst providing a very useful tool for coming to grips with the differences between the two standpoints, it is open to the possibility of misinterpretation, in that the different adjectives mean different things to different people. Nowhere is this more evident than in the way in which the notion of *conflict* has been treated in the sociological literature. Since Coser's demonstration of the functions of social conflict, for example, the role of conflict as an integrating mechanism has received a great deal of attention. In effect, the whole notion of 'conflict' has often been incorporated within the notion of integration. Dahrendorf's integration/conflict dimension has been conveniently telescoped so that it is brought within the bounds of sociology's traditional concern for the explanation of order. The fallacy of this position becomes clear if one considers certain extreme forms of conflict, such as class conflict, revolution and war, which can only be incorporated in the integrationist model by the wildest stretch of one's imagination. Examples such as these suggest that it is misleading to equate this type of macrostructural conflict with the functional conflict identified by Coser. There is an important question of degree involved here, which emphasises the dangers of the dichotomisation of integration and conflict; realistically the distinction between the two is much more of a continuum than the majority of writers have recognised.

Another strand of the Dahrendorf scheme which can be regarded as somewhat problematic lies in the distinction between *consensus* and *coercion*. At first sight the distinction appears obvious and clear-cut, focusing upon shared values on the one hand and the imposition of some sort of force on the other. On closer inspection there is a certain ambiguity. Where do the shared values come from? Are they acquired autonomously or imposed on some members of society by others? This question identifies the possibility that consensus may be the product of the use of some form of coercive force. For example, as C. Wright Mills has pointed out, 'What Parsons and other grand theorists call "value orientations" and "normative structure" has mainly to do with master symbols of legitimation' (1959, p. 46).

A normative structure here − what Dahrendorf would view as consensus − is treated as a system legitimising the power structure. From Mills's point of view, it reflects the fact of domination. In other words, shared values may be regarded not so much as an index of the degree of integration which characterises a society as one which reflects the success of the forces of domination in a society prone to disintegration. From one point of view, extant shared ideas, values and norms are something to be preserved; from another, they represent a mode of domination from which man needs to be released. The consensus/coercion dimension can thus be seen as focusing upon the issue of social control. Consensus − however it may arise − is identified in Dahrendorf's scheme as something independent of coercion. This we believe to be a mistaken view since, as suggested above, it ignores the possibility of a form of coercion which arises through the control of value systems.

In distinguishing between *stability* and *change* as respective features of the order and conflict models Dahrendorf is again open to misinterpretation, even though he explicitly states that he does not intend to imply that the theory of order assumes that societies are static. His concern is to show how functional theories are essentially concerned with those processes which serve to maintain the patterns of the system as a whole. In other words, functional theories are regarded as static in the sense that they are concerned with explaining the *status quo*. In this respect conflict theories are clearly of a different nature; they are committed to, and seek to explain, the process and nature of deep-seated structural change in society as opposed to change of a more superficial and ephemeral kind. The fact that all functional theories recognise change, and that change is an obvious empirical reality in everyday life, has led Dahrendorf's categorisation in relation to stability and change to lose its potential radical force and influence. It can be argued that different labels are required to identify Dahrendorf's two paramount concerns: first, that the order view of society is primarily *status quo* orientated; second, that it deals with change of a fundamentally different nature from that with which conflict theorists are concerned.[3]

Dahrendorf's notions of *functional co-ordination* and *disin-*

tegration can be seen as constituting one of the most powerful strands of thought which distinguish the order and conflict perspectives. Here again, however, there is room for misinterpretation. The concept of integration in Dahrendorf's work derives from the functionalists' concern with the contribution which constituent elements of a system make to the whole. In many respects this is an oversimplification. Merton (1948) introduced the idea of manifest and latent functions, some of which may be dysfunctional for the integration of society.[4] Again, Gouldner (1959), writing shortly after the publication of the German edition of Dahrendorf's work, suggests that various parts of a system may have a high degree of autonomy and may contribute very little by way of integration to the system as a whole. The term 'functional co-ordination' is thus something of an oversimplification and, given the existence of the points of view expressed above within the functionalist camp itself, it is not surprising that the concept of 'disintegration' should be seen as relevant and capable of being used from a functional standpoint. 'Disintegration' can be very easily viewed as an integrationist concept and, as with other aspects of Dahrendorf's scheme, this dimension has often been telescoped and brought within the bounds of the theories of order. For this reason it may well have been clearer if the position of conflict theory on this dimension had been presented in more radical and distinctive terms. There is much in Marxian theory, for example, which refers to the notion of 'contradiction' and the basic incompatibility between different elements of social structure. Contradiction implies heterogeneity, imbalance and essentially antagonistic and divergent social forces. It thus stands at the opposite pole to the concept of 'functional co-ordination', which must presuppose a basic compatibility between the elements of any given system. To argue that the concept of contradiction can be embraced within functional analysis requires either an act of faith or at least a considerable leap of imagination.

Dahrendorf's work has clearly served a very useful purpose in identifying a number of important strands of thought distinguishing theorists of order from theorists of conflict. However, as will be apparent from the above discussion, in many respects the distinctions which have been drawn between the two meta-theories do not go far enough. In particular, the insights of some twenty years of debate suggest that the characterisation of the conflict perspective has not been sufficiently radical to avoid confusion with the 'integrationist' perspective. This has allowed theorists of order to meet the challenge which Dahrendorf's scheme presents to their frame of reference within the context of their order-orientated mode of thought. In order to illustrate this point, let us return to the work of Cohen (1968) referred to earlier.

In advocating his viewpoint Cohen appears to be misinterpreting the distinction between the two models. His interpretation of concepts telescopes the different variables into a form in which they can be seen as consistent with each other. In effect his whole analysis reflects an attempt to incorporate the conflict model within the bounds of the contemporary theory of order. He thus loses the radical essence of the conflict perspective and is able to conclude that the two models are not mutually exclusive and do not need to be reconciled. He argues that the two models are not genuine alternatives and in effect suggests that each is no more than the reciprocal of the other. He is therefore able to leave Dahrendorf's analysis with the central concern of his book – the problem of order – largely intact. The incorporation of conflict into the bounds of the model of order de-emphasises its importance.[5]

In line with the analysis which we presented earlier, we argue that the attempt to reduce the two models to a common base ignores the fundamental differences which exist between them. A conflict theory based on deep-seated structural conflict and concerned with radical transformations of society is not consistent with a functionalist perspective. The differences between them, therefore, are important and worthy of distinction in any attempt to analyse social theory. With the benefit of hindsight, it is possible to see that many of the misinterpretations which have arisen have done so because the models in Dahrendorf's analysis were not sufficiently differentiated. We wish to propose, therefore, that certain modifications be made in order to articulate the differences in a more explicit and radical form. Since much of the confusion has arisen because of the ambiguity of the descriptions associated with the two models we wish to suggest the use of a somewhat different terminology.

'Regulation' and 'Radical Change'

Our analysis has shown that the order—conflict distinction is in many senses the most problematic. We suggest, therefore, that it should be replaced as a central theme by the notions of 'regulation' and 'radical change'.

We introduce the term '*sociology of regulation*' to refer to the writings of theorists who are primarily concerned to provide explanations of society in terms which emphasise its underlying unity and cohesiveness. It is a sociology which is essentially concerned with the need for regulation in human affairs; the basic questions which it asks tend to focus upon the need to understand why society is maintained as an entity. It attempts to explain why society tends to hold together rather than fall apart. It is interested in understanding the social forces which prevent the Hobbesian vision of 'war of all against all' becoming a reality. The work of Durkheim with its emphasis upon the nature of social cohesion and solidarity, for example, provides a clear and comprehensive illustration of a concern for the sociology of regulation.

The '*sociology of radical change*' stands in stark contrast to the 'sociology of regulation', in that its basic concern is to find explanations for the radical change, deep-seated structural conflict, modes of domination and structural contradiction which its theorists see as characterising modern society. It is a sociology which is essentially concerned with man's emancipation from the structures which limit and stunt his potential for development. The basic questions which it asks focus upon the deprivation of man, both material and psychic. It is often visionary and Utopian, in that it looks towards potentiality as much as actuality; it is concerned with what is possible rather than with what is; with alternatives rather than with acceptance of the *status quo*. In these respects it is as widely separate and distant from the sociology of regulation as the sociology of Marx is separated and distant from the sociology of Durkheim.

The distinction between these two sociologies can perhaps be best illustrated in schematic form; extreme points of view are counter-posed in order to highlight the essential differences between them. Table 2.2 summarises the situation.

We offer this regulation—radical change distinction as the second principal dimension of our scheme for analysing social theories. Along with the subjective—objective dimension developed in the previous chapter, we present it as a powerful means for identifying and analysing the assumptions which underlie social theories in general.

The notions of 'regulation' and 'radical change' have thus far been presented in a very rough and extreme form. The two models illustrated in Table 2.2 should be regarded as ideal-typical formulations. The seven elements which we have identified lend themselves to a much more rigorous and systematic treatment in which their overall form and nature is spelt out in detail. We delay this task until later chapters. Here, we wish to address ourselves to the broad relationships which exist between the sociologies of regulation and radical change. We maintain that they present fundamentally different views and interpretations of the nature of society. They reflect fundamentally different frames of reference. They present themselves, therefore, as *alternative* models for the analysis of social processes.

To present the models in this way is to invite criticism along the lines of that levelled at Dahrendorf's work. For example, it could be suggested that the two models are the reciprocals of each other − no more than two sides of the same coin − and that relationships

Table 2.2

The regulation—radical change dimension

The sociology of REGULATION is concerned with:	*The sociology of RADICAL CHANGE is concerned with:*
(a) The status quo	(a) Radical change
(b) Social order	(b) Structural conflict
(c) Consensus*	(c) Modes of domination
(d) Social integration and cohesion	(d) Contradiction
(e) Solidarity	(e) Emancipation
(f) Need satisfaction†	(f) Deprivation
(g) Actuality	(g) Potentiality

Notes
* By 'consensus' we mean voluntary and 'spontaneous' agreement of opinion.
† The term 'need satisfaction' is used to refer to the focus upon satisfaction of individual or system 'needs'. The sociology of regulation tends to presume that various social characteristics can be explained in relation to these needs. It presumes that it is possible to identify and satisfy human needs within the context of existing social systems, and that society reflects these needs. The concept of 'deprivation', on the other hand, is rooted in the notion that the social 'system' prevents human fulfilment; indeed that 'deprivation' is created as the result of the *status quo*. The social 'system' is not seen as satisfying needs but as eroding the possibilities for human fulfilment. It is rooted in the notion that society has resulted in deprivation rather than in gain.

between the sub-elements of each model need not be congruent, that is, an analysis may pay attention to elements of both.

The answer to both criticisms follows our defence of Dahrendorf's work. To conflate the two models and treat them as variations on a single theme is to ignore or at least to underplay the fundamental differences which exist between them. Whilst it may be possible to use each model in a diluted form and thus obtain two analyses of the middle ground which approximate each other, they must remain essentially separate, since they are based upon opposing assumptions. Thus, as we have illustrated, to discuss the 'functions' of social conflict is to commit oneself to the sociology of regulation as opposed to that of radical change. However close one's position might be to the middle ground, it would seem that one must always be committed to one side more than another. The fundamental distinctions between the sociologies of regulation and radical change will become clear from our analysis of their intellectual development and constituent schools of thought in later chapters. We conceptualise these two broad sociological perspectives in the form of a polarised dimension, recognising that while variations within the context of each are possible, the perspectives are necessarily separate and distinct from each other.

Notes and References

1. Among the numerous theorists primarily concerned with the problem of order, Dawe cites Parsons (1949), Nisbet (1967), Bramson (1961), Cohen (1968), and Aron (1968).
2. For a discussion of the Marxism versus social science debate, see Shaw (1975). The division between Marxist theorists and orthodox sociologists is now so deep that they either ignore each other completely, or indulge in an exchange of abuse and accusation regarding the political conservatism or subversiveness commonly associated with their respective points of view. Debate about the intellectual strengths and weaknesses of their opposing standpoints is conspicuous by its absence.
3. Later in this chapter we suggest that the descriptions of 'concern with the *status quo*' and 'concern for *radical change*' provide more accurate views of the issues involved here.

4. Dahrendorf acknowledges Merton's distinction between latent and manifest functions but does not pursue the consequence of 'dysfunctions' for the concept of integration (Dahrendorf, 1959, pp. 173–9).
5. Other 'order' theorists who have addressed themselves to Dahrendorf's model tend to follow a similar path in the attempt to embrace conflict theory within their perspective. See, for example, van den Berghe (1969).

3. Two Dimensions: Four Paradigms

In the previous two chapters we have focused upon some of the key assumptions which characterise different approaches to social theory. We have argued that it is possible to analyse these approaches in terms of two key dimensions of analysis, each of which subsumes a series of related themes. It has been suggested that assumptions about the nature of science can be thought of in terms of what we call the subjective—objective dimension, and assumptions about the nature of society in terms of a regulation—radical change dimension. In this chapter we wish to discuss the relationships between the two dimensions and to develop a coherent scheme for the analysis of social theory.

We have already noted how sociological debate since the late 1960s has tended to ignore the distinctions between the two dimensions – in particular, how there has been a tendency to focus upon issues concerned with the subjective—objective dimension and to ignore those concerned with the regulation—radical change dimension. Interestingly enough, this focus of attention has characterised sociological thought associated with both regulation and radical change. The subjective—objective debate has been conducted independently within both sociological camps.

Within the sociology of regulation it has assumed the form of a debate between interpretive sociology and functionalism. In the wake of Berger and Luckmann's treatise on the sociology of knowledge (1966), Garfinkel's work on ethnomethodology (1967) and a general resurgence of interest in phenomenology, the questionable status of the ontological and epistemological assumptions of the functionalist perspective have become increasingly exposed. The debate has often led to a polarisation between the two schools of thought.

Similarly, within the context of the sociology of radical change there has been a division between theorists subscribing to 'subjective' and 'objective' views of society. The debate in many respects takes its lead from the publication in France in 1966 and Britain in

1969 of Louis Althusser's work *For Marx*. This presented the notion of an 'epistemological break' in Marx's work and emphasised the polarisation of Marxist theorists into two camps: those emphasising the 'subjective' aspects of Marxism (Lukács and the Frankfurt School, for example) and those advocating more 'objective' approaches, such as that associated with Althusserian structuralism.

Within the context of the sociologies both of regulation and radical change, therefore, the middle to late 1960s witnessed a distinct switch in the focus of attention. The debate *between* these two sociologies which had characterised the early 1960s disappeared and was replaced by an introverted dialogue *within* the context of each of the separate schools of thought. Instead of 'speaking' to each other they turned inwards and addressed their remarks to themselves. The concern to sort out their position with regard to what we call the subjective—objective dimension, a complicated process in view of all the interrelated strands, led to a neglect of the regulation—radical change dimension.

As a consequence of these developments, recent debate has often been confused. Sociological thought has tended to be characterised by a narrow sectarianism, from which an overall perspective and grasp of basic issues are conspicuously absent. The time is ripe for consideration of the way ahead, and we submit that the two key dimensions of analysis which we have identified define critical parameters within which this can take place. We present them as

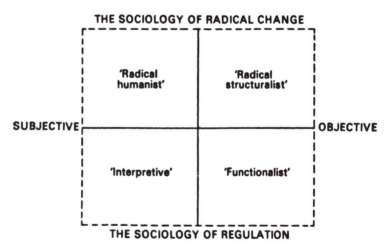

Figure 3.1   Four paradigms for the analysis of social theory

two independent dimensions which resurrect the sociological issues of the early 1960s and place them alongside those of the late 1960s and early 1970s. Taken together, they define four distinct sociological paradigms which can be utilised for the analysis of a wide range of social theories. The relationship between these paradigms, which we label 'radical humanist', 'radical structuralist', 'interpretive' and 'functionalist', is illustrated in Figure 3.1.

It will be clear from the diagram that each of the paradigms shares a common set of features with its neighbours on the horizontal and vertical axes in terms of one of the two dimensions but is differentiated on the other dimension. For this reason they should be viewed as contiguous but separate – contiguous because of the shared characteristics, but separate because the differentiation is, as we shall demonstrate later, of sufficient importance to warrant treatment of the paradigms as four distinct entities. The four paradigms define fundamentally different perspectives for the analysis of social phenomena. They approach this endeavour from contrasting standpoints and generate quite different concepts and analytical tools.

The Nature and Uses of the Four Paradigms

Before going on to discuss the substantive nature of each of the paradigms, it will be as well to pay some attention to the way in which we intend the notion of 'paradigm' to be used.[1] We regard our four paradigms as being defined by very basic meta-theoretical assumptions which underwrite the frame of reference, mode of theorising and *modus operandi* of the social theorists who operate within them. It is a term which is intended to emphasise the commonality of perspective which binds the work of a group of theorists together in such a way that they can be usefully regarded as approaching social theory within the bounds of the same problematic.

This definition does not imply complete unity of thought. It allows for the fact that within the context of any given paradigm there will be much debate between theorists who adopt different standpoints. The paradigm does, however, have an underlying unity in terms of its basic and often 'taken for granted' assumptions, which separate a group of theorists in a very fundamental way from theorists located in other paradigms. The 'unity' of the paradigm thus derives from reference to alternative views of reality which lie outside its boundaries and which may not necessarily even be recognised as existing.

In identifying four paradigms in social theory we are in essence suggesting that it is meaningful to examine work in the subject area in terms of four sets of basic assumptions. Each set identifies a quite separate social-scientific reality. To be located in a particular paradigm is to view the world in a particular way. The four paradigms thus define four views of the social world based upon different meta-theoretical assumptions with regard to the nature of science and of society.

It is our contention that all social theorists can be located within the context of these four paradigms according to the meta-theoretical assumptions reflected in their work. The four paradigms taken together provide a map for negotiating the subject area, which offers a convenient means of identifying the basic similarities and differences between the work of various theorists and, in particular, the underlying frame of reference which they adopt. It also provides a convenient way of locating one's own personal frame of reference with regard to social theory, and thus a means of understanding why certain theories and perspectives may have more personal appeal than others. Like any other·map, it provides a tool for establishing where you are, where you have been and where it is possible to go in the future. It provides a tool for mapping intellectual journeys in social theory − one's own and those of the theorists who have contributed to the subject area.

In this work we intend to make much use of the map-like qualities of the four paradigms. Each defines a range of intellectual territory. Given the overall meta-theoretical assumptions which distinguish one paradigm from another, there is room for much variation within them. Within the context of the 'functionalist' paradigm, for example, certain theorists adopt more extreme positions in terms of one or both of the two dimensions than others. Such differences often account for the internal debate which goes on between theorists engaged in the activities of 'normal science' within the context of the same paradigm.[2] The remaining chapters of this work examine each of the four paradigms in some detail and attempt to locate their principal theorists in these terms.

Our research suggests that whilst the activity within the context of each paradigm is often considerable, inter-paradigmatic 'journeys' are much rarer. This is in keeping with Kuhn's (1970) notion of 'revolutionary science'. For a theorist to switch paradigms calls for a change in meta-theoretical assumptions, something which, although manifestly possible, is not often achieved in practice. As Keat and Urry put it, 'For individual scientists, the change of allegiance from one paradigm to another is often a "conversion experience", akin to *Gestalt*-switches or changes of religious faith' (1975, p. 55). When a theorist does shift his position in this way, it stands out very clearly as a major break with his intellectual tradition and is heralded as being so in the literature, in that the theorist is usually welcomed by those whom he has joined and often disowned by his former 'paradigm colleagues'. Thus we witness what is known as the 'epistemological break' between the work of the young Marx and the mature Marx – what we would identify as a shift from the radical humanist paradigm to the radical structuralist paradigm. At the level of organisational analysis, a distinct paradigm shift can be detected in the work of Silverman – a shift from the functionalist paradigm to the interpretive paradigm. We will analyse such intellectual journeys in more detail in later chapters.

Before we progress to a review of the four paradigms, one point is worthy of further emphasis. This relates to the fact that the four paradigms are mutually exclusive. They offer alternative views of social reality, and to understand the nature of all four is to understand four different views of society. They offer different ways of seeing. A synthesis is not possible, since in their pure forms they are contradictory, being based on at least one set of opposing meta-theoretical assumptions. They are alternatives, in the sense that one *can* operate in different paradigms sequentially over time, but mutually exclusive, in the sense that one cannot operate in more than one paradigm at any given point in time, since in accepting the assumptions of one, we defy the assumptions of all the others.

We offer the four paradigms for consideration in these terms, in the hope that knowledge of the competing points of view will at least make us aware of the boundaries within which we approach our subject.

The Functionalist Paradigm

This paradigm has provided the dominant framework for the conduct of academic sociology and the study of organisations. It represents a perspective which is firmly rooted in the *sociology of regulation* and approaches its subject matter from an *objectivist* point of view. Functionalist theorists have been at the forefront of the order—conflict debate, and the concepts which we have used to categorise the sociology of regulation apply in varying degrees to all schools of thought within the paradigm. It is characterised by a concern for providing explanations of *the status quo, social order, consensus, social integration, solidarity, need satisfaction* and *actuality*. It approaches these general sociological concerns from a standpoint which tends to be *realist, positivist, determinist* and *nomothetic*.

The functionalist paradigm generates regulative sociology in its most fully developed form. In its overall approach it seeks to provide essentially rational explanations of social affairs. It is a perspective which is highly pragmatic in orientation, concerned to understand society in a way which generates knowledge which can be put to use. It is often problem-orientated in approach, concerned to provide practical solutions to practical problems. It is usually firmly committed to a philosophy of social engineering as a basis of social change and emphasises the importance of understanding order, equilibrium and stability in society and the way in which these can be maintained. It is concerned with the effective 'regulation' and control of social affairs.

As will be apparent from our discussion in Chapter 1 the approach to social science characteristic of the functionalist paradigm is rooted in the tradition of sociological positivism. This reflects the attempt, *par excellence*, to apply the models and methods of the natural sciences to the study of human affairs. Originating in France in the early decades of the nineteenth century, its major influence upon the paradigm has been through the work of social theorists such as Auguste Comte, Herbert Spencer, Emile Durkheim and Vilfredo Pareto. The functionalist approach to social science tends to assume that the social world is composed of relatively concrete empirical artefacts and relationships which can be identified, studied and measured through approaches derived from the natural sciences. The use of mechanical and biological analogies as a means of modelling and understanding the social world is particularly favoured in many functionalist theories. By way of illustration consider, for example, the work of Durkheim. Central to his position was the idea that 'social facts' exist outside of men's consciousness and restrain men in their everyday activities. The aim was to understand the relationships between these 'objective' social facts and to articulate the sociology which explained the types of 'solidarity' providing the 'social cement' which holds society together. The stability and ordered nature of the natural world was viewed as characterising the world of human affairs. For Durkheim, the task of sociology was to understand the nature of this regulated order.

Since the early decades of the twentieth century, however, the functionalist paradigm has been increasingly influenced by elements from the German idealist tradition of social thought. As will be recalled from our discussion in Chapter 1, this approach reflects assumptions about the nature of social science which stand in opposition to those of sociological positivism. As a result of the work of such theorists as Max Weber, George Simmel and George Herbert Mead, elements of this idealist approach have been utilised within the context of social theories which have attempted to bridge the gulf between the two traditions. In so doing they have forged theoretical perspectives characteristic of the least objectivist region of the paradigm, at its junction with the interpretive paradigm. Such theories have rejected the use of mechanical and biological analogies for studying the social world and have introduced ideas which place emphasis upon the importance of understanding society from the point of view of the actors who are actually engaged in the performance of social activities.

Since the 1940s there has been also an infusion of certain Marxist influences characteristic of the sociology of radical change. These have been incorporated within the paradigm in an attempt to 'radicalise' functionalist theory and rebuff the general charge that

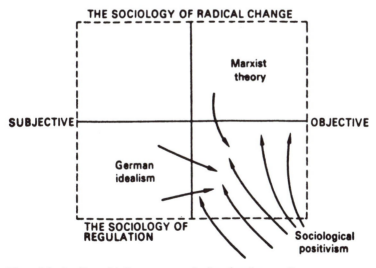

Figure 3.2 Intellectual influences upon the functionalist paradigm

functionalism is essentially conservative and unable to provide explanations for social change. These attempts underwrite the debate examined in the previous chapter as to whether a theory of 'conflict' can be incorporated within the bounds of a theory of 'order' to provide adequate explanations of social affairs.

Put very crudely, therefore, the formation of the functionalist paradigm can be understood in terms of the interaction of three sets of intellectual forces, as illustrated in Figure 3.2. Of these, sociological positivism has been the most influential. The competing traditions have been sucked in and used within the context of the functionalist problematic, which emphasises the essentially objectivist nature of the social world and a concern for explanations which emphasise 'regulation' in social affairs. These cross-currents of thought have given rise to a number of distinctive schools of thought within the paradigm, which is characterised by a wide range of theory and internal debate. By way of overview, again somewhat crudely, Figures 3.3 and 3.4 illustrate the four paradigms in terms of the constituent schools of sociological and organisational theory which we shall be exploring later on. As will be apparent, most organisation theorists, industrial sociologists, psychologists and industrial relations theorists approach their subject from within the bounds of the functionalist paradigm.

The Interpretive Paradigm

Theorists located within the context of the interpretive paradigm adopt an approach consonant with the tenets of what we have described as the *sociology of regulation*, though its *subjectivist* approach to the analysis of the social world makes its links with this sociology often implicit rather than explicit. The interpretive paradigm is informed by a concern to understand the world as it is, to understand the fundamental nature of the social world at the level of subjective experience. It seeks explanation within the realm of individual consciousness and subjectivity, within the frame of reference of the participant as opposed to the observer of action.

In its approach to social science it tends to be *nominalist, anti-positivist, voluntarist* and *ideographic*. It sees the social world as an emergent social process which is created by the individuals concerned. Social reality, insofar as it is recognised to have any existence outside the consciousness of any single individual, is regarded as being little more than a network of assumptions and

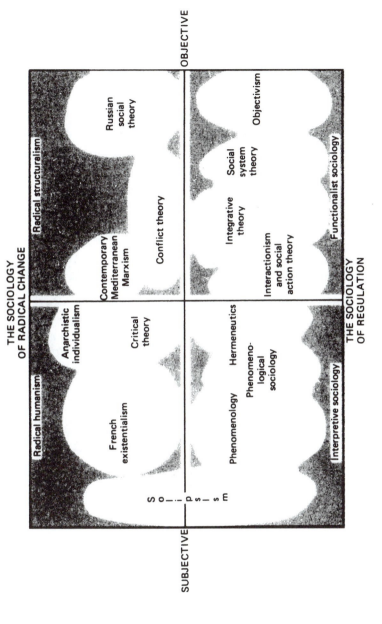

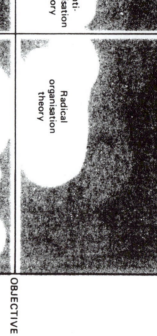

SUBJECTIVE

OBJECTIVE

THE SOCIOLOGY OF RADICAL CHANGE

THE SOCIOLOGY OF REGULATION

Ethnomethodology and Phenomenological symbolic interactionism

Anti-organisation theory

Radical organisation theory

Action frame of reference

Pluralism

Theories of bureaucratic dysfunctions

Social system theory

Objectivism

intersubjectively shared meanings. The ontological status of the social world is viewed as extremely questionable and problematic as far as theorists located within the interpretive paradigm are concerned. Everyday life is accorded the status of a miraculous achievement. Interpretive philosophers and sociologists seek to understand the very basis and source of social reality. They often delve into the depths of human consciousness and subjectivity in their quest for the fundamental meanings which underlie social life.

Given this view of social reality, it is hardly surprising that the commitment of the interpretive sociologists to the sociology of regulation is implicit rather than explicit. Their ontological assumptions rule out a direct interest in the issues involved in the order—conflict debate as such. However, their standpoint is underwritten by the assumption that the world of human affairs is cohesive, ordered and integrated. The problems of conflict, domination, contradiction, potentiality and change play no part in their theoretical framework. They are much more orientated towards obtaining an understanding of the subjectively created social world 'as it is' in terms of an ongoing process.

Interpretive sociology is concerned with understanding the essence of the everyday world. In terms of our analytical schema it is underwritten by an involvement with issues relating to the nature of *the status quo, social order, consensus, social integration and cohesion, solidarity* and *actuality*.[3]

The interpretive paradigm is the direct product of the German idealist tradition of social thought. Its foundations were laid in the work of Kant and reflect a social philosophy which emphasises the essentially spiritual nature of the social world. The idealist tradition was paramount in Germanic thought from the mid-eighteenth century onwards and was closely linked with the romantic movement in literature and the arts. Outside this realm, however, it was of limited interest, until revived in the late 1890s and early years of this century under the influence of the so-called neo-idealist movement. Theorists such as Dilthey, Weber, Husserl and Schutz have made a major contribution towards establishing it as a framework for social analysis, though with varying degrees of commitment to its underlying problematic.

Figures 3.3 and 3.4 illustrate the manner in which the paradigm has been explored as far as our present interest in social theory and the study of organisations is concerned. Whilst there have been a small number of attempts to study organisational concepts and situations from this point of view, the paradigm has not generated much organisation theory as such. As will become clear from our analysis, there are good reasons for this. The premises of the interpretive paradigm question whether organisations exist in anything but a conceptual sense. Its significance for the study of organisations, therefore, is of the most fundamental kind. It challenges the validity of the ontological assumptions which underwrite functionalist approaches to sociology in general and the study of organisations in particular.

The Radical Humanist Paradigm

The radical humanist paradigm is defined by its concern to develop a *sociology of radical change* from a *subjectivist* standpoint. Its approach to social science has much in common with that of the interpretive paradigm, in that it views the social world from a perspective which tends to be *nominalist, anti-positivist, voluntarist* and *ideographic*. However, its frame of reference is committed to a view of society which emphasises the importance of overthrowing or transcending the limitations of existing social arrangements.

One of the most basic notions underlying the whole of this paradigm is that the consciousness of man is dominated by the ideological superstructures with which he interacts, and that these drive a cognitive wedge between himself and his true consciousness. This wedge is the wedge of 'alienation' or 'false consciousness', which inhibits or prevents true human fulfilment. The major concern for theorists approaching the human predicament in these terms is with *release* from the constraints which existing social arrangements place upon human development. It is a brand of social theorising designed to provide a critique of the *status quo*. It tends to view society as anti-human and it is concerned to articulate ways in which human beings can transcend the spiritual bonds and fetters which tie them into existing social patterns and thus realise their full potential.

In terms of the elements with which we have sought to conceptualise the sociology of radical change, the radical humanist places most emphasis upon *radical change, modes of domination, emancipation, deprivation* and *potentiality*. The concepts of *structural conflict* and *contradiction* do not figure prominently within this perspective, since they are characteristic of more objectivist views of the social world, such as those presented within the context of the radical structuralist paradigm.

In keeping with its subjectivist approach to social science, the radical humanist perspective places central emphasis upon human consciousness. Its intellectual foundations can be traced to the same source as that of the interpretive paradigm. It derives from the German idealist tradition, particularly as expressed in the work of Kant and Hegel (though as reinterpreted in the writings of the young Marx). It is through Marx that the idealist tradition was first utilised as a basis for a radical social philosophy, and many radical humanists have derived their inspiration from this source. In essence Marx inverted the frame of reference reflected in Hegelian idealism and thus forged the basis for radical humanism. The paradigm has also been much influenced by an infusion of the phenomenological perspective deriving from Husserl.

As we shall illustrate in our detailed discussion of this paradigm, apart from the early work of Marx, interest remained dormant until the 1920s, when Lukács and Gramsci revived interest in subjectivist interpretations of Marxist theory. This interest was taken on by members of the so-called Frankfurt School, which has generated a great deal of debate, particularly through the writings of Habermas and Marcuse. The existentialist philosophy of Sartre also belongs to this paradigm, as do the writings of a group of social theorists as widely diverse as Illich, Castaneda and Laing. All in their various ways share a common concern for the release of consciousness and experience from domination by various aspects of the ideological superstructure of the social world within which men live out their lives. They seek to change the social world through a change in modes of cognition and consciousness.

Figures 3.3 and 3.4 again provide a somewhat rough and ready summary of the manner in which this paradigm has been explored in terms of social theory and the study of organisations. As we shall argue in Chapter 9, the writers who have something to say on organisations from this perspective have laid the basis of a nascent *anti-organisation theory*. The radical humanist paradigm in essence is based upon an inversion of the assumptions which define the functionalist paradigm. It should be no surprise, therefore, that anti-organisation theory inverts the problematic which defines functionalist organisation theory on almost every count.

The Radical Structuralist Paradigm

Theorists located within this paradigm advocate a *sociology of radical change* from an *objectivist* standpoint. Whilst sharing an approach to science which has many similarities with that of functionalist theory, it is directed at fundamentally different ends. Radical structuralism is committed to *radical change, emancipation,* and *potentiality,* in an analysis which emphasises *structural conflict, modes of domination, contradiction* and *deprivation.* It approaches these general concerns from a standpoint which tends to be *realist, positivist, determinist* and *nomothetic.*

Whereas the radical humanists forge their perspective by focusing upon 'consciousness' as the basis for a radical critique of society, the radical structuralists concentrate upon structural relationships within a realist social world. They emphasise the fact that radical change is built into the very nature and structure of contemporary society, and they seek to provide explanations of the basic interrelationships within the context of total social formations. There is a wide range of debate within the paradigm, and different theorists stress the role of different social forces as a means of explaining social change. Whilst some focus directly upon the deep-seated internal contradictions, others focus upon the structure and analysis of power relationships. Common to all theorists is the view that contemporary society is characterised by fundamental conflicts which generate radical change through political and economic crises. It is through such conflict and change that the emancipation of men from the social structures in which they live is seen as coming about.

This paradigm owes its major intellectual debt to the work of the mature Marx, after the so-called 'epistemological break' in his work. It is the paradigm to which Marx turned after a decade of active political involvement and as a result of his increasing interest in Darwinian theories of evolution and in political economy. Marx's basic ideas have been subject to a wide range of interpretations in the hands of theorists who have sought to follow his lead. Among these Engels, Plekhanov, Lenin and Bukharin have been particularly influential. Among the leading exponents of the radical structuralist position outside the realm of Russian social theory, the names of Althusser, Poulantzas, Colletti and various Marxist sociologists of the New Left come to mind. Whilst the influence of Marx upon the radical structuralist paradigm is undoubtedly dominant, it is also possible to identify a strong Weberian influence. As we shall argue in later chapters, in recent years a group of social theorists have sought to explore the interface between the thought of Marx and Weber and have generated a distinctive perspective which we describe as 'conflict theory'. It is to this radical structuralist perspective that the work of Dahrendorf belongs, along with that of other theorists such as Rex and Miliband.

Figures 3.3 and 3.4 again provide a general overview of the schools of thought located within the paradigm, which we shall be examining in some detail in Chapters 10 and 11. In British and American sociology the radical structuralist view has received relatively little attention outside the realm of conflict theory. This paradigm, located as it is within a realist view of the social world, has many significant implications for the study of organisations, but they have only been developed in the barest forms. In Chapter 11 we review the work which has been done and the embryonic *radical organisation theory* which it reflects.

Exploring Social Theory

So much, then, for our overview of the four paradigms. Subsequent chapters seek to place flesh upon the bones of this analytical scheme and attempt to demonstrate its power as a tool for exploring social theory.[4] Hopefully, our discussion will do justice to the essentially complex nature of the paradigms and the network of assumptions which they reflect, and will establish the relationships and links between the various perspectives dominating social analysis at the present time. Whilst the focus in Chapters 5, 7, 9 and 11 is upon organisational analysis, the general principles and ideas discussed in the work as a whole clearly have relevance for the exploration of a wide variety of other social science disciplines. The scope for applying the analytical scheme to other fields of study is enormous but unfortunately lies beyond the scope of our present enquiry. However, readers interested in applying the scheme in this way should find little difficulty in proceeding from the sociological analyses presented in Chapters 4, 6, 8, and 10 to an analysis of the literature in their own sphere of specialised interest.

Notes and References

1. For a full discussion of the role of paradigms in scientific development, see Kuhn (1970). In his analysis, paradigms are defined as 'universally recognised scientific achievements that for a time provide model problems and solutions to a

community of practitioners' (p. viii). Paradigms are regarded as governing the progress of what is called 'normal science', in which 'the scientist's work is devoted to the articulation and wider application of the accepted paradigm, which is not itself questioned or criticised. Scientific problems are regarded as puzzles, as problems which are known to have a solution within the framework of assumptions implicitly or explicitly embodied in the paradigm. If a puzzle is not solved, the fault lies in the scientist, and not in the paradigm' (Keat and Urry 1975, p. 55). 'Normal science' contrasts with relatively brief periods of 'revolutionary science', in which 'the scientist is confronted by increasingly perplexing anomalies, which call into question the paradigm itself. Scientific revolution occurs when a new paradigm emerges, and becomes accepted by the scientific community' (ibid., p. 55).

We are using the term 'paradigm' in a broader sense than that intended by Kuhn. Within the context of the present work we are arguing that social theory can be conveniently understood in terms of the co-existence of four distinct and rival paradigms defined by very basic meta-theoretical assumptions in relation to the nature of science and society. 'Paradigms', 'problematics', 'alternative realities', 'frames of reference', 'forms of life' and 'universe of discourse' are all related conceptualisations although of course they are *not* synonymous.

2. Some *inter*-paradigm debate is also possible. Giddens maintains 'that all paradigms ... are mediated by others' and that within 'normal science' scientists are aware of *other* paradigms. He posits that: 'The process of learning a paradigm ... is also the process of learning what that paradigm is not' (1976, pp. 142–4).

    Interestingly, he confines his discussion to the mediation of one paradigm by another one. We believe that a model of *four* conflicting paradigms within sociology is more accurate and that academics' knowledge of 'scientists' within the other three paradigms is likely to be very sketchy in some cases. Relations between paradigms are perhaps better described in terms of 'disinterested hostility' rather than 'debate'.

3. The notion of need satisfaction derives from the use of a biological analogy of an organism and plays no part in interpretive sociology.

4. The sociological concerns of recent years have resulted in a

number of works which have aimed to chart a path through the social science literature by reducing the variables of sociological analysis to a number of key dimensions. Those of Dahrendorf (1959), Wallace (1969), Gouldner (1970), Friedrichs (1970), Dawe (1970), Robertson (1974), Keat and Urry (1975), Strasser (1976) and Benton (1977) all readily come to mind. In a sense our work adds to this literature. Had space permitted, we would have liked to demonstrate the precise way in which the schemes proposed by these various authors all fall, in a partial way, *within* the bounds of the scheme developed here.

Part II

The Paradigms Explored

4. Functionalist Sociology

Origins and Intellectual Tradition

The mode of social theorising which characterises this paradigm has a long history. Indeed, its pedigree can be traced back to the very roots of sociology as a discipline, and the early attempts of social philosophers to apply the ideas and methods of natural science to the realm of social affairs. It is a paradigm which, in many respects, has developed as a branch of the natural sciences and, to this day, in disciplines as avowedly 'social' as sociology, psychology, economics, anthropology and the like, natural science models and methods reign supreme in various areas of enquiry.

Given such an extensive history, it is difficult to locate a precise starting point. Elements of the paradigm can be traced back to the political and social thought of the ancient Greeks but, for convenience, we shall commence our analysis with the work of Auguste Comte (1798–1857), commonly regarded as the founding father of 'sociology' – in name if not entirely in substance.

As Raymond Aron has suggested, Comte may be regarded, first and foremost, as 'the sociologist of human and social unity' (Aron, 1965, p. 59). He believed that knowledge and society was in a process of evolutionary transition, and that the function of sociology was to understand the necessary, indispensable and inevitable course of history in such a way as to promote the realisation of a new social order. From Comte's point of view this evolution passed through three stages of development – 'the Theological, or fictitious; the Metaphysical, or abstract; and the Scientific, or positive'. He defined the positive mode of thought in the following terms: 'In the final, the positive state, the mind has given over the vain search after absolute notions, the origin and destination of the universe and the causes of phenomena, and applies itself to the study of their laws, i.e. their invariable relations of succession and resemblance. Reasoning and observation duly combined are the means of this knowledge' (Comte, 1853, vol. I, pp. 1–2). Comte's vision was of a world in which scientific 'rationality' was in the ascendancy, underlying the basis of a well regulated social order. For Comte the 'positive' approach provided the key to man's destiny or, as Aron has put it, the 'one type of society which is absolutely valid' and at which 'all mankind must arrive' (Aron, 1965, p. 59).

Comte believed that all sciences passed through his three phases of development but did so at different times according to their complexity. He felt that the 'positive' method which had already triumphed in mathematics, astronomy, physics and biology would eventually prevail in politics and culminate in the founding of a positive science of society, which is called sociology. His vision was of a sociology based on the models and methods employed in the natural sciences, addressing itself to the discovery of scientific laws which explain the relationships between various parts of society – 'social statics' – and the way in which they change over time – 'social dynamics'. In his writings Comte made much of the link between biology and social science. He saw biology as marking a decisive point of transition between sciences, in that it marked a distinction between the 'organic' and 'inorganic' and placed emphasis upon understanding and explanation within the totality of the living whole (Comte, 1853, vol. II, pp. 111–26).

Comte thus laid the foundations for the mode of social theorising characteristic of the functionalist paradigm. Based upon the 'positive' model of the natural sciences, utilising mechanical and organic analogies, distinguishing between statics (structure) and dynamics (process), and advocating methodological holism, Comte initiated important ground rules for a sociological enterprise geared to an explanation of social order and regulation.

Herbert Spencer (1820–1903) had a major influence on developments in sociology in the 1870s and 1880s. A 'positivist' in the Comtian tradition, his principal contribution was to develop in a more detailed and extensive manner the implications of the biological analogy for sociology. Influenced by the work of Darwin, he saw the study of sociology as the study of evolution in its most complex form. Whilst regarding society as a sort of organism, he used the analogy flexibly, as an explanatory instrument yielding, in his words, a 'treasure of insights and hypotheses'. His work did much to lay the foundations for the analysis of social phenomena in terms of 'structure' and 'function', elaborating Comte's notion of totality and the need to understand the parts in the context of the whole. In this respect, however, he was more of a methodological individualist than Comte, maintaining that the properties of the aggregate are determined by the properties of its units.

Many of the notions underpinning what we now know as structural functionalism derive from Spencer's work. In particular the parallels which he drew between societies and organisms, and the view that the parts of society function in ways which contribute to the maintenance of the whole, have been highly influential. Spencer's view of society was that of a self-regulating system which could be understood through study of its various elements or organs and the manner in which they are interrelated. He saw society as being set on an evolutionary course of development in which changes of structure were characterised by a process of increasing differentiation and increasing integration. The highly developed social form was, for him, characterised by both diversity and integration. The idea of evolution had universal applicability and was the key to the understanding of both the social and the natural world.

It is a point of considerable importance that in developing the analogy between the biological and social, Spencer's focus of attention was primarily, though not exclusively, directed at the level of the organism rather than the species. Societies were seen as 'super-organisms'. This organismic frame of reference emphasises the unity, interdependence and ordered nature of constituent relationships. A somewhat different view emerges from an analysis conducted at the level of the species. As Buckley has noted, 'the particular level of biological organisation that is chosen as the basis for a model of society determines (or may be determined by) whether we see society as pre-eminently co-operative or basically conflictual. If society is like an organism, then its parts co-operate and do not compete in a struggle for survival, but if society is like an ecological aggregate, then the Darwinian (or Hobbesian) model of competitive struggle is more applicable' (Buckley, 1967, pp. 12–13). Whilst Spencer did draw parallels between the evolution of societies and the evolution of species – emphasising the role of conflict, including warfare, as a force for social change – it was within the context of a theoretical perspective which emphasised the inevitable march towards more complex and integrated social systems. Industrial society was viewed at its most advanced form. As Parsons has commented, 'Spencer's god was Evolution, sometimes also called Progress. Spencer was one of the most vociferous in his devotions to this god, but by no means alone among the faithful. With many other social thinkers he believed that man stood near the culminating point of a long linear process extending back unbroken, without essential changes of direction, to the dawn of primitive man' (Parsons, 1949, p. 4).

Emile Durkheim (1858–1917) explicitly recognised the influence of Comte and Spencer upon his sociological thought, but he approached their work in a critical vein. As Lukes (1973) has noted, Comte's influence on Durkheim was a formative rather than a continuing one, the extension of the 'positive', or scientific attitude to the study of society probably being most important. Although Durkheim specifically dissociated himself from many of Comte's beliefs, he was firmly influenced by the Comtian notion of a concrete social reality capable of rational scientific investigation. This is reflected in the Durkheimian notion of the objective reality of 'social facts'. Durkheim recognised that Comte had oversimplified this reality, ignoring the way in which 'society' comprised different 'types' and 'species'. In this respect Durkheim found Spencer's analysis more acceptable, and he incorporated many of Spencer's insights, derived from the use of the organic analogy, into his analysis of social institutions.

For Durkheim, however, sociology had to go much further. He did not believe that an analysis of the parts which existed in the social organism and the role they performed was adequate as an end of sociological analysis. In particular, he criticised those sociologists who 'think they have accounted for a phenomenon once they have shown how they are useful, what role they play, reasoning as if facts existed only from the point of view of this role and with no other determining cause than the sentiment, clear or confused, of the services they are called to render' (Durkheim, 1938, p. 89). Durkheim believed that *causal* analysis was required in addition to what we would now call *functional* analysis: 'To show how a fact is useful is not to explain how it originated or why it is what it is. The uses which it serves pre-suppose the specific properties characterising it but do not create them ... When, then, the explanation of a social phenomenon is undertaken, we must seek separately the efficient cause which produces it and the function it fulfills' (Durkheim, 1938, p. 89). In terms of method, therefore, Durkheim, following Comte and Spencer, borrowed freely from the natural sciences. A methodological holist, distinguishing between causes, functions and structures, he added much in terms of sophistication to the thought of these earlier theorists and, as will become apparent later, provided a firm foundation for subsequent work within the context of the functionalist paradigm.

In terms of the nature of his social theorising, Durkheim is firmly located within the context of the sociology of regulation. From the early 1880s Durkheim addressed himself to the study of the relations between the individual and society and the relations between individual personality and social solidarity. He was concerned with nothing less than the nature of social solidarity itself – with the nature of the bonds which unite men. As Lukes has noted,

> This, indeed, was the problem that remained central to the whole of Durkheim's life work: as he was to write in a letter to Bouglé, 'the object of sociology as a whole is to determine the conditions for the conservation of societies'. At this early period the problem posed itself as a question of determining the nature of social solidarity in industrial societies, as opposed to that in traditional or pre-industrial societies, and of accounting for the historical transition from the latter to the former. Later he was to turn to the study of 'elementary' or tribal societies, and in particular, primitive religion, in order to determine the nature of social solidarity in general. (Lukes, 1973, p. 139)

Durkheim saw, 'traditional societies' as being held together on the basis of a 'mechanical solidarity' deriving from similarity of parts, with the individual's 'conscience' a 'simple appendage of the collective type, following it [the collective conscience] in all its movements' (Durkheim, 1938, p. 148). The 'conscience collective' was based on a system of shared values, norms and beliefs. In the 'industrial' society, with its extensive system of 'division of labour' and functional differentiation, he saw an 'organic solidarity' arising from the interdependence of parts. It was a solidarity based upon a normative system of values, beliefs and sentiments. Durkheim recognised that in the process of transition from 'traditional' to 'industrial' societies solidarity could break down, creating a state of 'anomie' or normlessness. However, he saw this as an abnormal state of affairs, a 'pathological' deviation from the natural course of development. As Lukes notes, a major problem with Durkheim's account of anomie was that

> although it pinpointed the central ills of capitalism – unregulated competition; class conflict; routinised, degrading, meaningless work – it characterised them all as 'abnormal'. This procedure tended to hinder any full-scale investigation of their causes (which were assumed not to be endemic), especially given the evolutionary optimism Durkheim espoused at this stage. They were to be explained by the temporary and transitional lack of the appropriate economic controls, the appropriate norms governing industrial relations and the appropriate forms for work organisation – a lack that would in due course be

remedied by allowing the operation of interdependent functions to produce its natural consequences. (Lukes, 1973, p. 174)

Durkheim's sociology thus reflects a powerful predilection for 'order' as the predominant force in social affairs. Judged by the yardstick by which we have defined the 'sociology of regulation' (a concern for 'the *status quo*', 'social order', 'consensus', 'social integration and cohesion', 'solidarity', 'need satisfaction' and 'activity'), Durkheim emerges as a sociologist of 'order' and 'regulation' *par excellence.*

A fuller account of the origins of the functionalist paradigm would call for the analysis of the thought of a number of other social theorists. Alfred Marshall, Max Weber, Vilfredo Pareto, John Stuart Mill, Georg Simmel, George Herbert Mead and William James, among others, all have a strong claim to be considered here along with the founding fathers. To pursue such a task, however, would convert this work into a historical treatise well beyond the requirements of its present purpose. We will give specific consideration to the work of Simmel and Mead later in the chapter, since their ideas are of direct relevance to an understanding of the schools of sociological thought which are located in the least objectivist regions of the functionalist paradigm. The work of Weber is of similar importance, but we shall delay a full discussion of this until Chapter 6. Weber's work can only be adequately understood against the detailed background of German idealism, which provided the foundations for the development of the interpretive paradigm. Thus, although Weber's work belongs within the functionalist paradigm, we also discuss it in our chapter on the interpretive paradigm, to aid the presentation and intelligibility of our analysis as a whole. Readers who are unfamiliar with Weber's sociology are invited to consult Chapter 6 at appropriate points of discussion in this and the next chapter.

We conclude our discussion of the foundations of the functionalist paradigm here with a discussion of certain aspects of the work of Pareto.[1] It can be argued that the attention which he is often given in reviews of the development of social theory perhaps inflates his true importance in terms of the originality and sophistication of his ideas. His significance derives mainly from the considerable impact which his work has had upon the development of twentieth-century sociological thought, particularly through L. J. Henderson and the Harvard School of sociologists, who fostered what came to be known as the 'Pareto cult' during the 1930s at a particularly important and formative stage in the history of sociology. As will become apparent from our discussion in this and the next chapter, for this reason alone Pareto's influence calls for consideration in any review of the background to the functionalist paradigm.

Vilfredo Pareto (1848–1923) came to sociology from economics, with a view to supplementing the scientific theories of economics, based on their assumptions of logical and rational conduct, with a scientific theory of non-logical or non-rational conduct. The object of his main sociological work *A Treatise on General Sociology,* first published in 1916, was to construct a rigorous sociology which gave due recognition to the irrational elements in human behaviour. In his words, its sole purpose was 'to seek experimental reality, by the application to the social sciences of the methods which have proved themselves in physics, in chemistry, in astronomy, in biology, and in other such sciences' (Pureto, 1934, p. 291).

Among the main features of his work which are relevant for comment here are the fact that after establishing the extent and significance of the non-logical in social affairs, he proceeded to explain it in terms of a social systems model based upon the notion of equilibrium. His view of society was that of a system of interrelated parts which, though in a continual state of surface flux, were also in a state of unchanging equilibrium, in that movements away from the equilibrium position were counterbalanced by changes tending to restore it. Pareto saw in the concept of equilibrium a useful tool for understanding the complexities of social life. In the physical sciences it had provided a means of analysing the relationship between variables in a state of mutual dependence, and it had been used successfully in the field of economics. Pareto extended it to the social sphere, viewing society as determined by the forces acting upon it.

Pareto's equilibrium model of society was thus based upon a mechanical as opposed to a biological analogy. In contrast to the theories of Spencer and Durkheim, he took his main point of reference from the physical sciences. This is not to say that Pareto saw the physical and social worlds as being identical in nature; rather, he saw models derived from the former as having heuristic utility for the analysis of the latter. This is the role which the notion of equilibrium played in his scheme. It was a scientific construct to be used for the analysis of social reality. This distinction between equilibrium as an analytical construct and equilibrium as an empirical reality was by no means always spelt out as clearly as it might have been, and subsequent social theorists who followed Pareto's lead often adopted the equilibrium notion in its entirety.

As far as the development of the functionalist paradigm is concerned, it is through the notion of equilibrium that Pareto has had most influence. Whereas it was implicit in many earlier social theories, after Pareto it became much more explicit as a guiding principle. The distinction which he drew between the logical and non-logical elements in human conduct has, as we shall see, also been of some importance.

The Structure of the Paradigm

The functionalist paradigm has provided the dominant framework for academic sociology in the twentieth century and accounts for by far the largest proportion of theory and research in the field of organisation studies.

Its structure reflects the dominant influence of sociological positivism, as described in the previous section, fused at its junction with the interpretive paradigm with elements of German idealism. It contains many separate schools of thought, each occupying a distinctive relationship one with another. Our task in the remainder of this chapter is to trace these relationships in terms of the two dimensions which define the paradigm.

To facilitate this task, we identify four broad categories of functionalist thought and address each in turn. We describe them as: (a) social system theory, (b) interactionism and social action theory, (c) integrative theory, (d) objectivism.

Each of these broad categories occupies a distinctive position within the paradigm, as illustrated in Figure 3.3 *Social system theory* represents a direct development of sociological positivism in its most pure form. Adopting mechanical and biological analogies for the study of social affairs, it is most clearly represented in the schools of thought described as *structural functionalism* and *systems theory*.

Interactionism and *social action theory* is the category of thought which directly combines elements of sociological positivism and German idealism and, as such, can be considered as defining the most subjectivist boundary of the paradigm.

Integrative theory occupies a central location within the paradigm, seeking to bridge the gap between social system theory and interactionism. It is not fully committed to either of these two categories; it takes something from both and contributes something to both. It is truly a brand of theory characteristic of the middle ground, and is reflected in the schools of thought which we describe as *conflict functionalism, morphogenic systems theory, Blau's theory of exchange and power,* and *Mertonian theory of social and cultural structure.*

The category of thought which we describe as *objectivism* (comprising *behaviourism* and *abstracted empiricism*) is very closely related to social system theory, in that it again is firmly committed to the tradition of sociological positivism. We identify it as a separate category, in recognition of the fact that it reflects a particularly extreme form of commitment to the models and methods of the natural sciences. Behaviourism, for example, derives from physiological models employed in psychology. Abstracted empiricism is dominated by quantitative methodologies which often have no distinctly social qualities.

We commence our analysis with a consideration of social system theory.

Social System Theory

Under this heading we consider two schools of thought which, in many respects, have provided the dominant framework for analysis in contemporary sociology – structural functionalism and systems theory. Both have had a particularly important impact upon the field of organisational analysis.

The terms 'structural functionalism' and 'systems theory' are often seen as interchangeable. Whilst there is some measure of justification in equating the two as far as the majority of current systems applications are concerned, to do so represents an oversimplification, since systems theory is consistent with theoretical perspectives which extend beyond the confines of the functionalist paradigm. However, these remain largely undeveloped at the present time. In the following sections we trace the development of the two perspectives and the relationships which exist between them, arguing that the similarities only exist if they draw upon a similar analogy, that of the biological organism. Whereas structural functionalism inevitably draws upon this analogy, systems theory is in principle consistent with the use of many others.

Structural functionalism

It is through the notion of structural functionalism that the use of the biological analogy in the tradition of Comte, Spencer and Durkheim has had its major impact upon sociological thought. Building upon the concepts of holism, interrelationship between parts, structure, functions and needs, the biological analogy has been developed in diverse ways to produce a social science perspective firmly rooted in the sociology of regulation. Treating the external social world as a concrete reality, governed by observable functional relations amenable to scientific investigation through nomothetic methods, structural functionalism developed as the dominant paradigm for sociological analysis during the first half of the twentieth century. Indeed, by the 1950s its influence was so pervasive that in certain quarters functional analysis was equated with sociological analysis *per se* (Davis, 1959).

Significantly, it was not within sociology itself that structural functionalism received its first coherent expression as a theory and method of analysis. This took place within the realm of social anthropology, an area of enquiry which, in addressing itself primarily to the study of small-scale societies, provided an ideal situation for the application of holistic views of society in a manageable empirical context. Two names stand out as particularly influential in this endeavour – those of Malinowski and Radcliffe-Brown.[2]

Malinowski's overriding contribution was to establish the importance of field-work. Surprising as it may now seem, social anthropology was predominantly an 'armchair' discipline. As Jarvie notes, 'with the exception of Morgan's study of the Iroquois (1851), not a single anthropologist conducted field studies till the end of the nineteenth century' (Jarvie, 1964, p. 2). Malinowski's call was in effect to 'get off the verandah' and get involved in field-work and direct observation. In opposition to the 'evolutionist' and 'diffusionist' explanations of primitive society prevalent in the early 1920s, Malinowski advocated a 'functionalist' explanation, which argued that the unusual or special characteristics of primitive social systems could be understood in terms of the *functions* which they performed. His view was that society or 'culture' should be regarded as a complex whole and understood in terms of the relationships between its various parts and their ecological surroundings. Social organisation, religion, language, economy, political organisation, etc., were to be understood not so much as reflecting a primitive mentality or stage of 'underdevelopment' but in terms of the functions performed. In Malinowski's own words, the functional analysis of culture.

> aims at the explanation of anthropological facts at all levels of development by their function, by the part which they play within the

integral system of culture, by the manner in which they are related to each other within the system, and by the manner in which this system is related to the physical surroundings. It aims at the understanding of the nature of culture, rather than at conjectural reconstructions of its evolution or of past historical events. (Malinowski, 1936, p. 132)

Malinowski developed the notion of functional analysis against the prevailing orthodoxy in anthropology but without specifically grounding it within the context of earlier social theory. Radcliffe-Brown, on the other hand, was much more systematic in this respect. He specifically recognised that the concept of function, as applied to human societies, was based upon an analogy between social life and organic life, and that it had already received a certain amount of consideration in philosophy and sociology. He took his own particular starting point from the work of Durkheim and sought to elaborate the parallels which existed between biological organisms and human societies.[3]

Radcliffe-Brown's analysis was a sophisticated one. He argued that the concept of function in social science involved the assumption that there are necessary conditions of existence for human societies. Developing the analogy with animal organisms, he argued that societies could be conceptualised as networks of relations between constituent parts − 'social structures' − which had a certain continuity. In animal organisms the process by which this structural continuity is maintained is called life. The same applies in societies. Whilst recognising that societies in normal circumstances do not die in the manner of organisms, Radcliffe-Brown argued that the ongoing life of a society could be conceived in terms of the functioning of its structure − hence the notion of 'structural functionalism'. He illustrates his position as follows:

> To turn from organic life to social life, if we examine such a community as an African or Australian tribe we can recognise the existence of a social structure. Individual human beings, the essential units in this instance, are connected by a definite set of social relations into an integrated whole. The continuity of the social structure, like that of our organic structure, is not destroyed by changes in the units. Individuals may leave the society, by death of otherwise; others may enter it. The continuity of structure is maintained by the process of social life, which consists of the activities and interactions of the individual human beings and of the organised groups into which they are united. The social life of the community is here defined as the *functioning* of the social structure. The *function* of any recurrent activity, such as the punishment of a crime, or a funeral ceremony, is the part it plays in the

social life as a whole and therefore the contribution it makes to the maintenance of the structural continuity.

The concept of function as here defined thus involves the notion of a *structure* consisting of a *set of relations* amongst *unit entities*, the *continuity* of the structure being maintained by a *life-process* made up of the *activities* of the constituent units. (Radcliffe-Brown, 1952, p. 180)

Radcliffe-Brown saw this type of analysis as focusing attention upon three sets of problems relevant to the investigation of human society and of social life:

(a)   *The problems of social morphology* – what kinds of social structure are there? What are their similarities and differences? How are they to be classified?

(b)   *The problems of social physiology* – how do social structures function?

(c)   *The problems of development* – how do new types of social structure come into existence?

In specifying these problem areas, however, he was careful to recognise that the organismic analogy had a number of limitations as far as the study of society was concerned. First, whereas in the case of organisms it was possible to study organic structure independently of its functioning, in the case of societies it was not. As he put it, 'in human society the social structure as a whole can only be *observed* in its functioning' (Radcliffe-Brown, 1952, p. 181). In other words, he placed emphasis upon the essentially processual nature of social life, arguing that a social morphology could not be established independently of a social physiology. Second, he drew attention to the problem of morphogenesis. Societies are able to change and elaborate their structural types without any breach of continuity; organisms cannot. As he put it, 'a pig does not become a hippopotamus' (1952, p. 181). Third, he drew attention to the fact that the functional analysis of society, with its emphasis upon the contribution which the part makes to the continued existence and functioning of the whole, is based upon the *hypothesis* of functional unity. It implies that society has a 'functional unity' in which 'all parts of the social system work together with a sufficient degree of harmony or internal consistency, i.e. without producing persistent conflicts which can neither be resolved or regulated' (1952, p. 181). Radcliffe-Brown argued that functionalists should test this hypothesis by systematic examination of the facts.

With Radcliffe-Brown, therefore, we arrive at a quite sophisticated statement of the nature and limitations of the structural functionalist perspective. It is a point of view which recognises the processual relationship of mutual influence between structure and its functioning, and the dangers involved in pursuing the analogy between societies and organisms to an extreme. Not all functionalists were in complete agreement with Radcliffe-Brown, notably Malinowski, and it is as well to draw attention to some of the differences in points of view. Malinowski, for example, tended to seek explanations of society in terms of basic human needs. His version of functionalism tended to pursue the organismic analogy to an extreme and often resulted in teleological explanations. This was something Radcliffe-Brown consciously sought to avoid. He recognised the self-fulfilling nature of explanations based on 'needs' at both the individual and social level, and preferred to talk in terms of 'necessary conditions of existence'. This allowed for the possibility of the existence of some social phenomena which did not necessarily have a function to perform. Radcliffe-Brown had a preference for explaining social phenomena in terms of their 'survival value' to the *society*. He saw social institutions as contributing to the 'integration', 'stability' and 'maintenance' of the social system as a whole. He explained the nature of society in 'social' terms above and beyond the needs of its individual members. Though avoiding the problem of teleology, he ran dangerously close to the problem of reification.[4]

Subsequent developments in the functionalist tradition have drawn heavily upon the work of Malinowski and Radcliffe-Brown and have fanned out in many directions. Indeed, there has been considerable debate over whether functionalism or structural functionalism can be regarded as a unified approach, and a number of varieties of functionalism have, in fact, been identified (Demerath, 1966). The major distinction commonly drawn between approaches revolves around the issue of level of analysis: whether the focus in functional analysis is on the part or the whole, on the individual institution or the social system. In addition to this distinction, however, it is also desirable to draw attention to at least two other lines of development. The first follows on from Radcliffe-Brown's focus on structure in the tradition of 'social morphology'. In defiance (or at least ignorance) of his warning that 'the social structure as a whole can only be observed in its functioning', the notion of structure has become increasingly reified as some social theorists sought to identify its key elements. The 'search for structure' has led to an increasingly hard and indiscriminate application of the models and methods of the natural sciences to the study of social phenomena. In an extreme though pervasive form, much of contemporary structural functionalism manifests itself in terms of a host of empirical snapshots of reified social structures.[5] In the attempt to focus upon, define and measure 'structures', the notion of functional process − so central to the conceptualisations of both Malinowski and Radcliffe-Brown − has been lost. There has been a swing towards a highly objectified and static view of social reality − towards a positivism of an extreme, narrowly empirical and, indeed, atheoretical form. We shall pursue this in our discussion of abstracted empiricism later in this chapter.

The second line of development has focused upon what Radcliffe-Brown called the 'problems of social physiology', that is, upon explaining the way in which social systems function. For the most part these studies have drawn heavily upon the organismic analogy, attempting to understand the functioning of social systems in terms of system needs or conditions of existence. This is particularly evident, for example, in the work of Talcott Parsons and his analysis of the social system (1951).[6] Parsons takes as his point of departure the system as a whole and analyses the conditions necessary for its survival, functioning, evolution and change. As Rocher notes, in Parsons' perspective 'the term function refers to *various solutions to a particular complex of problems that a system can adopt in order to survive,* and 'survival' here includes persistence, evolution and transmutation. So for Parsons, functional analysis consists in establishing *a classification of the problems which every system must resolve* in order to exist and keep itself going' (Rocher, 1974, p. 155). This leads Parsons to the notion of what are called 'functional prerequisites' or 'functional imperatives' − the functions which must be performed if a society is to survive. As Parsons has put it, 'any social system is subject to four independent functional imperatives or "problems" which must be met adequately if equilibrium and/or continuing existence of the system is to be maintained' (Parsons, 1959, p. 16). These are most clearly illustrated in his so-called AGIL scheme, which identifies the four basic functional imperatives which Parsons regards as being relevant to the analysis of all social systems.[7] Simply put, these are:

Adaption   the complex of unit acts which serve to establish relations between the system and its external environment.

Goal attainment

the actions which serve to define the goals of the system and to mobilise and manage resources and effort to attain goals and gratification.

Integration   the unit acts which establish control, inhibit deviancy, and maintain co-ordination between parts, thus avoiding serious disturbance.

Latency or pattern maintenance

the unit acts which supply actors with necessary motivation.

As Radcliffe-Brown noted, the notion of needs or conditions of existence is implicit in the use of the analogy of a biological organism for social analysis. In placing them at the centre of analysis, however, Parsons ignores the limitations of this analogy for the study of society which Radcliffe-Brown was so careful to specify and redirects the main thrust of functionalist enquiry. Both Malinowski and Radcliffe-Brown had assumed that social 'structures' were implicit in the operation of social systems, and that the problem of empirically based social analysis was to identify the functions which the various elements of structure performed. Parsons in effect inverts this problematic: starting with the functions which must be performed, the problem of empirical social science becomes that of identifying the structures or elements of social systems which serve given imperative functions.[8] As David Lockwood (1956) has observed, Parsons' approach to the analysis of the social system has been heavily weighted by assumptions and categories which relate to the role of *normative* elements in social action, and especially to the processes whereby motives are structured normatively to ensure social stability. This normative orientation has attracted the charge that Parsons' scheme is inherently conservative, geared to a reaffirmation of the *status quo* and unable to deal with change.[9] Parsons, in the tradition of Comte, Spencer and Durkheim, has underwritten his approach by the implicit assumption that modern industrial society rests at the pinnacle of human achievement, and that the predominant problem is that of regulation. As Lockwood notes, one of the central themes emerging from Parsons' classic early work *The Structure of Social Action* is that 'order is possible through the existence of common norms which regulate "the war of all against all" ' (Lockwood, 1956, p. 137). Parsons' later work strongly reflects this basic orientation, though he has in fact been aware of the need to make his model a dynamic one capable of accommodating and explaining change.

Valid as the charge of a normative orientation in Parsons' work might be, it is also important to recognise that a certain degree of conservatism is imposed by adherence to the organismic analogy itself.[10] This is a point of particular significance in view of the fact that many structural functionalists do not specifically follow Parsons' normative orientation. Although the Parsonian model is often seen as dominating the contemporary structural functionalist perspective, there are other models which have developed independently. These other models also encounter difficulty in handling high degrees of change. As Radcliffe-Brown noted, this is a limitation inherent in the use of the organismic analogy. Radcliffe-Brown identified as his third set of problems those of development – that is, how do new types of social structure come into existence? It is of great significance that the structural functionalists have had the most difficulty with this issue and that it remains the least well explored.

Interestingly enough, the principal contributions to this problem area have come from theorists who have sought to provide a critique of structural functionalism as a whole or to provide alternative methods of analysis. Merton's contribution, for example, provides a good illustration of the former and Buckley's morphogenic systems theory an example of the latter. We will examine both later in this chapter under the broad heading of integrative theory. The positions which they develop represent a move away from the dominant perspectives which characterise social system theory; it takes these theorists to a different location within the functionalist paradigm.

By way of summary, therefore, we conclude our discussion of structural functionalism with the observation that from its start it has been dominated by the use of biological analogy for the study of society. Different varieties can be observed in practice. There are those approaches which focus upon system parts rather than upon systems as a whole. There are approaches in the tradition of Malinowski and Radcliffe-Brown which are most concerned with establishing the functions which various elements of society perform. There are those which focus upon 'social morphology' and often result as abstracted empiricism. There are those which focus upon functional imperatives or system needs and which seek to analyse society in whole or part with this perspective in mind. All these approaches adopt an approach to social science characteristic of the objectivist region of the functionalist paradigm. Ontologically, epistemologically and methodologically, structural functionalism has been based upon models derived from the natural sciences. For the most part, this has carried with it a relatively determinist view with regard to human nature. In terms of its characterisation of society, the overriding fact that the 'needs' or 'necessary conditions of existence' of social systems underwrite the very notion of function has inevitably committed structural functionalism to a perspective located within the sociology of regulation.

The current state of structural functionalism ranges from 'grand theory' to 'abstracted empiricism' with a general emphasis in the latter upon structure rather than function. The notion of functional *process* which was so important to its founding fathers has, for the most part, either been ignored or lost. The qualifications which were identified in drawing analogies between biological and social phenomena seem largely to have gone astray. Fostered by utilitarian demands for pragmatic theory and research geared to piecemeal social engineering – political, managerial, and the like – theoretical insights have been largely submerged under a deluge of empirical research. Indeed, structural functionalism as represented in the work of Radcliffe-Brown has proved a rare and transient phenomenon.

Systems theory

Since the early 1950s the 'systems approach' has assumed increasing importance in various branches of social analysis. In sociology, psychology, anthropology, archaeology, linguistics, organisation theory, industrial relations and many other social science subjects, systems theory has become established as an important method of analysis. Among the more prominent studies, it is worth citing by the way of illustration the work of Parsons *(The Social System*, 1951)*, Homans *(The Human Group*, 1950)*, Katz and Kahn *(The Social Psychology of Organisations*, 1966)*, Easton *(The Political System*, 1953)* Dunlop *(Industrial Relations Systems*, 1958)* and Buckley *(Sociology and Modern Systems Theory*, 1967)*.

Despite its popularity, however, the notion of 'system' is an elusive one. Many books on systems theory do not offer a formal definition of the systems concept, and where a definition is attempted, it is usually one of considerable generality.[11] For example, Angyal suggests that 'there is a logical genus suitable to the treatment of wholes. We propose to call it system' (Angyal, 1941, p. 243). Again, in the words of von Bertalanffy, the founding father of general systems theory, 'there are correspondences in the principles which govern the behaviour of entities that are intrinsically, widely different. This correspondence is due to the fact that they all can be considered, in certain respects, as "systems", that is, complexes of elements standing in interaction' (von Bertalanffy, 1956, pp. 1–2).

The notions of 'holism' and 'interaction' of parts are not exclusive to systems theory, and skeletal definitions such as these have led many social scientists to the view that systems theory often represents little more than old conceptualisations dressed up in new and needlessly complex jargon. For many, it is another case of the emperor having no clothes.

However, the situation is, in fact, much more sophisticated than this. Von Bertalanffy wishes to use the notion of 'system' as a means of cutting through the substantive differences which exist between different academic disciplines. The subject matter of chemistry, physics, biology, sociology, etc., are linked in his view by the fact that they study 'complexes of elements standing in interaction', that is, 'systems'. The task of his general systems theory is to discover the principles of organisation which underlie such systems. One of his general aims is to achieve a 'unity of science' based upon 'the isomorphy of laws in different fields' (von Bertalanffy, 1956, p. 8).

In many respects von Bertalanffy's aim can be regarded as archetypical of the positivist perspective: it is based upon epistemological assumptions dominated by a concern to search for and explain the underlying regularities and structural uniformities which characterise the world in general. However, his perspective differs from that of most positivists, in that he does not take his point of departure from the traditions of conventional science. Indeed, the contrary is true. Von Bertalanffy is firmly set against the reductionism which characterises most areas of scientific endeavour, with its emphasis upon modes of enquiry based upon the methods and principles of conventional physics. He views his general systems theory as providing an alternative to this; instead of reducing all phenomena of study to physical events, he advocates that we study them as systems. His positivism is thus of a non-traditional kind and is dominated by the metaphor of 'system' as an organising concept.

Von Bertalanffy makes much use of 'the limitations of conventional physics' as a means of advocating his general systems approach. In this the difference between 'closed' and 'open' systems plays a very important part. Von Bertalanffy argues that conventional physics deals mainly with closed systems, that is, systems which are considered to be isolated from their environment. The method of the controlled experiment, in which the subject of study is taken out of its environment and subjected to various tests, provides a very good example of this. Such closed systems are characterised by equilibrium. As von Bertalanffy puts it, 'a closed system *must*, according to the second law of thermodynamics, eventually attain a time independent equilibrium state, with maximum entropy and minimum free energy, where the ratio between its phases remains constant' (von Bertalanffy, 1950).

Open systems are quite different, in that they are characterised by an exchange with their environment. They engage in transactions with their environment, 'importing' and 'exporting' and changing themselves in the process.[12] A living organism provides a good example of an open system, since it maintains itself through a process of exchange with its environment, during the course of which there is a continuous building up and breaking down of component parts. The concept of an open system is thus essentially processual. Whilst a closed system *must* eventually obtain an equilibrium state, an open system will not. Given certain conditions, an open system *may* achieve a steady state, homeostasis, in which the system remains constant as a whole and in its phases, though there is a constant flow of the component materials. However, such a steady state is *not* a necessary condition of open systems.

This is a point of the utmost importance, and it needs to be emphasised. An open system can take a wide variety of forms. There are no general laws which dictate that it must achieve a steady state, be goal directed, evolve, regress or disintegrate. In theory, anything can happen. One of the purposes of open systems theory is to study the pattern of relationships which characterise a system and its relationship to its environment in order to *understand* the way in which it operates. The open systems approach does not carry with it the implication that any one particular kind of analogy is appropriate for studying all systems, since it is possible to discern different types of open system in practice.

The above point has not been clearly articulated and stressed in the literature on systems theory, at least not in the systems literature most often read by social scientists. As far as most social scientists are concerned, there are two types of system perspectives – open and closed. The fact that the former encompasses a whole range of possibilities is hardly ever recognised.

As a theoretical perspective in social science, the notion of a closed system tends to be avoided like a dreaded disease. Von Bertalanffy's argument that closed systems are characterised by isolation from their environment has proved overwhelmingly successful in persuading social theorists that the closed systems approach is inappropriate as a guiding principle for the conceptualisation of social phenomena. Indeed, it has become almost obligatory for social systems theorists to decry the inadequacies of closed system theorising, and the sport of attacking exponents of this now redundant perspective has become an extremely popular one. In the field of organisation studies, for example, an attack upon the closed system thinking implicit in Weber's model of bureaucracy or classical management theory provides a convenient springboard for lauding the praises of the contemporary perspective of open systems theory.

Paradoxically, however, as a method of analysis the notion of a closed system is still dominant in many areas of social enquiry. The use of controlled experiments and interview programmes, and the attempt to measure social phenomena through attitude questionnaires, all provide examples of closed system methodologies based upon the assumption that the environment generated by the investigation has no impact upon the subject of study. The paradox is compounded by the fact that such closed system methodologies are often employed within the context of theoretical perspectives which emphasise the importance of an open systems approach. This link between theory and method is an extremely problematic one in many areas of social science.

Despite the widely recognised deficiencies of the closed system as a theoretical construct in social science, the full implications of an open systems approach have not been pursued in any real depth. The concept has been adopted in a very partial and often misleading way. For many theorists, the adoption of an open systems perspective has been a very limited venture, confined to recognising and emphasising the environment as an influence upon the subject of study and reformulating traditional models in terms of systems concepts. More than anything, the call to adopt an open systems approach has been interpreted as a call to take heed of the environment and often little else. As Buckley has noted, 'though there is a fair amount of superficial (and often incorrect) use of the newer terminology (it is almost *de rigueur* to mention ''boundary-maintenance'', input-output, ''cybernetic control'' (sic), feedback and the like), the underlying conceptions show little advance over the mechanical equilibrium model of earlier centuries' (Buckley, 1967, p. 7). As we will argue below, the openness of the majority of systems models has been fundamentally constrained by the nature of the analogy used as a basis of analysis.

The majority of systems models used in the social sciences tend to be based upon mechanical and biological analogies, though in recent years increasing attention has been paid to cybernetic models as a basis of analysis.[13] The mechanical models have been derived directly from the physical sciences and tend to be underwritten by the assumption that the system has a tendency to achieve an equilibrium state. Since, as we have already noted, equilibrium is only possible in closed systems, does this imply that all those theorists using mechanical models are working upon closed system principles? To the extent that most of these theorists recognise the influence of the environment, the answer is no. Though adhering to the underlying concept of equilibrium − albeit mistakenly in theoretical terms − they modify their analysis to allow for the fact that *disequilibrium* is a very common feature of the system; or that the situation is one of *dynamic equilibrium*, with the system moving from one equilibrium state to another; or that the system is characterised by *homeostasis*. All these three strategies can be understood as attempts to save the notion of equilibrium as an organising concept in open system situations where it is fundamentally inappropriate. Homeostasis is an acceptable open systems concept, but it implies an organismic as opposed to a mechanical analogy as an organising principle. Mechanical models of social systems, therefore, tend to be characterised by a number of theoretical contradictions and are thus of very limited value as methods of analysis in situations where the environment of the subject of study is of any real significance.

Among the most sophisticated and systematically developed mechanical equilibrium models in social science are those developed by the Harvard School of sociologists, who took their lead from Pareto and L. J. Henderson. Of these the models of Parsons (1951), Homans (1950), Barnard (1938), Mayo (1933) and Roethlisberger and Dickson (1939), are perhaps the best known and most readily recognised. It will be recalled from our discussion earlier in this chapter that Pareto saw society as a system of interrelated parts which, though in a continual state of surface flux, were also in a state of underlying equilibrium. His notions were avidly received by Henderson at Harvard and, through him, by the whole generation of social theorists who came under his strong influence during the 1920s and 1930s.[14] Henderson was a biochemist who, through the now famous Fatigue Laboratory, developed his contact with the Business School and with social theory. He was particularly interested in the potential contribution which Pareto's equilibrium systems analysis could make to sociology, particularly as a means of studying complex social phenomena comprising many variables in a state of mutual dependence. The notion of equilibrium had provided a powerful analytical tool for research in the physical sciences, and its extension to the social sciences appeared a natural and logical development. Cannon's use of the notion of homeostasis to describe equilibrium in the blood, also developed at Harvard, was seen as extending the power and relevance of the equilibrium notion.

As we noted earlier, in Pareto's work the concept of equilibrium had an ambiguous status, in that it is not always entirely clear whether he intended it to serve as an analytical tool or as a description of reality. In the work of the Harvard Group this ambiguity disappears, and the concept is used to serve both purposes. Mayo's analysis of industrial problems, Homans' study of the human group, Barnard's study of the organisation, and Parsons' study of the social system all reflect the assumption that their subject of study has a tendency to achieve a state of equilibrium. Given that the notion of equilibrium plays such a central role in their analysis, the influence of the environment, whilst recognised as important, is necessarily reduced to a secondary and very limited role. Environmental change is of principal significance as a source of disequilibrium. The possibility that environmental change may influence the very structure and essential nature of the system is negated to some extent by assumptions that equilibrium will eventually be restored. The use of a mechanical equilibrium analogy thus severely constrains the openness of the system under investigation.

Similar problems relate to the use of biological analogies in systems analysis. Since von Bertalanffy's advocacy of the merits of an open systems approach, the choice of a biological organism as a model for systems analysis has proved increasingly popular and has more or less replaced the older mechanical analogies. Indeed, the biological analogy of an organism – with its emphasis upon characteristic features such as energic input, throughput and output, homeostasis, negative entropy, differentiation, and equifinality[15] – has often been equated with the open systems approach *per se*. Von Bertalanffy's enthusiasm for illustrating the open systems notion with analogies drawn from biology, his former discipline, has led many social systems theorists to confuse what was intended as an illustration with a point of principle. For many, the adoption of an open systems approach has been equated with the adoption of an organismic analogy as a basis of analysis. As we are arguing here, this represents but one of a number of possible open systems analogies.

As noted earlier, the organismic analogy is built into Parsons' (1951) analysis of the social system.[16] It is also found in the work of Katz and Kahn (1966), the Tavistock group of researchers, for example, Miller and Rice (1967), and countless other systems theorists, particularly those who have addressed themselves to the study of organisations.

Such analyses are usually organised around general principles such as the following:

(a)   that the system can be identified by some sort of *boundary* which differentiates it from its environment;

(b)   that the system is essentially *processual* in nature;

(c)   that this process can be conceptualised in terms of a basic model which focuses upon *input, throughput, output* and *feedback;*

(d)   that the overall operation of the system can be understood in terms of the satisfaction of *system needs* geared to survival or the achievement of *homeostasis;*

(e)   that the system is composed of *subsystems* which contribute to the satisfaction of the system's overall needs;

(f)   that these subsystems, which themselves have identifiable boundaries, are in a state of mutual *interdependence*, both internally and in relation to their environment;

(g)   that the operation of the system can be observed in terms of the *behaviour* of its constituent elements;

(h)   that the critical activities within the context of system operation are those which involve *boundary transactions*, both internally between subsystems and externally in relation to the environment.

Most of these general principles apply to open systems of all kinds. Of particular importance as far as the organismic analogy is concerned are those which imply that the system has 'needs'; that these are necessarily geared to survival or homeostasis; and that the subsystems contribute to the well-being of the system as a whole. As will be recalled from our discussion of the structural functionalism of Radcliffe-Brown, the notion that a system has needs which must be fulfilled and the notion of functional unity both derive directly from the use of the analogy of the biological organism for the study of society. The notions of homeostasis and survival are characteristic of biological analogies at the level both of the organism and of the species.

As in the case of the mechanical equilibrium systems model, the use of the organismic analogy constrains the manner in which the system is viewed in relation to its environment. First, the system, like an organism, is cast in a responding role. Despite the fact that the relationship between system and environment is seen in theory as one of mutual influence, the organismic analogy encourages the view that it is the environment which influences and the system which responds. The emphasis is upon the environment acting upon the system rather than the other way around. Secondly, the organismic analogy tends to presume a relatively stable system structure. The system responds through recognisable channels, the constituent elements of which have a function to perform within the context of the system as a whole. Third, the general nature of the response is seen as being determined by the 'needs' of the system. These needs act as a reference point for interpreting the activities of the system as a whole. Full openness, however, requires that the system be allowed to act unfettered by such assumptions.

There are thus many points of similarity between the perspective of the systems theorist who adopts the organismic analogy as a basis for analysis and that of the structural functionalist. The models of Malinowski and Radcliffe-Brown, for example, are very similar to the notion of a homeostatic open-systems model. Both emphasise the processual nature of social affairs, 'structure' being a very transient phenomenon, temporarily expressing a relationship between system parts and their 'ecological' context. Whilst some systems models perhaps provide a more rigorous statement of the implications of the biological analogy – for example, with regard to concepts such as input, throughput, output, homeostasis, negative entropy, equifinality, etc. – at a conceptual level they usually add little to the structural functionalist's insight with regard to the essence of social affairs. Radcliffe-Brown's view that 'the social structure as a whole can only be observed in its functioning' well anticipates the essential nature of the systems view. Indeed, the parallels between the two perspectives can be seen as being even closer than this. As in the case of the structural functionalists, social systems theorists have largely restricted themselves to two of the problem areas identified by Radcliffe-Brown, those of social morphology and social physiology. Many theorists working under the banner of systems theory, for example, have concerned themselves with the measurement of structures, with the social morphology of systems. There are many prominent examples within the field of organisation studies. The work of the Aston group of researchers, for example, Pugh and Hickson (1976), Richard Hall (1972) and almost any issue of *Administrative Science Quarterly* present excellent illustrations. Their systems models are constructed around *structural* notions such as size, configuration, centralisation, technology, environmental domain, etc. Systems theorists who have concerned themselves with the problem of social physiology have usually followed Parsons' lead and have focused upon the notion of functional imperatives in one form or another. Examples reflected in the work of Katz and Kahn (1966), and the notion of the socio-technical system (for example, Trist and Bamforth, 1951; Rice, 1958), among others, will be discussed in some detail in the next chapter. Both these lines of development are open to the same sort of evaluation and criticism which we have discussed in relation to structural functionalists who have focused upon social morphology and social physiology. The social morphologists have tended to emphasise structure at the expense of process and, along with the social physiologists, have tended to provide explanations of social affairs which are geared to providing explanations of the *status quo*. Both have largely ignored or underplayed the third set of problems identified by Radcliffe-Brown — those of social development. Systems theorists who base their work upon mechanical and organismic models are not well equipped to explain situations in which the elaboration and change of basic structure are the essential features of the phenomena under investigation. They find difficulty in handling the problem of morphogenesis and discontinuous forms of change which lead to system disintegration, disappearance or destruction.

Walter Buckley (1967) has provided a critique of the inadequacies of conventional models used in social science in similar terms. He argues that in the realm of human activity it is the morphogenic nature of social arrangements which is all important, and that systems models adequate for the task of analysing these processes need to be adopted. Buckley's morphogenic view of society takes him away from that of the majority of more conventional social systems theorists, in that he sees social structure as emerging from the process of social interaction. This view of social process is in line with that of Radcliffe-Brown, though Buckley is not constrained by any adherence to the organismic analogy. His morphogenic systems theory is consistent with a more subjectivist position within the context of the functionalist paradigm, and we shall thus consider it in more detail in a later section of this chapter.

Buckley's analysis opens up new horizons as far as systems theory in social science is concerned. It illustrates that systems analysis need not be confined to the use of a particular kind of well-worn analogy, such as that of the organism. Other choices offer themselves for consideration. One of these, which has already been explored to a certain extent, is that of the cybernetic model.[17] Cybernetics has concerned itself with the study of phenomena which behave as if they had goals. More specifically, it is concerned with the theory of complex interlocking 'chains of causation' from which goal-seeking and self-controlling forms of behaviour emerge. Cybernetic models seek to cut through the substantive differences which exist between, for example, machines and organisms, in an attempt to focus upon common organisational principles which define the nature of self-regulating systems. Such models offer a useful alternative to the traditional social system analogies in situations where the study of social regulation or social engineering is a primary concern.

Other analogies also offer themselves as a basis for systems analysis. As we shall argue in later chapters, if the concern is to study situations in which conflictual relationships tend to predominate, then an analogy which emphasises that the system has a tendency to break up or divide may be more appropriate. 'Factional' or 'catastrophic' systems models may provide a better explanation of the subject under study. One of the central problems facing the systems analyst is that of choosing an analogy which reflects the basic nature of the phenomena to be investigated.

Figure 4.1 presents an array of systems models arranged along a continuum describing the extent to which they emphasise order and stability as opposed to conflict and change as a normal tendency in system operation. In certain respects a rough parallel can be drawn between this continuum and the regulation—radical change dimension of the analytical scheme which we are using to differentiate between paradigms in social theory. Generally speaking, the mechanical, organismic and morphogenic models are consistent with a perspective characteristic of the functionalist paradigm; the other two models are more characteristic of the radical structuralist paradigm.

The emphasis in our discussion here has been placed upon the fact that systems theory in principle is not linked to the use of any one particular type of analogy. The fact that most applications

TYPE OF SYSTEM ANALOGY	Mechanical	Organismic	Morphogenic	Factional	Catastrophic
PRINCIPAL TENDENCY	Equilibrium	Homeostasis	Structure elaboration	Turbulent division	Complete reorganisation

ORDER AND STABILITY ←———————————→ CONFLICT AND CHANGE

Figure 4.1 Some possible types of system models

have been based upon the mechanical and organismic models, especially the latter, has often disguised this fact. The focus in modern systems theory is upon the way in which a system is organised internally and in relation to its environment. It seeks to penetrate beyond the substantive nature of machine, organism or whatever to reveal its principle of organisation. Systems theory is about organisation – the organisation of 'complexes of elements standing in interaction', to use von Bertalanffy's words (1956, p. 2). The automatic selection of one particular kind of analogy to represent a system pre-empts systems analysis, since each kind of analogy presumes a specific kind of structure and concommitant pattern of information process, exchange, behaviour and the like. The selection of a particular type of analogy to represent a system in advance of a detailed analysis of its structure and mode of operation is akin to prescription in advance of diagnosis. This has been the principal problem with systems analysis in social science. Social theorists have generally reached for some simple mechanical or organismic analogy in advance of any study of the system to which it is to be applied. In doing so, they have meted out rough justice to the essential nature of the social phenomena which they are investigating.

It will be clear from the above discussion that systems theory is not intrinsically tied to any specific view of social reality, except insofar as its general positivist orientation implies a social world characterised by some form of order and regularity which can be captured in the notion of 'system'. Insofar as it has been applied through use of mechanical and biological models, however, it has been committed to a highly objectivist view of the social world. By implication, the principles of physics and biology have been seen as capable of explaining the nature of the social world. In this respect there are direct parallels with structural functionalism and the development of a functionalist perspective stretching back to Durkheim, Spencer and other theorists before. We represent this overall perspective under the notion of social system theory, which occupies an area of that functionalist paradigm akin to that illustrated in Figure 3.3. Its relatively objectivist location will become all the more apparent as we move to consideration of other schools of thought located within the paradigm.

Interactionism and Social Action Theory

In terms of intellectual tradition, interactionism and social action theory can both be understood as representing a fusion of certain aspects of German idealism and Anglo-French sociological positivism. We have already considered sociological positivism in some detail and will be devoting attention to the idealist tradition in Chapter 6. As a means of presenting the essential characteristics of interactionism and action theory here, therefore, we will confine our attention to their immediate intellectual history. We will show how the foundations of interactionism were largely laid by Georg Simmel and George Herbert Mead, two theorists whose thought is characteristic of what has come to be known as the neo-idealist tradition. We will show how action theory derives from the work of Max Weber, another neo-idealist. Whilst sharing a similar position in relation to the subjective—objective dimension of our analytical scheme, their thought is differentiated because they focus upon different elements of social process.

Interactionism

Georg Simmel (1858–1918) was, to use Merton's words, a man of innumerable seminal ideas.[18] A philosopher and historian turned sociologist, he contributed freely to a wide range of areas of enquiry, and his thought defies simple and straightforward classification. His eclectic approach led to the development of a brand of sociology containing many strains and tensions which have never been fully reconciled. Essentially he was an academic renegade, shunning many aspects of both major contemporary schools of thought. He drove a middle way between idealism and positivism, retaining only those aspects of each which lent themselves to his own particular needs.

The German idealist tradition held that there was a fundamental difference between nature and culture and that natural laws were inappropriate to the realm of human affairs, which were characterised by the autonomy of the human spirit. Society was regarded as having no real existence above and beyond the individuals which composed it; no social *science* was possible. As we have seen, the Anglo-French tradition, on the other hand, held that society did have an objective existence and in many respects could be likened to a biological organism. Accordingly, it was characterised by the operation of laws which were amenable to investigation through the methods of natural science. Simmel rejected the extremes of both positions and argued in favour of an analysis of human association and interaction. Beneath the variety and complexity of individual affairs, he argued, there was a pattern. Beneath the content, an underlying form. He favoured a sociology focusing upon an intermediate level of analysis. In Coser's words, he was concerned with the study of society as

> an intricate web of multiple relations established among individuals in constant interaction with one another... The larger superindividual structures — the state, the clan, the family, the city, or the trade union — turn out to be but crystallizations of this interaction, even though they may attain autonomy and permanency and confront the individual as if they were alien powers. The major field of study for the student of society is, hence, *association* rather than society. (Coser, 1965, p. 5)

Simmel thus focused his attention upon human beings in their social context, a theme which reverberates throughout his many works. He was interested, above all else, in what he describes as 'interactions among the atoms of society'. As he put it,

> They account for all the toughness and elasticity, all the colour and consistency of social life, that is so striking and yet so mysterious. Sociology asks what happens to men and by what rules they behave, not insofar as they unfold their understandable individual existences in their totalities, but insofar as they form groups and are determined by their group existence because of interaction. (Simmel, 1950, pp. 10–11)

Beneath the mystery and individual character of interactions lay the 'form', or what Coser describes as the 'geometry' or 'grammar', of social life. For Simmel, the basic patterns lay hidden beneath the 'content' of social life and had to be extracted through formal analysis. Much of his work was devoted to an analysis of these forms and their influence upon human action and behaviour. His analysis of social forms such as dyadic and triadic relationships, group processes and the influence of group size on activities, provide good illustrations of the general orientation of his relativist, though firmly nomothetic, approach to the study of social life.

Despite his concern for form and pattern in social affairs, Simmel was by no means a strict determinist. In his view of human nature he again occupies a middle ground between the German and Anglo-French traditions. He saw social life as being characterised by a continuous conflict between the individual and his social world. His work is characterised by what Coser describes as an emphasis on a 'dialectical tension between the individual and society', in which the individual, though a product of his social world also stands apart. 'The individual is determined, yet determining, acted upon, yet self-actuating' (Coser, 1965, pp. 10, 11).

In terms of the subjective–objective dimension of our analytical scheme, therefore, Simmel occupies an interesting and complex position. On the ontological strand, he stands mid-way between the Anglo-French 'realism' and German 'nominalism'. On the epistemological strand, his belief in underlying form and pattern in human affairs places him towards the positivist position. In terms of the methodological strand his position is clearly nomothetic. On the human nature strand, he occupies an intermediate position. For these reasons we identify his brand of theorising as characteristic of the least objectivist fringe of the functionalist paradigm.

Simmel's interest in sociology at a micro-level of analysis led to many insights with regard to the dynamics of social life. The theme of conflict between the individual and the institutional context, for example, is one which runs throughout many aspects of Simmel's work and provides a valuable guideline as to where he stands in relation to the regulation—radical change dimension of our analytical scheme.

For Simmel, conflict was inherent in social life. As Coser notes,

> Simmel would have rejected any attempt to understand societies by way of models emphasising exclusively those processes making for harmony, consensus, and balance among component individuals and groups. To Simmel, sociation always involves harmony *and* conflict, attraction *and* repulsion, love *and* hatred. He saw human relations as characterised by ambivalence, precisely because those who are connected in intimate relations are likely to harbour for one another not only positive but also negative sentiments.
>
> An entirely harmonious group, Simmel argued, could not exist empirically. It would not partake of any kind of life process; it would be incapable of change and development. Any social relationship needs attractive and repulsive forces, harmony and disharmony, in order to attain a specific form. (Coser, 1965, p. 12)

The inherent conflict between the individual and his situation provides the basis of a penetrating analysis of the alienated state of modern man, particularly in works such as *The Stranger* and *The Metropolis and Mental Life*. Simmel presents the trend to modernity as reflecting a preponderance of what Nisbet has called 'the tyrany of objectivism' – the preponderance of 'the object spirit' over the 'subjective spirit' (Nisbet, 1967, pp. 305–12).

The individual, for Simmel, had 'become a mere cog in an enormous organisation of things and powers which tear from his hands all progress, spirituality, and value in order to transform them from their subjective form into the form of a purely objective life' (Simmel, 1950, p. 422). His analysis of 'alienation' could well have led him to a sociological perspective diametrically opposed to the interests of the *status quo*. However, he did not follow this path. As Nisbet notes, the notion of 'alienation' became for Simmel a kind of methodological tool with which 'ever more minute aspects of the social order are brought into view' (Nisbet, 1966, p. 311).

Within the context of his overall sociological perspective 'conflict' and 'alienation' were interpreted as playing an essential and positive role in society. This view was an essential aspect of his notion of the 'fallacy of separateness'. For Simmel, each aspect of interaction had to be understood in terms of its reciprocal context. Thus conflict and order were two aspects of the same reality; a measure of alienation was an essential ingredient of man's awareness of himself as a person. From this point of view, all social phenomena could be interpreted as playing an essential part in the maintenance of the wider society. This aspect of his thought brings Simmel very close to a functionalist interpretation of society, a view clearly reflected in his view of the latent positive functions of conflict.[19] As Coser notes, Simmel argued that

> Social conflict necessarily involves reciprocal action and is, hence, based on reciprocity rather than unilateral imposition. Conflict might often bind parties which might otherwise withdraw. It might serve as a safety valve for negative attitudes and feelings, making further relationships possible. For example, conflict might lead to a strengthening of the position of one or more parties to the relationship, increasing their dignity and self-esteem through self-assertion. Thus, conflict might produce new ties among the participants, strengthening their existing bonds or establishing new ones. In this sense, conflict might be considered a creative force rather than a destructive one ... The good society − far from conflict-free − is, on the contrary, 'sewn together' by a variety of criss-crossing conflicts among its component parts. (Coser, 1965, p. 12)

Simmel's brand of social theorising, therefore, is firmly rooted within the context of the sociology of regulation. Whilst recognising alienation and conflict as essential ingredients of social affairs, he incorporates them within an explanation of the *status quo* rather than as forces for radical change. Simmel's view of conflict has been particularly influential in establishing the 'problem of order' as the central problem of sociological analysis.[20] His writings have influenced developments in a number of areas, particularly those of urban sociology, experimental small-group research, reference group behaviour, role theory and conflict functionalism. In these diverse ways, Simmel's influence upon the functionalist paradigm has been of a major importance.[21]

The second theorist whom we identify as having made a major contribution to the interactionist movement is George Herbert Mead (1863–1931). Mead was an American social philosopher who, like Simmel, was influenced by the major cross-currents of thought flowing in the latter decades of the nineteenth century and the early decades of the twentieth century. In his wide-ranging contribution to social philosophy and social psychology, we again witness a fusion of the biological models derived from the Anglo-French tradition of social theorising with elements of German idealism. The product is a distinctive and complex system of thought containing many strains and tensions and is one which defies simple and straightforward treatment. The position is complicated by the fact that Mead published relatively little of his work. The books which appear under his name were assembled and edited posthumously from various notes and manuscripts held by former students and associates. Mead's position has thus necessarily been greatly influenced and modified by the interpretations placed upon it by students and editors alike and, as we shall argue below, his impact upon developments in social theory have been rather one-sided. Certain aspects of his thought have been developed at the expense of others.

Mind, Self and Society (1934), Mead's most influential work, is subtitled 'From the Standpoint of a Social Behaviourist'. Although Mead only used this term on one occasion (1934, p. 6), it is the term by which he and his work are most often identified and described. In point of fact, his work is much more wide-ranging than this, and a strong claim can be made that in his other books he moves away from this position towards a much more phenomenological stance.[22]

In *Mind, Self and Society* Charles Morris, its editor, suggests that 'philosophically, Mead was a pragmatist; scientifically, he was a social psychologist' (Mead, 1934, p. ix). The pragmatist movement sought to interpret the concepts of mind and intelligence in biological, psychological and sociological terms, in line with post-Darwinian views of the evolutionary nature of change and development.[23] It was a movement which can be clearly identified with the Anglo-French tradition of social theory. Mead, through his social psychology, sought to combine the biological models being used in psychology with the notion of 'society' or 'social interaction'.[24] His theories, as reflected in *Mind, Self and Society*, combined a modified form of behaviourism with elements of German idealism, such as the Hegelian notion of the social nature of self and morality.[25]

In *Mind, Self and Society* Mead seeks to establish how 'mind' and 'self' arise within the context of social conduct and interaction. His explanation places emphasis upon the role of gestures in the interaction process. Mead views the notion of 'gesture' in social terms – as part of an 'act'. In interaction between animals the social act or 'conversation of gestures' can be understood in terms of a series of symbols to which the various parties respond according to the interpretation placed upon the various gestures. Such action can be regarded as a form of communication, in which the various gestures or symbols involved influence later stages of the act. However, in the case of animals the meanings are not in the mind. Animals are not consciously communicating selves. Each animal determines its behaviour according to what the other is beginning to do.

With human beings the situation is somewhat different, since through 'vocal gestures' or language the individual has the capacity to become conscious of what he is doing. For Mead, it is the mechanism of language which underlies the development of 'mind'. Through the operation of 'mind', the individual can become the object of his own thoughts. It is this process which underlies the development of 'self'. In Morris's words, 'Mead's endeavour is to show that mind and the self are without residue social emergents; and that language, in the form of the vocal gesture, provides the mechanism for their emergence' (Mead, 1934, p. xiv).

Thus, for Mead, the conscious human being evolves through a social process, a process of interaction which involves the development of language and hence 'mind' and 'self'. The human being, unlike other animal organisms, has the capacity to become aware of what he is about. For this to happen, he must be able to interpret the meaning of his personal gestures. This involves an internal 'conversation' or process of thinking from the standpoint of what Mead called 'the generalised other' (Mead, 1934, p. 155). As Morris puts it,

> Behaviouristically, this is to say that the biological individual must be able to call out in himself the response his gesture calls out in the other,

and then utilise this response of the other for the control of his own further conduct. Such gestures are significant symbols. Through their use the individual is 'taking the role of the other' in the regulation of his own conduct. Man is essentially the role-taking animal. The calling out of the same response in both the self and the other gives the common content necessary for community of meaning (Mead, 1934, p. xxi).

In providing a bio-social explanation of the emergence of 'mind' and 'self', Mead drives mid-way between the idealist view of society as a subjectively constructed entity and a biological view which ignores the influence of the social aspects of human development. Ontologically, Mead's views, as expressed in *Mind, Self and Society*, are predicated upon the existence of an external world which influences human thought and action. Society is ontologically prior to 'mind' and 'self'.[26] However, his position is far from being deterministic. Rejecting the notion of simple stimulus-response models of human behaviour,[27] Mead recognises the role played by human beings in influencing their environment, particularly through symbolic interpretation of the consequences of various types of environmental conditions and modes of interaction. Individual actors are thus accorded at least a mediating and interpretive, if not entirely controlling or creative, role in relation to their environment. Epistemologically, on the basis of Morris's interpretation, Mead again occupies a middle ground. The world of science is conceived as essentially social in nature:

> composed of that which is common to and true for various observers — the world of common or social experience as symbolically formulated... The experienced world is conceived by Mead as a realm of natural events, emergent through the sensitivity of organisms, events no more a property of the organism than of the things observed. Philosophically the position here is an objective relativism: qualities of the object may yet be relative to a conditioning organism. A certain portion of the world, as experienced, is private, but a portion is social or common, and science formulates it. Private experience and common experience are polar concepts; the private can only be defined over against that which is common. (Mead, 1934, p. xix)

Mead's position is presented by Morris as being essentially that of 'objective relativism in regard to universals . . . By making universality relative to the act it is brought within the scope of an empirical science and philosophy' (Mead, 1934, p. xxviii). Mead was essentially a theorist who drew upon empirical examples to illustrate his concepts and point of view.

In terms of the four strands of the subjective—objective dimension of our analytical scheme, therefore, Mead's position as reflected in *Mind, Self and Society* can be interpreted as being close to that of Simmel. Although their theories and ideas differ in many important respects,[28] they are both committed to an interactionist form of analysis focusing upon individuals in a social context. For both, the realm of social affairs is essentially processual in nature, characterised by an underlying form expressed through social interaction. The study of this interaction is central to their social theories, which in the case of both writers are firmly geared to providing an explanation of the *status quo*.

For these reasons we could identify Mead as essentially a theorist of 'regulation', whose thought, along with that of Simmel, can be regarded as characteristic of the least objectivist fringe of the functionalist paradigm. On the basis of the way in which Mead's thought has been interpreted and used by subsequent theorists and researchers, there is a large measure of justification for doing this, since, as we shall argue later, Mead's work as interpreted above has had a considerable influence upon various aspects of interactionist thought. However, this whole mode of interpretation has been criticised as unrepresentative of Mead's true position and, following this line of argument, a case can be made for locating Mead within the interpretive paradigm – even though the work of most of his so-called followers and adherents would, without question, remain firmly located within the context of the functionalist paradigm.[29]

Maurice Natanson (1973c), in a very clear and coherent analysis of Mead's work, argues that the categorisation of Mead as a 'social behaviourist' misrepresents his position, and that his theory of social reality is of a more open-ended and developmental character. He argues that *Mind, Self and Society, The Philosophy of the Present* (1932b) and *The Philosophy of the Act* (1938) signify three implicit directions in Mead's overall position, and that the fundamental themes explored 'bear amazing resemblance to the problems of phenomenological philosophising in the tradition of Edmund Husserl' (Natanson, 1973c, p. 4). Natanson's view is that as Mead moved in his development away from 'pragmatic' philosophers such as James, Cooley and Dewey, to philosophers such as Bergson, Alexander and Whitehead, the nature of his thought moved 'from a problematic empiricism toward an idealistic and subjectivistic account of the nature of social reality' (Natanson, 1973c, p. 4). The three major directions in Mead's development are seen as:

(a) 'the attempt to explore and describe experience within society, treating consciousness, language, communication, and meaning as emergents from the social process';

(b) 'the re-approach to the same phenomena in terms of subjectivity, treating the given in experience as arising epistemologically and experientially within what Mead terms the "Act"';

(c) 'the attempt to describe what is given in experience by means of a radical theory of temporality which takes the present as the locus of reality' (Natanson, 1973c, p. 5).[30]

In terms of our analytical scheme the three directions represent a progressive movement away from the context of the functionalist paradigm towards the interpretive paradigm. In the course of his intellectual development Mead's meta-theoretical assumptions with regard to our subjective—objective dimension changed substantially, and it is this change which accounts for many of the strains and contradictions which Natanson and others have identified in his work. In other words, Mead's adherents have interpreted his work from the context of *their* meta-theoretical assumptions. As Douglas (1970b, p. 17) has noted, and our above analysis suggests, it is possible to distinguish between 'two parallel, but conflicting strains of interactionist thought: "behavioural interactionism" and "phenomenological interactionism" '. The 'behavioural interactionists' have interpreted Mead within the context of the functionalist paradigm; the 'phenomenological interactionists' within the context of the interpretive paradigm. Whilst recognising their indebtedness to a common heritage, they have used Mead's work in fundamentally divergent ways.

So much, for the moment, for the theories and ideas of Mead and Simmel. To many readers the attention which we have devoted to them may appear disproportionate within the context of our work as a whole. We justify our position on the basis that their theories and ideas have provided important foundations for developments in sociology and social psychology which are not always fully recognised. Simmel is given little prominence in modern sociological texts; in the literature on social psychology he is rarely mentioned. Yet his pioneering work underpins much contemporary theory in both these fields. The influence of Mead, though often recognised, is rarely treated comprehensively and his ideas are interpreted in a partial and often misleading way.

It is through the melting pot of what has come to be known as 'Chicago sociology' that the influence of Simmel and Mead have had the greatest impact upon contemporary sociological theory.[31]

Under the influence of leading intellectual figures such as Albion Small, W. I. Thomas, James Dewey, G. H. Mead, R. E. Park, E. W. Burgess and E. Faris, the Department of Sociology at Chicago had a major impact upon developments in American sociology from the 1890s until at least the beginning of World War II. Although each of these men made an original and distinctive contribution to philosophical and sociological thought, it is the work of Mead and Simmel which has had the most lasting influence.[32] Many of the interactionist ideas which characterise Chicago sociology can be directly traced to one or other of these two key figures or seen as representing a fusion of their respective contributions.[33] A full account of interactionist theory and research would call for a volume in itself. Our discussion here, therefore, will be restricted to an analysis of its dominant form – symbolic interactionism.

Symbolic interactionism

The term 'symbolic interactionism' has come to be associated with a very wide range of interactionist thought. Essentially, the notion derives directly from the work of Mead and the distinction which he drew between 'non-symbolic' and 'symbolic' interaction. As Herbert Blumer, one of Mead's ex-students and most prominent interpreters, has put it:

> In non-symbolic interaction human beings respond directly to one another's gestures or actions; in symbolic interaction they interpret each other's gestures and act on the basis of the meaning yielded by the interpretation. An unwitting response to the tone of another's voice illustrates non-symbolic interaction. Interpreting the shaking of a fist as signifying that a person is preparing to attack illustrates symbolic interaction. Mead's concern was predominantly with symbolic interaction. Symbolic interaction involves *interpretation*, or ascertaining the meaning of the actions or remarks of the other person, and *definition*, or conveying indications to another person as to how he is to act. Human association consists of a process of such interpretation and definition. Through this process the participants fit their own acts to the ongoing acts of one another and guide others in doing so. (Blumer, 1966, pp. 537–8)[34]

Whilst owing general allegiance to this notion, the symbolic interactionist movement in sociology and social psychology has not developed in anything like a consistent manner and has no single integrated body of theory which defines its position.[35] Rather, it constitutes a general orientation which is concerned to understand social phenomena through the micro-analysis of human affairs. Mead's basic ideas and concepts appear under the guise of 'role theory',[36] 'reference group theory',[37] 'self theory',[38] 'dramaturgical theory',[39] and the like. All represent varieties of symbolic interactionist thought which tend to emphasise one aspect of Mead's work at the expense of another.

Although one can identify a range of symbolic interactionist thought in terms of categories such as those listed above, this misses a very important point, since the fundamental issue which divides symbolic interactionists relates to the position which they occupy on the subjective—objective dimension of our analytical scheme. As has been suggested earlier, it is possible to distinguish between so-called 'behavioural interactionism' and 'phenomenological interactionism'. The differences between these two modes of theorising and research are so fundamental that it is definitely misleading to regard symbolic interactionism as a coherent school of thought.

The distinctions between these two strains of symbolic interactionism can be clearly illustrated by comparing the views of Rose and Blumer presented in the former's collection of specially commissioned readings on interactionism (Rose, 1962). In the introductory· chapter Rose, recognising that there is no complete agreement on concepts, premises and propositions among those who regard themselves as symbolic interactionists, seeks to restate Mead's theory as expressed in *Mind, Self and Society* in 'simple, systematic and researchable form'. More specifically, he is concerned to state it 'in terms that will fit the frame of reference of the behaviourist or Gestaltist so as to make it more generally understandable'. In order to do this Rose identifies (and elaborates upon) the following assumptions and propositions:

ASSUMPTION 1 *Man lives in a symbolic environment as well as a physical environment and can be 'stimulated' to act by symbols as well as by physical stimuli* ...

ASSUMPTION 2 *Through symbols, man has the capacity to stimulate others in ways other than those in which he is himself stimulated* ...

ASSUMPTION 3 *Through communication of symbols, man can learn huge numbers of meanings and values – and hence ways of acting – from other men* ...

GENERAL PROPOSITION (DEDUCTION) 1 *Through the learning of a culture* (and subcultures, which are the specialised cultures found in particular segments of society), *men are able to predict each other's*

*behaviour most of the time and gauge their own behaviour to the
predicted behaviour of others . . .*
ASSUMPTION 4 *The symbols* − and the meanings and values to
which they refer − *do not occur only in isolated bits, but often in
clusters, sometimes large and complex . . .*
GENERAL PROPOSITION (DEDUCTION) 2 *The individual defines*
(has a meaning for) *himself as well as other objects, actions, and
characteristics . . .*
ASSUMPTION 5 *Thinking is the process by which possible symbolic
solutions and other future courses of action are examined, assessed for
their relative advantages and disadvantages in terms of the values of
the individual, and one of them chosen . . .* (Rose, 1962, pp. 5−12).[40]

This interpretation of Mead's work is clearly in the mould of the
'social behaviourist'. The essential concepts relating to symbolic
interactionism are interpreted within the context of a framework
which views man as living within an essentially 'realist' world of
symbolic and physical objects. It is a world to which man reacts
and which he influences, though the emphasis in Rose's work
appears to be on the former. The concern to deduce propositions
reflects a predilection for a positivist epistemology; specific
hypotheses are put forward in other contributions to Rose's book
and the methodologies employed are usually of a firmly nomothetic character. Rose's overall standpoint provides a clear illustration of Strauss's observation that sociologists who tend to be social
determinists read Mead as if he too were a social determinist
(Strauss, 1964, pp. xii−xiii).

By way of contrast, Blumer, in an article in the same book of
readings, adopts a more subjectivist position. He argues that recognition of the process of interpretation in human affairs has
fundamental implications for an understanding of the human
being, human action and human association, and, in consequence,
he adopts an ontology which is much more nominalist than that of
Rose. As Blumer puts it, 'Instead of the individual being surrounded by an environment of pre-existing objects which play
upon him and call forth his behaviour, the proper picture is that he
constructs his objects on the basis of his ongoing activity' (Blumer,
1962, p. 182). His view on human nature is also much more voluntarist: 'The second important implication of the fact that the human
being makes indications to himself is that his action is constructed
or built up instead of being a mere release' (Blumer, 1962, p. 182).
In line with this analysis, Blumer develops a view of society which
constitutes a process of symbolic interaction, in which individual
'selves' interpret their situation as a basis for action. Group or
collective action is seen as consisting of an alignment of individual

actions 'brought about by the individuals' interpreting or taking into account each other's actions' (Blumer, 1962, p. 184). In this article, Blumer is concerned to establish the credentials of symbolic interaction in preference to other elements of sociological thought, particularly those based on organic rather than interactionist models (structural functionalism and social systems theory, for instance). Accordingly, he does not elaborate his particular view of symbolic interaction in any real depth.[41] This is left to later works, in which he adopts an increasingly subjectivist orientation. In his 1966 article discussing the work of G. H. Mead, for example, he presents Mead as advocating a distinctly nominalist ontology and goes on to draw out its implications for individual and group action:

> for Mead objects are human constructs and not self-existing entities with intrinsic natures. Their nature is dependent on the orientation and action of people toward them . . . This analysis of objects puts human group life into a new and interesting perspective. Human beings are seen as living in a world of meaningful objects – not in an environment of stimuli or self-constituted entities. This world is socially produced in that the meanings are fabricated through the process of social interaction. Thus different groups come to develop different worlds – and these worlds change as the objects that compose them change in meaning. Since people are set to act in terms of the meanings of their objects, the world of objects of a group represents in a genuine sense its action organisation. To identify and understand the life of a group it is necessary to identify its world of objects; this identification has to be in terms of the meanings objects have for the members of the group. Finally, people are not locked to their objects; they may check action toward objects and indeed work out new lines of conduct toward them. This condition introduces into human group life an indigenous source of transformation. (Blumer, 1966, p. 539)

Blumer goes on to present symbolic interactionism as being essentially concerned with the meanings which underlie the process of interaction and as an attempt to understand society in these terms.[42] It is presented as a form of analysis geared to understanding the way in which people align themselves with different situations. This essentially phenomenological standpoint is developed further in his 1969 study and reinforced by a call for interactionist methodology to 'respect the nature of the empirical world' (Blumer, 1969, p. 60).

This split in orientation between behavioural and phenomenological symbolic interactionism which we have illustrated in relation to the work of Rose and Blumer is mirrored on a wider scale in the work of the so-called Iowa and Chicago approaches to symbolic interaction.[43] The former have been particularly concerned to operationalise their approach and, in so doing, have become increasingly committed to a structural as opposed to a processual view of the phenomena which they are concerned to investigate. As Manis and Meltzer have observed, this is very evident in the work on self theory, where there has been a tendency to abandon the non-empirical concepts in Mead's thought and focus upon the measurement of essentially abstract concepts (Manis and Meltzer, 1967, p. vi). It also characterises a great deal of the work on role theory, where the concern has been to identify and measure the nature of the external situation in which the particular actors under investigation find themselves. Essentially, the Iowa interactionists, as a result of their commitment to a positivist epistemology and nomothetic methodology,[44] have tended to violate their ontological assumptions.

It is this distinction which lies at the heart of the difference between behavioural and phenomenological symbolic interactionism. The difference between the two approaches is largely one of epistemology and methodology. Whilst both recognise, at a conceptual level, the processual nature of symbolic interaction, and the significance of meaning and interpretation from the point of view of the actors involved, their empirical work often fails to do full justice to the nature of their theory.[45] Indeed, on occasions it bears little relation to the theory from which it is derived and ends up as little more than an 'abstracted empiricism'. There is a parallel to be drawn here with developments in the fields of structural functionalism and systems theory. We noted in our discussion of these approaches how the notion of 'functional process' became lost in an empirical 'search for structure'. Interactionism has often suffered the same fate, many studies resulting in little more than a series of empirical snapshots of reified concepts which defy the processual nature of the interactionist perspective *per se*.

Social action theory

The theory of social action, sometimes described as 'the action frame of reference', derives largely from the work of Max Weber (1864–1920) and the notion of *verstehen*. As we argue in some detail in Chapter 6 on the sociology of the interpretive paradigm, the method of *verstehen* or interpretive 'understanding' plays a crucial role in neo-idealist social thought. Introduced by Wilhelm Dilthey, and elaborated by Weber, it was seen as a method of analysis particularly suited to the investigation of social affairs, for which the subjective meanings of events was all important. In contrast to the natural sciences, the cultural or social sciences were viewed by the neo-idealists as being concerned with subject matter of a fundamentally different kind. Whereas the natural sciences were seen as dealing with the study of external processes in a material world, the cultural sciences were seen as being concerned with the internal and intangible processes of human minds. Special approaches and methods were regarded as necessary for an understanding of this world of human affairs. The method of *verstehen* – of placing oneself in the role of the actor – was seen as a means of relating inner experience to outward actions.

As we argue in our discussion of the interpretive paradigm, Weber was something of a positivist in his general epistemology, in that he wished to construct an objective social science capable of providing causal explanations of social phenomena, yet one which avoided what he regarded as glaringly obvious deficiencies in positivist explanations of society. He saw the sociological positivists of his day as drawing too close an analogy between the natural and social worlds.

For Weber, explanations of the social world had to be 'adequate on the level of meaning'. Explanations of social affairs, he argued, had to take account of the way in which individuals attached subjective meaning to situations and orientated their actions in accordance with their perceptions of those situations. Sociology, from his point of view, had to be essentially 'interpretive' in nature. Social action theory is based upon this Weberian view of the nature of social science, but Weber's methods are not always taken up in a systematic fashion.

Weber, in line with his method of analysis based on ideal types, constructed a typology of social action which distinguished between: (a) action orientated to *tradition*; in essence this was conceived as action dominated by a habitual response; (b) action dominated by *emotional* factors – that is, spontaneous expressions of feelings; (c) action which was rationally orientated towards some absolute value – *wertrational* action; and (d) action which was rationally orientated towards the achievement of specific ends, and in which the relative advantages and disadvantages of alternative means are taken into account – *zweckrational* actions. It was Weber's view that these 'types of action', albeit oversimplifications, could provide a useful sociological tool for analysing the modes of orientation of social action in practice (Weber, 1947, pp. 115–24). This scheme has normally been neglected in favour of a more generalised interpretation of the action perspective, which focuses upon the way in which individuals interpret the situation in which they find themselves. For example, Cohen has suggested that the theory of action can be regarded as consisting of a number of assumptions which provide a mode of analysis for explaining the action and conduct of typical individuals (actors or social actors) in typical situations. These assumptions are stated as follows:

(i) The actor has goals (or aims, or ends); his actions are carried out in pursuit of these.

(ii) Action often involves the selection of means to the attainment of goals; but even where it appears that it does not, it is still possible for an observer to distinguish analytically between means and goals.

(iii) An actor always has many goals; his actions in pursuit of any one affect and are affected by his actions in pursuit of others.

(iv) The pursuit of goals and the selection of means always occurs within situations which influence the course of action.

(v) The actor always makes certain assumptions concerning the nature of his goals and the possibility of their attainment.

(vi) Action is influenced not only by the situation but by the actor's knowledge of it.

(vii) The actor has certain sentiments or affective dispositions which affect both his perception of situations and his choice of goals.

(viii) The actor has certain norms and values which govern his selection of goals and his ordering of them in some scheme of priorities. (Cohen, 1968, p. 69)

Interpreted from this viewpoint, the effect of Weberian action theory has been to inject a measure of voluntarism into theories of social behaviour by allowing for the fact that individuals interpret and define their situation and act accordingly.[46] Within the context of the functionalist paradigm, Weberian action theory defines a position which stands in contrast to the determinism which characterises theories in the most objectivist regions, such as Skinner's behaviourism, which we shall discuss in a later section of this chapter.

Most prominent among the social action theorists is the name of Talcott Parsons, who in his classic work, *The Structure of Social Action* (1949), argued that there was a tendency for the work of Durkheim, Marshall, Pareto and Weber to converge in terms of a 'voluntaristic theory of action'. Parsons advocated this 'voluntaristic theory' as a general sociological perspective, but in point of fact it was relatively short-lived. In Parsons' hands the theory of social action became steadily more deterministic and was eventually incorporated into his theory of the social system which, as we have argued earlier in this chapter, is located in a more objectivist region of the paradigm. There has been much debate over the nature of the changes reflected in Parsons' thought.[47] In terms of our analytical scheme, he has journeyed across the functionalist paradigm from a position on its subjectivist boundary consonant with Weber's theory of social action to a position firmly located within the bounds of social system theory. This positivist inclination has always been evident in Parsons' work. *The Structure of Social Action* is undoubtedly an impressive piece of scholarship, thoroughly deserving of the description 'classic', but, given the range of social theorists whom Parsons considered, it is hardly surprising that their thought converges within the boundaries of the functionalist paradigm. Durkheim, Marshall, Pareto and Weber are all located in terms of their meta-theoretical assumptions within this perspective. Giddens (1976, p. 16) has observed that *'there is no action in Parsons' "action frame of reference"*, only behaviour which is propelled by need-dispositions or role expectations. The stage is set, but the actors only perform according to scripts which have already been written out for them.' Such is the nature of the functionalist perspective; its underlying meta-theoretical assumptions only allow for a limited measure of voluntarism in human behaviour. As will become apparent from our discussion of the social thought characteristic of the interpretive paradigm, the social action perspective reflected in the Weberian and Parsonian theories represents a very limited excursion into the realm of the subjective. Weber, in attempting to synthesise idealism and positivism within the bounds of an epistemology orientated towards the latter, necessarily committed himself to an intermediate position in terms of the subjective—objective dimension of our analytical scheme.

Social action theory has never really obtained a firm footing in the USA. In addition to Parsons's intellectual journey away from the Weberian position towards social system theory, other factors account for the lack of interest and popularity. First, and perhaps most important, Weber's work was not available in English until the mid 1940s. Second, the dominant influence was that of the symbolic interactionist movement. As we have argued

earlier in this section, as a result of the efforts of the Chicago
School, interactionism in the Meadian and Simmelian traditions
became firmly established from the early 1920s onwards. Their
position with regard to the subjective—objective dimension of our
analytical scheme was broadly equivalent to that of Weber and
provided a happy compromise position between raw idealism and
sociological positivism. The focus was placed firmly upon 'interaction', within which the study of 'action' and subjective meaning
played an important part. Given the interest in micro-social processes, the thought of G. H. Mead in particular was immeasurably
richer than that of Weber, infused as it was with much stronger
elements of the phenomenological tradition.[48] Weber had moved
towards positivism; Mead was moving towards phenomenology.
Weber's typology of social action appears pale when compared
with Mead's notions about the genesis of self. In addition, W. I.
Thomas's ideas on 'the definition of the situation' had close links
with Weber's notion of meaningful action. In the USA the
Weberian theory of social action thus confronted a strong, popular, tailor-made alternative and made relatively little impression as
far as its potential adherents were concerned. It was Weber's fate
to be embraced by his critics. As we shall discuss in the next
chapter, the notion of the 'ideal-type' bureaucracy and the concept
of purposive rationality were utilised by objectivists, social system
theorists and bureaucracy theorists in a way Weber never
intended. His conceptual tools were used by theorists located
within the objectivist region of the functionalist paradigm which he
had devoted much of his intellectual energy to avoiding at all costs.
Moving in the opposite direction, his work was used as a starting
point for Schutz's development of 'existential phenomenology'.
As we shall see in our chapter on the interpretive paradigm,
Schutz's analysis, whilst full of praise for Weber, revealed
Weber's position for what it was – a compromise between subjectivist and objectivist views of social life. With the resurgence of
interest in the subjective approach to sociology which took place
on the West Coast of the USA during the 1960s, therefore, it was
the work of Schutz rather than that of Weber which provided the
stimulus for further developments. Ethnomethodology and
phenomenological symbolic interactionism had little use for
Weber's analysis. In addition, as will become clear from our discussion of radical humanism in Chapter 8, Weber's work was also
subjected to a through-going critique from yet another perspective
in the work of Herbert Marcuse. As far as the USA is concerned,
therefore, the Weberian influence has been perverse; the critics of

Weber have arguably been more influential than Weber himself.

In Europe the Weberian tradition has achieved quite a lot more prominence, though here again the interpretations placed upon Weber's work are in many cases contrary to those Weber would have wished. In particular, his work has been used by what we shall call radical Weberians operating within the context of the radical structuralist paradigm in their debate with Marxist theory, who have produced a radical conflict theory of society. The work of Dahrendorf (1959), which we have already discussed to an extent in Chapter 2, provides a prominent example of this perspective, though we shall have yet more to say about it in our discussion of radical structuralism in Chapters 10 and 11. As far as Weber's theory of social action is concerned, since the early 1960s it has received attention, in general terms, in the work of Rex (1961) and Eldridge (1971) and is reflected in the empirical studies conducted by Goldthorpe and his colleagues (1968) on orientations to work. It has also achieved prominence through Silverman's (1970) advocacy of the action frame of reference as an alternative to the 'systems orthodoxy' in organisation theory. We shall devote further attention to some of these works in our discussion of organisation theory in Chapter 5.

By way of conclusion, we note here that social action theory, like the interactionist thought of Mead and Simmel, can be understood in terms of an attempt to weld together idealist and positivist approaches to the study of society. In essence, they define an intermediate position in relation to the subjective—objective dimension of our analytical scheme, characteristic of the subjectivist boundary of the functionalist paradigm. However, as we have seen, they are often employed in practice in a manner consistent with a whole range of ontological, epistemological and methodological assumptions.

Integrative Theory

We use the term 'integrative theory' to characterise the brand of sociological theorising which occupies the middle ground within the functionalist paradigm. In essence, it seeks to integrate various elements of interactionism and social systems theory and, in certain cases, to counter the challenge to the functionalist perspective posed by theories characteristic of the radical structuralist paradigm, particularly those of Marx. It is by no means a coherent body of theory, and we shall discuss it under the following four headings, which identify its most important variations: (a) Blau's exchange and power model; (b) Mertonian theory of social and cultural structure; (c) conflict functionalism; (d) morphogenic systems theory.

Each of these four strains of thought rests upon the assumption that the achievement of social order within society is in some way problematic and calls for explanations which are not normally provided within the bounds of social systems theory.

Blau's theory emphasises the role of *exchange and power* as a central source of integration in social life. Merton's theory of social and cultural structure tends to emphasise the functions performed by elements of *social structure* in the integrative process. Conflict functionalism tends to focus upon the 'positive' functions served by *conflict*. Morphogenic systems theory emphasises the importance of *information* transmission as a central variable of analysis. In the following sections we will briefly discuss each in turn, demonstrating how they have drawn upon various aspects of the cross-currents of sociological thought reviewed earlier in the chapter and have been shaped into a distinctive theoretical perspective.

Blau's exchange and power model

Blau's theory of exchange and power in social life (1964) sets out to analyse the processes which govern human association, with a view to establishing the basis for a theory of social structure. His theory attempts to link the micro- and macro-levels of social analysis — to build a bridge between interactionism and social system theory. In this Blau draws heavily upon the perspectives generally developed by Simmel and by Homans (1958 and 1961).

Blau, following Simmel, regards the study of social association as the central task of sociology, and in this respect he is clearly 'interactionist' in his approach. However, he is firmly set against reductionist explanations of society, since they ignore what he calls the 'emergent properties' of human interaction. For Blau, society is more than the sum of its parts. Social structure cannot be reduced to a series of constituent elements; it has to be understood as an emergent social process.

In Blau's hands the notion of 'exchange' is given a limited but powerful role and is used as an analytical tool for tracing the emergent properties of social interaction.[49] For Homans, all human behaviour and interaction can be understood in terms of exchange based upon a form of economic calculus. Blau rejects this. He recognises that what he identifies as 'social exchange'[50] only accounts for a part of the whole range of human action and behaviour and that Homans's economic calculus only applies to an element of this. His analysis of the process of social exchange leads him to identify the ways in which status and power become differentiated, and the way in which power makes it possible to organise collective effort. He traces the manner in which the legitmation of power has its source in the social approval its fair exercise evokes among subordinates. His analysis recognises that normative consensus is by no means automatic, and that the exercise of power will not always be legitimised. Power, legitimised or not, is thus a central variable in his analysis, providing a major factor in accounting for social integration and control.[51]

Blau is concerned to shift the balance in sociological theory away from an emphasis upon normative consensus-orientated explanations of social integration towards analysis of social associations, the processes that sustain them, the forms they attain and the complex social forces and structures to which they give rise. He summarises the situation as follows:

> A concern with social action, broadly conceived as any conduct that derives its impetus and meaning from social values, has characterised contemporary theory in sociology for some years. The resulting preoccupation with value orientations has diverted theoretical attention from the study of the actual associations between people and the structures of their associations. While structures of social relations are, of course, profoundly influenced by common values, these structures have a significance of their own, which is ignored if concern is exclusively with the underlying values and norms. Exchange transactions and power relations, in particular, constitute social forces that must be investigated in their own right, not merely in terms of the norms that limit and the values that reinforce them, to arrive at an understanding of the dynamics of social structures. (Blau, 1964, p. 13)

His analysis emphasises the role of exchange and power in the emergence of social structure and thus their role as integrative forces in any explanation of society as an ongoing process. The Simmelian view of society as 'sewn together' by a variety of cross-cutting conflicts between its component parts is prominent in Blau's work. He analyses the relationships between sub-elements of society and the way in which conflicts produce a pattern of dialectical change. As he puts it,

The cross-cutting conflicts and oppositions in complex modern societies, with many intersecting organised collectivities and interlocking memberships in them, are a continual source of social reorganisation and change. The pattern of change is dialectical, since each basic reorganisation has wide repercussions that create new problems and stimulate fresh oppositions. The cross pressures resulting from multigroup affiliations and the recurrent alignments of overlapping collectivities in different controversies prevent conflicts over issues from becoming cumulative and producing a deep cleavage between two hostile camps. (Blau, 1964, p. 311)

Blau's analysis thus builds from an interactionist view of association towards a theory of social change which, in *his* interpretation of the spirit of a dialectic, involves neither evolutionary progress in a straight line nor recurring cycles but alternating patterns of intermittent social reorganisation along different lines. It is a perspective which sees society oscillating under the influence of recurrent dis-equilibrating and re-equilibrating forces. Although recognising conflict as inherent in all social affairs, Blau's view is thus firmly rooted in the sociology of regulation. His work on exchange and power in social life represents an attempt to develop the interactionist perspective into an 'integrative theory' of social structure.

Mertonian theory of social and cultural structure

This second brand of integrative theory builds upon the work of Robert Merton, who in many respects can be regarded as the integrative sociologist *par excellence*. His work reflects the direct influence of writers as widely diverse as Durkheim, Marx, Mead, Parsons, Simmel and Weber, and has been subject to a wide range of interpretations.[52] As we shall argue, Merton's work is integrative in the sense that it seeks to link a number of conceptually distinct theories within the context of the functionalist paradigm. It is also integrative in the sense that it seeks to link micro- and macro-levels of analysis, empiricism and grand theory, through what Merton has described as theories of the 'middle range' (Merton, 1968). Although integrative theory as defined here would for the most part correspond with Merton's specification of the 'middle range', it is not identical with it, since it is possible to develop 'middle-range' theories in a number of areas within the functionalist paradigm.

We take our point of departure here, from Merton's early work on 'reference groups' and 'anomie theory', which seeks to understand how sub-groupings arise within the context of the social structure (Merton, 1968). In his paper 'Social Structure and Anomie', first published in 1938, Merton seeks to discover how social structures exert a definite pressure upon certain persons in a society to engage in non-conforming behaviour. His perspective is described as that of a 'functional analyst who considers *socially deviant behaviour* just as much a product of social structure as *conformist behaviour*' (Merton, 1968, p. 175). In essence, his paper represents a direct attempt to counter the tendency prevalent within functional analysis of explaining social behaviour in terms of its orientation towards a system of central normative values. Merton's work thus stands out against the sort of explanations offered in Parsonian systems theory and attempts to modify the functionalist perspective so as to introduce elements capable of explaining the process of social change. By tracing the possible relationships between two elements of social structure − 'cultural goals' and the 'institutionalised means' of achieving them − Merton is able to develop a typology of individual adaptation which, in addition to 'conformity', allows for aberrant behaviour associated with 'innovation', 'ritualism', 'retreatism' and 'rebellion' (Merton, 1968, p. 194).

Merton's analysis must be understood as an attempt to strengthen functionalism. His treatment of aberrant or deviant behaviour stands in stark contrast to a symbolic interactionist view, which would stress the emergent character of norms and values. From an interactionist perspective, norms and values are socially generated and sustained by human beings in their everyday interaction with others. For Merton, they are part of a predefined social context within which social action takes place. Thus, whilst Merton's functional analysis of deviance moves some way from social system theory towards an interactionist perspective, it remains fundamentally distinct in terms of the position occupied on the subjective—objective continuum of our analytical scheme.

This intermediate position is also evident in Merton's analysis of reference group behaviour. As he suggests, his work in this area represents an effort to utilize functional analysis in the study of reference groups as an important component of social structure (Merton, 1968, p. 181). According to Merton, 'reference group theory aims to systematise the determinants and consequences of those processes of evaluation and self-appraisal in which the individual takes the values or standards of other individuals or groups as a comparative frame of reference' (Merton, 1968, p. 288).

This view of reference groups is a direct development of Mead's 'generalised other' – a notion used by Mead to explain the emergence of self through interaction (Mead, 1934, pp. 152–64). Merton thus uses an interactionist concept for the analysis of social structure. In doing so, he again integrates certain aspects of interactionism with social system theory. This is clearly evident in his concern for the problem of identifying 'functional types' of reference groups and subsequent research directed towards this endeavour. Kelley (1968), for example, has distinguished between two kinds of reference groups according to the two functions they perform in the determination of attitudes. The first of these – the *normative function* – is seen as being concerned with the setting and enforcing of standards, a possibility which arises whenever a group is in a position to deliver rewards or punishments for conformity or non-conformity.[53] The second – the *comparison function* – refers to the role of a reference group in providing a standard or point of comparison against which a person can evaluate himself or others.

Merton's contribution to both reference group theory and anomie theory has provided a fruitful basis for further detailed theorising and empirical research. As an examination of Hyman and Singer's (1968) collection of readings on reference groups and Clinard's (1964) readings on anomie and deviant behaviour will reveal, the manner and context in which the notions have been applied is quite diverse. Some of it is true to the integrative style characteristic of Merton's work and occupies a similar position within the context of the functionalist paradigm. The remainder is often much more objectivist in orientation and in certain cases is more appropriately classified as abstracted empiricism. As in other areas of the functionalist paradigm, positivist methodology has often done rough justice to the more subjectivist elements of the underlying theory on which the research is ostensibly based.

Merton's sociology is complex and wide-ranging. In the areas of theorising discussed above, emphasis tends to be placed upon the problematic nature of social order. Merton seeks to demonstrate that whilst the process of social integration is not as straightforward as many social systems theorists have presumed, an analysis of the relationship between human behaviour and social structure can demonstrate the ways in which order or deviance arise. In the work which we have discussed thus far problems of change and conflict are recognised but not pursued in any depth. In later work Merton becomes increasingly involved with these problems and lays the basis for another brand of integrative theory – conflict functionalism. His article 'Bureaucratic Structure and Personality' (Merton, 1968, pp. 249–60) marks the point of transition to this perspective. Using functional theory in the analysis of bureaucratic activities, he demonstrates how conformity to regulations can be dysfunctional for realising the objectives of the structure and the groups in society the bureaucracy is intended to serve.[54] In other words, Merton demonstrates that conformity to normative standards can actually provide a force for the disintegration of the social order, a perspective which is further developed in his analysis of manifest and latent functions discussed below.

Conflict functionalism

This third category of integrative theory developed as a response to the charges that functionalist theories of society are unable to provide explanations of social change and are essentially conservative in orientation. It represents a fusion of the functionalist tradition with the theories of Simmel and an incorporation of the work of Marx. Whilst most of its leading proponents, such as Merton and Coser, pose as critics of functionalism, they have perhaps done more than its enthusiastic adherents to establish the overall dominance of the functionalist approach over the last twenty-five years. Their 'radical' critique has done much to remedy the deficiencies of more conventional approaches to the extent that certain theorists have argued that there is now a convergence between the analytical characteristics of Marxism and functionalism.[55]

The basis of conflict functionalism was in many respects laid in Merton's classic article of 1948, 'Manifest and Latent Functions' (reproduced in Merton, 1968). This piece set out to codify and bring together the diverse strands of functionalism and to provide a comprehensive critique. Merton's argument was directed against three central postulates of traditional functional analysis which he argued were debatable and unnecessary to the functional orientation as such. These were (a) the 'postulate of the functional unity of society' – that is, 'that standardised social activities or cultural items are functional for the *entire* social or cultural system'; (b) the 'postulate of universal functionalism' – that is, 'that *all* social and cultural items fulfil sociological functions'; (c) the 'postulate of indispensability' – that is, 'that these items are consequently indispensable' (Merton, 1968, pp. 79–91).

Merton discussed each of these postulates in relation to cases drawn from functionalist anthropology and demonstrated that they were by no means always true. In essence he argued that (a) societies are not unitary in nature – certain elements may be functionally autonomous and hence the degree of integration is an empirical variable; (b) societies may have non-functional elements, such as 'survivals' from the past, which need not necessarily make a positive contribution; (c) societies are quite capable of dispensing with certain activities without prejudice to their survival and, in any case, are capable of developing alternatives.

This critique of traditional functionalism led to a focus upon a number of factors which are usually excluded from consideration. Most importantly, it introduced the notion of 'dysfunctions' and the problematical nature of social integration, and it recognised that a particular social unit or activity may have negative consequences for society as a whole or for some particular part of it. It also attacked the concept of 'functional prerequisites' or 'preconditions functionally necessary for a society', thus questioning the 'indispensability' of certain cultural forms. It opened the way for a consideration of 'functional alternatives', 'functional equivalents' or 'functional substitutes'. Merton recognised that functional needs are permissive rather than determinant and that there is a range of variation in the structures which fulfil any given function (Merton, 1968, p. 88).

Merton's critique paved the way for an approach to functional analysis which, in contrast to traditional functionalism, sees the nature of social order as essentially problematic, allows analysis to take place from a variety of perspectives and gives full recognition to the process of social change. As Gouldner has noted, one of the strengths of Merton's approach is that it 'prevents either premature commitment to, or premature exclusion of, any given structure as an element in the social system' (Gouldner, 1959, p. 194). Merton is concerned to establish functionalism as an essentially neutral analytical tool. He recognises that its previous use has been tainted with ideology and demonstrates how in different hands it has attracted the charges of being both 'conservative' and 'radical'. On the basis of this he argues that functional analysis does not entail any necessary or intrinsic ideological commitment – ideology is an extraneous factor resulting from the manner in which functionalism is used. In order to demonstrate this he presents a detailed point-by-point comparison of dialectical materialism and functional analysis. Taking Marx and Engels' statements on dialectical materialism as a starting point, Merton specifies an equivalent statement in terms of functional analysis. His overall purpose in doing so is unclear. Whilst it directly illustrates his point about ideology, it also leaves the reader wondering whether Merton is suggesting that functional analysis can be substituted for the Marxist dialectic or whether he is merely seeking to introduce certain Marxist notions to his functionalist audience. Whatever the motive, its impact on sociological thought is clear. Merton's article has above all served the purpose of suggesting that the problems addressed by Marxism can be handled through appropriate forms of functional analysis. As will become evident from our discussion below, conflict functionalism, in essence, can be seen as the functionalists' response to Marx.

Perhaps significantly, Merton did not choose to follow the 'radical' implications of his critique of traditional functionalism. As we shall argue later, the notions of 'dysfunction' and 'functional autonomy', if followed to their logical conclusion, lead towards the notion of contradiction. The task of following this path was left for one of his students, Alvin Gouldner (1959). In the remainder of his article Merton contents himself with an analysis of the problem of the items to be subjected to functional analysis and the issue of manifest and latent functions.[56] As Merton notes, the notions of manifest and latent functions have a particularly important contribution to make to functional analysis. In particular, they can clarify the analysis of 'seemingly irrational social patterns' and also direct attention to theoretically fruitful fields of investigation. Indeed, the notions have provided sociologists with a means of directing their enquiry beyond the familiar and superficially related patterns of social activities towards analysis of unrecognised functions. The discovery of latent functions provided yet another means of explaining the ordered pattern of social affairs — through the identification of ways in which the 'unintended consequences' of social action perform positive functions within its context of the wider social system.

The influence of these ideas is particularly evident in the work of Coser (1956 and 1967). His analysis of social conflict represents in large measure an attempt to extend Simmel's insights into the subject through the perspective developed by Merton. In essence, it represents an analysis of the latent functions of social conflict.

Coser builds upon a central thesis running through Simmel's work — that 'conflict is a form of socialisation' and that no group can be entirely harmonious. Paraphrasing Simmel, he suggests that:

no group can be entirely harmonious, for it would then be devoid of process and structure. Groups require disharmony as well as harmony, dissociation as well as association; and conflicts within them are by no means altogether disruptive factors. Group formation is the result of both types of processes ... both 'positive' and 'negative' factors build group relations. Conflict as well as co-operation has social functions. Far from being necessarily dysfunctional, a certain degree of conflict is an essential element in group formation and the persistence of group life. (Coser, 1956, p. 31)

In his essay Coser takes a series of propositions from Simmel's work and systematically analyses the manner and 'conditions under which social conflict may contribute to the maintenance, adjustment or adaption of social relationships and social structures' (Coser, 1956, p. 151). As the title of his work suggests, Coser is specifically concerned with the functions of social conflict, and he builds up to a conclusion which emphasises the fundamental importance of the relationship between conflict and its institutional context in determining the stability of the overall social system. Coser's essay ends with a classic formulation of the pluralist perspective on social organisation, in which conflict is viewed as an essential ingredient of social life, creating strains and tensions with which the institutional structure must cope if the social system is to stabilise itself and evolve in an ordered manner. As we shall show in Chapter 5, this pluralist view is of considerable significance as far as the study of organisations is concerned.

In an essay written at the same time as 'The Functions of Social Conflict', Coser extends his analysis to cover situations in which social systems actually break their boundaries and lead to the establishment of new ones (Coser, 1967, pp. 17–35). The focus is upon the problems of social change, and an attempt is made to 'specify the structural conditions under which social conflicts lead to inner adjustments of social systems or the break-up of existing social orders and the emergence of a new set of social relations within a new social structure' (Coser, 1967, p. 18). In addition to generating new norms and new institutions, conflict is seen as stimulating technological innovation and economic change. Coser's analysis draws simultaneously on the work of such diverse theorists as Weber, Marx, Parsons and Veblen, although the ideas of none are followed in depth to their logical conclusion. Coser seems less interested in understanding the process of social change than in identifying the situations in which change can be constrained by institutional mechanisms. Whilst Coser follows Merton in his views on the ideological misuse of functionalism, there is, in fact, a strong normative undertone in his writings. His analysis of change is strongly orientated towards the development of a theory which explains how conflicts can be controlled and channelled through a system of normative regulation. This general orientation is very evident in Coser's other papers on, for example, the termination of conflict, the social functions of violence and its role in conflict resolution, and the functions of deviant behaviour and normative flexibility (Coser, 1967). Coser's whole theory of conflict is essentially pluralist in its ideological stance.

Both Merton and Coser, though critical of functionalism, are in essence committed to its problematic. It is for this reason that we identify their work as conflict functionalism. They recognise that social integration is by no means the straightforward process implicit in the work of normative functionalists such as Parsons, and they do much to recognise the role of conflict in social life. However, their view is firmly rooted in the sociology of regulation, a paradox clearly illustrated by the way in which conflict, particularly in Coser's hands, can be used as a conceptual tool for explaining social order. Despite their protestations to the contrary, their problematic is that of social order — they are principally concerned to explain why it is that society tends to hold together rather than fall apart.

Their position in this regard is clearly illustrated when compared with the critique of functionalism presented by Gouldner (1959). Taking the concept of system as a starting point, Gouldner argues that if one compares the work of Merton and Parsons, one finds many differences in approach but an underlying similarity with regard to the 'strategic place of the concept of a system, especially as an *explanatory* tool' (Gouldner, 1959, p. 198). He demonstrates that Merton, like Parsons, is concerned with explaining the persistence of social factors and in so doing tends to provide a 'partial and one-sided' explanation, since he fails to give specific attention to the concept of 'functional reciprocity'. For this reason explanations are likely to be incomplete, since, as he puts it, 'the only logically stable terminal point for a functional analysis is not the demonstration of a social pattern's function for others, but the demonstration of the latter's reciprocal functionality for the problematic social pattern' (Gouldner, 1959, pp. 199–200).

In other words, it is necessary to demonstrate functionality within a reciprocal context. This concept of 'functional reciprocity' is crucial to the notion of interdependence of parts which is so central to functional analysis. It is quite remarkable, therefore, that it has not been given more systematic consideration by functional analysts, since if functional reciprocity is asymmetrical, then the whole notion of interdependence becomes open to question. In recognising this, Gouldner arrives at a conclusion similar to Merton's but by a different route. For Merton, it is the recognition of 'dysfunctions' that leads him to view social integration as problematic.

However, in contrast to Merton, Gouldner carries the logic of his analysis much further. The notion of varying degrees of interdependence among the parts of a system leads him to the concept of 'functional autonomy' which, operationally speaking, relates to the probability of a system part's survival in separation from the system. High system interdependence means low functional autonomy of parts, and vice versa. This notion of functional autonomy is important, since it reflects a view which focuses upon the *parts* of a system (albeit in their relation to each other). This is in direct contrast to the more usual systems view, which tends to focus upon the whole and sees the parts in their relation to the whole. Gouldner's analysis is important, in that it focuses attention upon interchanges where functional reciprocity may not be symmetrical and thus directs analysis to tension-producing relationships. In this way Gouldner, starting from a systems perspective, arrives at the notion of 'contradiction', with a focus upon incompatible elements of a social system. Building upon the idea that the parts of a system may seek to maintain their functional autonomy, he shows how attempts at system control are likely to generate conflict. Moreover, system parts may take positive steps to resist incorporation and containment, and may generate changes in the system itself which are consistent within their overall autonomy. Different parts are likely to have 'greater or lesser vested interest in system maintenance' (Gouldner, 1959, p. 211).

This focus upon functional autonomy thus raises many issues which contradict the tenets of traditional systems theory and functional analysis. It places the parts rather than the whole at the centre of analysis. The focus upon contradictions provides an explanation of change and conflict which contributes to the interests and independence of the constituent elements of a system rather than the abstract whole. Although Gouldner only makes passing reference to Marx on two occasions in the whole of the article and couches his discussion almost exclusively in terms of the functionalist problematic, this piece of work represents a cautious but, in essence, truly radical critique of the functionalist approach to social analysis. It contains many signs and elements of the thought of the 'Marxist outlaw' which finds much clearer and more direct expression in some of Gouldner's later work.[57]

Gouldner's critique clearly serves to illustrate the extent to which Merton and Coser are committed to a view of society rooted in the sociology of regulation. Although they recognise the problematic nature of social integration and the relevance of Marxist theory, they do not pursue the full implications of these issues. As in the case of other conflict functionalists who have followed in their footsteps, they have incorporated and reinterpreted the concerns of Marx within the problematic of functionalism. Although they have recognised the existence of 'dysfunctions' within social systems and some of the consequences which this entails, they have stopped short of a theory of contradiction. As Gouldner has suggested, they have remained 'functionalists' at heart, in that they have not chosen to develop 'dysfunctionalism' as an alternative (Gouldner, 1970, p. 336). As we shall see, this would have led to a perspective characteristic of the radical structuralist paradigm.

Morphogenic systems theory

This brand of integrative theory is principally associated with the work of Buckley (1967) and the 'process model' which he advocates for the study of society. In essence, Buckley's work attempts to introduce to the social sciences the modern systems theory reflected in cybernetics, information and communication theory and general systems research. His work attempts to present a systems model with the capacity to explain the way in which societies change and elaborate their basic structures. His process model embraces and attempts to synthesise the whole range of thought contained within the functionalist paradigm – from interactionism to social systems theory – and makes passing reference to some of the ideas of Marx. It represents an extremely sophisticated attempt to develop an integrative systems model characteristic of the middle ground of the paradigm.

Buckley begins his analysis by recognising that the usual mechanical and organic systems models employed in the social sciences are inherently inadequate for their task, particularly when it comes to analysing factors such as 'structurally induced and maintained conflict and dissensus; the structure elaborating and changing feature of all societies; the theoretical status of less structured "collective" behaviour as a neglected but important aspect of the social system; the systemic status of "deviance" and "social control"' (Buckley, 1967, p. 4). He is thus essentially interested in the same kinds of functionalist issues as other integrative theorists, especially Merton, though his analysis and proposed solutions are quite different.

Buckley maintains that mechanical and organic systems models are inadequate, since they are based upon an outdated view of science and do not recognise the special qualities of socio-cultural systems.[58] He argues that in the twentieth century there has been a shifting scientific perspective, reflected in the growth of cybernetics, information and communication theory and general systems research, which 'marks the transition from a concern for eternal substance and the dynamics of energy transformation to a focus on *organisation* and its dynamics based on the "triggering" effects of information transmission' (Buckley, 1967, pp. 1–2). He argues that the social sciences need to adopt this perspective in recognition of the true character of socio-cultural systems whose morphogenic properties distinguish them from other types of biological and physical systems.

After providing a comprehensive critique of the mechanical and organic systems models, with specific reference to those of Parsons (1951) and Homans (1950), Buckley develops a process model which, in essence, represents a fusion of various strains of interactionism and modern systems theory. Buckley seeks to reinterpret the work of theorists such as G. H. Mead, Simmel, Small, Park, Burgess, Blumer and other members of the Chicago School of sociology within the context of cybernetics and information theory.

Buckley's model attempts to link micro- and macro-levels of analysis, building from the Meadian notion of the 'act' and the basic symbolic interaction process, through the notion of 'role' and role dynamics, to the emergence of organisations and institutions. The socio-cultural system is viewed as a 'set of elements linked almost entirely by way of the intercommunication of information (in the broad sense) rather than being energy- or substance-linked as are physical or organismic systems' (Buckley, 1967, p. 82). It emerges from a network of interaction among individuals in which information is selectively perceived and interpreted in accordance with the meaning it holds for the actors involved. The model is processual rather than structural in nature. 'Information', for example, is regarded as a 'carrier of meaning' rather than as 'an entity that exists some place or flows from one place to another' (Buckley, 1967, p. 92). It is a relation rather than a thing. Society is viewed as an organisation of meanings which emerge from the process of interaction between individuals dealing with a more or less common environment. Meanings may be sufficiently stable or clear to become generalised as codes, rules or norms for behaviour. However, these norms are not to be confused with 'the actual organisational process they partly inform' (Buckley, 1967, p. 94). Society remains an intangible process of interaction which ultimately rests with the actors directly involved and the way in which they choose to interpret and respond to their environment. The essentially processual nature of socio-cultural systems is not to be confused with the structure or organisation its components may take on at any particular time.

Buckley has undoubtedly made an important contribution to the application of systems theory in the social sciences. His argument that socio-cultural systems are not amenable to adequate study through the use of equilibrium or homeostatic models challenges the validity and usefulness of virtually all the social systems studies which have been made to date. Conceptually, his process model represents a considerable advance over these earlier approaches, restoring the processual element so essential to the very notion of system.

At first sight Buckley's interest in interactionist thought could be seen as an argument for locating him on the subjectivist boundary of the functionalist paradigm. This, however, would be an error. Buckley gives a great deal of attention to the work of interactionists such as Mead, because he interprets their work as being consistent with his own, at least in contrast to that of social theorists such as Parsons. Buckley is able to argue that the interactionist perspective represents a step in the right direction as far as social research is concerned, being 'congenial to — even anticipative of — basic principles of cybernetics' (Buckley, 1967, p. 17). If one has to rank his priorities, one can fairly conclude that Buckley is systems theorist first, interactionist second. His main concern is to translate the work of the interactionists into the concepts and language of cybernetics, which, as part of a general systems perspective, he sees as providing a framework for organising the insights derived from interactionist research. Buckley's work can best be understood as that of a systems theorist concerned to synthesise various elements within the functionalist paradigm. He attempts to bridge the gulf between interactionism and social systems theory from a systems perspective.

Our discussion of Buckley's work concludes our brief review of integrative theory. In their different ways, all four of the brands which we have considered seek to bridge the gap between interactionism and social system theory. Conflict functionalism also attempts to bridge the gap between the functionalist and radical structuralist paradigms. Placing emphasis upon different analytical variables, they have all made a substantial contribution to the development and general sophistication of functionalist theory by seeking to synthesise its potentially divergent elements.

Objectivism

We use the term 'objectivism' to refer to the considerable amount of sociological work located on the objectivist boundary of the functionalist paradigm. It is characterised by an extremely high degree of commitment to models and methods derived from the natural sciences.

The relationship between social systems theory and objectivism is thus obviously a close one. The difference between them hinges upon what may be described as the difference between metaphor and reality. Social systems theorists use the biological and physical world as a source of analogies for studying the social world, as a source of hypotheses and insight. Objectivists, on the other hand, treat the social world exactly as if it were the natural world; they treat human beings as machines or biological organisms, and social structure as if it were a physical structure. We identify two broad types of objectivism – behaviourism and abstracted empiricism.

Behaviourism

The notion of behaviourism is most often associated with the work of B. F. Skinner, who has attempted to develop causal theories of behaviour based upon an analysis of stimulus and response.[59] For this purpose man is treated, like any other natural organism, as entirely the product of his environment. Man, in essence, is regarded as little more than a machine, responding in a deterministic way to the external conditions to which he is exposed. In Skinner's work all reference to subjective states of mind are considered irrelevant – indeed, counterproductive – as far as scientific enquiry is concerned. As Skinner has put it,

> the practice of looking inside an organism for an explanation of behaviour has tended to obscure the variables which are immediately

available for scientific analysis. These variables lie outside the organism, in its immediate environment and in its environmental history. They have a physical status to which the usual techniques of science are adapted, and they make it possible to explain behaviour as other subjects are explained in science. (Skinner, 1953, p. 31)

Skinner's approach to the study of human behaviour is very much geared to the use of experimental methods typical of those utilised in the natural sciences. He is committed to the view that one learns about phenomena under investigation by careful manipulation of particular stimuli in controlled situations in which all other environmental influences are either excluded or accounted for in some way. It is a method which approximates a closed system form of analysis. The study of human behaviour from this perspective is very much an activity aimed at the discovery of universal laws and regularities which underlie the science of man. These laws exist out there in the external world. The social scientist's task is to discover them.

Skinner's perspective is a highly coherent and consistent one in terms of the four strands of the subjective—objective dimension of our analytical scheme. Ontologically, his view is firmly realist; epistemologically, his work is the archetype of positivism; his view of human nature reflects a determinism of an extreme form; the highly nomothetic methodology reflected in his experimental approach is congruent with these other assumptions.

On the regulation—radical change dimension Skinner occupies an equally extreme position. His view of the social world is one which emphasises the possibility and desirability of both prediction and control. He has been greatly concerned to develop a technology of behaviour modification and to spell out its relationships in a wider social context (Skinner, 1972). His theory is truly regulative in orientation, in that, given the correct conditioning environment, Skinner believes that human behaviour can be moulded and transformed into a perfectly ordered and regular pattern. We argue that Skinner's behaviourism occupies a position at the extremities of both dimensions of the functionalist paradigm.

Skinner's theorising reflects a behaviourism of an extreme form which, outside the realm of experimental psychology, has not served directly as a model for theory and research in the social sciences. However, there are a number of behavioural theories which are directly related to Skinner's model, such as the exchange theory developed by Homans (1958 and 1961). There are also many theories which share Skinner's assumptions in relation to the subjective—objective dimension of our analytical scheme. Those which attempt to explain behaviour in terms of universal psychological laws fall into this category. For example, many studies examining work group behaviour and motivation at work are based upon this type of thinking.[60] Wider social or environmental influences are ignored, and indeed in many experimental and research designs a deliberate attempt is made to exclude them; the rationale of 'controlled' experiments and research constitutes the epitome of such closed system thinking. Another related category of theory is found in the work of those theorists sometimes labelled determinists. Their focus of interest rests not upon the psychological make-up of the individuals to be studied but upon the environment in which they operate. Their energies are addressed to establishing situational laws which determine human behaviour. Studies of the relationship between work behaviour and technology, leadership styles, payment systems, etc., often provide illustrations of this perspective. The 'situational determinant' is viewed as all-important; individuals are assigned essentially passive and responding roles in relation to the conditions which they encounter in their immediate environment.

These types of theorising and research have had considerable influence in the field of organisational studies and will receive further attention in Chapter 5. We close our discussion here by re-emphasising their behaviouristic nature and the close parallels which exist with Skinner's work. Like Skinner, the theorists who advocate such views occupy a clear and consistent position in terms of the four strands of the subjective—objective dimension of our analytical scheme. Their determinist stance is paralleled by equally objectivist assumptions in relation to ontology, epistemology and methodology. However, in relation to the regulation—radical change dimension they are usually committed to a position which allows for more flexibility and variation than Skinner's model.

Abstracted empiricism

At certain points in our discussion of the schools of thought associated with interactionism, integrative theory, and social system theory, we have referred to the fact that the work of various theorists and researchers has ended up as abstracted empiricism. Systems theorists who spend their energies measuring 'structures'; interactionists who utilise static measurements of 'attitudes' and 'role situations'; integrative theorists who attempt to produce quantitative indices of 'power', 'conflict', 'deviancy' and the like – all provide illustrations of abstracted empiricism, in that they engage in empirical research which violates the assumptions of their theoretical perspective.

The term 'abstracted empiricism' has entered popular usage largely through the work of C. Wright Mills (1959) who, in his critique of theory and method in the social sciences, has used it to describe the output of researchers who have allowed methodologies derived from the natural sciences to *dominate* their work.[61] We use it here in a related but more specific and limited sense. Stating the position in terms of the subjective—objective dimension of our analytical scheme, abstracted empiricism represents a situation in which a highly nomothetic methodology is used to test a theory which is based upon an ontology, an epistemology and a theory of human nature of a more subjectivist kind. It represents a situation in which a nomothetic methodology is incongruent with the assumptions of the other three strands of the subjective—objective dimension. It is with regard to this incongruence that abstracted empiricism differs from behaviourism. As we have illustrated, Skinner and other behaviourists adopt a perfectly coherent and congruent perspective in relation to the four elements of the subjective—objective dimension. Their engagement in the wholesale use of experimental and other research methods derived from the natural sciences is consistent with the nature of their theorising. Abstracted empiricism arises in situations where the methods used are inconsistent with the underlying theory.

It is a regrettable fact that a major proportion of research work in the social sciences at the present time results in abstracted empiricism. The drive to obtain research funding to sustain teams of research workers tends to favour the collection of large quantities of empirical data. Indeed, the collection and processing of such data is often equated with the total research effort and is regarded as an essential ingredient of any proposal likely to meet the 'quality control' requirements of research funding institutions. The demands for pragmatic results from social science research programmes also tends to favour some form of substantive information output. Under the pressure of such forces, research programmes often become tailored to the requirements and methods of their data base, to the extent that theoretical assumptions with regard to basic ontology, epistemology and human nature are relegated to a background role and are eventually violated by the demands of empiricism. It is no exaggeration to suggest that there is scarcely a theoretical perspective within the context of the functionalist paradigm which has not been translated into abstract empiricism of one form or another.

We identify abstracted empiricism as being characteristic of the objectivist boundary of the functionalist paradigm. We locate it here in recognition of the fact that the bulk of such work arises as a result of extreme commitment to nomothetic methodologies in which quantitative measures of reified social constructs dominate the reseach endeavour. It represents research in which the social world is treated methodologically as if it were a world of hard, concrete, tangible reality, whereas theoretically it is conceived as being of a more subjectivist nature. The problem of adopting methodologies appropriate to the nature of the phenomena under investigation is a crucial one in contemporary social science. As we shall see, it is also encountered by sociologists working within the context of the interpretive paradigm. Problems of incongruence between theory and method raise issues of concern to sociologists of all kinds.

The Underlying Unity of the Paradigm

The functionalist paradigm contains a wide range of theorising. At a superficial level, it is its diversity which is most apparent. The contrasts between social system theory and interactionism, for example, cannot fail to catch one's attention. The differences between the many schools of thought which we have identified are clear. Beneath the diversity, however, there is an underlying unity and form. The paradigm is characterised by a fundamental commonality of perspective in terms of basic, 'taken for granted' assumptions, which provide a hidden link between its constituent theories and which distinguishes them from those in other paradigms. Indeed, it is this underlying unity which the very notion of paradigm reflects.

Theorists located in the functionalist paradigm are linked by a shared view of the fundamental nature of the socio-scientific reality to which their work is addressed. They are committed to a view of the social world which regards society as ontologically prior to man and seek to place man and his activities within that wider social context. Merton has noted that 'the concept of function involves the standpoint of *the observer*, not necessarily that of the participant' (Merton, 1968, p. 78). Theorists located within the context of the functionalist paradigm tend to assume the standpoint of the observer and attempt to relate what *they* observe to what *they* regard as important elements in a wider social context. This perspective is common to the interactionist, the integrative theorist, the social system theorist and the objectivist.

The functionalist view of this wider social context also tends to have many common reference points. It is a view which assumes a continuing order and pattern. It is geared to providing an explanation of what is. Allowing for various but *limited* degrees of order and disorder, consensus and dissensus, social integration and disintegration, solidarity and conflict, need satisfaction and frustration, the overall endeavour is to provide an explanation of why the social fabric of society tends to hold together. It is geared to providing an explanation of the regulated nature of human affairs.

The paradigm is based upon an underlying norm of purposive rationality. This concept provides a direct link between the two dimensions which define the paradigm's regulative and objectivist view of the social world. The conception of science which underlies the paradigm emphasises the possibility of objective enquiry capable of providing true explanatory and predictive knowledge of an external reality. It is a conception which assumes that scientific theories can be assessed objectively by reference to empirical evidence. It is a conception which attributes independence to the observer – an ability to observe what is, without affecting it. It is a conception which assumes there are general external and universal standards of science which can serve as a basis for determining what constitutes an adequate explanation of what is observed. It is a conception which, above all else, assumes that there are external rules and regulations governing the external world.

The essential rationality reflected in this view of science is put to use by the functionalist to explain the essential rationality of society. Science provides a frame of reference for structuring and ordering the social world, a frame of reference which emphasises an order and coherence similar to that found in the natural world. The methods of science are used to generate explanations of the social world consistent with the nature and philosophy of science itself. Science, in the functionalist's hands, becomes a tool for imposing order and regulation upon the social world – order and regulation from the standpoint of the observer.

The diversity of thought which exists within the context of the functionalist paradigm is a diversity within the confines of this overall view of science and society. The various broad categories and schools of thought differ in the degree and manner in which they subscribe to and address themselves to common basic assumptions. It is important to emphasise this. The difference between theories within the paradigm is one of degree rather than of fundamental perspective, a feature which becomes clearly evident when theories are compared with those located in other paradigms.

As we have attempted to show, differences within the paradigm reflect the intellectual response to the interaction between the main currents of sociological thought which have come into prominence in the nineteenth and twentieth centuries. Building upon basic models derived from the natural sciences (as modified by Comte, Spencer, Pareto and Durkheim), sociologists have responded to the external challenge and threat posed by alternative intellectual traditions through both fusion and incorporation. As we have seen, elements of German idealism have been fused with the Anglo-French tradition to produce interactionism. Aspects of the work of Marx has been incorporated into integrative theory. In each case the rival intellectual tradition has been sucked into the paradigm and used in a manner which defies certain of its basic assumptions. In other words, these different intellectual traditions have been reinterpreted from a functionalist perspective.

This process of fusion and incorporation is reflected in the position which the resulting theory occupies on the two analytical dimensions of the paradigm. The German idealist tradition has influenced the emergence of functionalist theories of a more subjectivist orientation. The Marxist tradition is reflected in functionalist theories which focus upon conflict and change. The differences thus generated account in large measure for the ongoing debate within the paradigm between rival schools of thought, and also for the nature of the issues discussed. Thus integrative theorists criticise structural functionalists and systems theorists on the grounds that the latter cannot handle the problems of conflict, change and deviancy. The interactionists criticise them for being too orientated towards structural considerations and for ignoring the emergent nature of social organisation. Process versus structure, voluntarism versus determinism, become the issues for debate here. We end this chapter by emphasising the limited nature of this debate. Conducted within the paradigm, it reflects little more than a disagreement about the variations which characterise a commonly accepted theme.

Notes and References

1. Our review of the intellectual foundations of the functionalist perspective has been necessarily terse. Readers interested in more extensive analyses of Comte, Spencer and Durkheim and the relationships between them might usefully consult Parsons (1949), Aron (1965), Gouldner (1970), Lukes (1973) and Keat and Urry (1975). For a general discussion of Pareto, see Parsons (1949), Homans and Curtis (1934) and Russett (1966), pp. 85–101.

2. For a discussion of the emergence of functionalism in social anthropology, see Jarvie (1964). The concept of functionalism in psychology predates its appearance in anthropology – see, for example, James (1890) and Angell (1902). Psychology at this time was, of course, primarily physiological in orientation.

3. For a clear exposition of his views, see Radcliffe-Brown (1952), especially his article 'On the Concept of Function in Social Science', pp. 178–87.

4. For a further discussion of these issues, see, for example, Jarvie (1964) pp. 182–98 and Cohen (1968) pp. 37–45.

5. The literature on sociology is replete with studies which focus upon the empirical measurement of 'social structure' in one aspect or another. See, for example, our discussion of research on organisations in Chapter 5.

6. For two excellent analyses of Parsons's writings, see Rocher (1974) and Black (1961).

7. Rocher (1974) presents a very clear analysis of the AGIL scheme. Our categorisation here draws upon this source.

8. It is never entirely clear in Parsons's work whether these functional imperatives exist empirically or whether they are purely analytic constructs for making society intelligible from a functionalist standpoint. Although he maintains a posture of 'analytical realism', he does not appear to discourage others from engaging in empirical research in relation to his theoretical scheme. It is from this dualism that ambiguity regarding his position arises.

9. See, for example, Gouldner (1970) and C. Wright Mills (1959). Other writers however, have argued to the contrary. See, for example, Rocher (1974) and Martins (1974).

10. Parsons's own version of structural functionalism builds largely upon the work of Durkheim and Pareto, and on Weber's notion of the action frame of reference. It fuses the

biological approach of Durkheim with the mechanical equilibrium approach of Pareto. In this his scheme is somewhat inconsistent. *The Social System* contains no reference to Radcliffe-Brown, and it is clear that Parsons differs quite considerably in the way in which he uses the concept of structure and function.In his later work Parsons prefers to be identified with systems theory rather than structural functionalism as such.

11.   A common approach is to take the concept of 'system' as self-evident and confine discussion to the difference between 'closed' and 'open' systems.

12.   Buckley (1967) adds to this definition: 'That a system is *open* means not simply that it engages in interchanges with the environment, but that this interchange is an *essential factor* underlying the system's viability, its reproductive ability or continuity, and its ability to change' (p. 50).

13.   For an excellent and detailed analysis of this field, see Buckley (1967).

14.   For a discussion of Henderson and his influence, see, for example, Russett (1966), pp. 111–24.

15.   For a discussion of these concepts, see Katz and Kahn (1966), pp. 19–26.

16.   In point of fact, Parsons' model fuses the mechanical and organismic analogies.

17.   For a clear discussion of the principles of cybernetics, see Wisdom (1956) and Dechert (1965).

18.   For a clear and comprehensive discussion of some of the major aspects of Simmel's work, see Coser (1965) and Wolff (1950).

19.   A detailed presentation of his views on conflict can be found in Simmel (1955).

20.   As will be apparent from our discussion in Chapter 2, Simmel, particularly through the work of Coser (1956), has provided the main platform for sociologists to argue that the order—conflict debate is dead.

21.   A short time before his death Simmel wrote: 'I know that I shall die without intellectual heirs – and that is as it should be. My legacy will be, as it were, in cash, distributed to many heirs, each transforming his part into use conformed to *his* nature: a use which will reveal no longer its indebtness to this heritage' (Georg Simmel, 1919, p. 121). As Coser notes (1965, p. 24), this is indeed what happened. No clear-cut school of thought has emerged around Simmel's work, and his influ-

ence is not always specifically recognised. Yet his impact has been important and diverse, particularly through the work of Coser (1956), Merton (1949), Blau (1964), the work of the Chicago School of sociologists and the 'formal sociology' of von Wiese at Cologne.

22. See, for example, Natanson (1973a, b and c). If *Mind, Self and Society* is interpreted within the context of Mead's other work, the term 'social behaviourist' becomes increasingly inappropriate as a means of describing his overall position. Mead takes the behaviourism of Watson as a starting point for his analysis, but from the outset recognises the necessity for a much wider approach.

23. For a discussion of pragmatism, see 'The Philosophies of Royce, James and Dewey in their American Setting', *International Journal of Ethics*, XL (1930); its historical genesis is discussed in Mead's *Movements of Thought in the Nineteenth Century* (1932).

24. In *Mind, Self and Society* Mead traces the process by which biological considerations forced psychology through the stages of associationism, parallelism, functionalism and behaviourism, and, against this background, introduces essentially 'social' concepts (for example, the notion of the gesture derived from Wundt) to formulate his own distinctive position. As noted above, his 'social behaviourism' can only be regarded as a behaviourism in the very widest of senses.

25. Early in his intellectual development, Mead became interested in Hegelian idealism, largely through the influence of Royce. Indeed, there are indications that at one time (*circa* 1887–8) Mead was more attracted to idealism than to pragmatism (see, for example, Miller, 1973, p. xiv). It is also likely that he was influenced by other aspects of German idealism, in the same manner as Simmel, during a period of study at Leipzig and Berlin (1888–91).

26. In Morris's words, 'instead of beginning with individual minds and working out to society, Mead starts with an objective social process and works inward through the importation of the social process of communication into the individual by the medium of the vocal gesture' (Mead, 1934, p. xxii).

27. In this Mead, along with Dewey and the ideas expressed in the latter's paper of 1896, 'The Reflex Arc Concept in Psychology', stressed the correlation between stimulation and response.

Aspects of the world become parts of the psychological environment, become stimuli, only in so far as they effect the further release of an ongoing impulse. Thus, the sensitivity and activity of the organism determine its effective environment as genuinely as the physical environment affects the sensitivity of the form. The resulting view does more justice to the dynamic and agressive aspects of behaviour than does Watsonism, which gives the impression of regarding the organism as a puppet, whose wires are pulled by the physical environment. (Mead, 1934, pp. xvii – xviii)

28. Their interactionist perspective served different purposes. For Mead, the study of human interaction provided a key to understanding the genesis of 'self'. For Simmel, it was more of an end in itself – reflecting the underlying 'form' and characteristics of human association.

29. See, for example, our discussion of symbolic interactionism later in this chapter.

30. The account which we have presented of Mead's work in the preceeding pages draws heavily upon *Mind, Self and Society* and largely relates to point (a) above. Points (b) and (c) are reflected more clearly in *The Philosophy of the Act*, and *The Philosophy of the Present*. An analysis of the thought contained in the latter two works is beyond the scope of the present enquiry (the reader is referred to Natanson's (1973c) extremely comprehensive discussion). Since the phenomenological aspects and interpretations of Mead's work have largely been neglected, it is significant that Natanson's excellent analysis from this point of view has only recently been republished in the wake of the 1960s' enthusiasm for phenomenological ideas. In the present work we shall confine discussion of Mead's 'phenomenology' to the impact it has had upon symbolic interactionism, particularly through the work of Herbert Blumer.

31. For a discussion of the background and dynamics of 'Chicago sociology' during the period 1920–32, see Faris (1967).

32. Simmel's ideas had an important impact upon 'Chicago sociology' through Robert Park, who was arguably the leading figure at Chicago during the 1920s. Park, like other Chicago scholars such as Mead, studied in Germany and was directly influenced by Simmel's ideas. In their famous *Introduction to the Science of Sociology* (1921) Park and Burgess present a view of sociology which Faris has described as geared to 'the pursuit of objective scientific knowledge con-

cerning the nature of society and social organisation, groups, and institutions, the nature and effects of processes of social interaction, and the effects of these forms and processes on the behaviour of persons' (Faris, 1967, p. 41). This approach to sociology has a distinctly Simmelian flavour. Interestingly though, Park's teachings in the 1920s paid little attention to the work of Mead (Strauss, 1964, p. xi).

Although interactionist thought is sometimes presented as having developed independently at Chicago and in Germany, a strong claim can be made that the two schools of thought derive from a common Germanic source.

33. Simmel and Mead have also had an influence upon the development of the integrative theories relating to social exchange, social control and conflict functionalism which will be discussed in a later section of this chapter. These theories build upon interactionist concepts.

34. Although Blumer is generally recognised as interpreting Mead's thought from a more phenomenological perspective than many other theorists, there would probably be little dispute over the essentials of symbolic interactionism as described in this quotation.

35. The variety of thought can be clearly seen by consulting one of the popular readers on symbolic interaction; see, for example, Rose (1962), and Manis and Meltzer (1967). For a review of the trends in symbolic interactionism theory in the twenty-five years from 1937–62, see the article by Manford H. Kuhn in Manis and Meltzer (1967), pp. 46–7.

36. The development of role theory owes much to the Chicago School of sociologists, including Mead, and also, though this is rarely recognised, to Simmel. For a discussion of role theory and concepts such as role taking, role sets, role conflicts, see, for example, Gross *et al.* (1958) and Newcomb (1950 and 1953).

37. The notion of reference groups owes much to Mead's notion of 'the generalised other', and has been most systematically developed by Merton in the classic articles 'Contributions to the Theory of Reference Group Behaviour' and 'Continuities in the Theory of Reference Groups and Social Structure' in Merton (1968). This work also draws very heavily upon S. A. Stouffer's *The American Soldier* (1949), particularly the concept of 'relative deprivation', and Simmel's concept of the 'completeness' of a group (Merton, 1968, pp. 242–6).

For a further selection of writings on reference group

analysis, see the articles in Rose (1962), Manis and Meltzer (1967) and Hyman and Singer (1968).

38. Self theory in symbolic interaction (not to be confused with the psychological theory of Carl Rogers) embraces a wide range of research directed at analysis and application of this aspect of Mead's work. As Manis and Meltzer (1967) point out, it includes those who see 'self' as a dynamic process of viewing and responding to one's own behaviour; those who see 'self' as a structure of internalised roles; and those who conceive 'self' as a set of attitudes or evaluations (p. 215).

    For a selection of articles reflecting these points of view, see Manis and Meltzer (1967), pp. 215–366.

39. Dramaturgical theory, closely related to self theory, is most often associated with the work of Erving Goffman and his studies of the active self in social situations. His perspective presents the individual as an actor shaping his social situation through the images which he presents. See, for example, Goffman (1959, 1961, 1963 and 1967).

40. In addition to these general assumptions and propositions, Rose goes on to specify four further assumptions in relation to the process of socialisation of the individual child (Rose, 1962, pp. 13–18).

41. Indeed, it could be argued that in his attempt to meet the structural functionalists on their own ground, Blumer is drawn into a position which to an extent goes against his view of ontology quoted earlier (Rose, 1962, p. 182). For example, towards the end of his article he places much more emphasis upon action 'with regard to a situation' (p. 187) and the fact that 'human society is the framework inside of which social action takes place' (p. 189).

42. In his 1966 article Blumer presents symbolic interactionism as an approach which is capable of covering 'the full range of the generic forms of human association. It embraces equally well such relationships as co-operation, conflict, domination, exploitation, consensus, disagreement, closely knit identification, and indifferent concern for one another. The participants in each of such relations have the same common task of constructing their acts by interpreting and defining the acts of each other' (Blumer, 1966, p. 538). He goes on to criticise those theorists who tend to impose a particular frame of reference on the nature of interaction: 'Their great danger lies in imposing on the breadth of human interaction an image derived from the study of only one form of interac-

tion. Thus, in different hands, human society is said to be fundamentally a sharing of common values; or, conversely, a struggle for power; or, still differently, the exercise of consensus and so on' (Blumer, 1966, p. 538).

Blumer is thus, in essence, advocating symbolic interactionism as an approach capable of occupying a wide range of positions in relation to the vertical dimension of our analytical scheme. Theoretically, it can be conceptualised as ranging along the whole of the vertical dimension within the context of the sociology of regulation.

43. For an analysis of the distinctions between these two versions, see, for example. Meltzer and Petras (1973), and Meltzer *et al.* (1975).

44. As Reynolds and Meltzer (1973) have put it, the Chicago interactionists 'tend to prefer phenomenological approaches, participant observation and "sensitising concepts", all linked with a logic of discovery'. This is in contrast with the Iowa researchers who 'have preferred operational approaches, The Twenty Statements Test and "definitive concepts", all linked with a "logic of verification"'.

45. For a clear and articulate discussion of some of the issues involved here, see Williams (1976).

46. Cohen (1968), p. 69. This statement of the assumptions of the theory of action draws upon the work of von Mises and Parsons, as well as that of Weber. It provides a good illustration of the way in which Weber's ideas are adapted to suit the purposes of individual authors. Cohen provides a good description and critique of action theory in general, and rightly emphasises that it should be regarded as a method rather than a theory as such (Cohen, 1968, pp. 70–94).

47. See, for example, the analysis of Parsons's epistemological and other movements presented in Scott (1963).

48. On the other hand, the strength of Weber's work (as opposed to that of the interactionist tradition) lay in its conscious attempt to link the concept of social action to wider aspects of social structure, particularly through the notion of 'legitimate order'. Given the priorities of the functionalist paradigm, this is indeed a strength of Weber's work; social action, with its emphasis on the individual's interpretation of the situation, is always related to the wider context of that action.

49. Blau's version of exchange theory is often linked to that of Homans (1958 and 1961). Whilst the work of these two writers has developed through a process of mutual influence,

they are, in fact, quite different and occupy conceptually distinct locations within the functionalist paradigm.

50. Blau's notion of 'social exchange' is restricted to behaviour orientated towards ends that can only be achieved through interaction with other persons and which seeks to adapt means to achieve those ends. It thus represents action which is purposive and calculative. It is wider than the notion of economic exchange because of the unspecified obligations incurred within it and the trust both required for and promoted by it. It excludes behaviour based on the 'irrational push' of emotional forces, that based on coercion and that orientated towards ultimate values and issues of conscience rather than towards immediate rewards (Blau, 1964, pp. 4–8).

51. The conceptualisation of power found in Blau is very similar to that of Emerson (1962). Emerson stresses the need to see power as a relationship, as the property of interaction rather than as the attribute of individuals or of groups.

52. See, for example, the interpretations of Gouldner (1970), Horton (1964) and Strasser (1976).

53. The concept of 'normative function' in relation to reference groups builds upon another Meadian idea – that of the socialised 'self' – and converts it into an instrument for explaining social control. Mead was interested in 'self' as a process. As Strauss notes, in the theory of reference groups (and also in Parsonian functionalism) the notion is used in a very restricted way, largely for the purposes of explaining how norms get internalised and how self-control is, in essence, a reflection of social control (Strauss, 1964, p. xii).

54. Applying Veblen's concept of 'trained incapacity', Merton argues that bureaucrats may develop blind spots – abilities function as inadequacies. He suggests that bureaucratic personnel may overconform to the normative structure of the enterprise which emphasises strict devotion to regulations. This process stifles initiative and, under changed conditions, produces inappropriate responses and impairs the efficient performance of organisational tasks.

55. See, for example, the argument put forward by van den Berghe suggesting that the basic postulates of functionalism and the Hegelian-Marxian dialectic are capable of synthesis (van den Berghe, 1963).

56. Merton defines 'manifest functions' as 'those objective consequences contributing to the adjustment or adaption of the

system which are intended and recognised by participants in the system. 'Latent functions' are 'those which are neither intended nor recognised' (Merton, 1968, p. 105). The distinction is introduced to differentiate and avoid confusion 'between conscious *motivations* for social behaviour and its *objective consequences*' (Merton, 1968, p. 114).

57. See, for example, Gouldner (1973 and 1976).
58. The term 'socio-cultural' is used by Buckley 'to make explicit the difference between the human level of organisation and the lower, merely "social", level of certain animal or insect species' (Buckley, 1967, p. 1). As Buckley argues in dealing with socio-cultural systems, one is not only concerned with the issue of structure maintenance, as in biological systems, but also with the structure-elaborating and structure-changing feature of the inherently unstable system, i.e. morphogenesis (Buckley, 1967, pp. 14–15, 58–62).
59. See, for example, Skinner (1953, 1957 and 1952).
60. See, for example, some of the work presented in Cartwright and Zander (1968) and Landy and Trumbo (1976), pp. 293–335.
61. Mills uses the term to castigate those researchers who, along with 'grand' theorists, have abandoned what he sees as being the central task of sociology, that of grasping 'history and biography and the relations between the two within society . . . To recognise this task and this promise is the mark of the classic social analyst . . . No social study that does not come back to the problems of biography, of history and of their intersections within a society, has completed its intellectual journey' (Mills, 1959, p. 12). On the basis of this criterion, the work of most theorists who engage in empirical work would be categorised as abstracted empiricism. Our definition is more limited, in that it relates to empirical work which is abstracted from its theoretical context.

5. Functionalist Organisation Theory

In recent years the study of organisations has established itself as an increasingly significant area of social-scientific investigation. In terms of the number of research studies conducted, the volume of literature produced and its establishment as a recognised field of study within academic institutions, the study of organisations has a good claim to being regarded as a distinct branch of social science of some importance.

Yet in many respects it is a confusing field. It is usually presented as comprising of at least three lines of development, each drawing upon a number of different intellectual traditions. First, there is what may be described as organisation theory, which addresses itself to the study of 'formal organisations' and builds upon the work of the so-called 'classical school' of management and administrative theory. As Salaman and Thompson have noted, this is often seen as the 'orthodox approach' to the study of organisations and 'tends to adopt theories and models of organisational functioning, and to focus on areas of empirical investigation, that are highly oriented towards managerial conceptions of organisations, managerial priorities and problems, and managerial concerns for practical outcomes' (Salaman and Thompson, 1973, p. 1). The foundations of classical theory were largely laid by practising managers with little or no social science background. Second, there is the approach which is sometimes described as the sociology of organisations. For the most part this builds upon the foundations laid by Max Weber, and it approaches the study of organisations from a sociological as opposed to a managerial perspective. Third, there is the approach which is essentially concerned with the study of the behaviour of individuals within organisations. This builds upon the work of the human relations movement and for the most part approaches the subject from a psychological standpoint, though a significant number of industrial sociologists have also contributed to work conducted from this point of view.

These three lines of development thus draw upon a variety of perspectives and academic disciplines. In the course of their development they have often had a significant influence upon each other, and it is not uncommon for them to be fused and described under the guise of a multi-disciplinary approach to the study of 'organisational behaviour'. Many theorists shy away from this fusion, recognising that the different theories are not always compatible and that the term 'organisational behaviour' reflects a reification of the subject of study. However, the term is often used to denote interest in a whole range of organisation studies, embracing theories of organisation, theories of the individual in the work situation and the way in which both relate to the wider social environment.

In this chapter we intend to examine a wide range of these theories, particularly with regard to the assumptions on which they are based. As we have noted earlier, all theories of organisation are founded upon a philosophy of science and a theory of society, whether the theorists are aware of it or not. To many this may appear an unduly banal and simplistic statement. However, within the context of an analysis of the field of organisation studies it seems more than justified. Many theorists appear to be unaware of, or at least ignore, the assumptions which various theories reflect.

This is particularly evident, for example, in the way in which reviewers of the field are normally content to rely upon simple linear explanations of the historical development of the subject as a means of presenting the current state of the art. It is also reflected in the host of rival typologies which attempt to classify the subject area. Both are symptomatic of a reluctance to penetrate to the foundations of the discipline. The typical analysis of the historical development of the subject, for example, usually traces how classical management theory, Weber's theory of bureaucracy and human relations theory existed side by side until synthesised in terms of open systems theory during the 1950s, and how subsequent research has sought to explore the ramifications of the systems approach at an empirical level. Theorists who choose typologies as a means of organising the subject area vary quite considerably in approach. Pugh (1966), for example, identifies six approaches: management theory, structural theory, group theory, individual theory, technology theory and economic theory. Whyte (1969) identifies seven schools of thought and activity: event—process analysts, structuralists, organisational surveyors, group dynamicists, decision making theorists, psychiatric analysts and technological structuralists. Eldridge and Crombie (1974), in a review of the typologies which have been used by various organisation theorists, differentiate between typologies based on functions (for example, Katz and Kahn, Tavistock, Blau and Scott), technology (for example, Woodward, Blauner, Thompson), regulation (Etzioni) and structure (for example, Ackoff, Vickers). As many of the authors who engage in the construction of such typologies readily recognise, the classifications thus produced are rough and ready and have many imperfections. They tend to emphasise certain aspects of the work under review whilst ignoring others. Again, it is not uncommon to find that a particular theory can be legitimately classified under more than one of the typologies produced.

It is our view that although they are helpful in identifying some of the detailed differences between various approaches to the study of organisations, both the simple linear historical description and the construction of descriptive typologies are inherently limiting in perspective *unless they seek to explore the basic theoretical assumptions of the work which they purport to describe.* Unless they do this, such analyses can be positively misleading, in that in emphasising differences between theories, they imply a diversity in approach. Insofar as these differences are identified in terms of superficial characteristics rather than fundamental assumptions, the diversity is more apparent than real. As will become clear from the discussion conducted in the rest of this work, we believe this to be the case in the field of organisation studies. Whilst superficially there appears to be a dazzling array of different kinds of theory and research, in point of fact the subject tends to be very narrowly founded indeed. This becomes evident when the theories which comprise the field are related to the wider background of social theory as a whole. As will become apparent, most are located within the context of what we have called the functionalist paradigm. The other social science paradigms remain almost completely unexplored as far as theories of organisation are concerned. Moreover, within the context of the functionalist paradigm, the majority of existing theories tend to be located within a relatively narrow range of academic territory. Despite the apparent diversity reflected in current debate, the issues which separate the parties in academic controversy often tend to be of minor rather than of major significance. The really big issues are rarely discussed, lying hidden beneath the commonality of perspective which induces organisation theorists to get together and talk with each other in the first place.

Theories of Organisation within the Functionalist Paradigm

Figure 5.1 presents a very rough overview of the location of contemporary theories of organisation within the context of the functionalist paradigm. It identifies four principal theoretical perspectives.

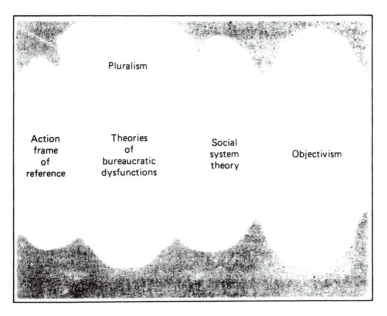

Figure 5.1   Functionalist approaches to the study of organisations

1. *Social system theory and objectivism*

This perspective, which characterises the most objectivist region of the paradigm, is of overwhelming significance as far as contemporary theories of organisation are concerned. The vast majority of writers on organisational issues adopt a perspective located here. It corresponds with the categories of social theory identified in Chapter 4 as social system theory and objectivism. In the field of organisation studies there has been a continuous interaction between these two categories of theory, since the conceptual distinctions between them have not often been recognised. We will attempt to follow some of these interactions and show how various theories have evolved. The overall perspective broadly corresponds to what Silverman (1970) has described as the 'systems orthodoxy', though, as we shall argue, it is positively misleading to view many of the theories located within it as systems theories in anything but name. It embraces a small amount of genuine social system theory and a larger element of behaviourism, but it is dominated by abstracted empiricism.

2. *The action frame of reference*

This perspective, which occupies the subjective boundary of the paradigm, is considerably less developed. Deriving principally from the work of Weber, it has received its clearest expression and formulation in the work of Silverman (1970). Contrary to Silverman's view, we do not see it as constituting an alternative paradigm for the study of organisations. We see it as an alternative perspective which remains essentially within the context of the functionalist paradigm. It is a perspective which, in terms of the analysis contained in Chapter 4, is akin to symbolic interactionism and social action theory.

3. *Theories of bureaucratic dysfunctions*

This perspective builds upon the category of integrative theory described in Chapter 4 as Mertonian theory of social and cultural structure. It embraces a relatively small number of theorists, who have specifically developed Merton's work and have carried the perspective to a position approaching that of conflict functionalism.

4. *Pluralist theory*

This is another category of integrative theory akin to the 'conflict functionalism' discussed in Chapter 4. Theorists have arrived at this perspective by different routes. In terms of numbers they are relatively few, but the perspective is of growing importance within the subject area as a whole.

The rest of this chapter is devoted to a systematic analysis of theories of organisation against the theoretical background defined by the functionalist paradigm as discussed in Chapter 4. We attempt to penetrate beyond simple historical and typological analysis to the essential theoretical foundations which underlie contemporary work in the subject.

Social System Theory and Objectivism

The dominant perspective within the field of organisation studies is characterised by a close and interactive relationship between social system theory and objectivism. In the rest of this section we intend to sketch the relationships between some of its prominent landmarks. In order to provide an overview, albeit in rough and ready terms, Figure 5.2 illustrates the general course of development.

Our plan for negotiating this complex field of theory and research is as follows. We take our starting point from the work of the *classical management theorists* and the *industrial psychologists* who were the fore-runners of the human relations movement. We argue that, despite the detailed differences in the theories which they expounded, both occupied a similar position hard against the most objectivist boundary of the functionalist paradigm. The perspective of both sets of theorists reflected a raw determinism, in which objective factors in the work environment were treated as of paramount importance to the analysis and explanation of behaviour in organisations. As we have attempted to illustrate in Figure 5.2, both approaches are alive and well today. They have flourished throughout the period and are most evident in the work of ergonomists, work study theorists and the management theorists who continue to prescribe rules of organisation.

We move from these early examples of objectivism to a consideration of the social system theory reflected in *The Hawthorne Studies*. We argue that the theoretical model which emerged from this work was, for its time, quite sophisticated, though the insights it offered were largely lost in the ensuing debate which tended to focus upon the empirical results of the study. As a result, post-Hawthorne research on work behaviour usually reverted to the objectivism of earlier years. We devote our next section to a

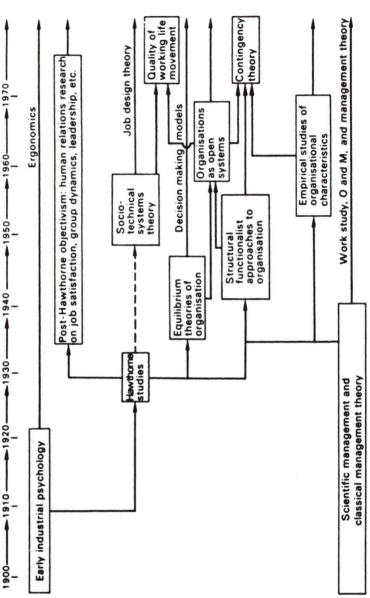

Figure 5.2 The development of social system theory and objectivism

consideration of this *post-Hawthorne objectivism* which has dominated the human relations movement and research on job satisfaction, group dynamics, leadership and managerial styles, etc., right up to the present day. This is followed by a short section on *socio-technical systems theory*, which in essence represents a direct development of the theoretical insights generated in the Hawthorne research, and which has had such a major influence upon the theory of job design.

A consideration of socio-technical systems theory leads naturally to an examination of the open systems approach to the study of organisations. In order to provide an adequate account of this, however, it is necessary to return to the Hawthorne studies and trace another line of development, which begins with Barnard's theory of organisation. Barnard's work represented one of the first attempts at developing a comprehensive model of an organisation. All the other research which we have just mentioned focuses attention upon behaviour within organisations and is concerned with the individual, social group and work environment. Barnard's work represented a clear move towards an organisational level of analysis. Later in this chapter we consider Barnard's theory, along with the work of Herbert Simon, as *equilibrium theories of organisation*.

Barnard's theory, heavily influenced by the Hawthorne research, tended to emphasise social aspects of organisation. He was concerned, first and foremost, to see the organisation as a social enterprise. This tendency was modified by subsequent theorists such as Philip Selznick and Herbert Simon who, influenced by Weber and some of the classical theorists, gave the rational/legal or bureaucratic aspects of organisation greater prominence. Simon did so within the context of an equilibrium model embracing rational and social factors. Selznick did so within the context of a structural functionalist approach to organisation. Developing certain principles derived from the use of an organismic analogy, structural functionalism has had an important influence upon organisation theory. Our next section, therefore, is devoted to a consideration of Selznick's early work as an example of the *structural functionalist approach to organisation*.

Having considered these foundations for a theory of organisations, we will then be in a position to link up with our previous discussion of socio-technical systems theory, and we devote a section to a consideration of some of the theories which emerged in the 1960s treating *organisations as open systems*. These models incorporate the insights of earlier approaches and tend to place primary emphasis upon the relationship between organisation and environment.

In the following section we consider some *empirical studies of organisational characteristics* which reflect a movement away from social system theory and towards objectivism. These studies, along with the open systems models of the 1960s, paved the way for a major synthesis in terms of *contingency theory*. This approach, which has dominated organisation theory during the 1970s, is the subject of our penultimate section.

We conclude our analysis with a discussion of the *quality of working life movement*. This too has come into prominence in the 1970s and in essence fuses the perspectives of job design theorists with those deriving from open systems theory. Drawing upon the notion of post-industrialism, it links the traditional concerns of the human relations movement and socio-technical systems theory with changes taking place within the context of contemporary society as a whole.

Classical management theory and industrial psychology

F. W. Taylor (1856 – 1915), the founder of 'scientific management' was very much a man of practical affairs. A chief engineer of a large steel works who had worked his way up from the position of ordinary labourer on the shop floor, he was interested in managerial action and its immediate measurable results. We learn that he developed the work study techniques for which he has become so famous as a result of problems experienced as a gang boss seeking to increase output by putting pressure on the men. A serious struggle ensued which Taylor finally won but at the expense of considerable soul-searching. He gave the matter thought and decided that the primary cause of such conflict was that management, without knowing what constituted a proper day's work, tried to secure output by pressure. He felt that if management knew what work was possible, they could then ascertain output by demonstration. He decided to experiment to discover what was a proper day's work for every operation in the steel shop (Taylor, 1947).

Taylor continued his experiments throughout his career in the steel industry and later as a consultant, communicating his findings to other managers through meetings of the American Society of Mechanical Engineers, for example, and through the publication of papers such as 'Shop Management' (1903) and 'The Principles of Scientific Management' (1911) (see Taylor, 1947). These works bristle with a meticulous concern for the detailed analysis of everyday work activities, such as the process of earth shovelling, pig-iron handling, etc. Taylor realised that by matching men, tools and the tasks they were required to perform, it was possible to increase productivity without placing increased physical burdens upon the men. He sought to convert the process of management from an art form based upon experience and rule of thumb to 'a true science, resting upon clearly defined laws, rules, and principles, as a foundation' (Taylor, 1947, p. 7).

Most of Taylor's work was conducted in relation to shop floor management. Whilst recognising that the scientific approach could be applied to all kinds of human activities, even 'the work of our great corporations, which call for the most elaborate co-operation', Taylor did not pursue the latter to any real extent. This was left to other members of the so-called classical school of administrative and management theory, many of whom found great inspiration in Taylor's work.

Henri Fayol (1841–1925) was a French mining engineer who rose to the top of the managerial hierarchy. After thirty years as managing director of a group of coal mines he turned his attention to popularising his 'theory of administration' which articulated various principles relating to the task of general management (Fayol, 1949). Whereas Taylor had concentrated on work conducted on the shop floor, Fayol concentrated upon the problems of work at a managerial level. Planning, organisation, command, co-ordination and control were the focus of his interest; he defined various principles which could be taught to managers. He saw the need for a theory of management.

Subsequent members of the 'classical school' for the most part built upon the foundations laid by Taylor and Fayol. Gulick, Mary Parker Follett, Mooney, Urwick and others concerned themselves with formulating and popularising principles of management. Their work related broadly to what would now be regarded as problems of organisation structure, leadership style and efficiency, and constituted a guide to managerial action rather than a theory of organisation in any formal sense.

The theories of Taylor, Fayol and the classical management school as a whole are founded upon assumptions which characterise the most objectivist region of the functionalist paradigm. The world of organisations is treated as if it were the world of natural phenomena, characterised by a hard concrete reality which can be systematically investigated in a way which reveals its underlying regularities. Above all else it is a world of cause and effect; the task of the management theorist is seen as the identification of the fundamental laws which characterise its day-to-day operation. Given this overall view, the individual is assigned an essentially passive and responding role; the individual and his behaviour at work is seen as being determined by the situation to which he is exposed. From this, the golden rule of scientific management emerges: 'Get the situation right, and the appropriate human behaviour and organisational performance will follow'.[1]

By the beginning of World War I another movement which was to have a considerable impact upon theories of behaviour in organisations was well under way in the USA, Britain and certain other European countries. Unlike scientific management, however, which was the subject of controversy from its earliest days,[2] the industrial psychology movement adopted a lower profile. For the most part it was a consultancy-orientated concern, supplying advice to industrial managers on problems associated with industrial fatigue, employee selection, individual differences and the like.[3] As such, most of the work conducted was practice- rather than research-orientated and its results often confidential. As an academic discipline, therefore, its development was severely constrained until after 1915, when as part of the war effort in Britain, the Health of Munitions Workers Committee was established. The Committee and its successor, the Industrial Fatigue Research Board (established in 1918), did much to sponsor research into problems of fatigue and health at work, with a view to contributing to the general efficiency of industry. The results of the research studies conducted were published on a systematic basis and did much to launch industrial psychology as a field of enquiry. The research papers stimulated discussion of the psychological problems of industry and further research, particularly in the USA.

From its earliest days the industrial psychology movement was at pains to emphasise its humanitarian as well as its managerial interests. In particular it was anxious to disassociate itself from any connection with Taylor and scientific management, with which it was often identified by working men. As Lupton has noted, when the National Institute of Industrial Psychology (a private foundation supported mainly by industry) was set up in Britain in 1921, 'there was some suspicion that it was practising Taylorism under another name, whereupon it was explained that the work of the NIIP was based upon sound psychology rather than on a mechanical analogue of the human being. It sought not to push the worker from behind but to ease his difficulties, and by this to increase his output and his personal satisfaction' (Lupton, 1971, p. 30). The industrial psychology movement has adhered to this standpoint as a guiding principle more or less throughout the sixty or so years of its history. It has always presented itself as vigorously humanitarian and opposed to Taylorism. Indeed, the attacks upon Taylor and his system have at times been particularly scathing, as Taylor's notion of 'The One Best Way' and his oversimplified model of 'economic man' have been subjected to systematic criticism and sometimes ridicule.[4] In most comparisons of scientific management and industrial psychology it is the differences between the two approaches which tend to be given prominence,[5] and any casual observer of the debate may well be forgiven for believing that it is the differences rather than the similarities between the two approaches which are all-important.

However, probing well beneath the surface, one finds many points of similarity between Taylor's approach and that of the industrial psychologists. The work of the early psychologists, for example, was largely directed at establishing the causes of fatigue and monotony at work and their effects upon performance and efficiency. Among the factors studied one finds the degree of mechanisation and routineness of work, methods of payment, job rotation, hours of work, the introduction of rest pauses and the influence of social groups receiving attention. All these factors (which, incidentally, are still, fifty years on, receiving much attention from industrial psychologists) had been the subject of research by the late 1920s. There can be little doubt that Taylor would have been interested in the results of these studies and would have applauded the attempt to bring science to bear upon these problems, even though it has not been the science of the stop-watch which was reflected in his predilection for time and motion study. Taylor himself had, in fact, addressed some of the problems examined by the psychologists (for example, payment systems, rest pauses, job design, etc.). The research reported by Elton Mayo (1933) on the problems of telegraphists' cramp, the performance of 'spinning mule' workers (who were all provided with sacking so that they could lie down in comfort by their machines during rest pauses) and the illumination experiments which preceded the Hawthorne studies are all reminiscent of Taylor's interest in earth shovelling and pig-iron handling.

The work of the industrial psychologists, like Taylor's, was based upon the assumption that objective factors in the work situation have a major influence upon behaviour in organisations.

This view, as we have indicated earlier, is informed by a highly objectivist ontology and epistemology. The world of work is treated as a world of hard concrete reality characterised by uniformities and regularities which can be understood in terms of cause and effect. Given these assumptions, the individual is accorded an essentially passive role; his behaviour is regarded as being determined by the work environment. The main difference between Taylorism and the work of the early industrial psychologists is thus one not so much of principle as of detail. They differ in the sophistication of their determinism. Within the context of Taylor's scheme it is crude; man is no more than a machine. Within the industrial psychologists' scheme man is a more complex psychological entity; the relationship between his environment and his behaviour can only be unravelled and understood through the use of a more complex psychological model. It is this which lies at the heart of the difference between Taylorism and traditional industrial psychology and gives rise to the different conclusions which they draw from their research. Among the psychologists a behavioural as opposed to a mechanical analogy is preferred; man is treated as a sophisticated machine which can only be understood through detailed analysis of the complex relations of stimulus and response. As will become clear from subsequent discussion, the history of industrial psychology largely reflects a sequence of attempts to plug different models of man into an essentially deterministic theory of work behaviour characteristic of the objectivist boundary of the functionalist paradigm.

The Hawthorne studies

Over the last twenty-five years or so the Hawthorne studies have been subjected to an increasing barrage of criticism, to the extent that in many quarters they are now largely discredited as a piece of social research. They have been criticised for ignoring the role of conflict in the work place; for being ideologically biased in favour of management; for being paternalistic; for adopting an inappropriate view of man and society; for ignoring unions and the role of collective bargaining; for giving insufficient attention to the role of factors in the outside environment; for being very unscientific in their approach to their research; and for misinterpreting the evidence which they collected (Landsberger, 1958; Carey, 1967). Given these criticisms, almost all of which are valid in varying degrees, it is often difficult to know precisely what to make of the

Hawthorne studies. Most theorists would agree that their significance from a historical viewpoint is beyond dispute. Whether right or wrong, they have drawn the attention of researchers to the role of social factors within the work place and what has been called the informal organisation. The Hawthorne studies have had a massive impact upon subsequent developments in industrial psychology and sociology, particularly in relation to the so-called human relations movement.[6]

In many respects the Hawthorne research has entered the realm of mythology. Few students of organisations now read either Mayo's *The Human Problems of an Industrial Civilisation* (1933) or the more comprehensive report *Management and the Worker* by Roethlisberger and Dickson (1939). They tend to learn about the Hawthorne studies at second or third hand. The literature is replete with oversimplified accounts and reports of the Hawthorne investigations which tend to focus for the most part upon their practical implications for management. Schein presents a good illustration of this, concluding that:

> what this study brought home to the industrial psychologist was the importance of the *social* factor − the degree to which work performance depended not on the individual alone, but on the network of social relationships within which he operated. As more studies of organisations were carried out, it became highly evident that informal associations and groups are to be found in almost any organisational circumstances and that these profoundly affect the motivation to work, the level of output, and quality of the work done. The Hawthorne studies were one of the major forces leading to a redefinition of 'industrial psychology as industrial *social* psychology'. (Schein, 1970, p. 34)

From the point of view of this sort of interpretation, the main significance of the Hawthorne studies is that it identified the existence of 'social man' in the work situation.

To focus upon what the Hawthorne studies found out about man in the work situation is, however, to miss the point. Its substantive conclusions, given all the criticisms of the way in which the studies were conducted, do not stand up to detailed cross-examination. Moreover, subsequent research in the human relations tradition bears out this point, in that its results have proved equally ambiguous with regard to the identification of any relationship between the satisfaction of social needs and behaviour at work.[7] In evaluating the studies some fifty years after they began, it now seems less important to discuss them in terms of their results than in terms of the theoretical approach upon which they were based. This is important because, despite all the criticism which has been levelled at the Hawthorne studies, the model which the researchers finally adopted for *explaining* their results has been used in more or less unchanged form by numerous subsequent theorists and researchers. This point has been clouded by the smoke screen generated in the debate about their ideology, results and detailed methodology. As we shall show below, the explanatory model presented by Roethlisberger and Dickson moves away from the narrowly behavioural and deterministic approach characteristic of scientific management and early industrial psychology and towards a mechanical equilibrium systems model based upon the ideas of Pareto. It represents a conscious shift from objectivism to social system theory, albeit of a limited kind, which contains within it the core notions characteristic of what later came to be known as socio-technical systems theory. Whilst criticising and often dismissing the contribution of the Hawthorne research, a large proportion of the theorists and researchers working within the field of organisation studies have continued to base their perspectives upon elements of the Hawthorne model, elevating the importance of different parts to meet their own particular research interests. The Hawthorne studies are thus of principal significance, not so much because they focused attention upon 'social man' as because they constituted an important landmark in the application of the systems approach to organisational situations. As we shall see, despite all the criticisms, organisation theory has not progressed far beyond the perspective emerging from the Hawthorne work; indeed, in some areas of enquiry it has actually regressed. With these points in mind, we will proceed to a brief examination of the Hawthorne model. Needless to say, the reader unfamiliar with the original work can unmask many myths by consulting it for himself and is strongly encouraged to do so.

The Hawthorne experiments reported by Roethlisberger and Dickson (1939) began in 1927. As they state, 'at the beginning of the enquiry the general interest was primarily in the relation between conditions of work and the incidence of fatigue and monotony among employees. It was anticipated that exact knowledge could be obtained about this relation by establishing an experimental situation in which the effect of variables like temperature, humidity and hours of sleep could be measured separately from the effect of an experimentally imposed condition of work' (Roethlisberger and Dickson, 1939, p. 3). The experiments were thus initially cast in the highly objectivist mould which characterised Taylor's scientific management and early industrial psychology.

The experimenters were simply concerned to identify cause and effect relationships between physical work conditions and employee performance and efficiency. In the course of the experiments the influence of rest pauses, hours of work, wage incentives, supervision and social factors all came to play a part, whether by design or by default.

Roethlisberger and Dickson's lengthy report on the research is packed with background information and details of the experiments conducted and the results obtained. The emphasis in the first half is upon reporting what happened and the way in which the research changed as the initial hypotheses failed to command the expected support. They report that the results of the experiments were very confused, and that the controlled experiment approach was replaced by an attempt to describe and understand the social situations under examination as 'a system of interdependent elements' (1939, p. 183). Gradually attention shifted from the physical characteristics of the work environment towards factors such as supervision and the attitudes and preoccupations of employees. In order to investigate these latter factors, the Hawthorne management, impressed by 'the stores of latent energy and productive co-operation which clearly could be obtained from its working force under the right conditions', agreed to the initiation of an interview programme with employees (1939, p. 185). It was conducted as a sort of action research project designed to improve supervisory training. As Roethlisberger and Dickson note, this interviewing programme marked a turning point in the research and for a time overshadowed all the other activities of the research group. After describing at length the approach and findings of the interview programme, the authors finally set out their systems model which informs the second half of their work. It is this model which literally stands at the centre of their analysis. Derived from the early Hawthorne work, and informing and directing interest in the later stages of research, it provides the best statement of their research perspective as a whole.

The model is presented as part of a conceptual scheme for the understanding of employee dissatisfaction.[8] Like the rest of their substantive conclusions, the model is almost submerged beneath a deluge of data presenting the approach and empirical findings of the interview programme. In their analysis of employee attitudes they make much of the difference between 'fact' and 'sentiment', and between 'manifest' and 'latent' complaints. These distinctions are important, since they led the researchers to treat certain complaints no longer 'as facts in themselves but as symptoms or indicators of personal or social situations which needed to be explored' (1939, p. 269). Employee complaints characterised by exaggeration and distortion came to be seen as symptomatic of states of personal disequilibrium. It is worth reproducing the conclusions of the researchers in full. They report that

> in order to fit their findings into a coherent whole, the investigators had to evolve a new way of thinking about the worker and those things about which he complained. Their conclusions emerged in terms of a conceptual scheme for the interpretation of employee complaints, which can be stated as follows:
>
> 1. the source of most employee complaints cannot be confined to some one single cause, and the dissatisfaction of the worker, in most cases, is the general effect of a complex situation;
> 2. the analysis of complex situations requires an understanding of the nature of the equilibrium or disequilibrium and the nature of the interferences;
> 3. the interferences which occur in industry can come from changes in the physical environment, from changes in the social environment at work, or from changes outside the immediate working environment, and the 'unbalances' which issue from such interferences may be organic (changes in the blood stream), or mental (obsessive preoccupations which make it difficult to attend to work), or both;
> 4. therefore, to cloak industrial problems under such general categories as 'fatigue', 'monotony', and 'supervision' is sometimes to fail to discriminate among the different kinds of interferences involved, as well as among the different kinds of disequilibrium;
> 5. and if the different interferences and different types of disequilibrium are not the same ill in every instance, they are not susceptible to the same kind of remedy. (1939, p. 3)

Roethlisberger and Dickson illustrate this position with the aid of a diagram which has been reproduced here as Figure 5.3. They suggest that this schema

> shows the major areas from which interference may arise in industrial situations and the kind of responses which can be expected if unbalance arises. It is apparent that this way of thinking substitutes for a simple cause and effect analysis of human situations the notion of an interrelation of factors in mutual dependence: that is, an equilibrium such that any major change in one of the factors (interference or constraint) brings about changes in the other factors, resulting in a temporary state of disequilibrium until either the former equilibrium is restored or a new equilibrium is established. (1939, p. 326)

POSSIBLE SOURCES OF INTERFERENCE   RESPONSES

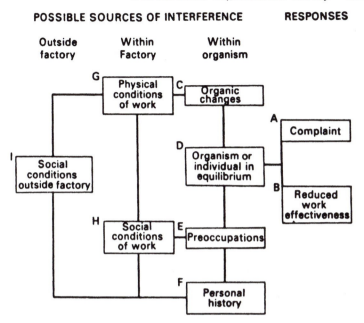

Figure 5.3 Scheme for interpreting complaints and reduced work effectiveness
SOURCE: F. J. Roethlisberger and W. J. Dickson, *Management and the Worker*
(Harvard University Press, 1939) p. 327.

Before proceeding to a full critique and evaluation of this overall position, it will be as well if we pause awhile and consider the advances over earlier thinking reflected in this model.[9]

(a) It is quite explicit in rejecting the utility of the traditional approach of scientific management and industrial psychology as a means of investigating social situations within organisations. In terms of the model presented in Figure 5.3, these approaches had tended to concentrate upon the relationships between the elements in boxes C, D and G. The Hawthorne model emphasises that employee attitudes and work behaviour can only be understood in terms of a complex network of interacting elements both within and outside the work situation and also within the individual himself.

(b) This systems approach is consciously 'open' in nature, in that it recognises the influence of outside forces (box H), though attention is mainly paid to them insofar as they affect the personal history of individuals (box F), and their possible effects are moderated by the concept of equilibrium.

(c) The analysis of factors within the factory identifies the elements of the socio-technical systems approach to the study of organisations (boxes G and H).

(d) In line with point (a) above, the investigators specifically reject the view that any one factor can be identified as a source of industrial problems. They mention 'fatigue', 'monotony' and 'supervision'; with hindsight they would undoubtedly have added 'social needs'.

Roethlisberger and Dickson proceed to apply this model to the evidence collected in the research and then develop certain aspects in more detail. In brief, they suggest that the evidence collected shows that the set of relationships characterised by boxes G, C, D, A and B and those characterised by boxes F, E, D, A and B are less important as a source of disequilibrium at work than those associated with I, H, E, D, A and B. In other words, they conclude that the balance of evidence of their research places most emphasis upon social factors both outside and within work as influences upon employee attitudes and work effectiveness. On the basis of this conclusion, they focus upon these factors in their subsequent investigations and analysis, and they identify the notions of the 'formal' and 'informal' organisation and the contribution made by social factors to equilibrium in the work place. It is important to stress that these conclusions, for which the studies are best remembered, result from the empirical aspect of the enquiry and the interpretations placed upon the evidence collected.

One further point in relation to their theoretical model is worthy of note. Having identified the importance of individual attitudes in the work situation, Roethlisberger and Dickson go on to elaborate a further conceptual scheme for understanding employee satisfaction and dissatisfaction, reproduced here as Figure 5.4. It

attempts to show in terms of their relations to one another those factors which have to be taken into account when considering employee content or discontent. According to this interpretation it is not possible to treat, as in the more abstract social sciences, material goods, physical events, wages, and hours of work as things in themselves, subject to their own laws. Instead they must be interpreted as carriers of social value. For the employee in industry, the whole working environment must be looked upon as being permeated with social significance. Apart from the social values inherent in his environment the meaning to the employee of certain objects or events cannot be understood. (1939, p. 374)

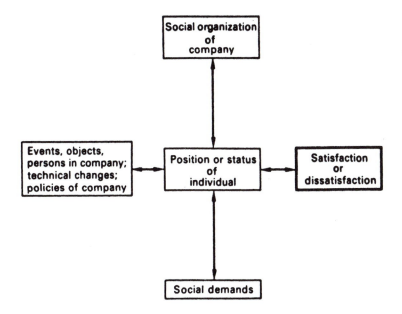

Figure 5.4   Scheme for interpreting complaints involving social interrelationships of employees
SOURCE: F. J. Roethlisberger and W. J. Dickson, *Management and the Worker* (Harvard University Press, 1939) p. 375.

To the list of advances over earlier thinking reflected in the Hawthorne model, we can thus add:

(e) An anticipation of what has later come into prominence as the 'action frame of reference'. The Hawthorne researchers emphasised that explanations must be adequate at the level of meaning to the individual involved.[10] Their insights here, however, were clouded by their euphoria about the importance of the social organisation, which led them to view meaning and significance as arising primarily from within the context of the internal organisation. As they put it:

to understand the meaning of any employee's complaints or grievances, it is necessary to take account of his position or status within the company. This position is determined by the social organisation of the company: that system of practices and beliefs by means of which the human values of the organisation are expressed, and the symbols around which they are organised – efficiency, service, etc. . . .

But the relation of the individual employee to the company is not a closed system. All the values of the individual cannot be accounted for by the social organisation of the company. The meaning a person assigns to his position depends on whether or not that position is allowing him to fulfill the social demands he is making of his work. The ultimate significance of his work is not defined so much by his relation to the Company as by his relation to the wider social reality. (1939, pp. 374 – 5)

These important theoretical insights relating to the employee's interpretation of his situation were not developed and, along with many other aspects of the Hawthorne model, were largely buried under the deluge of empirical research generated by the study.

In any evaluation of the Hawthorne studies, therefore, it seems important to be clear about whether one is assessing them in terms of their contribution to theory or in terms of their substantive conclusions. Whilst there is undoubtedly a relation between these two factors, they are by no means synonymous, and much of the current confusion over the value of the studies has arisen because critics have not always distinguished between these factors.

In theoretical terms the Hawthorne model can best be understood as representing a fusion of elements from the sociology of Pareto and Durkheim. As we noted in Chapter 4, Pareto had a massive impact upon the 'Harvard Group' of sociologists in the 1920s and 1930s, and his idea of a social system in equilibrium provides the core notion underlying the Hawthorne model. The research also reflects Pareto's interest in 'non-logical' conduct. The notion of 'sentiments' derives directly from Pareto's work and is used by the Hawthorne team to describe attitudes which are not based upon 'facts'. The distinction between 'facts' and 'sentiments' plays an important part in guiding the Hawthorne analysis.

The notion of 'social facts' is, of course, reminiscent of Durkheim's work, and Roethlisberger and Dickson duly acknowledge his influence upon the way in which they sought to analyse the situations encountered in the research.[11] However, the Durkheimian influence is much more extensive than this. It will be recalled from our discussion in Chapter 4 that Durkheim addressed himself to the study of the relations between the individual and society, and the relation of the individual personality to social solidarity. Now, it is precisely this theme which dominates the substantive content of the Hawthorne research. Whilst Pareto's notion of a system in equilibrium provides an organising framework for the research, it is the Durkheimian notion of anomie that receives central attention. The Hawthorne studies address themselves to what is perceived as a situation of anomie − the disjuncture between the individual and his work. It is this Durkheimian influence which accounts for the emphasis placed upon social factors. Crudely put, the Hawthorne interest in 'social man' does not derive so much from the researchers' interest in the psychological make-up of man (as much of the post-Hawthorne literature would lead us to believe) as from an interest in Durkheim's analysis of the process of social change.

Interestingly enough, in Roethlisberger and Dickson's account of the studies, the Durkheimian influence upon their theoretical perspective is not specifically elaborated in any degree.[12] In Mayo's (1933) account, however, it receives much greater attention. The spirit of Durkheim is present throughout and is clearly reflected in Mayo's suggestion that human problems are to be understood in relation to the erosion of social values brought about by the dictates of economic and technical change. Concluding his review of some of the findings of the Hawthorne experiments, for example, Mayo remarks that

> Human collaboration in work, in primitive and developed societies, has always depended for its perpetuation upon the evolution of a non-logical social code which regulates the relations between persons and their attitudes to one another. Insistence upon a merely economic logic of production − especially if the logic is frequently changed − interferes with the development of such a code and consequently gives rise in the group to a sense of human defeat. This human defeat results in the formation of a social code at a lower level and in opposition to the economic logic. One of its symptoms is 'restriction'. (Mayo, 1933, pp. 120−1)

This statement clearly reflects the central principles which inform the theoretical perspective of the Hawthorne studies. Society is to be understood in terms of a system tending towards equilibrium; if this equilibrium is disturbed, forces are set in motion to restore it. The equilibrium of modern society has been upset by technological change prompted by the dictates of an economic logic; as a result social forces have been set in motion to restore the balance. This equilibrium model, as applied at the societal level, is transferred in more or less unchanged form to an analysis of the work situation. The individual now becomes an equilibrating system, influenced by the various elements which comprise the situation within and outside work. Behaviour at work is understood in terms of attempts to maintain or restore an equilibrium position. In the work place where the influence of technology and economics are paramount the social organisation acts as one of the principal forces for restoring equilibrium. It is this fusion of Paretian and Durkheimian perspectives which gives the Hawthorne model of the organisation as a social system its own distinctive flavour.

In evaluating the theoretical contribution of the Hawthorne studies, therefore, it is important to distinguish between the Paretian and Durkheimian influences upon their model. Both elements are open to criticism. As will be apparent from our discussion in Chapter 4, the Paretian equilibrium model is not particularly well equipped for the study of an open system such as that envisaged by the Hawthorne researchers. As we have argued, the notion of equilibrium is indeed incompatible with an open systems view, but in the case of the Hawthorne analysis this may amount in the end to no more than a semantic confusion. The Paretian model is infused with the notion of the individual as an organism; it thus reflects a fusion of mechanical and biological analysis. In this situation the notion of homeostasis rather than equilibrium provides the relevant organising concept. (This is perhaps a fine point and one which should not be pursued too far.)

The real limitation of both equilibrium and homeostatic models for the study of open systems is that they place severe constraints upon the openness of the system. The system is only allowed to vary within fairly narrow constraints in predefined ways. The equilibrium notion is particularly restrictive in this respect, since it focuses attention almost exclusively upon the internal relationships which characterise the system. External factors are generally considered only insofar as they cause disequilibrium; the causes of such disequilibrium and the mechanisms by which it is restored tend to be at the focus of interest. Indeed, the use of an equilibrium analogy encourages a search for these equilibrating mechanisms. The use of such a model thus carries with it a conservative orientation. The influence of the environment upon the system is constrained by the nature of the assumptions by which it is defined, and explanations of system operation are guided primarily by the assumption that some form of balance will be restored. As will be clear from our discussion of systems theory in Chapter 4, the Hawthorne model is open to its environment, but only partially so.

Thus in evaluating the model from this perspective one must recognise that, despite the advances which it reflects over the traditional theories of classical management and industrial psychology, as a social systems model it is severely constrained. However, as will become clear as we progress through this chapter, other social systems models employed for the study of organisations often show little advance over the Hawthorne model; sometimes they are considerably less sophisticated. In criticising Hawthorne on this ground, therefore, one is likely to be criticising social system theory in general. The biological analogies most commonly employed show little advance over the modified Paretian model described above.

Many of the criticisms directed at the Hawthorne model have, in fact, been of this nature. They represent criticisms of social system theory in general and have often been launched from the perspective of 'pluralist theory', which we shall be discussing later in this chapter. The major criticism from this point of view is that the Hawthorne model treats the organisation as a unitary system in which the normal state of affairs is characterised by co-operation and harmony; such a view underplays the role of power and conflict as factors in organisational affairs.[13]

Moving on to consider the Durkheimian elements of the model, it will be clear from our analysis, presented earlier, that the influence of Durkheim accounts in some measure for the focus upon social factors within the organisation. It is no doubt an oversimplification to suggest that the Hawthorne *analysis* was provided by Pareto and the *conclusions* by Durkheim, but it is an interesting proposition nonetheless. In all empirical research the results are largely determined by the nature of the 'problematic' or 'theoretical framework' adopted, and the suggestion that the Hawthorne researchers were guided in their interpretation of evidence by a Durkheimian interest in social solidarity remains highly persuasive. As we have noted earlier, the notion of 'social man' as it emerged from the Hawthorne studies owes more to Durkheim than to any analysis of psychological needs. This is a point which has often been lost in the post-Hawthorne mythology. The psychologists who have dominated the human relations movement have made Hawthorne so much their own that many students of organisations may be forgiven for not realising that the studies were primarily informed by a sociological rather than a psychological perspective.

Insofar as criticisms of the Hawthorne model are directed at its detailed conclusions and results about the relative influence of economic, social and other factors upon work behaviour, therefore, it is the Durkheimian influence upon the model that is being challenged. A number of critics have attacked the studies on these grounds, without necessarily recognising the Durkheimian influence.[14] The attack is launched on the basis of detailed methodology and the interpretation of results. Interestingly enough, in not addressing the assumptions built into the Hawthorne model – its equilibrium tendencies, for example – such criticisms implicitly endorse the model used as a legitimate method of analysis. The problem with the studies, from this point of view, lies in the way they have been implemented; whilst endorsing the theoretical framework, criticism is levelled at the way in which it has been used.

Hopefully, the above discussion goes some way towards sorting out the confusion which surrounds the interpretation of the Hawthorne studies. The view that they are worthless in themselves and merely of importance because of their historical impact derives largely from the fact that they are judged only from the point of view of their conclusions and results. The majority of criticisms have been of this sort. This can be explained to some extent by the fact that the results of the studies were available before the theoretical model. Roethlisberger and Dickson's detailed account, for example, was preceded by numerous publications. Those of Mayo were of a polemical nature and undoubtedly did much to provoke criticism of the studies. Whitehead's (1938) detailed presentation of results also drew attention to their substantive conclusions rather than to their theoretical orientations. Numerous other publications have laid stress upon their practical relevance. As a result, the Hawthorne studies have been judged largely in terms of their contribution to the empirical knowledge of work behaviour as opposed to the analysis of work situations. In terms of the latter, their record fares much better. The quality of the systems theory propounded, whilst highly deficient when judged from a perspective outside the bounds of social system theory as a whole, stands up well to many contemporary models of the work place. By way of redressing the unfavourable balance against the Hawthorne model, but at risk of presenting the model in too favourable a light, we conclude our discussion here by re-emphasising that the research, whatever its drawbacks, marked a clear advance in sophistication over the simple factor explanations offered by the classical management theorists and industrial psychologists. The research represented one of the first attempts at viewing an organisational situation in terms of a system of interrelated parts, and anticipated a number of future developments in relation to the notion of socio-technical systems theory and, to a lesser extent, the action frame of reference.

Post-Hawthorne objectivism: job satisfaction and human relations

Despite the basic *theoretical* insights implicit in the Hawthorne social systems model, the majority of social theorists interested in the study of work behaviour remained largely uninfluenced by the systems notion until some twenty years later, when the idea of 'socio-technical' system began to hold sway. In the interim, and to a lesser extent throughout the post-Hawthorne period as a whole, research on work behaviour has been characterised by a return to the objectivism of traditional industrial psychology discussed earlier in this chapter. From the point of view of most researchers, it was the *results* of the Hawthorne work which commanded attention, and the studies were used largely as a source of new hypotheses for informing and guiding further empirical enquiries in the traditional mould. The systems model was largely left behind in favour of a continued search for causal relationships between new variables identified in the Hawthorne work.

As will be recalled from our previous discussion, the early industrial psychologists had concerned themselves with the study of relationships between employees, their work environment and their work performance. In this endeavour concepts such as 'fatigue' and 'monotony' had provided the central focus of interest. In the post-Hawthorne era the notion of 'job satisfaction' has replaced them at the centre of attention. Interest has been directed towards the identification of the determinants of job satisfaction and its relationship to work performance. Thus, whereas the pre-Hawthorne concern was for studying the relationships between *work, fatigue, monotony* and *performance*, post-Hawthorne concern has been for studying the relationship between *work, satisfaction* and *performance*.

The first comprehensive study of job satisfaction was conducted by Hoppock (1935). It focused upon general job satisfaction among employed adults within a small community, and concluded that factors such as occupational level, fatigue, monotony, working conditions and achievement could all have an influence upon job satisfaction. This was followed by a host of other empirical studies focusing upon specific work variables such as supervision, leadership style, promotion opportunities, remuneration, status, job content, working conditions, social environment, attitudes to the company and technology.[15] Many of these studies also sought to link job satisfaction, both in relation to specific job factors and in general terms, to levels of employee work performance, absence from work, rate of employee turnover, accidents, etc. The method of analysis adopted in these studies focused upon measurement of the variables involved and a study of inter-correlation coefficients. As Vroom noted, whilst these studies suggested some sort of negative relationship between job satisfaction and the probability of resignation, absence from work and accidents, there was no simple relationship between job satisfaction and job performance (Vroom, 1964, pp. 101–5). Subsequent reviewers of job attitudes and motivation have also concluded that the field is characterised by studies yielding a host of unrelated fragments but little real understanding of the subject area (for example, Miner and Dachler, 1973).

The absence of a clear relationship between factors in the work environment and job satisfaction has inevitably led to an increasing focus upon the nature of man. The attempts to identify and define what constitutes job satisfaction has carried with it a need to understand the process of motivation at work. In the light of post-Hawthorne research the classical view of economic man has been increasingly discredited. The research of Roethlisberger and Dickson (1939), Whyte's study of the restaurant industry (1948), Walker and Guest's study of the assembly line (1952), Likert's work on leadership and supervision (1961 and 1967), and the work of Lewin *et al.* on leadership and group dynamics (1939), among countless other research studies, have been interpreted as evidence in support of the view of man at work as a social being motivated by affective needs. These and other researches, such as the job satisfaction studies of Herzberg *et al.* (1959), have also been used in support of the view that man at work attempts as well to satisfy higher-level psychological needs for recognition, achievement, self-actualisation, etc.

In essence, the attempt to identify and test through empirical research the validity of different models of man can be understood as a search for a substitute for Taylor's 'economic man'. Behaviourist and determinist theories of human behaviour only have utility if it can be shown that man is predictable. Much of the objectivist research on work behaviour has aimed essentially to show precisely this. It has been underwritten by the assumption that the nature of man can be revealed through systematic empirical investigation of his attitudes and behaviour.

In the attempt to identify an appropriate model of man for the study of work behaviour, industrial researchers have made much use of the work of humanistic psychologists such as Abraham Maslow, whose theory of a hierarchy of human needs has proved influential (Maslow, 1943). Some specific attempts have been made to test his model at an empirical level,[16] though the more common approach has been to use it as a point of reference for interpreting results achieved independently of the model as such. In both cases the data generated has proved inconclusive. Even in the case of Herzberg *et al.* (1959) simple two-factor theory of job satisfaction, which is in essence related to Maslow's ideas, research has again proved inconclusive. Its results are consistently supported only when those authors' own highly idiosyncratic method of testing the theory is used.[17]

Since the 1960s the inability of such models of man to provide consistent explanations of work motivation and behaviour has led to increasing interest in cognitive models of the motivational process, particularly 'expectancy theory'.[18] This is a theory based essentially upon what Locke has described as 'a form of calculative, psychological *hedonism* in which the ultimate motive of every human act is asserted to be the maximisation of pleasure and/or the minimisation of pain. The individual always chooses that course of action which he expects will lead to the greatest degree of pleasure or which will produce the smallest degree of pain' (Locke, 1975, p. 459). In effect, expectancy theory has given the kiss of life to objectivism in the waning years of the Hawthorne influence. It has generated a spate of empirical studies and now stands as the most popular approach to motivation among industrial researchers (Locke, 1975, p. 457). Somewhat paradoxically, it turns the wheel of industrial psychology right back to the days of Taylorism, in that in place of rational economic man it seeks to substitute rational, calculative, hedonistic man.

This course of development clearly underlines the essentially objectivist nature and orientation of industrial psychology, even in the post-Hawthorne era. As will be recalled from our discussion of the work of the early industrial psychologists, the distinction between their concerns and Taylorism largely boils down to different conceptions of what the industrial worker was like. The differences in the substantive conclusions which their theories generate arise as a result of the different models of man included in their analytical schemes. The industrial psychologists have come to see the nature of man as increasingly complex and problematic as far as explaining behaviour in organisations is concerned. They have searched for solutions in humanistic and cognitive psychology, primarily with a view to slotting complex psychological man into the framework of a deterministic theory of work behaviour, albeit one based upon a contingency rather than a universal mode of explanation. This essentially determinist stance is the classic mark of objectivist theory, and it is for this reason that much contemporary work in this area, along with the theory and research of the early industrial psychologists, Taylor, and the classical management theorists, can be regarded as representative of the most objectivist region of the functionalist paradigm.

Socio-technical systems theory

As we have noted, the elements of socio-technical systems theory were built into the structure of the Hawthorne model for analysing work situations. In the immediate post-Hawthorne years, however, these important insights were largely neglected in favour of objectivist studies of job satisfaction, group dynamics, leadership style and other factors of interest to the human relations movement. Certain studies had paid attention to the relationships between technology and social structure,[19] but it was not until the 1950s that anything approaching what might be called a socio-technical systems approach came into being.

The term 'socio-technical system' was first used by members of the Tavistock Institute to characterise the interaction of technological and social factors in industrial production systems. It derived largely from a study conducted by Trist and Bamforth (1951), which was directed at examining the effects of the introduction of the long-wall method of coal mining in certain British mines. This mechanised, mass production-type system of coal mining, which replaced the traditional 'hand-got' method, involved a complete reorganisation of work and social relationships within the pit. The study, which was heavily informed by a psycho-analytical perspective focusing upon the importance of group relationships, led the researchers to view the work situation in terms of the interrelations between social and technological factors. The working group was regarded not as just a technical system or a social system, but as an interdependent socio-technical system. Like the Hawthorne studies, the Tavistock work was underwritten by the assumptions of an equilibrium model. The technological change reflected in the new long-wall method was seen as disturbing the 'pre-mechanised equilibrium', and the responses of the miners interpreted as reactions to this disturbance. The situation in the pit was analysed in terms of a field of psychological and social forces, the balance of which was influenced by the interaction between technical and human factors.

The study was of importance in recognising that socio-psychological factors were built into the nature of work technology, and that the work organisation also had social and psychological properties of its own which were independent of technology. However, the socio-technical systems notion remained in an embryonic rather than an explicit and well developed form, awaiting refinement through further research. This was conducted by various members of the Tavistock group throughout the 1950s and resulted in a number of important publications.[20] These reflect an increasing preoccupation with the notion of system as an organising concept, not just at the level of the work group but for the study of the organisation as a whole, and a move away from the equilibrium model to one based upon an organismic analogy.

The notion of the socio-technical system has had a major impact upon developments within the field of job design, particularly since the middle 1960s, and upon the quality of working life movement which we shall be considering later in the chapter. For a number of years, however, its use was most prominent in British research, particularly that of the Tavistock Institute. Research conducted in the USA during the 1950s was not so clearly informed by the systems concept, though it addressed itself to similar considerations. The work of Argyris provides the most impressive and outstanding example. As early as 1952 Argyris published his study of *The Impact of Budgets upon People*, followed in 1957 by *Personality and Organisation*. Both these studies investigate the conflicts between the needs of human personality and the characteristics of formal organisation, recognising that an adequate analysis of behaviour in organisations must take account of individual factors, small informal group factors and formal organisation factors (staff-line, chain of command, specialisation of tasks, production layout and control, etc.).[21] Argyris is concerned to integrate relevant behavioural science research through the use of a systematic framework for the study of what he describes as organisational behaviour, and he generates many insights which parallel those which characterise socio-technical systems theory. His work, like its British counterpart, is underwritten by the notion of equilibrium. Certain elements anticipate an open systems view of organisations, and indeed the underlying model is specifically updated and rewritten within the context of this open systems approach in a subsequent volume (Argyris, 1964).

Equilibrium theories of organisation: Barnard and Simon

Chester Barnard (1886–1961) was for many years a prominent figure in management thought in the USA. A president of a large corporation, he had a great deal of contact with the 'Harvard Group' of sociologists led by Henderson and Mayo during the 1930s, and in response to their encouragement, set out his thoughts on management and organisation in his famous essay *The Functions of the Executive*, published in 1938. This work reflects the dominant perspectives and orientations of the Harvard Group, in that it is underwritten by a concern to analyse organisations as social systems whose activities can be understood with reference to the concept of equilibrium. Barnard's essay represented one of the first systematic attempts to lay the basis of an academic theory of organisations and has been extremely influential upon subsequent thought. Indeed, Perrow has gone so far as to suggest that 'it would not be much of an exaggeration to say that the field of organisational theory is dominated by Max Weber and Chester Barnard, each presenting different models, and that the followers of Barnard hold numerical superiority' (Perrow, 1972, p. 75).

Barnard argues that his work presents two treatises. The first is described as an 'exposition of a theory of co-operation and organisation', and the second as 'a study of the functions and of the methods of operation of executives in formal organisations' (Barnard, 1938, p. xii). The underlying theme is that organisations are by nature essentially co-operative systems but require sensitive management to maintain them in states of equilibrium. His essay as a whole seeks to establish the basis of a theory of management which will contribute to this overall aim.

Barnard defines a formal organisation as 'a system of consciously co-ordinated activities or forces of two or more persons' (1938, p. 73), and argues that 'an organisation comes into being when (1) there are persons able to communicate with each other, (2) who are willing to contribute action, (3) to accomplish a common purpose' (1938, p. 82). Barnard argues that these three factors

– communication, willingness to serve and common purpose – are necessary and sufficient conditions found in all formal organisations. The organisation, therefore, is a co-operative enterprise of individuals in pursuit of a common purpose. It is essentially 'unitary' in nature. In Barnard's work the notions of co-operation and purpose assume a moral flavour. Barnard argues that it is the natural state of affairs for human beings to co-operate, and he cites physical, biological, psychological and social arguments in support of his case. He regards people 'unfitted for co-operation' as pathological cases, insane and not of this world (1938, p. 13). For Barnard, the fact that members of an organisation participate and co-operate willingly is taken as an endorsement of the purpose of the organisation. As he puts it, 'a purpose does not incite co-operative activity unless it is accepted by those whose efforts will constitute the organisation' (1938, p. 86).

It is against this sort of background that Barnard develops his theory of executive functions. In his scheme executives within organisations are charged with the task of sustaining the organisation in a state of equilibrium and hence ensuring its survival. Barnard recognises that disequilibrium is a very common state of affairs and that in practice even the willingness of persons to co-operate may be in doubt. He thus devotes considerable attention to considering ways in which equilibrium can be restored through appropriate executive management. The executive is urged to give consideration to necessary adjustments in relation to the environment and within the organisation. In relation to the latter he is urged to alter the conditions of behaviour of individuals, including conditioning of the individual by training, by the inculcation of attitude and by the construction of incentives (1938, p. 15).

Thus, although the co-operation of individuals is seen as the defining characteristic of an organisation, Barnard's theory of executive functions is based upon somewhat contradictory assumptions. This is a major weakness in his theory and one which has not perhaps been recognised sufficiently clearly by those theorists who have built upon Barnard's work. His theory of 'inducements' and 'contributions', which is developed to explain the continued participation of members of the organisation, seems particularly paradoxical within the context of an organisation characterised by a common purpose. Similarly Barnard's view that one of the functions of the executive is to 'indoctrinate' those at lower levels of the organisation with its general purposes seems equally paradoxical (1938, p. 233). Again his view that 'the final test' of his 'conceptual scheme is whether its use will make possible a more effective conscious promotion and manipulation of co-operation among men' (1938, p. 74), also contradicts his basic assumptions about the co-operative nature of organisations.

Barnard's theory of organisations, like the Hawthorne studies to which it was so closely related, is of some importance but must be approached with caution. Given that Weber's theory was not yet available to the English-speaking world, Barnard's contribution was for many students the first theory of organisation which they encountered. Its influence has been enormous and its assumptions are reflected in much contemporary theory, particularly that which approaches organisation from a managerial perspective. It offered a view of and an approach to the study of organisations which differed quite remarkably from the conventional approach of management theorists of the day. Although a major section of his book is devoted to the theory and structure of formal organisations, there is, in point of fact, very little discussion of structure in the classical management sense. Barnard was less concerned with describing managerial hierarchies, lines of command, spans of control, job design, etc., than with delineating the relationship of individual members to the ongoing executive process. Whilst interested in the co-ordination of activities in pursuit of the general purpose of the organisation, Barnard approached the problems which this posed in terms of the motivation of individual members. For Barnard, the theory of formal organisation was largely concerned with the relationships between people.

This perspective, then, differed substantially in emphasis from the approach of the classical theorists. Whilst being at one with these theorists in viewing organisations as goal-seeking entities, Barnard devoted considerably less attention to the formal and technical aspects of organisation in terms of structure. On their part, the classical theorists paid very little attention to the role of individuals, their motivation and behaviour. By the 1940s, therefore, the time was ripe for a fusion of these two perspectives and the creation of a goal-orientated theory of organisation which took due consideration of both human and structural factors. The foundations of such a perspective were laid in two quite different ways by Herbert Simon and Philip Selznick.

Simon, in his famous book *Administrative Behaviour*, first published in 1945, integrates the motivational and structural approaches to organisation within the context of a theory of equilibrium. His analysis, like Barnard's, is comprehensively underwritten by Paretian ideas, though this is not specifically acknowledged. Simon focuses upon decision making within organisations, and he seeks to reconcile the principle of rationality which underwrites the theory of formal organisation and administration with the fact that the behaviour of individuals never reaches any high degree of rationality. For Simon, the notion of 'economic man' characteristic of classical theory is plainly at odds with the view of man revealed by the psychologists and, indeed, that which emerges from observations in everyday work experience. One of his solutions is to introduce a new model of man — 'administrative man' — based upon the notion of 'bounded rationality' and the assumption that man 'satisfices' rather than 'maximises' in his work behaviour.

Thus, for Simon, *'the central concern of administrative theory is with the boundary between the rational and non-rational aspects of human social behaviour.* Administrative theory is peculiarly the theory of intended and bounded rationality — of the behaviour of human beings who *satisfice* because they do not have the wits to *maximise'* (Simon, 1957, p. xxiv). Simon is specifically concerned to build a theory of administrative behaviour around a theory of human choice or decision making which is sufficiently broad and realistic to accommodate the rational aspects of choice which have interested economists and the elements of decision making and behaviour which have interested psychologists. It is this theory which is placed at the centre of his equilibrium (inducement—contribution) model of the organisation and from which he derives various propositions of interest to the administrator.

Simon's theory of administration has proved tremendously influential and has stimulated considerable interest in decision-making approaches to the study of organisations. The basic themes implicit in Simon's analysis were updated in an important volume by March and Simon (1958), which in essence sought to codify and define the field of organisation theory in terms of a series of formal propositions. The bounded rationality of 'administrative man' as opposed to the maximising behaviour of 'economic man' again emerges as the focus of analysis and is used to develop links with the structure of organisations. The characteristics which are seen as defining human problem-solving processes and rational human choice are seen as determining the basic features of organisation structure and function (March and Simon, 1958, p. 169). In this way the model of organisation which emerges from the authors' analysis reflects their assumptions with regard to the nature of man. Essentially the theory presented reflects a modified form of behaviourism. Whilst allowing for an element of 'subjective rationality' deriving from the individual's frame of reference, human behaviour is seen as being shaped by influences in the environment. These provide the initial stimulus to which humans respond in the somewhat mechanistic manner of 'administrative man' – defining the situation in 'limited' ways, 'searching' and 'satisficing'.

The March and Simon model has been further developed by Cyert and March (1963), who view the organisation as an 'adaptively rational' system coping with a variety of internal and external constraints in arriving at decisions. It sees the firm as an information-processing and decision-making system which has to cope with various conflicts from both within and outside its boundaries. It focuses upon the internal operations of the firm, develops the analysis of conflict presented in March and Simon's work and arrives at a theoretical perspective which, although dominated by the notion of equilibrium, has many points of similarity with the pluralist theories of organisation discussed later in this chapter.

The structural functionalist approach to organisation

Philip Selznick (1948), like Simon, sought to develop a goal-orientated theory of organisation which took due consideration of both human and structural factors. However, whereas Simon focused upon organisations as decision-making entities, Selznick chose to develop a structural functionalist view.

Selznick begins his analysis by reviewing two definitions of an organisation, one from the work of J. M. Gaus, a classical theorist in the public administration field, and the other from Barnard's work. Gaus defined 'organisation' as 'the arrangement of personnel for facilitating the accomplishment of some agreed purpose through the allocation of functions and responsibilities' (1936, p. 66). Barnard, it will be recalled, defined a formal organisation as 'a system of consciously co-ordinated activities or forces of two or more persons' (Barnard, 1938, p. 73). Selznick suggests that 'viewed in this light, formal organisation is the structural expression of rational action' (1948, p. 25). As in the case of Simon, Selznick thus links his view of organisation with the notion of rationality and also recognises that organisations are far from rational in their actual operations. In line with the conclusions of the Hawthorne studies, Merton's research on bureaucratic dysfunctions, and Barnard's analysis of co-operative systems, he argues that 'as we inspect these formal structures we begin to see that they never succeed in conquering the non-rational dimensions of organisational behaviour. The latter remain at once indispensable to the continued existence of the system of co-ordination and at the same time the source of friction, dilemma, doubt and ruin' (Selznick, 1948, p. 25). In other words, Selznick argues that, although organisations are formally rational, in actual practice they are greatly influenced by the informal and social aspects of organisation. He argues that individuals never submit as 'wholes' to the dictates of formal structure. He also argues that the institutional environment within which an organisation finds itself exerts pressure upon the formal and social structure of the organisation, again deflecting it from the rational model.[22] He proceeds to suggest that organisations should be viewed as both '*an economy*' (that is, a system of relationships which define the availability of scarce resources and which may be manifested in terms of efficiency and effectiveness) and as an '*adaptive social structure*'. He argues for a combination of the perspectives reflected in Weber's view of bureaucracy and the classical management theorists' definition of organisation on the one hand, and on the other, that reflected in Barnard's co-operative system, which emphasises the importance of 'inducements' to members as a basis of ensuring the maintenance of the organisation and the authority system which it reflects. As Perrow (1972) has noted, Selznick's analysis goes right to the heart of many issues which have continued to attract the attention of organisation theorists to the present day. The relationships between formal and informal organisation, mechanistic and organic management (discussed in terms of the problems of delegation), individual and organisation goals and the problem of explaining the way in which changes in organisational structure come about are all briefly addressed.

Having integrated the social and the formal, economic or technical aspects of organisation in this way, Selznick then proceeds to advocate that a structural functional form of analysis be adopted. He recognises that a sociological analysis of formal structures is inadequate as an end in itself and that a theory of organisations capable of understanding adaptive processes is required. He views structural functional analysis as being adequate for this end and develops a model based upon the analogy of a biological organism. It is of importance, in that it represents a clear break from the use of the mechanical equilibrium model derived from Pareto which had characterised earlier theories. Selznick largely follows the

Parsonian scheme described in the previous chapter, in that he seeks to identify the functional 'imperatives' which serve the overall need of the 'maintenance of the system' as a whole.

Thus, whilst setting off from a position similar to Simon's, Selznick follows a different route in the development of his theory of organisation. However, in both theories the notion of rationality remains central. Simon begins and ends with rationality as a dominant concept, even to the extent that a new model of man – 'administrative man' – is developed to reconcile the contradictions between formal and informal aspects of organisational activities. 'Administrative man' (who satisfices because he does 'not have the wits to maximise') in essence preserves rationality as the pre-eminent concept. The nature of man is redefined to serve the theory of formal organisation. In Selznick's model the notion of rationality is allowed to occupy a background role though an extremely pervasive one in terms of the purposive nature of organisation. The organisation is presumed to operate in a goal-directed manner, geared to maintaining itself internally and in relation to its environment. The adoption of an organismic analogy as a basis of analysis leads to the identification of a series of functional imperatives which serve the needs of the organisation as an 'economic' and 'adaptive social system'. Purposive rationality is still the dominant concept, though – in contrast to Simon's scheme – the individual is conspicuously absent; purposive rationality becomes a characteristic of the system as a whole. As we shall see, the concept of purposive rationality, particularly in relation to the notion of organisational goals, is an important characteristic of many social system theory approaches to the study of organisations.

Organisations as open systems

Since the mid-1950s the open systems approach has established itself as a popular means of studying organisations. The reign of structural functionalism as a descriptive term in this field was relatively short-lived, though, as we have argued in Chapter 4, there is, in effect, little difference between structural functionalism and open systems theory when the latter is limited to the use of organismic system analogies. In the late 1950s, therefore, many structural functionalists began to describe themselves as open systems theorists and a number of old functionalist models began to appear in new guises. Theorists who had adopted equilibrium models also began to cast their analyses within the context of an open systems approach. In this section we will give specific consideration to some examples which illustrate the principles of open systems theory as it has been applied to the study of organisations and which illustrate the general trend referred to above.

It will be recalled from our discussion of the work of the Tavistock Institute that the concept of socio-technical system was formulated within the context of a study adopting a mechanical equilibrium model as a basis of analysis (Trist and Bamforth, 1951). By 1958 the concept had been incorporated into a much wider *open* socio-technical systems approach for the study of organisations based upon an organismic analogy. Rice's (1958) analysis of the Tavistock Institute's research in an Indian textile firm provides a clear illustration of this. The industrial enterprise is viewed as a socio-technical system which must satisfy the financial conditions of the industry of which it is part. The social, technological and economic dimensions of the organisation are all seen as interdependent but with values of their own. Stated more bluntly, the argument is that in an industrial system there are technological, social and economic *imperatives* which must be satisfied if an optimum industrial system is to be achieved. The aim of the Tavistock researchers, in their capacity as consultants, was to establish new systems in which all three elements were more adequately related than before.

Rice's analysis of the textile firm is explicitly based upon the model of a firm as a living organism which is 'open' to its environment. The firm is seen as maintaining itself through the exchange of materials with its environment — importing capital, raw materials, equipment and supplies, and exporting dividends, investments, waste products and finished goods. It is assumed that if there is neither import nor export, the organisation will die. The study is guided by the notion of 'primary task'. Each system, or subsystem is regarded as having, at any one given time, a 'primary task – the task which it is created to perform' (Rice, 1958, p. 32). In the case of private enterprise in a Western economy, the primary task is regarded as being that of making profits. Rice treats the primary task as a factor which unites the whole organisation, in a manner which is reminiscent of Barnard's concept of a co-operative system. As Rice puts it,

> *The performance of the primary task is supported by powerful social and psychological forces which ensure that a considerable capacity for co-operation is evoked among the members of the organisation cre-*

ated to perform it, and that, as a direct corollary, *the effective performance of a primary task can provide an important source of satisfaction for those engaged upon it.* In other words, there is, among the members of any organisation, a need, whether latent or manifest, to get on with the job. They take pride in doing it well. (Rice, 1958, pp. 33–4)

The organisation is thus viewed as a unitary system under the umbrella of a common task. The social system is viewed as a positive force contributing to task achievement. Technology is viewed as a force which imposes constraints upon possible modes of organisation, but within which choice is possible. The important variable, therefore, is organisational design. The design of an appropriate mode of work organisation which satisfies the demands of technology and the needs of employees is seen as the key to producing a harmonious and effective organisation. The notion of an open socio-technical system is used as a tool for analysing the textile firm with this overall perspective in mind. The complex relationships between systems and subsystems which are identified – 'operating systems', 'managing systems', 'governing systems', etc. – derive their significance as conceptual tools from the context of this overall view of the industrial firm.[23] It is a systems view which is based upon a philosophy of social engineering and which in essence seeks to ameliorate the problems created by technological change.[24]

The sophistication of the open socio-technical systems approach to the study of organisations has been further elaborated, within the context of the above problematic, through other research conducted by various members of the Tavistock Institute. In this work the relationship between the organisation and its environment is given more and more attention. In his book *The Enterprise and its Environment*, published in 1963, for example, Rice now defines the primary task of an organisation as 'the task that it must perform to survive' and the primary task of leadership as 'to manage the relations between an enterprise and its environment so as to permit optimal performance of the primary task of the enterprise' (Rice, 1963, pp. 13–15). The environment of the enterprise is regarded as consisting of its total political, social and economic surroundings; for a part of an enterprise the environment is regarded as including the other parts and the whole (Rice, 1963, p. 15). In line with the increased attention devoted to 'environment', the notion of boundary regulation and management is also given increased prominence, particularly in Miller and

Rice's work (1967). Boundary regulation is seen as 'the essential managerial control in any enterprise' and considerable attention is given to the problems and importance of boundary definition of control systems both within enterprises and between enterprises and their environment. This work explicitly views the organisation 'as a tool designed primarily for task performance', in which 'human needs — for satisfaction and for defence against anxiety — should be regarded as constraints upon task performance' (Miller and Rice, 1967, p. vi). The systems analysis which Miller and Rice offer is geared to a search for optimum solutions to the problems posed by the fact that the demands of an organisation's various subsystems do not always coincide.

The nature of organisational environments has also received a great deal of attention from the Tavistock team in recent years. In 1965 Emery and Trist published their well-known article, 'The Causal Texture of Organisational Environments'. This study shifted the focus of open systems theory away from a specific concern for what Dill (1958) has described as the 'task environment' towards a more general concern for the 'appreciation' of the social environment as a quasi-independent domain.[25] The turbulence of the world environment as a whole and its implications for the future have come to be seen as important contextual influences upon organisational activities. This wider concern for context has led to an interest in the field of 'social ecology' (Emery and Trist, 1972). The attempt to understand organisations as open socio-technical systems has carried with it a concern for understanding the patterns of life characteristic of post-industrial society, the manner in which these patterns are changing and the implications which they carry for the understanding and the influencing of the operation of organisations as complex adaptive systems. This interest in social ecology has led to a fusion between socio-technical systems theory and theories of 'post-industrialism', which has led the researchers involved away from an exclusive and narrowly based concern for theories of organisation and organisational change towards a concern for social theory and social change. Their theorising now reflects that of the social engineer operating on a truly macro-scale.

Our second illustration of the open systems approach to the study of organisations is taken from the work of Katz and Kahn. Their study *The Social Psychology of Organisations* (1966), has established itself as a classic in the field and provides one of the most frequently cited systems models of an organisation. In essence it constitutes a structural functionalist model of organisation, presented in the terminology and jargon of open systems theory. Their basic approach to the study of social phenomena is very much in the tradition of Radcliffe-Brown, in that they emphasise the need to regard a social system as a 'structuring of events or happenings rather than of physical parts' and as having 'no structure apart from its functioning' (Katz and Kahn, 1966, p. 31). They see the open systems approach as a means of analysing the social and institutional context within which people live, and they develop a processual model for understanding organisations in terms of energic 'input', 'throughput' and 'output'. Their analysis is largely based upon the assumption that social systems are homeostatic, possessing the characteristics of negative entropy, feedback, differentiation and equi-finality.[26]

Within the context of this open systems approach Katz and Kahn go on to argue that there are five generic types of subsystem:

PRODUCTION OR TECHNICAL SUBSYSTEMS
primarily concerned with organisational throughput;

SUPPORTIVE SUBSYSTEMS which carry on the environmental transactions in procuring the input or disposing of the output or aiding in these processes;

MAINTENANCE SUBSYSTEMS for attracting and holding people in their functional roles;

ADAPTIVE SUBSYSTEMS concerned with organisational change;

MANAGERIAL SUBSYSTEMS which direct and adjudicate among all the others.

(Katz and Kahn, 1966, pp. 39–47)

This classification is reminiscent of Parsons's four 'functional imperatives' discussed in the previous chapter and reflects Katz and Kahn's predilection for explaining the factors which they see as 'creating and maintaining a stable system' (1966, p. 107). They are primarily concerned with explaining the way in which social systems maintain themselves, and their whole analysis is geared to this endeavour. They explicitly recognise the limitations of the mechanical model as a means of studying social affairs, and argue that the use of such models ignores the significance of system openness with respect to production and maintenance inputs and neglects the overriding importance of the maintenance input for the social system (1966, p. 31). They argue that special attention must be given to these maintenance inputs.

Thus for Katz and Kahn the adoption of an open systems approach is linked to the traditional sociological concern for explaining order in social affairs. The openness of the system is constrained by the assumption that the system is stable. In point of fact, Katz and Kahn give relatively little substantive attention to the nature of the environment of organisations. Their main concern is with the process of input—throughput—output in a conceptual sense. For modelling this process they select what amounts to a qualified biological analogy – qualified in the sense that they recognise that social systems do not have a physical structure and are more complex in their maintenance requirements. However, it is the biological analogy, characteristic of much functionalist analysis in social science, that dominates their work.

The Tavistock and Katz and Kahn models represent two of the most prominent systems approaches to the study of organisations and serve the purpose of illustrating the state of the art at the present time. Open systems theory has undoubtedly had a major impact upon approaches to the study of organisations, particularly with regard to the emphasis which is now placed upon understanding the nature and influence of environment and in studying organisations as processes rather than as structures. Conceptually, these advances have become well embedded in contemporary organisation *theories*.

As we have noted, open systems models of organisation are invariably based upon the analogy of a biological organism. The organisation is regarded as essentially purposive in nature and as having certain needs or 'functional imperatives' which must be fulfilled if the organisation is to continue to exist.[27] Thus systems models of organisation are often predicated upon the assumption that organisations, like organisms, aim at survival. This is conceptualised in terms of a 'primary task' or in terms of some sort of goal-setting process. The organisation and its subsystems are then viewed as being orientated towards the achievement of this overall aim and assumed to be intelligible with this reference point in mind. A norm of purposive rationality, which this orientation to an end state implies, thus underwrites the whole approach. Subsystems are defined and their actions judged with reference to their influence upon the ability of the system to achieve its primary task. The approach is based upon the assumption that the system has a 'functional unity'. If the system is not working well, it is implied that certain 'imperatives' are not being met. Thus the whole approach is geared to defining the imperatives which make the system work. The notion of the socio-technical system, for example, is based essentially upon the idea that human and technical imperatives must be satisfied in the interests of the system as a whole. People, technology, resources, etc., are regarded as inputs to a purposively rational process geared to the achievement of end states.

The use of the biological analogy for the study of organisations is a popular one because it is well suited to the purposes of social engineering. It is this which accounts for its popularity within the context of management theory, a point to which we shall return at the end of this chapter.

We close our discussion of open systems approaches to the study of organisations with a point which has links with our next section: the problem of operationalising systems notions within an empirical context. Most systems analyses, such as that of Katz and Kahn, are pitched at a theoretical level and, with appropriate qualifications with regard to factors such as the dynamic and intangible nature of 'structure', the need to avoid 'reification' and 'oversimplification', are able to present systems theory in processual terms. Theorists who attempt to operationalise such a scheme within an empirical context, however, often find their open systems approach rapidly turning into a more traditional structural functional analysis, with an emphasis upon structure. As a heuristic device the dynamic essence of the systems concept can be maintained as events are conceptualised in terms of an open field of continuous action. At an empirical level, however, the issue of boundary definition almost inevitably leads to an attempt to identify relatively static system parts. Open systems theory, when put into practice at an empirical level, often ends up as an abstracted form of empiricism which defies the processual nature of the systems concept.

Empirical studies of organisational characteristics

In an earlier section we described how research into behaviour in organisations in the post-Hawthorne period reverted to the objectivism characteristic of early industrial psychology. The systems notions implicit in the Hawthorne studies were largely abandoned in favour of a search for correlations between individual behaviour, job satisfaction, work performance and 'objective' characteristics in the work situation. As we have argued, this objectivist search for the determinants of behaviour in organisations is alive and well today and in evidence in most of the leading journals in the subject area.

A similar approach is prominent in much of the empirical work directed at the study of organisations. Since at least the early 1950s there has been a distinct and growing trend towards the measurement and inter-correlation of organisational characteristics. Alongside developments in the systems approach there has been a strong surge of objectivism. This has fed upon two sources. First, it has sought to spell out, operationalise, measure and search for relationships between ideas deriving from the work of the classical management theorists and from the sociological writings of Max Weber. Second, it has sought to do the same with regard to insights and hypotheses generated within the context of systems theory. Somewhat paradoxically, the systems approach has spawned a fair number of empirical investigations characteristic of the objectivist mode of scientific enquiry which many systems theorists initially set out to counter and replace.

One of the earliest and certainly one of the most significant organisational studies in the objectivist tradition was that conducted by Joan Woodward in the early 1950s. Woodward (1958 and 1965) set out to discover whether the principles of organisation laid down by the classical management theorists correlated with business success when put into practice. Since most of these management principles were concerned with the design of organisation structures, her survey of firms in south-east Essex involved the collection of quite a wide range of quantitative data relating to the organisation of the firm, manufacturing processes and methods, commercial success and general history. The now-famous results of her study suggested that there was an empirical relationship between the nature of production systems (technology), patterns of organisation and business success. Whilst rejecting the hypotheses derived from classical management theory, the study generated a new one: that technical methods were the most important factor in determining organisation structure and had an important influence upon human relationships within the firm. This study and its results were very much in line with the conclusions emerging from research conducted elsewhere. The interest in the relationship between technology and social organisation was very much in the ascendency. The work of Trist and Bamforth (1951), Walker and Guest (1952), Burns and Stalker (1961), Sayles (1958) and many others was yielding similar findings. What is important about Woodward's work for our present purposes was that it focused upon an organisational level of analysis and employed simple quantitative descriptions of organisations which could be subjected to statistical analysis.[28] It opened the floodgates to a new style of research based upon the objectivist assumption that organisations are hard, concrete, empirical phenomena *which can be measured*. It was seen that the traditional methods of empirical science could be set to work in a new social terrain.

Our discussion of objectivist research on organisations since Woodward's study can be no more than illustrative. We shall confine our attention to the most prominent pieces of work, directing the reader interested in obtaining a more encompassing view to issues of *Administrative Science Quarterly* over the last ten years or so. This journal is literally packed with reports on research in the objectivist tradition; indeed, one might say that it has helped to raise objectivism as applied to the study of organisations to the status of an orthodoxy.

The work conducted by the Aston group of researchers on organisations in Britain during the 1960s and early 1970s represents one of the most prominent, systematic and sustained attempts to study organisations from an objectivist perspective. Their most important articles have recently been brought together in a number of edited volumes, which provide a convenient overview of their approach, areas of interest and detailed results (Pugh *et al.*, 1976).

In essence, the Aston research has sought to conceptualise and measure organisational *structures*, and the *context* in which they are set, with a view to examining the relationships between them through a multi-variate analysis of data. Organisational structures were conceptualised in terms of a number of dimensions – specialisation, standardisation, formalisation, centralisation, configuration and flexibility – which largely derive from Weber's conceptualisation of bureaucracy in terms of an 'ideal type'. The notion of 'context' was conceptualised in terms of factors such as origin and history, ownership and control, size, charter, technology, location, resources and interdependence (with other organisations). The empirical data generated through the research has led to revision and refinement of the various dimensions and associated scales for measuring organisational characteristics, and has permitted the comparison of 'profiles' of different types of organisations. It has shown that the notion of bureaucracy is by no means unidimensional, and an empirical taxonomy of organisational forms has been constructed upon the basis of key characteristics. The analysis of relationships between context and structure has drawn attention to factors such as size, dependence and what the researchers describe as the 'charter—technology— location nexus'. In subsequent work the influence of technology upon organisational structure has received particularly close attention and has led to detailed examination of the nature and measurement of technology in a wide range of studies.

In the USA work which shares many similarities with the Aston approach has been conducted by numerous researchers, of whom Richard Hall, Hage and Aiken and Peter Blau are among the most prominent. Much of this research is conveniently summarised in a recent text produced by Hall (1972), which, like the Aston volumes, gives a good overall perspective on the objectivist approach to the study of organisations. Hall has been concerned mainly with the empirical measurement of bureaucracy, using Weber's 'ideal type' as a reference point, and arrives at similar conclusions with regard to the multidimensional nature of the concept. He too has constructed an empirical taxonomy of organisations. Hage and Aiken (1967) have mainly concerned themselves with the measurement and explanation of organisational structure. Blau in recent years (1971 and 1974) has greatly concerned himself with the relationships between structure and size.[29]

The development of objectivist approaches to the study of organisations over the last ten years has consumed the intellectual energy of an increasing proportion of organisation theorists; indeed, it is possible that a majority of organisation researchers are now working within the context of this area of the functionalist paradigm. There is scarcely an organisational variable which has not been measured in some form and even correlated with itself in the objectivist search for 'significant' relationships which eventually will prove 'determinate'.[30] The 1976 and early 1977 issues of *Administrative Science Quarterly*, for example, contain objectivist research on the familiar topics of technology and structure, size and structure, structure and effectiveness and structure and environment, as well as many objectivist articles on the traditional human relations issues. Even romantic relationships within organisations have been subjected to this type of analysis (Quinn, 1977).

The extremely high degree of commitment to the models and methods of the natural sciences which characterises this sort of work has firmly established itself as a dominant perspective within organisation theory. It seeks to advance knowledge and understanding of organisations through empirical analysis of a reified social world. It is based upon an ontology, epistemology, methodology and view of human nature characteristic of the most objectivist region of the functionalist paradigm.

Contingency theory: the contemporary synthesis

The contingency approach to the study of organisations has come into increasing prominence during the 1970s as a loose sort of framework for synthesising the principal notions of open systems theory with the results of objectivist research conducted at all levels of organisational analysis. The results of empirical research on individual motivation, job satisfaction, leadership style, organisation structure, technology and many other organisational variables have been interpreted within the context of a managerially orientated set of propositions, which assert that the effective operation of an enterprise is dependent upon there being an appropriate match between its internal organisation and the nature of the demands placed upon it by its tasks, its environment and the needs of its members.

The idea of a contingency theory of organisation was first presented in an explicit way by Lawrence and Lorsch in their book *Organization and Environment* (1967), which reported the results of an empirical study of ten organisations operating in a variety of environmental conditions. The study was directed at answering the basic question 'What kind of organisation does it take to deal with various economic and market conditions?' The study adopted an open systems framework based upon an organismic analogy and viewed the organisation as a system of interrelated elements which were subject to influence by their environment. The authors express their view of the organisation as a system as follows:

> At the most general level we find it useful to view an organization as an open system in which the behaviors of members are themselves interrelated. The behaviors of members of an organization are also interdependent with the formal organization, the tasks to be accomplished, the personalities of other individuals, and the unwritten rules about appropriate behavior for a member. Under this concept of system, the behavior of any one manager can be seen as determined not

only by his own personality needs and motives, but also by the way his personality interacts with those of his colleagues. Further, this relationship among organization members is also influenced by the nature of the task being performed, by the formal relationships, rewards, and controls, and by the existing ideas within the organization about how a well-accepted member should behave. It is important to emphasize that all these determinants of behavior are themselves interrelated. (Lawrence and Lorsch. 1967, p. 6)

To this they add that the understanding of the behaviour of managers in large organisations necessitates a central concern with two other aspects of the functioning of systems. First, they argue that as systems have become large they have been divided into parts (differentiated), the functioning of which has to be integrated if the system as a whole is to be viable. They draw an analogy here with the organs of the human body, which are integrated through the nervous system and the brain. Second, they argue that an important function of any system is adaption to what goes on in the world outside (1967, p. 7).

Thus, the Lawrence and Lorsch study places emphasis upon the organisation as a system which is internally differentiated and which must achieve an adequate level of integration if it is to adapt to the conditions which it encounters in its environment.[31] On the basis of the results of their empirical research, the authors conclude that the most effective organisations are those which succeed in achieving a degree of differentiation and integration compatible with environmental demands. As they put it, 'in a more diverse and dynamic field, such as the plastics industry, effective organisations have to be highly differentiated and highly integrated. In a more stable and less diverse environment, like the container industry, effective organisations have to be less differentiated, but they must still achieve a high degree of integration' (1967, p. 10). The research results suggested that effective organisations in all environments employed effective methods of conflict resolution in order to maintain the required state of differentiation and still achieve the required integration (1967, pp. 109–32).

The findings of the Lawrence and Lorsch study provided a direct challenge to the tenets of both classical management and human relations theory. As we have suggested, the former sought to specify universal principles of organisation as a guide to managerial action. The Lawrence and Lorsch study suggested that different organisational principles were appropriate in different environmental circumstances and indeed within different parts of the *same* organisation. The human relations theorists had stressed the importance of adopting organisational structures and managerial styles which permitted the satisfaction of psychological needs through, for example, participation in decisions, the carrying of responsibility, etc. In other words, they were generally in favour of an approach to organisation which moved away from the formal and mechanistic bureaucratic model towards a more flexible, loosely structured and open organic model. The Lawrence and Lorsch study suggested that the highly structured bureaucratic model, from the point of view of business success, may be the most effective in certain circumstances.

The time was ripe, therefore, for a reconciliation of the detailed propositions of classical management theory and human relations, which for many years had stood in opposition to one another.[32] Lawrence and Lorsch's contingency approach appeared to show a way forward, suggesting that the appropriateness of management principles depended upon the nature of the situation in which they were applied. Moreover, other important empirical studies were generating similar results. Woodward's (1958) study had demonstrated that commercially successful firms organised themselves in a manner compatible with their technology. Burns and Stalker (1961) had demonstrated that successful firms adopted an approach to organisation and management which was consistent with demands placed upon them by their environment, particularly with regard to the degree of market and technological change. Emery and Trist (1965), were also drawing attention to the importance of environmental demands upon organisations and, along with other Tavistock colleagues, had long argued that organisation was a variable open to choice (Trist *et al.*, 1963). The empirical work on organisation structures conducted in the 1960s by the Aston group (Pugh *et al.*, 1976), and Richard Hall (1972), among many others (for example, Udy, 1959), was pointing to the range and diversity of organisational forms and directing attention to the need for some form of explanation. Fiedler (1967) had developed a contingency theory of leadership. Thompson had suggested that 'the basic function of administration appears to be co-alignment, not merely of people (in coalitions) but of institutionalised action − of technology and task environment into a viable domain, and of organisational design and structure appropriate to it' (Thompson, 1967, p. 157). Burns and Stalker had urged that 'the beginning of administrative wisdom is the awareness that there is no one optimum type of management system' (Burns and Stalker, 1961, p. 125). In short, it appeared that a contingency theory of organisations was necessary to provide an opportunity for reconciling and synthesising the conclusions emerging from the work of this diverse body of theorists studying organisations and behaviour from a managerial point of view. And this was precisely what Lawrence and Lorsch suggested. However, in the ten years since the Lawrence and Lorsch study was first published there has been little progress towards the articulation of a contingency *theory* as such. Lawrence and Lorsch devoted their own attention to the managerial implications of their contingency approach, particularly with regard to problems of organisational design (Lawrence and Lorsch, 1970, for example). Many others followed their lead, or confined themselves to further empirical tests of various aspects of the contingency model in its skeletal form.[33] As a result, there is within the subject of organisation theory at the present time a body of research which may be described as representative of a 'contingency view' or 'contingency approach', but no clear and consistent statement of the nature of 'contingency theory' at a conceptual level.[34] In its present state the contingency approach really stands for little more than a loosely organised set of propositions which in principle are committed to an open systems view of organisation, which are committed to some form of multivariate analysis of the relationship between key organisational variables as a basis of organisational analysis, and which endorse the view that there are no universally valid rules of organisation and management.

In the rest of this section we attempt to draw together the various strands of the contingency approach and provide a systematic statement of the principles upon which it is based. Insofar as one wishes to analyse organisations as social systems from a managerial point of view, the contingency model which we present goes a long way towards an integration of contemporary issues and concerns and provides a framework for examining the status and utility of theory and research in this area.

A contingency model for organisational analysis

1. The contingency theory of organisation postulates that organisations and their functioning can be understood in terms of principles which apply to biological organisms.

2. It is based upon an open systems view which regards an

organisation as existing within the context of a wider environment.

3. The organisation and its environment are seen as being in a state of mutual influence and interdependence. In principle the organisation is seen as representing a subsystem of a wider social system of which its environment is part.

4. However, as organisational analysts, contingency theorists focus upon the organisation as a unit in its own right, distinguished from this wider environment by a notional boundary.

5. The contingency theory of organisations is concerned to understand and represent the key associations which characterise relationships between the organisation and its environment.

6. It is assumed that the key relationship between organisation and environment can be understood in terms of the organisation's 'need' to survive.

7. The organisation, in line with the use of an organismic analogy, is viewed as comprising a series of interdependent subsystems, each of which has a function to perform within the context of the organisation as a whole.

8. In other words, the organisation as a system comprises a series of functional subsystems, each of which may interact with elements of the environment external to the organisation. Because of their importance to the survival needs of the organisation as a whole, each can be conceptualised in terms of a 'functional imperative'.

9. Contingency theorists are not in complete agreement as to which subsystems or functional imperatives characterise, or should be singled out to represent, the system as a whole. They also frequently confuse functional subsystems with their structural manifestations at any given point in time. However, the following subsystems are frequently identified in one form or another in the literature, and they are presented here as functional imperatives of direct relevance to the contingency theorists' concern to explain the survival of an organisation within the context of its wider environment.

The strategic control subsystem The organisation as a system is viewed as being in need of strategic guidance aimed at maintaining an appropriate balance between the organisation and its environment. This functional imperative is usually viewed as the role of the 'policy makers' or top management. As we have seen, it has been portrayed within the context of the work of some of the Tavistock researchers as a problem of managing the boundary between the enterprise and its environment. This is usually seen in terms of monitoring market, technological, economic, political and social change, with a view to taking key decisions which (a) set the goals and direction of the organisation as a whole, (b) set in motion the internal mechanisms which will produce an appropriate balance and relationship between subsystems within the organisation and thus (c) ensure the viability, legitimacy and survival of the organisation within the context of its wider environment.

The operational subsystem The organisation is viewed as being involved in some form of purposive activity geared to the achievement of the goals and objectives set by its policy makers. In industrial organisations this activity involves the *transformation* of inputs – labour, raw materials, capital, etc. – into outputs in the form of material goods. In non-industrial organisations this transformation process involves the conversion of inputs into service-type outputs. This transformation process reflects the 'operational imperative' characteristic of goal-orientated organisations. This imperative receives tangible expression through the way in which productive roles are organised. In broad terms it is often characterised as the technology employed. The concept of 'technology' as used by most organisation theorists is a partial and shorthand way of referring to the way in which the operational subsystem expresses itself through the 'structure' of the organisation. Technology is not consonant with the operational system, which is essentially processual; it is merely a partial structural expression of it.

The human subsystem The role of human beings in organisations is accorded a special status within most contemporary theories of organisation. Individuals are recognised as having certain needs which must be satisfied if they are to be attracted and encouraged to stay within the organisation and to apply themselves to their functional roles in a manner consistent with the requirements of the system as a whole. In other words, human needs have acquired the status of a functional imperative. Theorists differ with regard to the nature of this imperative, according to the model of man to which they subscribe. From a system standpoint, 'economic man', 'social man', 'self-actualising man' or whatever, implies a different form of human imperative, with implications for all the other subsystems which comprise the organisation as a whole. In all important respects, the debate about models of man within the context of contemporary organisation theory has in essence been a debate about the nature of the imperatives of the human subsystem.

The managerial subsystem The internal integration and control of the organisation is the function of the managerial subsystem. As has been argued, the functional differentiation of organisations calls for some method of integration, in order to satisfy the demands of, and reconcile conflicts within and between, the 'production' and 'human' subsystems and to ensure that they are in harmony with the requirements imposed by the 'strategic control' subsystem. In most contemporary theories of organisation, management is viewed as a functional imperative; the notion of self-regulating human and production subsystems is not often encountered, though the trend towards the use of autonomous work groups is something which moves in the direction of this state of affairs and, to some extent, undermines the notion of a managerial imperative. The operation of the managerial subsystem expresses itself in two principal ways. First, it receives structural expression through the organisation's authority structure as reflected, for example, in organisation charts, job descriptions, budgetary control systems and the like. Second, it is expressed through the managerial styles adopted by individual managers in day-to-day interpersonal relationships.

By way of summary of the above points, therefore, the organisation is viewed as a process of mutual influence and interaction between four functional imperatives or subsystems and the environment in which they are located.

10. Contingency theory assumes that each of the four subsystems is open to a range of variation; it stresses strategic choice, technological choice (that is, choice of operational methods) and organisational and managerial choice, and it recognises that the nature of the human subsystem is con-

tingent upon the personalities and orientations of organisational members. It also recognises that each of the subsystems can reflect a range of variation within any given organisation.

11. The variation in environments and organisational subsystems has received considerable attention in theory and research conducted over the last twenty years or so, and there appears to be an emerging consensus that the differentiation of these variables can be characterised in the following terms.

(a) *The environment*

A common theme running throughout recent research on the nature of organisational environments focuses upon the concept of *uncertainty* as a pre-eminent characteristic for distinguishing between different types of environment. The research and writings of Burns and Stalker (1961), Emery and Trist (1965), Lawrence and Lorsch (1967), Thompson (1967), Terreberry (1968) and Child (1972), among many others, all in their different ways characterise environments in terms of the degree of uncertainty.

One of the difficulties encountered in attempting to apply this concept of uncertainty to the analysis of an organisation's environment revolves around the definition of what constitutes a particular environment. The distinction between 'task environment' (Dill, 1958) and 'context' (Emery and Trist, 1965) is particularly relevant here. Viewed from the standpoint of the latter, all contemporary organisations are located in an uncertain and turbulent environment, in which technical, economic, market, social and political change is rapidly becoming a norm characteristic of post-industrial society. From this point of view, the age of the stable, certain organisational environment is over.

(b)   *Strategic control*

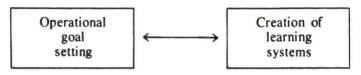

| Operational goal setting | ←——→ | Creation of learning systems |

Within the context of contingency views of organisation the primary task of top management – ensuring survival – has usually been interpreted in terms of the need to relate the organisation to its environment (Burns and Stalker, 1961; Rice, 1958 and 1963). From this point of view, the nature of this primary task is contingent upon environmental circumstances. Thus the primary strategic task of an organisation in a highly uncertain and turbulent environment may be regarded as being to facilitate organisational *learning* and adaption to change. In a more stable environment the primary task may be conceptualised in terms of the achievement of more static goals. Given stability, the primary task of an organisation can be much more operationally orientated towards the maintenance of this stability and survival of the organisation through the efficient and effective achievement of pre-set goals. The dimension of strategic control can thus be conceptualised from a contingency standpoint, in terms of operational goal setting versus the generation of learning within the organisation. This characterisation reflects the implications of environmental circumstance for strategic decisions.

(c)   *The operational subsystem*

| Routine low-discretion roles | ←——→ | Complex high-discretion roles |

The operational subsystem of an organisation, as defined here, relates to all activities – production, sales, personnel, finance, research and development – which contribute to the overall transformation process with which the organisation is concerned. The diversity of its elements, therefore, adds difficulties to its conceptualisation in terms of a single dimension, and this is very much reflected in the literature on organisation theory. Two related concepts are prominent in contemporary research – those of 'technology' and 'operational task'. The former term often causes confusion, since it is frequently identified in the popular eye with machine technology. However, in recent years steps have been made towards a conceptualisation of technology which has general applicability across all the activities of an organisation. Most prominent are the contributions of the Aston group of researchers (Hickson *et al.*, 1969 and Charles Perrow, 1967).

The Aston group have suggested a distinction between the following technologies:

'Operations technology':
> This refers to the techniques used in workflow activities. It is seen as having a number of characteristics, such as 'automation', 'workflow rigidity' and the exactness of standards against which operations can be evaluated. Other factors, such as the degree of 'continuity', are also seen as being relevant in certain cases.

'Materials technology':
> This concept, also used by Perrow, relates to the characteristics of the material used in the workflow, particularly its 'uniformity' and 'stability'.

'Knowledge technology':
> A concept, again used by Perrow, which relates to the knowledge used in the workflow, a factor greatly influenced by the predictability and familiarity of problems encountered.

All three of these elements of technology combine to influence the nature of individual jobs or 'tasks' within organisations, and many writers have chosen to analyse the impact of technology at this level of individual roles. The characteristics of the three dimensions of technology referred to above appear to correlate in terms of the 'routineness' or 'discretionary content' of work, a factor which has been investigated and conceptualised in various ways by Jaques (1962) and Turner and Lawrence (1965), among others. This 'degree of routineness' of work tasks provides a means of differentiating between the characteristics of operational subsystems, ranging from those dominated by the mass-production type of technology, which creates low-discretion work, to the complex, highly discretional form of work characteristic, for example, of many executive-type roles, or enriched jobs.

(d)   *The human subsystem*

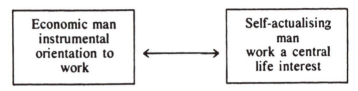

Ever since the Hawthorne studies, the needs of the human or social subsystem within an organisation have received increasing attention. The broad line of argument has been that Taylor's vision of 'economic man', who views work in a purely instrumental fashion, grossly misrepresents the needs and aspirations of people at work. Alternative visions of human motivation, which (following Maslow and other humanistic psychologists) emphasise the importance of the satisfaction of 'higher-level' needs, have been advocated by many theorists as providing a more realistic model of man for understanding work behaviour. The theories of Argyris (1957 and 1964), Herzberg *et al.* (1959) and many other neo-human relations theorists have presented this point of view and have argued that the satisfaction of higher-level needs at work is an imperative as far as human growth and development, job satisfaction and effective work performance are concerned. The different models of man advocated by Taylor on the one hand, and the neo-human relations theorists on the other, thus offer a way of conceptualising the nature of the human subsystem in terms of the imperatives set by the nature of human needs. However, the situation is more complicated than this, in that as our discussion of post-Hawthorne objectivism has shown, the empirical evidence in support of this imperative is far from clear-cut, and the relationship is not as deterministic as many theorists have suggested. One important supplementary idea, which certain theorists have drawn upon to maintain the validity of the 'model of man approach' in the light of this evidence, relates to the question of orientation to work. Research by a number of theorists, notably Dubin (1956) and Goldthorpe and his colleagues (1968), has demonstrated that work is by no means always a central life interest, and that people may seek to minimise their commitment to work and obtain satisfaction (in terms of psychological needs, goals and personal values, or whatever), elsewhere. Thus this 'orientation to work' factor must be placed alongside the 'model of man' analysis in any attempt to conceptualise the dimensions of the human subsystem. The psychological analysis in terms of needs is thus modified in terms of the sociological factors which influence attitudes to work.

(e)   *The managerial subsystem*

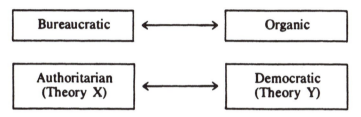

As we have argued, the managerial subsystem within an organisation expresses itself through the formal authority structure *and* through the nature of the personal styles of behaviour of individual managers. In principle, both are capable of varying independently, though it can be argued that particular types of organisations attract and develop particular types of managers.

The formal authority structure of organisations has received a considerable amount of attention in the literature on organisation theory, and it has become more or less orthodox to compare organisations in terms of their degree of bureaucratisation, using Weber's ideal-type 'bureaucracy' as a basis for analysis. The distinction offered by Burns and Stalker (1961) between mechanistic (bureaucratic) and organic organisations has become well established, and the research of Woodward (1958), the Aston group (Pugh *et al.*, 1976) and Richard Hall (1972), referred to earlier has added empirical substance to the notion that organisations do in fact vary in terms of formal structure.[35]

Managerial or leadership styles have also received considerable attention from researchers operating in the human relations tradition. McGregor's (1960) distinction between 'Theory X' as a label for highly authoritarian, directive styles of management and 'Theory Y' for flexible, open, democratic, 'motivating' styles provides a convenient way of characterising this dimension of the managerial subsystem. Further research has added considerable depth and sophistication to McGregor's original analysis which, in the neo-human relations tradition, placed principal emphasis upon 'human needs' as the primary determinant of the effectiveness of a managerial style. However, the authoritarian—democratic characterisation remains central and is reflected, for example, in the schemes offered by Likert (System 1 as opposed to System 4) (1967), Blake and Mouton's managerial grid (9.1 and 9.9 styles) (1964), the Ohio State leadership studies (initiating structure and consideration) (reviewed in Blum and Naylor, 1968). The distinction between Theory X and Theory Y will thus serve to capture the common element which distinguishes those managerial styles which seek to direct, coerce and control and those designed to integrate the individual and the organisation through a more open, democratic style which emphasises the importance of delegation, trust and intrinsic job satisfaction.

12. Contingency theory postulates that the effectiveness of the organisation in coping with the demands of its environment is contingent upon the *elements* of the various subsystems which comprise the organisation being designed in accordance with the demands of the environment (or, more accurately, sub-environments) with which they interact; this implies that the elements of different subsystems must be congruent in terms of the characteristics along each of the basic dimensions by which they are defined. We shall call this *the congruency hypothesis*.

The congruency hypothesis warrants further elucidation, which can be most easily achieved with the aid of Figure 5.5. This seeks to bring together the main elements of the contingency framework developed in the preceding paragraphs. The congruency hypothesis postulates that a necessary condition for the effectiveness of an organisation in meeting the demands of its environment is that the relationships between subsystem characteristics be congruent; it is postulated that organisations will be less effective in dealing with the demands of its environment when such relation-

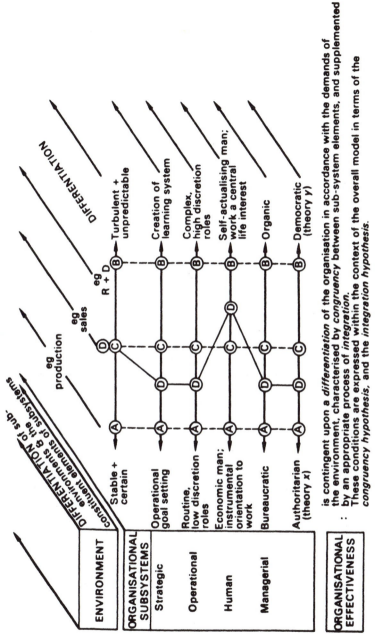

Figure 5.5 A contingency model for organisational analysis

ships are incongruent. It is hypothesised, for example, that an organisation or part of an organisation dealing with a highly stable and certain environment can operate effectively when:

(a) the strategic subsystem is geared to operational goal setting;
(b) the operational subsystem employs a technology which leads to high specialisation and division of labour in accordance, for example, with the principles of scientific management;
(c) employees are content with economic rewards and have low expectations with regard to work;
(d) the organisation is structured in a bureaucratic fashion;
(e) the organisation is managed in a highly authoritarian and directive way.

Conversely, it is hypothesised that when an organisation or an element of an organisation is dealing with a turbulent and unpredictable environment, the appropriate element of the organisation needs:

(a) strategic management which fosters the ability of the organisational unit to learn and respond to the environment by
(b) adopting an operational system characterised by complex, high-discretion roles, which are
(c) filled by 'organisation men' who see work as their central life interest and attempt to satisfy higher-level psychological needs through their work experience, and
(d) who are managed within the context of an organic form of organisation structure by
(e) managers who adopt an open and democratic style of management, and gear their efforts to creating a situation in which it is possible for the individuals being managed to satisfy their own personal goals through the achievement of organisational objectives.

These two hypothesised relationships characterise extreme positions with regard to modes of organisation and management, and are illustrated in Figure 5.5 by the broken lines marked A and B respectively. The contingency model allows for intermediate positions with regard to the nature of organisational environments and subsystems. Each dimension should be regarded as a contiuum rather than a dichotomy, varying in accordance with the characteristics discussed under point 11 above.

The congruency hypothesis applies to all these intermediate positions, maintaining that congruency with the demands of the environment is an essential characteristic of subsystem elements if an organisation is to succeed in its primary tasks. An intermediate stage of congruency is illustrated by the broken line marked C. The continuous line marked D illustrates a position characterised by incongruency; it is hypothesised that such an organisation would be less effective than that illustrated by line C, given that they operate under similar environmental conditions.

13. The adaption of subsystem elements to environmental demands leads to a differentiation within the organisation which calls for appropriate boundary management to achieve an adequate state of integration for the system as a whole. This integration is one of the ongoing functions of the managerial and strategic subsystems. As Lawrence and Lorsch (1967) have argued, integration is as important as differentiation in influencing an organisation's success in coping with the demands posed by its environment. Congruency between subsystem elements is thus a necessary condition for success but not a sufficient one. It needs to be supplemented by what may be called the *integration hypothesis*. This postulates that an organisation, once differentiated, must achieve an appropriate state of reintegration if it is to be fully effective.

    We have attempted to illustrate this requirement in Figure 5.5 by adding a third dimension to our model of the relationships between organisational environment and subsystems. This illustrates that various elements of an organisation may be differentiated in relation to the environment and all of the subsystems. We have chosen to demonstrate this by placing three departments in locations consistent with supposed environmental characteristics.[36] The congruency hypothesis requires that the nature of all subsystems be congruent with this environmental characteristic, as argued under point 12 above. The integration hypothesis calls for adequate boundary management to ensure appropriate links between these different elements of the organisation.

14. Bringing the congruency and integration hypotheses

together, therefore, the contingency model outlined above postulates that the success of an organisation in dealing with the demands made on it by its environment is contingent upon appropriate differentiation characterised by a congruency between subsystem elements *and* the achievement of an appropriate state of integration.

The contingency model outlined above provides a theoretical framework for analysing organisations from a managerial point of view, and represents a synthesis of the concepts and ideas implicit in a great deal of contemporary organisation theory. Much of the empirical research on organisations conducted during the 1960s and 1970s has been informed by various elements of the model, though it is very questionable whether it has been true to the basic ontological and epistemological foundations upon which the model is based. We have in mind here the distinction between 'process' and 'structure' (Cooper, 1976) which we have already referred to on a number of occasions in this and the previous chapter. The contingency model, based as it is upon an open systems approach, is essentially processual in nature. The subsystems are viewed in terms of functional imperatives which interact with the environment in a manner geared to achieve the survival of the system as a whole through appropriate adaption to environmental circumstances. This system *process* expresses itself in a partial and transient manner through various 'structural' characteristics such as 'technology' and the degree of 'bureaucratisation'. It is these temporary structural manifestations of a more fundamental and ongoing process which organisational researchers tend to seize upon for the purpose of empirical research. The organisation is often equated with these structural characteristics, while the processual aspects of system are ignored. Much of the research which has been conducted under the guiding notion of the contingency approach has been of this nature and as such stands as an abstracted form of empiricism.[37] The incongruence between theory and method which this reflects is a fundamental problem facing social systems theorists in general. The processual nature of 'system' does not lend itself to meaningful study through the use of quantitative snapshots of objectified social structures. Social systems theorists who wish to operationalise contingency theory thus face very real problems, in that a new methodology is needed which is consistent with the ontology and epistemology of a true open systems approach.

Our final remarks on contingency theory here will focus upon some of the conceptual implications of the model which we have presented. The first of these emerges from the role of the strategic control subsystem within the context of the model as a whole. As we have argued, one of the functions of this subsystem is to interpret what is happening in the environment and to guide and adapt the organisation in an appropriate manner. It follows that the relationship between elements of subsystems and their environment is contingent upon the decisions emerging from the strategic control subsystem and also, at a lower level within the organisation, those emerging from the managerial subsystem. Thus, a search for determinate relationships between contextual factors and organisational characteristics, and between the elements of different subsystems, is ill-founded. The pattern of relationships is the product of human decision, and is influenced by choice.[38]

The congruency hypothesis spells out many implications for theories of organisational change and development. It suggests, for example, that attempts to change the operational subsystem through some programme of job redesign has implications for all the other subsystems within the organisation. Any analytical framework for studying and prescribing organisational change must therefore pay due adherence to the elements of the model as a whole. We shall give further consideration to this point in the next section on the quality of working life movement.

A third point of some importance arises from the fact that the role of 'choice' draws attention to the issue of power as an organisational variable. Within the context of social systems theory the issue of power within organisations is virtually ignored. An organismic systems model stresses the functional unity of system parts, and views the organisation as being geared to the achievement of end states shared by the system as a whole. Functional imperatives and unity of purpose tend to dominate the analysis. Although the contingency model implicitly identifies power as a variable, it does not address it in any specific fashion. To do so in a meaningful sense involves a shift in perspective away from the bounds of social systems theory. We will discuss such perspectives later in this chapter, and in our discussion of the radical structuralist paradigm.

The quality of working life movement

We conclude our analysis of social system theory with a short discussion of the quality of working life movement which has come into prominence during the 1970s. In essence this movement seeks to apply the insights of open systems theory, particularly through the notions of open socio-technical systems theory and the theory of job design, to the problems which its followers see as characterising post-industrial societies. It is based upon a philosophy of piecemeal social engineering which seeks to solve the problems posed by the transition from the industrial to the post-industrial society.

The key perspectives are well illustrated in the recent volumes of readings edited by Davis and Cherns (1975). The authors argue that there is a growing crisis which calls into question the viability of present relationships between work, economic production, man and society, and the ability of organisations to adapt to the rapid pace of environmental change. The solution to many of these problems is seen as the creation of an improvement in the quality of working life. As they put it, 'confronting us is the need to accept, as a national goal, both public and private responsibility for the quality of working life in all of productive society, particularly in facing the transition into the post-industrial era, if we are to develop useful social policy and devise workable responses to problems' (Davis and Cherns, 1975, p. 5). They argue that the key to the problem revolves around the 'humanization of work', which 'far from imposing economic costs, yields societal, personal and economic gains' (1975, p. 6). They argue that there is a need to build upon the body of knowledge, research and techniques which is currently available and to formulate

> *a coherent body of theory and practice on how to create the conditions for a humane working life in its relevant social environments.* Researchers and practitioners must learn how to define the situation, how to study ongoing social systems, how to intervene in such situations with enhanced probability of success, how to identify and measure a successful outcome, how to develop conceptual bases within institutions which will support the diffusion of outcomes, and how to assure that continued adaptation will take place.' (1976, p. 8)

Viewed within the context of the contingency model presented in the previous section, therefore, the quality of working life movement urges a programme of organisational change based upon the assumption that a more humane working situation is a functional imperative within the context of the system as a whole. The argument is that social change within the wider environment is such that people are beginning to demand more satisfying work, and that organisations need to make operational and managerial subsystems congruent with these demands. This is a familiar theme, which has long been the concern of neo-human relations theorists and, more generally, those concerned with the theory of organisational development (for example, Bennis, 1966): the quality of working life movement represents a logical development of these traditions. Its propositions run counter to those of contingency theory, which stresses that in stable environments rigid, dehumanising work structures may be appropriate for achieving organisational effectiveness. The quality of working life theorists tend to stand against such a proposition, arguing that the nature of the post-industrial environment ('context' as opposed to 'task environment') is such that in the long run open, flexible organisational design and management will prove the more effective. The argument is pitched not merely at the organisational level: the organisation is seen as a subsystem of the wider society, and the view propounded is essentially that it is a functional imperative that the quality of working life be improved to sustain society as a whole. The notions of 'social responsibility' and 'individual responsibility' are often summoned to bridge the gap between organisational or personal interests on the one hand and societal interests on the other. Social responsibility thus becomes a functional imperative as far as the maintenance of the social system as a whole is concerned.

The quality of working life movement is often seen and presented as a radical action-orientated response to the current problems facing modern Western industrial societies. However, their stance is essentially a regulative one, concerned to make piecemeal adjustments designed to improve the viability of the technological society characteristic of the present era. Their fundamental commitment to existing social forms is evident when one compares their approach, for example, with the theories characteristic of the radical humanist paradigm discussed in Chapters 8 and 9. Although committed to humanitarian concern for the development of human growth and potential through the satisfaction of 'higher-level' psychological needs, their 'selling pitch' is invariably geared to the contribution which this will make to the stability and survival of the system as a whole. This is clear, for example, from the way in which Davis and Cherns emphasise the economic benefits to be derived from improving the quality of working life.

The 'hardware' or conceptual apparatus of the quality of working life movement is firmly based upon open socio-technical systems theory. The socio-technical approach to job redesign is given prominence, though the movement turns away from an exclusively psychological perspective to embrace wider sociological concerns. In particular, there are strong links with the industrial democracy movement, which at times approaches a pluralist view of organisations.

This review of the quality of working life movement completes our analysis of social system theory and objectivism. We shall return to an evaluation of the perspective as a whole at the end of this chapter. For the moment we will close with the somewhat oversimplified but at heart realistic observation that whereas contingency theory stands as the contemporary equivalent of classical management theory, the quality of working life movement stands as the contemporary equivalent of the industrial psychology and human relations movements. Whilst there has been a shift in perspective away from objectivism and towards a social systems approach, the dominant concern is still to provide an understanding of organisations, and the behaviour of individuals within them, from an essentially managerial point of view.

Theories of Bureaucratic Dysfunctions

In this section we wish to devote some attention to the work on organisations conducted by Robert Merton and three of his most prominent students, Selznick, Gouldner and Blau. A case could be made for treating this work as just one link within the overall chain of development of social system theory, as presented in Figure 5.2; indeed, we have already discussed the structural functionalist orientation which characterises some of Selznick's work in that context. However, separate treatment seems warranted on at least two grounds. First, much of the work of Merton and his colleagues is addressed to the theory of bureaucracy as developed by Max Weber. It does not specifically seek to develop a functionalist theory or organisations; it seeks to provide a critique of an important element of Weber's work. A second and related point is that the work of these theorists is primarily addressed to the study and explanation of 'dysfunctions'. Subject to a qualification with regard to some of Selznick's work, it reflects an explicit break with the use of an organismic analogy stressing the functional unity and functional interdependence of system parts. Merton and his colleagues have been less concerned with explaining the unity and interdependence of social systems than with explaining disequilibrium and change, in line with Merton's general sociological concern to explain how socially deviant behaviour can be seen as a product of social structure. As we have argued in Chapter 4, Merton's work characterises the middle ground of the functionalist paradigm and his work on the study of organisations is no exception. His influential study of the 'bureaucratic personality' provides an illustration of his approach to the analysis of 'deviant' or 'non-conforming' behaviour in action, and it lays the basis for further studies of the 'unanticipated consequences' and 'dysfunctions of bureaucracy' which stand at the centre of the analyses offered by Selznick, Gouldner and Blau. In the rest of this section we will review the essential features of these studies.[39]

Merton's article on 'Bureaucratic Structure and Personality' (1968) focuses upon the internal stresses and strains which he sees as characterising bureaucratic activities. Observing that the formal Weberian theory of bureaucracy places emphasis upon the positive attainments and functions of bureaucratic organisation, Merton seeks to approach the subject from the opposite point of view. As he puts it, 'Weber is almost exclusively concerned with what the bureaucratic structure attains: precision, reliability, efficiency. This same structure may be examined from another perspective... What are the limitations of the organisations designed to attain these goals?' (Merton, 1968, p. 252). Merton argues that bureaucratic operations, with their emphasis upon method, prudence, discipline and conformity, may have such an impact upon the bureaucrat that the adherence to rules and regulations, originally conceived as means to wider purposes, become ends in themselves. There thus occurs a 'displacement of goals' – 'an instrumental value becomes a terminal value' (1968, p. 253). This pattern of behaviour of the bureaucrat provides an example of what Merton classifies in his typology of adaption as 'ritualism'. It is an example of a ritualistic situation where culturally defined aspirations (in this case organisational goals) are abandoned, and behaviour is governed by an almost compulsive adherence to institutional norms (in this case bureaucratic rules and regulations). Merton goes on to argue that the problems which the rigidities create (for example, in dealing with the bureaucracy's clients) generate further responses within the organisation which reinforce the importance of conformity to rules and regulations. The situation thus becomes cumulatively worse, as bureaucrats proceed to defend their actions against outside pressures. Bureaucratic behaviour and operation becomes increasingly ritualistic in nature, characterised by the 'red tape' image so familiar to the public eye. Merton stresses, in line with his general sociological concern to explain the structural sources of deviancy, that the 'trained incapacity' of the bureaucrat is a product of the bureaucratic structure within which he works. His model of bureaucratic functioning is one which stresses the dysfunctions which emerge from the overall attempt to achieve *structural* control over the operations of the organisation.

Philip Selznick's famous empirical study of organisation, *TVA and the Grass Roots* (1949), is informed by the Mertonian concern for the study of unanticipated consequences and dysfunctions and by Robert Michels's ideas on the 'iron law of oligarchy'. It is also informed by Selznick's concern to construct a structural functionalist theory of organisations.

The Tennessee Valley Authority (TVA) was, at the time of Selznick's study, riding upon the crest of a wave. It was regarded as a model of democratic organisation and a symbol of the aspirations characteristic of the New Deal policy in the USA. Selznick's study in essence shows that behind the democratic façade lay a bureaucratic oligarchy. The main thrust of the study is the notion that 'all formal organisations are moulded by forces which are tangential to their rationally ordered structures and stated goals' (Selznick, 1966, p. 251). As we have discussed earlier in this chapter, Selznick believed that the formal aspects of organisation never succeed in conquering the non-rational human aspects of behaviour. His study of TVA demonstrates this, through a detailed analysis of administrative processes both within the organisation and in its relations with its environment. More specifically, he shows how the delegation of authority within the organisation leads to specialisation within limited spheres of activity and the orientation of groups of individuals to various sub-goals associated with these specialised interests. The division of labour within the bureaucratic structure in terms of expertise is thus seen as leading to a focus upon operational goals which may be in conflict with each other and detrimental to the overall purposes of the organisation as a whole. 'Commitment' is seen as a basic mechanism in the generation of unanticipated consequences. The struggle for control which results from these various commitments and conflicts of interest is seen as reinforcing the division of the organisation and commitment to sub-unit ideologies and goals. As in the case of the Merton model, therefore, the dysfunctional consequences are cumulative and self-reinforcing. They thus become increasingly embedded within the nature of the organisation as a whole, potentially diverting it further and further away from its formal objectives.

Thus far the analyses of Merton and Selznick show a high degree of similarity. Whilst Merton's study focused upon the dysfunctional influence of rules as a form of bureaucratic control, Selznick focused upon the dysfunctional consequences of delegation and specialisation. However, from this point on their studies diverge since, as we have noted, Selznick was also concerned to interpret organisation from a more conventional structural functionalist perspective. He thus resorts to the use of an organismic model which stresses the relevance of 'needs' and the process of adaption to the external environment in the interests of survival. The problem becomes that of establishing how the organisation limits the cumulative and potentially destructive influence of the dysfunctions. Selznick identifies two principal mechanisms. The first relies upon the use of 'ideology' to achieve conformity and loyalty in the organisation. The second relates to the process of 'co-optation', through which various sectional interests within the organisation and its environment are brought into a power-sharing situation. In these ways formal organisations such as TVA are seen as being able to stem their dysfunctions, adapt and survive. Selznick thus arrives at a structural functionalist view of organisations which also has many similarities with the pluralist theories discussed later in this chapter.

Alvin Gouldner's study of a gypsum factory reported in *Patterns of Industrial Bureaucracy* (1954a) and *Wildcat Strike* (1954b) provides a third example of the Mertonian approach to the study of bureaucratic dysfunctions. Gouldner addresses his work to certain 'obscurities' and 'tensions in Weber's theory' (Gouldner, 1954a, pp. 19–20), particularly with regard to the notion that the effectiveness of bureaucratic functioning depends upon organisational members accepting the legitimacy of the rules or 'legal norms', whether these are established by agreement or imposition. Gouldner points out that the manner in which rules are initiated (for example, by agreement *as opposed to* imposition) may have a fundamental influence upon the dynamics and effectiveness of bureaucratic operations. His empirical analysis of managerial succession within the gypsum factory, and the impact which this has upon bureaucratic rules and employee activities, leads him to conclude that the manner in which rules are initiated is of considerable importance. On the basis of his analysis he identifies three types of bureaucracy, 'mock', 'representative' and 'punitive', each of which is characterised by different patterns of rule setting and enforcement, different modes of social organisation and different levels of tension and conflict.

Gouldner's study thus leads to important modifications of the notion of bureaucracy as conceived by Weber. His mode of analysis focuses upon the way in which the human element of organisation modifies the formal or technical aspect. His study of the way in which bureaucracy develops through the creation and use of impersonal rules emphasises the unanticipated consequences which result because of their effect upon interpersonal relations within the organisation. Rules are shown as being used by managers and workers for fundamentally different ends and in ways which are dysfunctional for the formal aims of the organisation. In the process of his analysis Gouldner illustrates quite clearly that organisations as such only have goals or ends in an abstract or 'metaphorical' sense, and that the reality of organisational life is one dominated by individuals and groups striving towards different ends. As in the case of Selznick, therefore, insofar as the focus on dysfunctions takes the analysis of organisation away from the social system postulate of functional unity, a pluralist view of organisation emerges, though it is not developed to its full extent. Whose goals is the organisation trying to achieve? For whom are the rules useful as a rational device? Questions such as these are central to pluralist views and emerge quite clearly from Gouldner's analysis.

A fourth study relating to the dysfunctional aspects of bureaucratic organisation is presented in Peter Blau's *The Dynamics of Bureaucracy* (1955). In this work Blau sets out to apply the principles contained in Merton's 'paradigm for functional analysis' to the daily operations and interpersonal relations of government officials in two bureaucratic agencies. His analysis focuses upon the factors which generate disequilibrium and change within the organisation, and confirms many of the bureaucratic dysfunctions identified by Merton and his colleagues, such as overconformity and goal displacement. It demonstrates how bureaucracies, far from being the static structures supposedly envisaged in Weber's ideal type, are the scenes of an ongoing process of interpersonal relationships which generate new elements of organisation. The study also demonstrates the part played by the latent as opposed to the manifest functions of bureaucratic procedure. Blau's analysis of the way in which employee performance is evaluated through the use of statistical records, for example, demonstrates that in addition to serving as a performance control, the system also has the latent function of maintaining cordial relations between supervisors and subordinates. The study emphasises the importance of tracing these unanticipated consequences as a basis for understanding the true significance of any particular organisational characteristic. It clearly demonstrates the futility of confining attention solely to the rational or manifest functions of organisation. In Blau's analysis such factors are seen as lying at the heart of explanations of organisational change. Bureaucratic structure, like other aspects of social structure, is seen as generating forces which lead to its own transformation.

This work of Merton, Selznick, Gouldner and Blau thus presents a coherent and systematically developed critique of the notion of bureaucracy they saw as reflected in Weber's ideal type.[40] Coming as it did in the wake of the Hawthorne studies and the development of the human relations movement, it is understandable that so much attention should be devoted to the human or informal aspects of organisation. However, in contrast to the perspective reflected in the human relations movement and, indeed, social system theory in general, the work of Merton and his colleagues was specifically addressed to providing explanations of change in social systems. They sought to inject a dynamic element into the functionalist perspective. As we argued in Chapter 4, the notion of 'dysfunction' and its corollary, 'functional autonomy', contained the potential for a radically different theory of organisation. However, with the exception of Gouldner's steps in this direction in his article 'Reciprocity and Autonomy in Functional Theory' (1959), this path was not followed. As we shall argue in a later chapter, it was left to theorists approaching organisations from a fundamentally different standpoint to develop the implications of this line of enquiry.[41] Merton and his colleagues were largely content to dwell upon the implications which their modified version of functionalism suggested.

The Action Frame of Reference

As will be clear from our discussion in Chapter 4, social action theory or the action frame of reference is a perspective characteristic of the most subjectivist boundary of the functionalist paradigm. We have demonstrated how, along with behavioural symbolic interactionism, it has developed largely as a result of the fusion between positivist and idealist approaches to social science. Whereas the action frame of reference was first articulated by Max Weber, symbolic interactionism is largely the product of the theoretical perspectives of Simmel and Mead.

Strictly speaking, it would be appropriate to give consideration to both these schools of thought in any detailed analysis of the theory of organisations, since, as we have argued, whilst reflecting a similar perspective in terms of the subjective—objective dimension of our analytical scheme, their focus of attention is often somewhat different. However, we shall not do so here because, for one reason or another, symbolic interactionism has, in a pure sense, had relatively little impact upon the theory of organisations. Whilst there have been many studies of interaction at work, they have rarely been true to the assumptions characteristic of the subjectivist region of the paradigm. More often than not such studies have been conducted within the context of a systems approach to organisations (for example, Homans, 1950; Lupton, 1963) or have been cast as studies of 'deviant behaviour' or 'informal organisation' (for example, Roy, 1960). Yet others have ended up as an abstracted form of empiricism.

Similarly, the action frame of reference has rarely been conceptualised or implemented in the pure form envisaged by Weber. Its adherents have often taken as much of a lead from writers such as Schutz, Blumer, Mead or even Merton as they have from Weber.[42] The lack of appreciation of the basic ontological,epistemological and methodological assumptions which differentiate the perspectives of these key writers has often led to hybrid schemes of analysis which one can say are characteristic of the subjectivist boundary of the functionalist paradigm but no more. For this reason we are going to discuss them all under the heading of the action frame of reference which, at least in Britain, has been generally used as a label for describing a major proportion of the work to be considered here. Whilst the work of Goffman and Turner can be regarded as typical of symbolic interactionism, the work of Goldthorpe and Silverman is more explicitly aligned with the action frame of reference. However, this division, for the reasons discussed above, is by no means a rigid one, there being many points of overlap, particularly between the perspectives of Goffman, Turner and Silverman.

Erving Goffman has established himself as the foremost exponent of the 'dramaturgical' approach to symbolic interactionism. A product of the Chicago School of sociology, the principal orientation of his work has been to demonstrate the way in which individuals shape and influence their social reality. One of his earliest and most famous works, *The Presentation of Self in Everyday Life* (1959), offers a view of individuals in ordinary work situations as engaged in a 'theatrical performance', in a process of 'impression management', as putting on a show through which they attempt to guide and control the impressions which people form of them. The purpose of Goffman's analysis is to identify the features which characterise the patterns of everyday life. In line with the perspective of Simmel, he is concerned to penetrate to the underlying 'form' of human affairs. As he observes in the introduction to another of his books, he is interested in building up a picture of human interaction from basic elements such as glances, gestures, positioning and verbal statements, with a view to uncovering the normative order of social affairs (Goffman, 1967). His analyses focus upon the rituals and routines which characterise human interaction.

However, Goffman does not restrict himself merely to the study of the rules. He is also concerned to show how people relate to them, either conforming or adapting them to their purposes. Roles and institutional patterns are not seen as determining individual behaviour in any sense; rather, they provide a framework within which the *process* of social life is acted out. Ontologically, in the tradition of behavioural symbolic interactionism, society is seen as being prior to self, but the individual is accorded a creative role in the production of self, or at least the impression of self created as a result of performance management. In these respects Goffman's analysis of interaction is much more subjectivist in orientation than that of many other interactionists operating within the functionalist paradigm. Compare his work, for example, with the studies of behaviour in organisations offered by those theorists who cast their analysis within a more managerially orientated frame of reference and emphasise the systemic nature of life in an organisational context (for example, Lupton, 1963; Roy, 1960).

Goffman's approach to the analysis of human interaction clearly has implications for the study of behaviour in organisations in a general sense. In addition, Goffman himself has made a number of studies of institutional behaviour, particularly within the context of mental institutions. On the basis of these studies he has offered an analysis of the nature of 'total institutions', a term which is used to characterise organisations such as prisons, mental hospitals, concentration camps, ships, monastries, etc., in which people spend whole periods of their lives, sleeping, playing and working within institutional boundaries. Goffman depicts such institutions as being characterised by the fact that all aspects of life are conducted in the same place and under the same single authority; that each member is in the company of a large group of others who are treated alike and required to do the same things together; that the phases of the days' activities are tightly scheduled, with the patterns imposed from above; that the various enforced activities are brought together to form a single rational plan supposedly designed to fulfil the official aims of the institution (Goffman, 1961).

For Goffman one of the most important aspects of such institutions is that, whilst the authorities attempt to define the situation for the inmates – through rules, regulations, indoctrination, discipline, etc. – the individuals who live within them 'make out' by adjusting in various ways. They 'develop a life of their own that becomes meaningful, reasonable and normal once you get close to it' (Goffman, 1961, p. 7). Such adjustments take the form of 'conformity' (behaving as a 'normal' member) or it may be achieved through unauthorised means. Goffman's work focuses upon these adjustment processes, revealing what he calls the 'underlife' of the organisation – the ways in which inmates 'make out' in an attempt to defend themselves against the onslaught of the system upon their impressions of self.

As Eldridge and Crombie (1974), have noted, in addition to illuminating the concept of self, Goffman's study of 'total institutions' also informs us about the processes of social control within them and teaches us generally about the life and mechanisms which operate in all formal organisations. Those who are familiar with Goffman's work can approach the interactionist-type studies reflected in the work of more management-orientated theorists, such as those referred to earlier, with a fresh and critical eye. The difference in approach reflects their relative positions with regard to the subjective—objective dimension of our analytical scheme.

Another example of interactionist research, of relevance to the study of organisations and characteristic of the subjectivist region of the functionalist paradigm, is presented by Barry Turner in his monograph *Exploring the Industrial Subculture* (1971). Turner was a member of Joan Woodward's research team investigating management control within organisations, a piece of work characteristic of social system theory in the more objectivist region of the paradigm (Woodward, 1972). Turner informs us that his own particular book was written as a result of his dissatisfaction with the prevailing forms of organisational analysis in general and the management control project in particular. He was concerned about the high levels of abstraction which characterised much of this work and its remoteness from what seemed to him to be 'real' industrial life. He was more interested in developing a sociology of organisations which concerned itself 'with discovering the way in which people in industry define their life-positions, with learning the sets of symbolisms which they adopt in the definitions, and with examining the collective or organisational consequences of these views which they hold of themselves' (Turner, 1971, p. vii). In the course of his research for the management control project, he also kept notes on his own informal research observations of life in the organisation with which he was concerned. It is this informal material which provides the basis for his analysis of the industrial subculture.

Having collected his data, Turner searched the literature for relevant concepts and theories which would make sense of his field of observations, and he informs us in the course of his book that the ideas of Schutz, Berger and Luckmann, and Weber had particular relevance. From Schutz he seems to take the view that one of the tasks of sociologists should be to analyse the 'taken for granted' assumptions of everyday life. Turner sets out to do this with regard to what he calls the 'industrial subculture' – a feature of organisational life worthy of understanding in its own right but which most researchers take for granted or dismiss in summary terms.

Although Turner takes Schutz as his point of reference, his analysis is by no means representative of the phenomenological sociology to be discussed in our chapter on the interpretive paradigm. Rather, it is much more orientated towards an analysis of 'meaning', fused with the concerns of what we have described as 'behavioural symbolic interactionism'. The general orientation of Turner's study is clearly indicated in his opening paragraph, in which he defines his view of the notion of 'subculture' and the way in which it is maintained. As he puts it,

> A subculture is a distinctive set of meanings shared by a group of people whose forms of behaviour differ to some extent from those of wider society. The distinctive nature of the set of meanings is maintained by ensuring that newcomers to the group undergo a process of learning or socialisation. The process links the individual to the values of the group, and generates common motives, common reaction patterns and common perceptual habits. Distinctiveness is also maintained by the use of sanctions which are operated against those who do not behave in appropriate ways. (Turner, 1971, p. 1)

Turner is thus concerned to study the way in which subcultures evolve and are sustained. His focus is upon 'meaning' and the way in which it becomes shared through 'communicative exchanges'. In his analysis of meaning Turner again makes reference to the work of Schutz, particularly in relation to the notion of 'reflexivity', though, in point of fact, his overall perspective on this is much more closely related to the symbolic interaction model outlined by Rose discussed in Chapter 4. There is undoubted confusion with regard to ontology in this aspect of Turner's work. In contrast to the Schutzian position, Turner's ontology is much more realist in nature. However, this aside, his primary concern is to follow Schutz in the study of the nature of meaning patterns and the mechanisms by which they are conveyed. In this he pays considerable attention to the role of language and the ritualistic role of objects.

Turner's thorough and clearly presented analysis of basic concepts and their relationship to his empirical evidence results in a valuable study of the informal aspects of organisational life. His perspective is a very refreshing one. In contrast to most interactionist studies of informal organisation, which are often implicitly informed by a managerial perspective which regards 'informal' as 'deviant', Turner approaches the industrial subculture on its own terms. He is concerned to reveal it for what it is, without bringing in too many assumptions and preconceptions in advance of detailed analysis. Although aspiring to a phenomenological perspective, for reasons which have been argued above, it should be regarded as a piece of theory and research on organisational life typical of the subjectivist region of the functionalist paradigm.

A third example of theory and research typical of this region of the paradigm is found in the work of those members of the Chicago School who have concerned themselves with the sociology of occupations. Among these Everett Hughes is particularly prominent for the work which he himself has conducted (for example, Hughes, 1958) and for his influence upon other scholars who have chosen to follow his lead. Their work is characterised by an attempt to penetrate to the level of subjective meaning in an exploration of occupational roles. In contrast to other role theorists, who often tend to be concerned with the structural aspects of role and tangible role behaviour, the Chicago theorists have interested themselves in the study of what work means for the individual, and the way in which this is related to attitudes and relationships within the work place. These theorists tend to start with the individual and build out from there in the construction of his organisational world. Thus we are given an inside view of what it is like to be 'in the basement' as an apartment janitor or to be a cab-driver relating to his 'fares' (Gold, 1964; Davis, 1967). Taken together, such studies build up a picture of work experience in contemporary society, as viewed by the workers themselves rather than by a 'detached' observer.[43] The approach draws heavily upon ethnographic accounts and participant observation techniques, and tends to focus upon process as opposed to static structure as a means of characterising the principal features of the world of work and everyday life.

The work of the occupational sociologists moves very close to the use of an action frame of reference, in that they are primarily concerned with the general orientation of individuals to their roles and with the meaning of work at a subjective level. A similar perspective characterises the work of Goldthorpe and his colleagues (1968), in their study of industrial workers' orientations to work, though little explicit interest is shown in the analysis of subjective meaning as such, particularly in its processual and emergent aspects.[44] Their study of 'affluent' manual workers in the context of their industrial employment attempts to describe and explain 'orientations to work'. This perspective has much in common with Weber's attempt to construct a typology of social action based on four kinds of orientations – traditional, emotional, value-rational and purposively rational. Goldthorpe and his colleagues do not employ Weber's typology as such or, for that matter, make much reference to his work, though there are clear and obvious links. They argue that among the workers studied a particular orientation to work is predominant – one of a markedly instrumental kind. As Eldridge (1971) has noted, the analysis of Goldthorpe et al is closely linked to the use of reference group analysis, in that one of the primary concerns of the research is to examine the relationship between orientations to work and the worker's place in the class structure. This research on orientation to work is cast within the context of a wider study concerned to test the widely acknowledged thesis of working-class *embourgeoisement*: that is, as manual workers and their families become more affluent, they become progressively assimilated into the middle class. Thus in this study the action frame of reference is given a background role; it is a tool to be used in relation to but a small part of the research project as a whole. It does, however, present one of the few well-known British attempts to operationalise the action frame of reference, albeit in this limited sense.

Most prominent among the advocates of the action frame of reference as a basis for organisational analysis has been the name of David Silverman. Indeed, it was he who, for the most part, introduced the term to organisation theorists, arguing in his book *The Theory of Organisations* (1970) that it provides an alternative to systems theory. Silverman suggests that the systems approach, as applied to organisations, has 'severe logical difficulties', particularly in its assumption that organisations as systems have 'needs' or are 'self-regulating'.[45] He points out that to attribute such characteristics to organisations, except as a heuristic device, involves the problem of 'reification', a process whereby social constructs are accorded the power of thought and action. He argues that explanations of social change at a systems level usually involves these problems of reification, since attention is drawn to the purposive actions of the *system*, which is seen as recognising threats to its existence and as adapting accordingly. The systems view of organisations is thus seen as being pitched at a level of analysis which does not take into account, or provide explanations in terms of, the actions of the individual human beings who are its constituent members. In opposition to this systems view Silverman argues that social scientists should build their theories upon foundations which view social reality as being socially constructed, socially sustained and socially changed. In other words, Silverman wishes to place man as a social actor at the centre of the stage, insofar as the analysis of social phenomena such as organisations are concerned. In recognition of the fact that social life is an ongoing process, sustained and 'accomplished' by social actors, Silverman advocates the action frame of reference as providing an appropriate basis for analysis.

Silverman's view of the action frame of reference, which is based upon the work of a number of writers, is summarised in terms of the following seven propositions:

1. The social sciences and the natural sciences deal with entirely different orders of subject-matter. While the canons of rigour and scepticism apply to both, one should not expect their perspective to be the same.
2. Sociology is concerned with understanding action rather than with observing behaviour. Action arises out of meanings which define social reality.
3. Meanings are given to men by their society. Shared orientations become institutionalised and are experienced by later generations as social facts.
4. While society defines man, man in turn defines society. Particular constellations of meaning are only sustained by continual reaffirmation in everyday actions.
5. Through their interaction men also modify, change and transform social meanings.

6.   It follows that explanations of human actions must take account of the meanings which those concerned assign to their acts; the manner in which the everyday world is socially constructed yet perceived as real and routine becomes a crucial concern of sociological analysis.
7.   Positivistic explanations, which assert that action is determined by external and constraining social or non-social forces, are inadmissible. (Silverman, 1970, pp. 126–7)

In developing these propositions Silverman draws very heavily upon ideas characteristic of the work of Dilthey, Weber and Schutz.[46] His distinction between the subject matter which characterises the natural and social sciences (Proposition 1), for example, follows Dilthey's distinction between *Naturwissenschaften* (natural sciences) and *Geisteswissenschaften* (cultural sciences). As we argue in Chapter 6 on the interpretive paradigm, this distinction is central to an understanding of the German idealist tradition of social thought. The cultural sciences were seen as being distinguished by their essentially 'spiritual' character, and it was held that they could not be understood through the approaches and methods of the natural sciences. The idealists rejected positivist epistemology and the nomothetic methods employed by the natural scientists as simply inappropriate to the realm of social and cultural affairs. They held that man was 'free' and did not behave and act in accordance with positivist-type laws. As a means of bridging this gap between idealist and positivist perspectives, theorists such as Dilthey and Weber concerned themselves with problems of 'understanding' in the realm of human affairs. The notion of *verstehen* or 'interpretive understanding' which they developed was seen as providing a method appropriate to the social sciences. As developed by Weber, the notion of *verstehen* was used as a methodological tool which drew attention to the importance of understanding the subjective meaning which lay behind social action. For Weber explanations of social phenomena had to be 'adequate on the level of meaning'.

It is precisely this point which Silverman seeks to emphasise in a number of the propositions of his action schema. Proposition 2, for example, emphasises that 'sociology is concerned with understanding action rather than with observing behaviour', and that 'action arises out of meanings which define social reality'. This is firmly in line with the Weberian position. Social action is seen as deriving from the meaning which is attributed to the social world by individual actors. It is imperative, therefore, that the sociologist understand these subjective meanings if he is to understand the full significance of individual acts. Thus to focus upon the behaviour of individuals in the tradition of positivist social science is to miss the point, since patterns of behaviour may mean different things to different people. The action of men is meaningful to them. They construct their social world by attributing meaning to it. Action arises from meanings, so it is necessary to understand social activities at the level of subjective meaning. This point is again emphasised by Silverman in Proposition 6, which states that 'explanations of human actions must take account of the meanings which those concerned assign to their acts; the manner in which the everyday world is socially constructed yet perceived as real and routine becomes a crucial concern of sociological analysis'.

In Proposition 3 Silverman asserts that 'meanings are given to men by their society. Shared orientations become institutionalised and are experienced by later generations as social facts'. Here we are concerned with the issue of ontology, and we find Silverman adopting a 'realist' position in which society is seen as being ontologically prior to man. In developing his position on this point Silverman makes specific reference to Durkheim and the view that men are constrained by social facts which determine their actions and their consciousness. Following Durkheim, Silverman suggests that meanings reside in social institutions and that individuals play roles that are given to them as a result of their location upon the social map. As he puts it, 'by participating in society, they are given expectations about the appropriate acts of themselves and of others when in various status positions. They are able to apprehend the meanings associated with the actions of other people and to form a view of self based on the responses of others' (1970, p. 131). In order to explain why people should meet the expectations of others Silverman invokes explanations presented by Talcott Parsons in *The Social System*, which emphasise the tendency to order in social affairs — 'common values must predominate if the system is to survive' (1970, p. 131). Ontologically, therefore, Silverman's position appears to be as 'realist' as that of any other theorist within the functionalist paradigm. He argues, for example, that 'the social world is given to us by the past history and structure of our society', and that 'social reality is "predefined" in the very language in which we are socialised. Language provides us with categories which define as well as distinguish our experiences' (1970, p. 132). We are thus left in no doubt that individual actors occupy a 'realist' social world which is external to the individual and has a reality which is independent of any individual's social construction of it.

However, in Proposition 4 Silverman immediately proceeds to qualify this 'realism' by asserting that 'while society defines man, man in turn defines society'. He emphasises that 'particular constellations of meaning are only sustained by continual reaffirmation in everyday actions'. In developing this proposition Silverman emphasises that whilst individual actors may operate in accordance with the 'common-sense' belief that the social world exists outside themselves, in point of fact this common-sense notion only holds insofar as it is sustained and reinforced through the everyday actions of the actors directly involved in any given social situation. It thus has a precarious existence. 'The existence of society depends upon it being continuously confirmed in the actions of its members' (1970, p. 134). In support of this view he argues, following Berger and Pullberg (1966), that social structure 'has no reality except a human one. It is not characterisable as being a thing able to stand on its own . . . [and] exists only insofar and as long as human beings realise it as part of their world'. He goes on to argue that to attribute to society an existence separate from and above its members is to reify it. Again following Berger and Pullberg, Silverman suggests that 'social roles and institutions exist only as an expression of the meanings which men attach to their world − they have no "ontological status"' (1970, p. 134). In other words, Silverman is suggesting that reality is socially constructed. He is advocating an ontology which is essentially 'nominalist' in orientation.

Propositions 3 and 4 thus tend to qualify one another, in that the former suggests a 'realist' ontology, and the latter a 'nominalist' ontology. As we shall argue in Chapter 7, Silverman is unclear on this point in most of his work and he oscillates precariously from one position to another according to his purpose. His overall position seems to be that whilst recognising that there is an external world which is ontologically prior to man, its crucial significance as far as the study of social affairs is concerned lies in the way in which its 'meaning' resulted from the interpretations placed upon it by individual actors.

In emphasising the way in which individuals have the ability to interpret and attribute meaning to their social world, Silverman in effect directs attention to the voluntaristic nature of human activities. This receives specific attention in Proposition 5, which asserts that 'through their interaction men . . . modify, change and transform social meanings'. In elaborating this proposition he places emphasis upon the ways in which individuals can choose to interpret the roles which they play, and how they can disrupt prevailing views of reality by engaging in disruptive activities of one kind or another. In his analysis Silverman qualifies his position with regard to Parsons' view of the nature of social order referred to earlier, and recognises that because of the choices available to the individual, social integration may, in fact, be problematic.

In the elaboration of his action schema Silverman thus presents a view of the social world which emphasises the processual nature of human affairs. It is a world where human actors interpret the situation in which they find themselves and act in ways which are meaningful to them. Social reality is thus seen as being in a process of continual flux, as human beings interpret and redefine, through their actions, the world in which they live. It follows that special methods are required to study this social world. Thus Silverman, in line with his opening proposition on the distinction between the natural and social sciences, concludes by asserting that 'positivistic explanations, which assert that action is determined by external and constraining social or non-social forces, are inadmissible' (Proposition 7). Explanations of social affairs must be adequate, on the level of meaning, for the actors directly involved. The action frame of reference is offered as a perspective adequate for this end.

As will become apparent from our analysis in Chapter 6, Silverman's action approach has much more in common with the work of Weber than with that of Schutz. Although Silverman makes frequent reference to Schutzian concepts, his perspective is far removed from the 'existential phenomenology' which characterises Schutz's work. Silverman, in *The Theory of Organisations*, seems primarily concerned, like Weber, to develop a *method* of analysis appropriate to the nature of social phenomena, and he advocates the action frame of reference as a method of analysing social relations within organisations. It represents a perspective characteristic of the subjectivist boundary of the functionalist paradigm. While quite voluntarist in terms of its assumptions with regard to the way in which individuals define and interpret the situations in which they find themselves, it is based upon an ontology which is essentially realist in orientation. As advocated by Silverman, in terms of epistemology the perspective is set against the extreme form of positivism characteristic of the most objectivist region of the functionalist paradigm, but does not reject the positivist approach in its entirety. Silverman, for example, is in favour of a measure of 'generalisation' in the social sciences, but emphasises that the 'generalisations which the social sciences develop' are 'fundamentally different from the laws of the natural sciences' (1970, p. 128).

There has been a tendency in recent years for writers on organisations to equate the action frame of reference with schools of thought such as ethnomethodology and phenomenology. This represents a gross misstatement of the actual position. Whilst action theorists often make reference to the work of phenomenologists and ethnomethodologists, they do not follow the full implications of the latter's point of view. In the manner of other theorists within the paradigm, they tend to incorporate the insights of 'outsiders' insofar as they serve useful ends. Action theorists have used notions derived from the phenomenological perspective to shore up and support the functionalist point of view. As will be clear from our discussion in Chapter 6 this is clearly evident in the work of Weber, who used idealist notions in a positivist way. The same is true of Parsons and of Silverman. Silverman, for example, in addition to concluding that the action frame of reference is no more than a method of analysis, suggests that it may 'be a useful source of propositions in organisational analysis' (1970, p. 143). This view is firmly in line with the positivist attitude to the whole concept of *verstehen* and clearly emphasises its location within the context of the functionalist paradigm. In Silverman's work the action frame of reference becomes no more than a different way of studying the same reality. Emphasis is placed upon the importance of developing scientific explanations at an individual as opposed to a systems level of analysis, because of the problems of reification. The ontological and epistemological assumptions remain firmly grounded in the functionalist perspective. As will become clear in our discussion in Chapters 6 and 7, phenomenology and ethnomethodology in their true form are predicated upon fundamentally different views with regard to the ontological nature of social reality itself.

Silverman did not adhere to the position articulated in *The Theory of Organisations* for long. As we will see in Chapter 7, his subsequent work led him to a perspective firmly located within the context of the interpretive paradigm. A comparison of this later work with the approach presented in *The Theory of Organisations* clearly illustrates the essentially intermediate position which the latter reflects in terms of the subjective—objective dimension of our analytical scheme. Silverman's early and later works are paradigms apart.

Pluralist Theory

The issues of power and conflict within organisations have long attracted the attention of organisation theorists but have rarely received sustained and systematic consideration. We intend to argue here that many of the ideas and research findings which this interest has generated anticipate, and point the way towards, the development of a pluralist theory of organisations characteristic of the conflict functionalism discussed in Chapter 4. Taken together, they lay the basis for the analysis of organisations as pluralist political systems – according to which organisations and their environment are viewed principally as arenas of conflict between individuals and groups whose activities are orientated towards the achievement of their own personal goals, values and interests. Many current theories of organisation contain elements of this view but stop some way short of a fully developed pluralist theory of organisations. Power and conflict are often studied as isolated phenomena or used as concepts in schemes geared to wider ends. They are rarely regarded as defining the nature of organisation itself.

As Eldridge and Crombie (1974) have noted, the use of the term 'pluralism' is fraught with danger because of the wide range of interpretations which have come to be placed upon it. It will be as well, therefore, if we set out in a little more detail the way in which we intend to use it here. Broadly speaking, we see a 'pluralist' as opposed to a 'unitary' view of organisations as reflecting three sets of assumptions relating to what we shall describe as *interests*, *conflict* and *power*.[47]

The different assumptions with regard to *interests* are clearly reflected in the distinction which Fox (1966) has drawn between the industrial organisation as a 'team' striving towards the achievement of a common objective and as a coalition with divergent interests. Whereas the unitary view of organisations tends to stress that an organisation is a co-operative enterprise united in the pursuit of a common goal, the pluralist view stresses the diversity of individual interests and goals. Whereas from a unitary perspective organisations are viewed as instruments of rational and purposive activity, from a pluralist view they represent a network of sectional groups interested in the wider purpose of the organisation as a whole only insofar as it serves their own individual ends. From a pluralist perspective the formal goals of an organisation have the status of little more than a legitimising façade, an umbrella under which a host of individual and group interests are pursued as ends in themselves.

The unitary view of organisations regards *conflict* within organisations as a rare and transient phenomenon which, when present, can easily be eradicated or controlled through appropriate managerial action. Because interests are regarded as being characterised by a harmonious order, conflict within organisations is regarded as an alien, obstrusive and unwelcome force and one which is largely the creation of deviants and troublemakers. From a pluralist perspective, on the other hand, conflict within organisations is viewed as an inevitable and ineradicable feature of everyday life. The organisation is seen as a web of cross-cutting conflicts between the individuals and interest groups which give it life. Rather than advocating its removal, the pluralist view emphasises the possibilities of its playing a constructive role within the context of the organisation as a whole. For the pluralist, conflict must be institutionalised in some way, so that it can find expression and 'work itself through' without prejudice to the survival of the system as a whole.

Within the context of a unitary view of organisation the question of *power* is largely ignored. Since the organisation is viewed as a harmonious and conflict-free enterprise, striving uniformly towards the achievement of what is common and in the interests of all, questions about the source and use of power do not often arise. Concepts such as authority, leadership and control are preferred ways of describing the 'prerogative' of managers to guide the organisation as a whole towards desired goals and aims. Power in this sense is little more than a neutral resource which oils the wheels of the system as a whole. The pluralist view, on the other hand, regards the power of various groups within the organisation as a crucial variable for understanding what happens in everyday affairs. Power is seen as the medium through which conflicts of interest are settled. Organisational life, from a pluralist standpoint, is a power-play between individuals and groups who draw upon their various sources of power in order to control their work situations and to achieve whatever objectives they value. The organisation is viewed as a plurality of power holders who derive their influence from a plurality of sources. The organisation is regarded as a loose coalition which moves towards the achievement of its plurality of aims through an uncertain process of bargaining and mutual adjustment of respective claims. Considerable emphasis is placed upon the importance of devising a network of rules and regulations which allow this process to occur in an orderly fashion and without undue prejudice to the survival of the organisation as a whole.

Thus, by way of summary, the two views of organisation can be illustrated as in Table 5.1.

Table 5.1

The unitary and pluralist views of interests, conflict and power

	The unitary view	*The pluralist view*
Interests	Places emphasis upon the achievement of common objectives. The organisation is viewed as being united under the umbrella of common goals, and striving towards their achievement in the manner of a well integrated team.	Places emphasis upon the diversity of individual and group interests. The organisation is regarded as a loose coalition which has but a remote interest in the formal goals of the organisation.
Conflict	Regards conflict as a rare and transient phenomenon which can be removed through appropriate managerial action. Where it does arise it is usually attributed to the activities of deviants and troublemakers.	Regards conflict as an inherent and ineradicable characteristic of ·organisational affairs and stresses its potentially positive or functional aspects.
Power	Largely ignores the role of power in organisational life. Concepts such as authority, leadership and control tend to be preferred means of describing the managerial prerogative of guiding the organisation towards the achievement of common interests.	Regards power as a variable crucial to the understanding of the activities of an organisation. Power is the medium through which conflicts of interest are alleviated and resolved. The organisation is viewed as a plurality of power holders drawing their power from a plurality of sources.

The unitary view of organisation is epitomised in the classical theory of organisations which tends to view the organisation as a machine geared to the achievement of formal goals. From this point of view the organisation is an instrument of purposive rationality, which directs its members in an effective and efficient manner. The members of the organisation are viewed as responding to incentives which secure their commitment to the formal goals of the organisation. The enterprise is thus envisaged as a unitary phenomena in which the goals of all members can be simultaneously satisfied; the task of management is to ensure that the organisation is appropriately structured, directed and controlled so that effective operation is achieved.

The unitary view is also reflected in many of the other theories which we have reviewed in earlier sections of this chapter. Barnard's view of an organisation as a 'co-operative system', the human relations concern to integrate individual and organisational needs and the open systems view of an organisation as being geared to the process of survival, all in varying degrees reflect elements of this perspective. Above all else the organisation is viewed as a functionally integrated system, the operations of which can be understood with reference to the organisational goals which it is concerned to achieve. However, ever since the Hawthorne studies, increasing attention has been devoted to the role of conflict within organisations, and it is now rare to find theoretical perspectives which reflect the unitary view in an extreme sense. In broad terms, developments in organisation theory over the last fifty years have been away from the unitary and towards the pluralist view of organisations. However, as we noted earlier, this movement has been incomplete, so that many theories reflect elements of a pluralist perspective but stop some way short of a fully developed pluralist theory. To this extent many of the theories which we have discussed in earlier sections of this chapter are of a hybrid nature. Some are more pluralist than others. As a means of developing the pluralist perspective in a little more detail, therefore, it will be useful if we return to some of the theory and research which we have already considered and examine the way in which it has treated interests, conflict and power. We will then proceed to examine the work of other theorists who have contributed to the pluralist perspective.

Pluralist elements in social system theory

Many theories located within the bounds of social system theory tend to move towards the pluralist perspective with regard to conflict and, to a lesser extent, with regard to interests. But with regard to power they remain firmly embedded within the unitary standpoint. Conflict is recognised to occur in many forms. For example, theorists in the human relations tradition, or those who adopt a socio-technical systems perspective, have emphasised the conflicts which can arise between human needs and the characteristics of formal organisation structure (for example, Argyris, 1952 and 1957), technology (Trist and Bamforth, 1951) and the like. Other theorists and researchers have pointed towards the conflicts which can arise between formal organisational roles (for example, Dalton, 1959; Katz and Kahn, 1966) and to conflicts between the different sub-units of an organisation (Lawrence and Lorsch, 1967). Others have documented conflicts in the work place between individual workers, work groups and their supervisors (for example, Lupton, 1963; Whyte, 1955). Theorists who have focused upon decision-making processes within organisations have emphasised the conflicts which occur between managers (for example, Cyert and March, 1963). Social system theory thus contains many examples of theory and research which treat organisational life as based upon a plurality of conflicts.

However, these theories do not always recognise organisations as being characterised by a plurality of interests. The human relations theorists, for example, in focusing upon human needs, tend to underplay the fact that individuals may have goals which are in conflict with those of the organisation. Their perspective is based upon the premise that it is somehow possible to satisfy individual needs through the achievement of wider organisational goals. The emphasis upon needs thus tends to present the organisation as a unitary phenomena which has the capacity to operate as a well integrated team. The potential divergence of goals is de-emphasised as a consequence of the focus upon universal needs. Again, those theorists who have been concerned with the study of conflicts between organisational roles and sub-units often stress the structural determinants of conflict as opposed to the plurality of individual and group orientations and interests, which, as Dubin (1956) and Goldthorpe and his colleagues (1968) have demonstrated, may be brought into the organisation from outside. Similarly, the organisation theorists who have focused upon decision-making processes within organisations also often tend to de-emphasise the plurality of interests. This is particularly evident, for example, in the work of Simon (1957), March and Simon (1958) and Cyert and March (1963), and in the notions of 'bounded rationality' and 'administrative man'. Such conceptualisations attempt to reconcile the unitary view of organisation as a rationally ordered enterprise with the observations that organisational activities do not in practice follow the pattern that the rational model would lead us to expect. Their theories favour a unitary view of organisation, based upon a qualified principle of rationality, as opposed to a pluralist view, which gives *full* recognition to the variety of orientations and interests of individual members.[48]

Most social system theories completely ignore the issue of power within organisations. As we have argued at some length, these theories are usually based upon assumptions that organisations are social processes characterised by equilibrium or homeostasis. Theories based upon an organismic analogy, for example, tend to stress the functional interdependence and unity of the system and emphasise the functions which are performed in the interests of the survival of the whole. The exercise of authority and control is thus seen as an essential process geared to the achievement of this overall state of affairs. The emphasis upon common purpose and functional unity tends to deflect attention from a consideration of the power of constituent elements. Issues involving the use of power tend to be interpreted as issues or problems of authority and control which are of direct relevance to the effectiveness of the organisation in the achievement of its formal goals (see, for example, Tannenbaum, 1968).

Pluralist elements in theories of bureaucratic dysfunctions

Moving on to consider the theories of bureaucratic dysfunctions, we find that they usually reflect a pluralist view with regard to interests and conflict and tend, to an extent, to recognise the importance of power as a variable in organisational analysis. As we have seen, the work of Merton (1968), Selznick (1949), Gouldner (1954a and b) and Blau (1955) all demonstrated, in one way or another, the unintended consequences of formal organisation. In cases where these unintended consequences were dysfunctional as far as the formal goals of the organisation were concerned, it was usually because they were functional for other interests within the organisation. Merton's 'bureaucratic personalities' adopted a defensive and ritualistic posture to protect themselves from the possibility of criticism from outside the organisation; the dysfunctions of specialisation and goal displacement revealed by Selznick arose because the specialists sought to further their own interests; the bureaucratic rules in Gouldner's gypsum factory were used by the workers and managers to serve their own quite different purposes; Blau's study of government agencies revealed numerous examples of group and sectional interests. The very notion of dysfunction inevitably raises questions such as, functional or dysfunctional for whom? Whose goals is the organisation attempting to achieve? Whose interests are the rules rational for? A theory of interests is thus a direct corollary of the theory of dysfunctions. As Gouldner (1959) has noted, the notion of dysfunctions directs attention towards issues such as the degree of functional reciprocity which characterises the relationships between system parts. To the extent that reciprocal relationships are asymmetrical, interdependence of parts is less than perfect and gives rise to various degrees of functional autonomy or independence of parts within the context of the system as a whole. It is this principle of autonomy which lies at the heart of the pluralist theory of interests.

The role of conflict is also given considerable prominence in the theories of Merton and his colleagues. These studies of bureaucracy were, in many respects, stimulated by the Hawthorne findings on the relationship between formal and informal organisation, and they are permeated by the theme of conflict between the rational and human aspects of organisation. Conflicts between bureaucrats and their clients, between sectional groups and coalitions within the organisation, and between management and workers are all given prominence in one or more of these studies. Conflict is central to the theory of bureaucratic dysfunctions.

The work of Selznick (1949) and Gouldner (1954a and b), also draws attention to the plurality of power relationships within organisations, but the insights generated are not followed up to their full extent. Selznick traces the struggle for control which ensues from the different commitments and patterns of interest within the organisation, and the process of co-option through which they are brought within the bounds of the decision-making system. However, his general orientation is the study of the manner in which an organisation *limits* the influence of its dysfunctions and is not so much concerned with tracing them to their source, as a fully developed view of power would require. Similarly, Gouldner gives much attention to the process of subordination and control within 'punitive' bureaucratic structures, but stops short of a full analysis of the power relationships between the workers and managers under investigation. These studies both point the way towards a pluralist view of power, but since they are essentially orientated towards the specific study of the dysfunctions of bureaucratic structures, they only treat the subject insofar as it has relevance to this purpose. Their focus upon bureaucratic structure necessarily overemphasises the role and importance of formal authority as opposed to other forms of power relationships. Nonetheless, in terms of general orientation and approach their overall theoretical stance has much in common with, and has contributed immeasurably towards, more fully developed pluralist views of organisation, notably that of Crozier (1964).

Pluralism and the action frame of reference

Theorists who adopt the action frame of reference as a basis for their analysis of organisational situations usually do so in recognition of the fact that any social situation is characterised by a plurality of interests. They also frequently point to the conflicts which exist within the situations studied, and occasionally draw attention to the role of power as a variable worthy of analysis. However, their standpoint upon the last issue tends to be implicit rather than explicit, and is not developed systematically to any degree.

As will be clear from our earlier analysis, the action frame of reference owes much to the Weberian view that explanations in social science must be 'adequate on the level of meaning'. It is based on the view that the various actors in a social situation interpret and define that situation in ways which have meaning for them, and act accordingly. The idea that there will be a plurality of such definitions is central to this standpoint; if this were not so, then the action frame of reference would prove unnecessary. That organisational situations are characterised by a plurality of interests is clearly evident in the work of Goffman (1961), Turner (1971), Goldthorpe *et al.* (1968), and Silverman (1970), as discussed earlier. It is also evident in the work of many of the so-called behavioural symbolic interactionists referred to in Chapter 4.

The conflicts which arise as a result of the different definitions of organisational situations have often provided the action theorist with excellent case material for illustrating his particular point of view. It is clearly evident in Goffman's (1961) analysis of the 'underlife of total institutions' and in Eldridge's analysis of restrictive practices (Eldridge, 1971, pp. 45–9). Silverman's reinterpretation of Gouldner's *Wildcat Strike* in terms of a social action perspective also provides an excellent illustration of the ways in which conflicts in expectations, modes of involvement in an organisation and general conflicts in the definition of situations can account for change within organisations (Silverman, 1970, pp. 155–63). Indeed, the scheme which Silverman suggests for the comparative analysis of organisations from an action perspective has many characteristics which emphasise the pluralistic nature of organisations. He summarises the issues which ought to be addressed as follows:

1. The nature of the predominant meaning-structure and associated role-system in different organisations and the extent to which it relies on varying degrees of coercion or consent.
2. The characteristic pattern of involvement of the actors; differing attachment to rules and definitions of their situation.
3. The typical strategies used by different actors to attain their ends.
4. The relative ability of different actors to impose their definition of the situation upon others. The nature and sources of the symbolic 'sticks' (resources) available to the actors; their relative effectiveness.
5. The origin and pattern of change of meaning-structures (institutionalisation and de-institutionalisation of meanings) in different organisations. (Silverman, 1970, pp. 171–2)

Points 1 and 4 draw attention to the role of power within organisations, which is seen from an action standpoint largely in terms of the ability to impose one's definition of a situation upon others. Many action theorists have referred to this. Goffman's definition of 'total institutions', for example, emphasises that such organisations assume much of their special character because those in authority are able to impose their definitions of the situation upon inmates. However, action theorists do not tend to involve themselves in an analysis of the nature and sources of power as such. Power is often seen as a variable relevant to the explanation of the 'meanings' which prevail but is rarely analysed in detail. Nevertheless, the action theorists have much in common with more fully developed pluralist views of organisation.

Other movements towards pluralist theory

Since the early 1960s an increasing number of social theorists have concerned themselves with the development of theoretical perspectives which are essentially pluralist in nature. The work of Peter Blau (1964) on exchange theory, for example, provides a clear illustration of this. As will be apparent from our discussion in Chapter 4, Blau's 'Exchange and Power Model' provides a theory of social integration which is explicitly based upon the variables which are central to pluralist theory. Following Simmel, Blau focuses upon the emergent properties of human interaction and attempts to account for the nature and patterns which exist within society in terms of the process of exchange. Social exchange geared to the satisfaction of different needs and interests is seen as creating inequalities of power and as generating a host of cross-cutting conflicts and oppositions which lie at the heart of changes within society as a whole. Blau thus provides a processual theory of social interaction which is firmly based upon pluralist principles but which, as he recognises, allows for further development.[49]

Another step in the direction of a pluralist theory of organisation has been taken by Michel Crozier (1964). However, he approaches the subject from a different direction. Whereas Blau has developed his theory from an interactionist stance, Crozier's theory represents a direct development in the mould of the theories of bureaucratic dysfunctions discussed earlier. His analysis of the bureaucratic character of two French administrative organisations leads him to a theory of bureaucracy which identifies power as 'the new central problem of the theory of organisation' (Crozier, 1964, p. 145). His analysis traces the conflict of interests and the bargaining process which characterise relationships between groups within an organisation, particularly at different levels of the organisational hierarchy. It demonstrates how the various groups attempt to gain control of their work situations by drawing upon the various sources of power at their disposal, and the way in which this influences the organisation structure. In line with other theorists in the pluralist tradition, Crozier sees the power struggle within organisations as being limited by certain stabilising factors, such as the need to maintain minimum standards of efficiency, and other social factors which ensure that the organisation continues as an ongoing concern. In the true tradition of conflict functionalism, therefore, conflict is seen as having its limits.

A third example of the move towards a pluralist perspective is found in the work of Etzioni (1961), whose comparative analysis of organisations in terms of the 'nature of compliance' focuses upon the relationship between power and employee commitment. The nature of compliance is viewed as being related to many other organisational variables, such as the goals that organisations pursue, the kind, location, power and interaction of elites, the level of consensus attained, etc. Etzioni's analysis has done much to draw attention to the role of power as a variable in organisational analysis, but his treatment of the different 'interests' and 'conflicts' within organisations falls well short of what a more fully developed pluralist theory would require.

In the field of industrial relations pluralist-type theories have become well established. The perspective is clearly evident, for example, in the opening words of the *Report of the Royal Commission on Trade Unions and Employers' Associations* (1965–8; Chairman, Lord Donovan), which describes the nature of the business enterprise in the following terms:

> The running of large businesses is in the hands of professional managers ... While in the long term shareholders, employees and customers all stand to benefit if a concern flourishes, the immediate interests of these groups often conflict. Directors and managers have to balance these conflicting interests, and in practice they generally seek to strike for whatever balance will best promote the welfare of the enterprise as such.

This viewpoint is in line with an intellectual tradition which finds expression in other literature in the industrial relations field such as that of Clark Kerr and his colleagues (1964). Their view of 'pluralistic industrialism' emphasises a movement towards a society in which the state, organisations and employee associations will be united through a web of rules which govern and settle conflicts between interest groups. Others have built upon such a perspective – notably Alan Fox (1966), who has been prominent in advocating the pluralistic frame of reference as a means of understanding the nature of work organisations and, more recently (1973 and 1974), in emphasising its inherent weaknesses and deficiencies. Within the context of the industrial relations field the debate over pluralism has in many respects focused upon the nature of power. Those advocating the pluralist perspective have usually underwritten their views with the assumption that there is a rough balance of power between the competing interest groups, and that all groups are united in preserving the system as an ongoing concern. It is also assumed that the survival needs of the organisation, or those of society, impose limits on the degree and nature of conflict.

A fifth line of development which moves in the direction of a pluralist theory of organisations is witnessed in the increasing number of research studies which have focused upon the study of power as a variable in organisational analysis (for example, Kahn and Boulding, 1964; Zald, 1970, Hickson *et al.*, 1971). Most of these studies are cast within the wider perspective of social system theory but represent a temporary excursion outside the bounds of the dominant model. As we have argued, power as a variable does not figure prominently in functionalist systems theory, so the fascination of these theorists with it can be seen as especially significant. In many respects it can be understood as symptomatic of a desire to forge a radical perspective within the context of the functionalist paradigm akin to the movement towards conflict functionalism described in Chapter 4. Organisation theory has frequently attracted the charge of being conservative in orientation, unduly biased towards a managerial perspective and generally supportive of the *status quo*. A number of organisation theorists who have wished to avoid this charge have directed their attention to the study of power in organisational life. Yet other theorists, more firmly committed to a managerial view, have chosen to study power in the belief that an understanding of the subject may facilitate better managerial control. Whatever the reason, the result has been a series of studies in which power is the focus of interest and its underlying definition essentially pluralist in orientation.

A final trend in the direction of pluralist theory worthy of mention here is found in the work of those theorists who have sought to study decision making within organisations as an explicitly 'political' process. The recent study by Pettigrew (1973), for example, is illustrative of this general trend and goes a long way towards presenting a pluralist theory of decision making in which the relationships between interests, conflict and power are spelt out in some detail. In essence, it develops the elements of pluralism which we have described as characterising the decision-making theories of Herbert Simon and Cyert and March, taking them to their logical conclusion. In Pettigrew's theory man is accorded a 'political' rather than an 'administrative' orientation, which is consistent with the nature of the 'political system' within which he operates.

Towards a clearer statement of pluralist theory

In the previous sections we have sought to show how elements of functionalist organisation theory converge upon various factors which characterise a pluralist approach to the study of organisations. The movement to this position has been gradual and piecemeal rather than the response to the various research findings which have demonstrated that models based upon unitary assumptions are inadequate for an understanding of the dynamics of modern organisations. We have thus arrived at a point at which pluralist models of organisation have developed in advance of a clear statement of the pluralist perspective as such, except in its relationship to the unitary view.

The lack of a clear perspective is well illustrated in relation to the way in which the concept of power is handled in pluralist-type theories of organisation. Where it is recognised as a key variable, the major concern is usually to locate its source and measure the extent to which it exists. Relatively little attention is devoted to the *nature of power* as such. Many theorists favour Dahl's (1967) conceptualisation of power, namely, that the power of a person A over a person B lies in the ability of A to get B to do something that he would not have done otherwise, and go hardly any further in terms of an attempt to define the nature of the phenomenon under investigation. Yet the problem of defining power seems to be a crucial issue.

One of the few orthodoxies in the 'What is power?' debate is the view that power refers to a 'relationship' rather than a 'thing'. Ever since the publication of Emerson's influential paper, 'Power-Dependence Relations' (1962), it has become fairly well established that the concept of power inevitably involves the question: 'power over whom?' However, this still leaves many issues unresolved. Among the most important of these, we may cite the following:

(a) *Power or social control?* Is it possible or meaningful to identify power independently of a wider process of ongoing social control? For example, processes of socialisation have been shown to be important regulators of social behaviour. Where does one draw the line between social control and power? Is power utilised in the social control of a child's behaviour within the nuclear family? Is it meaningful to equate this with the type of control exercised by some form of elite through the mass media or the control of workers through board-room decisions? Wrong (1968) has suggested that it is necessary to restrict the use of power to the intentional efforts of groups or individuals to control others, and many pluralist theorists follow his lead. However, the concept of social control does undermine the utility of the notion of power. It shows it to be at best a partial and incomplete conceptual tool for the analysis of social affairs. The validity and utility of the notion of power as a concept for organisational analysis is thus worthy of much more detailed consideration and attention than it has received up to now.

(b) *Is power 'zero-sum' or 'non-zero-sum'?* Assuming that one accepts that it is valid to treat power as a variable in organisational analysis, the question of whether it is 'zero-sum' becomes an issue. Is power something which benefits one group at the expense of another, or is it something which can benefit everyone? Talcott Parsons (1963) supports the latter view, arguing that power is a resource generated by the social system in a manner akin to the generation of wealth, and whilst some people may have more of it than others, the use to which power is put is of as much interest as its distribution. Giddens (1972a) has referred to these as the 'collective' and 'distributive' aspects of power.

(c) *Illegitimate or legitimate power?* This distinction serves to undermine the simplistic equation found in some work that power equals coercion. Parsons (1963) has argued that the use of open force is an indication of a shallow and unstable power base. Where authority is pervasive, for example, power (in a coercive sense) will not be in evidence. Thus questioning of the relationship between power and coercion immediately draws attention to the distinction often made in the literature between authority and power. The term 'power' is often used simply to characterise the non-legitimised use of power. A full development of the concept of power must also concern itself with the way in which it becomes legitimised in the form of authority. Whilst organisation theory has paid considerable attention to the notion of 'authority', it has paid relatively little to the concept of power in a wider sense.

(d) *Negative or positive power?* An important distinction can be drawn between the notion of 'positive power' – the ability to get things done – and 'negative power' – the ability to stop things being done. A focus upon negative power is normally accompanied by an emphasis upon the role of 'veto groups' in organisational life. A fully developed conceptualisation of power must take account of both positive and negative elements of power.

(e) *Actual or potential power?* Power does not have to be exercised to be present. The distinction between actual and potential power is fundamental at both theoretical and methodological levels. Those who are concerned to operationalise power often restrict their attention to the visible use of objective manifestations of power, ignoring essential background elements which, whilst extremely potent in their effects, may be hidden from view. The distinction which we have in mind here is clearly related to Wrong's (1968) view of power as an 'episodic' as opposed to a 'dispositional' concept. The former refers to specific behavioural events, whereas the latter refers to the way in which situations are defined by the individuals concerned. The distinction between actual and potential power is thus very much influenced by the way in which the situation is perceived by the actors involved.

(f) *Intercursive or integral power?* Is power something which is spread around? Or does it derive from one source or a small number of sources? This distinction, which is again found in Wrong's discussion of power, is of crucial relevance to the pluralist perspective. Pluralism is based on the notion that power is intercursive and that no individual or group dominates totally. It regards power as deriving from many sources and as varying from situation to situation and issue to issue. In other words, it assumes that there are spheres of influence in which different individuals and groups have different degrees of power.

This brief and somewhat oversimplified overview of issues relevant to a theory of power, serves to illustrate some of the major problems facing pluralist organisation theory at the present time. The foundations have simply not yet been fully explored. Pluralist theory implicitly assumes that power is intercursive, and major attention is devoted to an identification of relevant sources. The classifactory scheme offered by French and Raven (1968), for example, and the 'strategic contingencies' theory of power offered by Hickson and his colleagues (1971), provide two prominent examples of this endeavour. Their search for the bases of power presumes answers to questions which they simply do not raise.

Future developments with regard to a pluralist theory of organisation would thus seem to call for a much more systematic statement of the theory of power upon which it is based.[50] It also calls for a much more systematic statement of the theory of interests and the theory of conflict upon which it is founded. At the present time assumptions with regard to these other two issues are vague and underdeveloped. Interests tend to be equated with individual, group or sub-unit goals; conflict tends to be seen as an endemic but bounded and potentially constructive element of organisational life. These and other related assumptions are in need of systematic elaboration, so that a systematic theory of the relationships between interests, conflicts and power can be developed.

Such an endeavour would lead to the consideration of some major issues. A theory of interests, conflict and power at an organisational level necessarily implies a theory of interests, conflict and power at a societal level. This focus would thus encourage organisation theorists to form a clearer idea of the relationship between organisations and society, within both a contemporary and a historical context. It would bring them to a direct consideration of the nature of the assumptions which define their location within the functionalist paradigm as opposed to the radical structuralist paradigm. As will become apparent from our discussion of radical structuralism in Chapters 10 and 11, theorists located there have also given consideration to a theory of interests, conflict and power, and their stance is radically different from that of the pluralist. At a sociological level, the confrontation of ideas drawn from the work of Marx and Weber has produced a conflict theory which offers a view of organisations substantially different from those reviewed here within the context of the functionalist paradigm.

So much, then, for our discussion of pluralist theory. Our review of this perspective completes our analysis of contemporary schools of thought located within the functionalist paradigm. Clearly, they vary considerably in terms of general orientations and underlying assumptions. In the concluding section of this chapter we will examine briefly the way in which these differences are reflected in terms of ongoing debate within the context of the paradigm as a whole.

Debate Within the Functionalist Paradigm

Having completed our review of the different approaches to the study of organisations characteristic of the functionalist paradigm, it will be useful by way of conclusion if we turn our attention to examine some of the issues of debate within the paradigm. Anyone familiar with the literature on organisational analysis cannot have failed to notice the differences of opinion which exist between members of different schools of functionalist thought. We intend to argue here that much of this debate can be understood in terms of the positions which its participants adopt in relation to the two dimensions of our analytical scheme. Whilst they are committed to the overall view of science and society which characterises the paradigm, they differ in the degree and manner in which they subscribe and address themselves to these common basic assumptions. It is these differences which underwrite the nature of the debate.

We will take the dominant perspective within the paradigm, social system theory and objectivism, as our starting point. Putting aside for the moment debate concerning 'levels of analysis' (that is, whether it is fruitful to focus upon individual, group, organisational or societal issues as topics of analysis),[51] we find that debate within this perspective tends to focus upon points of detail. It is usually 'friendly' and 'constructive' in tone, and it focuses upon the ways in which particular models can be refined and research methods improved, and what the precise meaning and significance of a particular set of empirical results might be. The debate is often about the technical improvements which might be made within the context of the perspective as a whole.

Criticisms that this dominant perspective is characterised by an undue and extreme commitment to positivism and a naïve empiricism, and that it is characterised by a complete disregard for the nature of the phenomena under investigation, tend to be of a different order. Whilst such charges are often levelled from outside the paradigm by interpretive theorists or radical humanists, they are also levelled within the paradigm by theorists who adhere to a subjectivist position typical, for example, of the action frame of reference. From the standpoint of action theory, the work of the social system theorist and objectivist is dubious because it reflects too strong a commitment to the models and methods of the natural sciences as a basis for social analysis. These criticisms are often founded on the charge that social system theorists and objectivists 'reify' their subject of study.

The charge that social system theorists and objectivists are overdeterministic in their view of human nature also arises from the same source. The voluntarism which characterises the action approach, for example, is often set in opposition to the technological or structural determinism characteristic of much of the theory and research located in the more objectivist regions of the paradigm.

Another charge levelled at social system theory and objectivism is that it is ideologically biased in favour of a managerial view of organisation. This charge has come from all directions. The action theorists have claimed that the meanings which managers attribute to organisations are given undue prominence and that the meanings and orientations of other organisational actors are, relatively speaking, ignored. The theorists who have focused upon bureaucratic dysfunctions have stressed the non-managerial interests which account for much of organisational activity. The pluralists have criticised social system theorists for adopting a unitary frame of reference and for ignoring the role of power as an organisational variable. All in their various ways have contributed to the view that social system theorists and objectivists are little more than the handmaidens and functionaries of those in control of organisational life.

For their part the social system theorists and objectivists are often at a loss to understand the basis of such charges. They may not be consciously aware of being managerially biased and may see their overall endeavour as directed at increasing the effectiveness of 'the organisation' or the satisfaction and productivity of the work force in the interests of all. Such is the nature of the unitary frame of reference which underwrites their approach. However, the issue runs much deeper than this. Their conservative or managerially orientated stance is rooted in the models which they adopt for the purpose of analysis. We have already devoted considerable space to a discussion of the assumptions which underwrite different approaches to the study of organisations, but it is worth re-emphasising them here.

Social system theory and objectivist approaches to the study of the organisations are built around the common-sense, 'taken for granted' assumptions that organisations are purposive, goal-seeking enterprises. The question 'What is an organisation?' is rarely given very much attention; the answer is taken to be self-evident. The problem of defining an organisation is usually tackled in three or four lines, which form a convenient springboard for moving on to the issues which are regarded as being of real concern. Yet it is the question 'What is an organisation?' that should lie at the heart of organisational analysis. Different paradigmatic locations yield different answers to this question.

If a social theorist takes the definition of the phenomena which he is attempting to investigate as largely self-evident, it is also likely that he will adopt a model for analysis which is similarly unquestioned. It is hardly surprising, therefore, that the mechanical and organismic models, particularly the latter, have proved such popular analytical tools for the study of organisations. The notion of equilibrium which characterises the mechanical analogy is well suited for the study of organisations – which, by definition, are *assumed* to be relatively stable entities. The notions of functional unity, homeostasis, adaptability and survival which characterise the organismic analogy lend themselves well to the study of organisations, if they are *assumed* to be rational, purposive, goal-seeking, adaptive enterprises coping with the demands of an environment. As we have argued in Chapter 4, as a result of the distinction drawn between 'closed' and 'open' systems, it has now become almost routine to view organisations as 'open' rather than 'closed' and to view the organismic analogy as providing an appropriate basis for analysis. The adoption of an open systems approach has been mistakenly regarded as synonomous with the use of an organismic analogy. As a result the use of organismic models for the study of organisations has been regarded as being as self-evident and obvious as the common-sense definition of the phenomenon which they are used to analyse.

The upshot of our argument, therefore, is that the conservatism or ideological and managerial bias which many theorists have suggested characterises social system theory and objectivism is built into the models which are used as a basis of analysis. For this reason many theorists are not conscious of being biased one way or another. This is nowhere better illustrated than in the work of many socio-technical system theorists or human relations theorists who, whilst attracting the charge of conservatism and managerialism, actually see themselves as perhaps taking a 'radical' stand in favour of employees and their job satisfaction. What they fail to realise is that their radicalism is constrained by the nature of the models upon which their work is implicitly based. Insofar as they adopt organismic models which presume a functional unity of system parts, with certain imperative functions which must be satisfied if the organisation is to survive, their analyses are constrained by the requirements chacteristic of a managerial point of view. It is this consonance between the nature of the organismic analogy and the requirements of managerialism which underwrites the dominance of organismic models within the field of organisation theory.

Notes and References

1. For an extended discussion of classical management theory, see, for example, Massie (1965).

2. Taylor, hard, direct and abrasive in approach, soon became embroiled in a battle with organised labour and was seen as the arch-enemy of the working man. By 1912 his system of scientific management had become the subject of a hearing before a Special Committee of the House of Representatives.

3. For an overview of the early work and history of the industrial psychology movement, see Rose (1975), pp. 65–100. For a discussion of some early research, see Mayo (1933), pp. 1–54.

4. See, for example, Myers (1924).

5. See, for example, Schein (1970), pp. 55–76.

6. For a critical discussion of the human relations movement, see Perrow (1972).

7. For a review of the research conducted, see Vroom (1964) and Locke (1975).

8. Part III of their book is devoted to this conceptual scheme (1939, pp. 255–376).

9. As we have mentioned earlier, and will discuss further later in this chapter, the model can be more accurately regarded as the product of the Harvard School under Henderson and Mayo. Mayo (1933) sets out some of the notions underlying the model in a somewhat crude and incomplete form. Barnard (1938) also uses the notion of an equilibrating social system, though his model is much more general in nature.

10. It is interesting to note that many early social researchers were at pains to avoid attributing to social phenomena too concrete a reality. See, for example, Mayo (1933), pp. 33–4.

11. Roethlisberger and Dickson (1939), p. 272. Other significant influences, in addition to those of Pareto and Durkheim, included Freud, Piaget, Jung, Lévy-Bruhl, Malinowski and Radcliffe-Brown.

12. Roethlisberger and Dickson refer to Durkheim on only two occasions in the whole of their work.

13. Many of the criticisms reviewed by Landsberger (1958) are launched from a pluralist perspective.

14. See, for example, the critique offered by Carey (1967). This is subtitled 'A "Radical" Critique', but in addressing itself to problems of methodology and interpretation of results operates within the problematic set by the Hawthorne model.

15. For an overview see, for example, the following collections of readings: Vroom and Deci (1970), Warr (1971), Davis and Taylor (1972).
16. For a review of these, see Miner and Dachler (1973).
17. For a review of recent evidence, see, for example, Locke (1975).
18. Most contemporary 'expectancy' models are based upon that developed by Vroom (1964).
19. See, for example, Warner and Low (1947), especially pp. 66–89, and Homans (1950).
20. See, for example, Rice (1958 and 1963) and Trist *et al.* (1963).
21. The relationship between human and structural aspects of organisation was also explored in a systematic fashion by Merton, Selznick, Gouldner, Blau and others. Taking their point of departure from the bureaucratic theory of Max Weber, they sought to show how dysfunctions arise as a result of the unanticipated responses of organisation members. As will be apparent from our discussion of Mertonian theory in Chapter 4, Merton's and his colleagues' study of dysfunctions reflects a perspective which falls outside the bounds of social system theory. We shall be considering this important work in detail in a separate section later in this chapter.
22. The non-rational or informal aspects of organisation are given detailed attention in some of Selznick's earlier works. See, for example, Selznick (1943).
23. See, for example, Miller and Rice (1967).
24. See, for example, Rice's discussion on the management of change (Rice, 1958, pp. 248–54).
25. The notion of 'appreciation' is derived from the work of Vickers (1966).
26. For a discussion of these terms, see Katz and Kahn (1965), pp. 25–8.
27. Most open systems models for the study of organisations can usually be expressed in terms of a series of assumptions about 'functional imperatives'. The apparent diversity of such systems models usually disappears when they are stripped down to the basic assumptions deriving from the use of an organismic analogy.
28. In point of fact, Woodward's work also involved case studies which incorporated the use of some interesting methodological approaches. However, it is the hard quantitative results of her survey which are given the most prominence in reports

of the research and which have been most influential.

29. The references cited here are illustrative. The writers concerned have produced a large number of publications in this area.

30. It can be argued, for example, that in attempting to correlate the technology and structure of organisations, researchers are examining two aspects of the same variable − viz. the method of control.

31. The notion of differentiation and integration of social systems was utilised by Herbert Spencer, who, as we have argued, was one of the earliest social theorists explicitly to develop the implications of the biological analogy.

32. As we have already discussed, the general *concerns* of the classical management school (structures) and those of the human relations school (human and social factors) had already been integrated within the context of a framework for the study of organisations by both Simon and Selznick. However, this synthesis did not reconcile the detailed propositions with regard to what constituted ideal management practice.

33. *Administrative Science Quarterly* contains numerous reports on research testing various aspects of the Lawrence and Lorsch model. See, for example, Osborn (1974).

34. Kast and Rosenweig (1973) present many good and relevant ideas on the contingency approach in a book of readings which brings together some of the well-known articles in this area.

35. The utility of and reliance which can be placed upon these studies is qualified later in this section in terms of the distinction which we draw between the importance of 'process' as opposed to 'structure'.

36. The choice of these departments is arbitrary and an oversimplification. It is unlikely that a whole department − a structural manifestation of process − would comprise an element on its own account. It is very easy to fall back upon structural characteristics as a means of describing the differentiation of an organisation, to the detriment of an overall systems view. See below our qualifications on this point in our discussion of the distinction between structure and process.

37. Even the research of Lawrence and Lorsch (1967) suffers from this problem. They virtually ignore the processual aspects of system and resort to hard quantitative measures of structures and attitudes as a means of testing their scheme.

The methodology employed in this study is nowhere near as sophisticated as the conceptual ideas which they present. They equate subsystems with structural features within the organisation; structure rather than system provides the starting point for their analysis. The same problem is found in the extension of the contingency approach presented in Lorsch and Morse (1974); this study does little to advance the concepts and methods presented in the earlier work. Insofar as it is presented under the guise of systems theory as opposed to determinism, the work of Pugh and Hickson (1976) and Hall (1972) also stands as abstracted empiricism.

38. A similar point of view is presented in the work of Burns and Stalker (1961), Rice (1963), Trist *et al.* (1963) and Child (1972). However, it could be argued that the choice available to the strategic decision makers is, in fact, fairly restricted, bounded by the structural constraints imposed by the environment.

39. For an excellent presentation of some of the central features of the work of Merton, Selznick, and Gouldner, see March and Simon (1958), pp. 36–47.

40. The work of these writers diverges quite considerably after the publication of these case studies on bureaucracy. We have already referred to the way in which Selznick follows the implications of a fairly traditional structural functionalist approach to organisation. Peter Blau makes a specific break with the case study as a method of organisational analysis in favour of empirical studies of formal organisational structures, as referred to in an earlier section of this chapter. In essence this line of development reflects an attempt to follow Merton's call for 'middle-range' activities linking theory to research. We would argue that much of Blau's recent work in this area represents a form of abstracted empiricism, in which methods dominate theoretical perspectives. We also referred in Chapter 4 to Blau's theory of exchange and power, which reflects another 'middle-range' investigation characteristic of a different region of the functionalist paradigm – that of interactionism. Blau's work is thus characteristic of a number of distinct areas. Blau presents a useful outline on the development of his general research interests in the introductory chapter of his book of essays *On the Nature of Organisations* (1974).

The work of Alvin Gouldner demonstrates the greatest change of all. Since his early work on bureaucracy, Gouldner has ranged very considerably in general orientations. From the cautious but potentially radical critique of functionalism presented in his 'Reciprocity and Autonomy in Functional Theory' published in 1959, he has moved to what constitutes an all-out attack upon the functionalist perspective. This is most clearly illustrated in *The Coming Crisis of Western Sociology* (1970), which provides a somewhat rambling 'reflexive sociology' characteristic of the general trend to individualism and subjectivism in sociology during the 1960s. It is a perspective which, whilst moving towards the view of a radical humanist seems much more concerned to develop a subjectivist attack upon functionalism than to focus upon a sociology of radical change. This dimension is much more evident in *The Dialectic of Ideology and Technology* (1976).

41. See, for example, our discussion of radical organisation theory in Chapter 11.

42. Schutz and Weber are discussed elsewhere in this text. The work of Berger and Luckmann, *The Social Construction of Reality* (1966), presents a strange mixture of sociological positivism and phenomenological sociology in the neo-idealist mould. Their ideas have influenced many theorists located in this area of the functionalist paradigm, including David Silverman, whose work we shall be considering in a later section.

43. See also, the collection of ethnographic accounts of work presented in Fraser (1968).

44. As we argue below, the action frame of reference only figures as an element in their overall work, which viewed in its totality draws heavily upon much more objectivist methodologies. We include it here as an example of the action framework with considerable qualification and, indeed, reservations. It is often cited as an example of the action approach, but its links with the Weberian perspective are at times very tenuous.

45. Silverman (1970), pp. 3–4. This view of the systems approach implies that it is necessarily associated with the use of a biological analogy. Whilst this is true in relation to the majority of systems applications within the field of organisation theory, it is not a necessary characteristic of the systems approach as such. Please see our discussion in Chapter 4 for further elaboration of this point.

46. Silverman acknowledges the influence of the following writers: Weber (1947), Schutz (1964), Berger and Luckmann

(1966), Berger and Pullberg (1966), Rose (1962), Goffman (1959), Cicourel (1964) and Cohen (1968).

47.   The distinction between 'unitary' and 'pluralist' frames of reference has come into prominence through the work of Fox (1966). It is also possible to introduce a third category – the 'radical' frame of reference (Fox, 1973, 1974a, 1974b). We are excluding the radical perspective from our discussion here because it belongs to a different intellectual tradition, one characteristic of the radical structuralist paradigm. See Chapter 11 for a discussion of this radical organisation theory.

48.   The view put forward in March and Simon (1958), for example, is that whilst members of an organisation have different goals and values, the major implication for a theory of organisations is that they have to be motivated to produce and to remain members of the organisation. Hence their elaboration of the 'inducement—contribution' theory first introduced by Barnard (1938).

49.   For a review of some of these developments, see Chadwick-Jones (1976).

50.   An extensive literature on the theory of power does already exist upon which organisation theorists can draw. See, for example, the wide range of articles in Olsen (1970) and the discussion presented by Lukes (1974). Lukes' distinction between different views of power has much in common with the distinction which we have drawn between the functionalist and radical structuralist paradigms.

51.   We will return to this in our concluding chapter.

6. Interpretive Sociology

Origins and Intellectual Tradition

The interpretive paradigm embraces a wide range of philosophical and sociological thought which shares the common characteristic of attempting to understand and explain the social world primarily from the point of view of the actors directly involved in the social process. Its history is firmly rooted in the German idealist tradition, and in the view that the ultimate reality of the universe lies in 'spirit' or 'idea' rather than in the data of sense perception. This tradition, which runs counter to that of sociological positivism, owes much to the work of Immanuel Kant (1724–1803), who was one of the first philosophers to articulate its basic ontological and epistemological foundations. Kant, whose philosophy is open to a wide range of interpretations, posited that *a priori* knowledge must precede any grasp or understanding of the sense data of empirical experience. He argued that there must be inherent, in-born organising principles within man's consciousness by which any and all sense data is structured, arranged and thus understood. *A priori* knowledge was seen as independent of any external reality and the sense data which it 'emits'; it was seen as the product of 'mind' and the interpretive processes which go on within it. Whilst the world in which men live may be the product of a complex interrelationship between *a priori* knowledge and empirical reality, for Kant the starting point for understanding this lay in the realm of 'mind' and 'intuition'. It is this basic, uncomplicated assumption which underlies the whole of German idealism.

The development of idealism has, however, been far from uniform. Subject to diverse influences ranging from the 'romantic' writings of Goethe and Schiller to the somewhat dogmatic philosophy of Hegel, its fortunes have been mixed. From a period of ascendency in European thought during the later eighteenth and early nineteenth centuries, it was thereafter more or less forced into a secondary place by the 'practical' achievements of sociological positivism. However, by the end of the nineteenth century a revivial of interest was underway, giving rise to the so-called neo-idealist, or neo-Kantian movement.

As H. Stuart Hughes has so clearly argued, the period 1890–1930 was a time of considerable intellectual ferment characterised by a concern with the subjective aspects of scientific enquiry. The major intellectual figures of the 1890s 'were obsessed, almost intoxicated, with a rediscovery of the non-logical, the uncivilised, the inexplicable' (H. S. Hughes, 1958, p. 35). This interest in the subjective and irrational was reflected in the work of writers as widely diverse as Freud, Weber and Husserl, each of whom responded in his own distinctive fashion.[1] In addition to focusing attention upon the essentially complex and problematic nature of human behaviour and experience, the work of this generation of theorists returned to the basic problems of epistemology identified by Kant, which confronted both the natural and social sciences. The positivist position came to be seen as increasingly unsatisfactory and problematic on at least two counts. First, within the natural sciences (*Naturwissenschaften*) it became clear that human values intruded upon the process of scientific enquiry. It was evident that scientific method could no longer be regarded as value-free; the frame of reference of the scientific observer was increasingly seen as an active force which determined the way in which scientific knowledge was obtained. Within the realm of the cultural sciences (*Geisteswissenschaften*) a second set of difficulties were also seen as arising, since their subject matter was distinguished by its essentially spiritual character. It was realised that man as an actor could not be studied through the methods of the natural sciences, with their concern for establishing general laws. In the cultural sphere, it was held, man was 'not subject to law in the physical sense, but was free. An intellectual apprehension of his life and action could be attained only by the speculative methods of philosophy, especially by a process of the intuition of the total wholes (*Gestalten*) which it was illegitimate to break down by "atomistic" analysis' (Parsons, 1949, p. 475). As a result of this disenchantment with sociological positivism, idealism assumed a new lease of life. In short, there was a distinctive shift in the focus of intellectual attention along the subjective—objective dimension of our analytical scheme, which involved certain theorists in clarifying the intellectual foundations of what we describe as the interpretive paradigm.

Among the theorists who have contributed to these intellectual foundations, we identify Wilhelm Dilthey, Max Weber and Edmund Husserl as having been particularly influential. In fundamentally distinct ways they have done much to define the character and issues which have commanded the attention of interpretive sociology during the twentieth century.

Dilthey (1833–1911) and Weber (1864–1920) were particularly concerned to bridge the gulf between idealism and positivism, or at least place the cultural sciences upon a firm foundation in terms of their 'objective validity'.[2] If the cultural sciences were defined by their spiritual character, then the 'spirit' of a social situation or type of institution was of key importance. This posed considerable problems for social philosophers, who were concerned to provide explanations of social and historical affairs without reverting to the methods of positivism. The idealist process of 'the intuition of total wholes' provided a means of organising the historical process but got no closer to an understanding of it. It often resulted in an entirely relativistic view of history as a series of unique and essentially unconnected systems. Explanations in the idealist tradition, it seemed, could only be provided through recourse to intuition or metaphysics.[3]

Dilthey's solution to the problem was found in the notion of *verstehen* (understanding). In drawing a distinction between the natural and cultural sciences, he maintained that the difference between them was essentially one of substance, and that the two types of science addressed themselves to fundamentally different kinds of subject matter. Whereas the natural sciences investigated external processes in a material world, the cultural sciences were essentially concerned with the internal processes of human minds. Even though these processes may be translated into relatively tangible cultural phenomena such as art, poetry, institutions and the like, it was maintained that they could only be fully understood in relation to the minds which created them and the inner experience which they reflected. Cultural phenomena were, in essence, seen as the external manifestations of such inner experience and hence, it was argued, could only be fully appreciated with this reference point in view. In these situations the approach and the methods of the natural sciences, with their emphasis upon the search for general laws and causal explanations, were deemed inappropriate. The cultural sciences needed a new analytical method based on *verstehen*, through which the investigator could seek to understand human beings, their inner minds and their feelings, and the way these are expressed in their outward actions and achievements. In short, the outward manifestations of human life needed to be interpreted in terms of the inner experience which they reflected through the *method* of *verstehen*.

We wish to place emphasis here upon the word *method* since, as conceptualised by Dilthey and later by Weber, this was its essential status. *Verstehen* was viewed as a method which could be used in the cultural sciences to generate scientific knowledge of an objectivity comparable with that obtained in the natural sciences. The notion of *verstehen* provided a means of studying the world of human affairs by reliving or re-enacting the experience of others. As we shall see, Dilthey's view of *verstehen* has had an important, direct and formative influence upon the hermeneutic school of thought which we discuss later in this chapter. In more general terms, his social philosophy had a marked but indirect influence upon the development of many other elements of thought characteristic of the interpretive paradigm. Indeed, the notion of 'understanding' in one form or another is a defining characteristic of all theories located within this paradigm.

Despite Dilthey's importance and underlying formative influence, it is through the work of Weber that the notion of *verstehen* as method has had the greatest impact on sociological thought, and nowhere is the bridge-building exercise between idealism and positivism more evident.[4] As Hughes (1958), Runciman (1972) and others have suggested, Weber was fighting a war on at least two fronts. He was dissatisfied with the superficialities which he regarded as characterising positivist explanations of society, and also greatly concerned with the subjective and 'unscientific' nature of idealist thought. His solution to the problem is found in his methodological writings, in which he develops the view that explanations of social affairs must be 'adequate on the level of meaning', and that the essential function of social science is to be 'interpretive', that is, to understand the subjective meaning of social action. He defines sociology as 'a science which attempts the interpretive understanding of social action in order thereby to arrive at a causal explanation of its courses and effects ... Action is social insofar as, by virtue of the subjective meaning attached to it by the acting individual (or individuals), it takes account of the behaviour of others, and is thereby oriented in its course' (Weber, 1947. p. 88).[5]

This definition clearly reflects the attempted fusion of idealist and positivist perspectives. He adheres to the positivists' concern for providing causal explanations of social phenomena but insists that such explanations must be reduced to the level of the individual. As Schutz notes, 'Weber reduces all kinds of social relationships and structures, all cultural objectifications, all realms of objective mind, to the most elementary forms of individual behaviour' (Schutz, 1967, p. 6). His view of sociology is thus one which is concerned to provide causal explanations of social phenomena whilst avoiding the pitfalls of reification. He is concerned to build an objective science of sociology upon the foundations of subjective meaning and individual action.

In this task Weber's notion of the 'ideal type' plays a central part.[6] Indeed, Weber insists that objectivity in the social sciences is only made possible through the use of ideal types, which allow for the ordering of elements of reality. Through the use of these constructs Weber attempts to reconcile the method of *verstehen* with the need to develop an objective social science. Ideal types incorporate the 'spirit' which characterises individual phenomena into a wider generalised whole. In certain important respects, therefore, the method of *verstehen* is assimilated into a typological scheme of analysis which provides a means of ordering and explaining human action.

Weber thus seeks to balance and reconcile the potentially divergent perspectives of idealism and positivism. Whilst stressing the importance of subjective meaning in explanations of social affairs, he at the same time seeks to contain and limit the role of these subjective factors. This is clearly evident, for example, in his classification of behaviour into different types such as 'rationally purposive', 'rationally value-orientated', 'emotional' and 'traditional'. Although the central task of his sociology is to understand and interpret social action, he constrains this endeavour by the implicit assumption that behaviour can be causally explained with reference to fairly narrowly defined typologies of action.

Viewed critically, therefore, Weber's stand with regard to 'interpretive sociology' can be seen as reflecting certain strains and tensions. Interpretation and the notion of *verstehen* in Weber's hands acts as little more than a methodological tool for overcoming obvious deficiencies in positivist method. Essentially, Weber is interested in developing a causal theory of social explanation rather than in pursuing the full implications of the idealist view of the nature of social reality. As Schutz (1967) has observed, Weber was most concerned with confronting concrete problems and was interested in the more fundamental epistemological issues only insofar as they had a contribution to make towards this end.

Weber can be seen as a 'sociologist of regulation', in that one of his central concerns was to provide a thorough-going analysis of social order. In this the notion of rationality was accorded a central role. Whether he can be more appropriately described as a positivist rather than an idealist will no doubt continue to be debated.[7] As far as the four strands of the subjective—objective dimension of our analytical scheme is concerned, he appears to occupy an intermediate and somewhat incongruent position. In terms of methodology, his interpretive perspective would suggest a location on the boundary of the interpretive paradigm, along with Dilthey's hermeneutics. His position with regard to ontology, epistemology and human nature would appear to be more objectivist. For Weber, the objective reality of the social world is not a central issue. It is the way in which it is interpreted by human actors that is important. In this his position directly parallels the theoretical perspective which we have described as behavioural symbolic interaction within the context of the functionalist paradigm. As we have suggested, theory and research based upon the action frame of reference, which derives more or less directly from Weber's explorations in methodology, is most appropriately located there, and it would seem that a similar case can be made in relation to much of Weber's other work.

What, then, is Weber's significance as far as the interpretive paradigm is concerned? We argue that it arises from his role as a point of departure for other writers, notably Schutz, who have taken Weber's work as a base from which to develop a much more subjectivist view of sociology. It will be apparent from our discussion later in the chapter that the notion of *verstehen* in other hands has assumed a significance beyond that of mere method. As Giddens has noted, from a phenomenological point of view 'it is the very ontological condition of human life in society as such' (Giddens, 1976, p. 19). This ontological status of *verstehen* is clearly evident, for example, in the work of Edmund Husserl, and it will be helpful if we conclude our discussion of the origins and intellectual traditions of the interpretive paradigm with a brief review of his work. The extremely subjectivist position which he adopts will also serve to illustrate the essentially intermediate perspective reflected in Weber.

Edmund Husserl (1859–1938) is widely regarded as the founder and leading exponent of the phenomenological movement in philosophy. As will become apparent from our discussion later in the chapter, it is not altogether a coherent movement and does not lend itself to any simple and straightforward definition. Maurice Natanson, one of phenomenology's leading contemporary spokesmen, offers the following characterisation:

> Phenomenology is a presuppositionless philosophy which holds consciousness to be the matrix of all phenomena, considers phenomena to be objects of intentional acts and treats them as essences, demands its own method, concerns itself with prepredictative experience, offers

itself as the foundation of science, and comprises a philosophy of the life world, a defence of Reason, and ultimately a critique of philosophy. (Natanson, 1973b, p. 19)

Husserlian phenomenology is based upon a fundamental questioning of the common-sense, 'taken for granted' attitudes which characterise everyday life and the realms of natural science. As Natanson has suggested, 'the central endeavour of phenomenology is to transcend [what Husserl calls] the natural attitude of daily life in order to render it an object for philosophical scrutiny and in order to describe and account for its essential structure' (Natanson, 1966, p. 3). The view that there is an objective external world which exists in space and time and is real for all men is subjected to thorough scrutiny. The presuppositions of science are reduced to implicit metaphysical commitments. In the process the external world is shown to be an artefact of consciousness; phenomena are shown to be willed into existence through intentional acts. Man is shown to live in a world created through consciousness.

Husserl thus adopts an extremely subjectivist position in relation to the subjective—objective dimension of our analytical scheme. Ontologically, the world constitutes a stream of consciousness; it is experiential; the subjective is the source of all objectivities. The task of epistemology is to explore and reveal the essential types and structures of experience. Phenomenology studies essences and clarifies the relationships between them; it seeks to delve into experiences and clarify the very grounds of knowledge. In this endeavour the methods of 'direct intuition' and 'insight into essential structures' are offered as the principal means of penetrating the depths of consciousness and transcending the world of everyday affairs in search of subjectivity in its pure form. The procedure of *époche* – whereby the phenomenologist suspends his complicity and participation in the 'natural attitude' – also plays a central role. As Natanson puts it, 'believing-in-the world is the paradigm of normality. The philosopher's task is not to ridicule it but to understand it and point out its implications. Any attempt to examine such believing will be prejudiced, however, by the philosopher's own believing unless he finds a way to free himself of the very attitude he seeks to elucidate' (Natanson, 1973b, p. 15). *Époche*, or suspended complicity, provides a means of entering the realm of subjectivity which phenomenology seeks to analyse and describe.

Compared with the philosophy of Husserl, Weber's

'interpretive sociology' thus emerges as a very limited excursion into the realm of the subjective. It is perhaps fair to say that it does little more than attribute an element of voluntarism to the individual's interpretation of his world which more positivist theories typical of the functionalist paradigm tend to deny, or at least ignore.

Interestingly enough, Husserl, like Weber, began to articulate his distinctive intellectual position as a result of his dissatisfaction with conventional science. He began his academic career as a mathematician and physicist but soon became concerned with what he regarded as defects in their essential foundations.[8] He was passionately committed to the ideal of a 'rigorous science' and looked to philosophy and logic for answers to what he saw as the fundamental problems. Disappointed with what he found, his desire to penetrate to the sources of science led him to an increasingly subjectivist position, and the conclusion that philosophy required a phenomenological reorganisation which would 'assist even the objective scientist in the clarification and critique of his unclarified fundamental concepts and assumptions' (Spiegelberg, 1965, p. 79).

Like Weber, Husserl was highly dissatisfied with positivist science, with its uncritical study of mere facts and its inability to cope with problems of ultimate truth and validity. However, whilst Weber concerned himself with the refinement of methodology and addressed himself to what he saw as the fundamental problems of social science, Husserl travelled in another direction. Addressing himself to fundamental problems of ontology, epistemology and methodology, he embarked upon an intellectual journey leading to a radically subjectivist form of transcendental phenomenology. In so doing he laid the foundations for further exploration in the highly subjectivist region of the interpretive paradigm.

The Structure of the Paradigm

Whilst its intellectual roots can be traced back to the work of the early German idealists, the interpretive paradigm has been most decisively shaped and influenced by the works of Dilthey, Husserl and Weber. For the most part, therefore, it can be regarded as a twentieth-century phenomenon.

We argue that the paradigm can be considered in terms of four distinct but related categories of interpretive theory, distinguished for the most part by their degree of 'subjectivity' in terms of the four strands of the subjective—objective dimension of our analytical scheme.[9] We identify them as (a) solipsism; (b) phenomenology; (c) phenomenological sociology; (d) hermeneutics. Their location within the paradigm is illustrated in Figure 3.3.

The Hermeneutic school occupies the least subjectivist region of the paradigm. Deriving largely from the work of Dilthey and the notion of *verstehen*, it first evolved as a method of study especially adapted to an idealist view of the world. More recently, under the influence of Gadamer, it has assumed a new dimension and has developed in broader theoretical terms, particularly in relation to the role and influence of language in social life. Its contemporary importance within the context of the interpretive paradigm is rapidly increasing, though up to now has been largely overshadowed by its use in critical theory within the context of the radical humanist paradigm. We identify *solipsism* in the most subjectivist region of the paradigm. It belongs to the realm of metaphysics rather than sociology and is included here to highlight the ultimate dilemma facing all philosophical and sociological perspectives which emphasise the subjective in an extreme form.

Phenomenology occupies the middle ground of the paradigm. We distinguish between the *transcendental phenomenology* of Husserl and the *existential phenomenology* of Schutz. The latter attempts to link themes drawn from the sociology of Weber and the philosophy of Husserl.

Closely related to phenomenology, but distinct from it, we identify two branches of sociological thought which combine the phenomenological perspective with elements drawn from elsewhere. *Ethnomethodology* fuses phenomenology and elements of ordinary language philosophy, particularly that typical of the work of the later Wittgenstein and Winch. *Phenomenological symbolic interactionism* interprets the work of G. H. Mead from a phenomenological perspective, in the manner discussed in an earlier chapter.

We will examine each broad category and school of thought in turn.

Hermeneutics

Hermeneutics is concerned with interpreting and understanding the products of the human mind which characterise the social and cultural world. Ontologically, its proponents adopt an 'objective idealist' view of the socio-cultural environment, seeing it as a humanly constructed phenomenon. Human beings in the course of life externalise the internal processes of their minds through the creation of cultural artefacts which attain an objective character. Institutions, works of art, literature, languages, religions and the like are examples of this process of objectification. Such objectifications of the human mind are the subject of study in hermeneutics.

As we have already noted, it is largely through the work of Dilthey that hermeneutics has achieved the status of a school of thought within the context of contemporary social theory.[10] In Dilthey's hands it was essentially a methodology for studying the objectifications of mind. It played a central role in his overall scheme for generating objectively valid knowledge in the *Geisteswissenschaften* through the method of *verstehen*. *Verstehen*, we recall, was the means by which we comprehend the meaning of a historical or social situation or cultural artefact. It was a method of understanding based upon re-enactment. In order to be comprehended, the subject of study needed to be relived in the subjective life of the observer. Through this process, Dilthey claimed, objective knowledge could be obtained.

Dilthey argued that one of the main avenues for *verstehen* was through the study of empirical life assertions – institutions, historical situations, language, etc. – which reflected the inner life of their creators. The study of these social creations was seen as the main avenue to an understanding of the world of objective mind. The method was that of hermeneutics. As he puts it,

> Re-creating and re-living what is alien and past shows clearly how understanding rests on special, personal inspiration. But, as this is a significant and permanent condition of historical science, personal inspiration becomes a technique which develops with the development of historical consciousness. It is dependent on permanently fixed expressions being available so that understanding can always return to them. The methodical understanding of permanently fixed expressions we call exegesis. As the life of the mind only finds its complete, exhaustive and, therefore, objectively comprehensible expression in language, exegesis culminates in the interpretation of the written records of human existence. This method is the basis of philology. The science of this method is hermeneutics. (Dilthey, 1976, p. 228)

Dilthey singled out hermeneutics as a key discipline and method in the human sciences. He advocated that social phenomena of all kinds should be analysed in detail, and interpreted as texts, to reveal their essential meaning and significance. The method of hermeneutics thus involved human scientists adopting the style of literary analysts rather than natural scientists. Textual analysis of meaning and significance was regarded as more appropriate than a scientific search for knowledge of general laws. Dilthey was concerned that the basic rules of hermeneutics should be defined, so that the insights of interpreters of rare genius could be utilised by others.

Dilthey's overall approach to hermeneutics is clearly illustrated in the notion of the so-called 'hermeneutic circle'. He recognised that the social whole cannot be understood independently of its parts, and vice versa. Words in a sentence have to be understood in terms of their total context. Whilst one can attribute a particular meaning to words on their own account, they may assume a different meaning in the context of other words. So, too, with social phenomena. Dilthey recognised that this part—whole relationship was characteristic of the social world and that a systematic approach was necessary. The desire to formulate methodical rules of interpretation, therefore, was accompanied by a recognition that 'there are no absolute starting points, no self-evident, self-contained certainties on which we can build, because we always find ourselves in the middle of complex situations which we try .to disentangle by making, then revising, provisional assumptions' (Rickman, 1976, p. 11). In this way the methodological rules of hermeneutics were seen to move in a circular and iterative fashion towards an increased understanding of the objectifications of mind.

In recent years the hermeneutic tradition has assumed a new line of development particularly through the work of Gadamer (1965).[11] He argues that the circle of understanding, as envisaged, for example, by Dilthey, is not a 'methodological' circle, but describes an ontological structural element in understanding. Taking Heidegger's description and existential account of the hermeneutic circle as a point of departure, he argues that we cannot relate, for example, to a historic tradition as if it existed as an object apart from us, since there is an interplay between the movement of tradition and the interpreter. In order to understand social or cultural phenomena, the observer must enter into a dialogue with the subject of study. As Giddens puts it,

> Understanding a text from a historical period remote from our own, for example, or from a culture very different from our own is, according to

Gadamer, essentially a creative process in which the observer, through penetrating an alien mode of existence, enriches his own self-knowledge through acquiring knowledge of others. *Verstehen* consists, not in placing oneself "inside" the subjective experience of a text's author, but in understanding literary art through grasping, to use Wittgenstein's term, the "form of life" which gives it meaning. (Giddens, 1976, p. 56)

With Gadamer, *verstehen* is not so much concerned with 're-living' or entering into the subjective experiences of others as it was for Dilthey. It is more concerned with appreciating the interchange of the frames of reference of the observer and the observed. In this process the role of language is given a central role 'as the medium of intersubjectivity and as the concrete expression of "forms of life", or what Gadamer calls traditions' (Giddens, 1976, p. 56). Language is the mediator between frames of reference or traditions, and is thus central to the process of understanding.

Extended and developed in this way, hermeneutics in Gadamer's hands becomes relevant to all areas of enquiry: 'a universal mode of philosophy' and not just a methodological foundation for the cultural sciences. The role of language assumes ontological status and brings Gadamer's view of hermeneutics close to a phenomenological perspective. Language, for Gadamer, is more than a system of symbols for labelling the external world; it becomes an expression of the human mode of 'being in the world'. As Gadamer says, 'Being is manifest in language'.[12]

From the perspective of sociology as opposed to that of philosophy, the hermeneutic school of thought has as yet received relatively little attention within the context of the interpretive paradigm. Its main impact has been upon the radical humanist paradigm, where the insights of Gadamer have generated interest in the role of language within the context of critical theory, particularly as developed by Habermas.

Solipsism

Solipsism represents the most extreme form of subjective idealism, in that it denies that the world has any distinct independent reality. For the solipsist, the world is the creation of his mind.

Ontologically, it has no existence beyond the sensations which he perceives in his mind and body.[13]

The solipsist view is most often associated with the work of the Irish cleric Bishop Berkeley (1685–1753), though in point of fact he did not adhere to such an extreme standpoint himself.[14] Berkeley questioned the common-sense belief that man is surrounded by a world of external objects such as trees, mountains, tables, streams, chairs, etc., and suggested that they may be merely the products of our perception. He argued that they may have no distinct existence, being no more than our ideas. They may exist only in our mind. What we mean when we say that a thing exists is that it is perceived. An object may have no existence beyond this ideal perception.

The solipsist perspective often attracts scorn and ridicule from those who wish to continue to subscribe to a common-sense view of an everyday world with a hard and fast external reality. However, Berkeley's argument is often equal to the challenge and not easily refuted. Boswell reports how Berkeley's contemporary, Dr Johnson, kicked a nearby stone saying, 'I refute it thus' (Boswell, 1953, p. 333). Dr Johnson's experience, however, in Berkeley's terms, was reducible to the *perception* of pain and bodily sensations which Johnson may have located in his toe. The attempted refutation was thus consistent with Berkeley's thesis that the world is no more than what we perceive it to be.[15]

The solipsist position results in a complete relativism and scepticism. Given that there is no external point of reference, knowledge must be limited to what we as individuals experience. It is an entirely individual and personal affair; there is nothing beyond oneself and one's ideas. The solipsist position is thus one which is logically permissible but inward-looking and self-sustaining, and it offers no scope for the development of a philosophy or social theory which can be shared in any realistic sense.

We characterise solipsism as occupying the most subjectivist region of the subjective—objective dimension of our analytical scheme. The notions of regulation and radical change clearly have no significance within a solipsist perspective; solipsism is thus consistent with both the interpretive and radical humanist paradigms. Its significance within the context of each is, for the most part, a negative one, in that it presents a potential danger to social theorists who wish to develop social theories with a subjective emphasis. Subjectivist philosophies run the danger of being grounded upon Sartre's 'reef of solipsism', of entering an entirely individualistic and subjectivist view of reality in which no meaningful discourse is possible. As we shall find in later discussion, the 'reef of solipsism' has been seen as a potential threat to a number of social philosophers, notably Husserl.

In a more positive sense, in emphasising extreme subjectivism solipsism defines the essentially intermediate and more moderate status of other subjectivist philosophies. In adopting a completely relativist position it illustrates the extent to which other views of social reality and knowledge of the world are based essentially upon shared meanings. It also highlights the equally extreme nature of the common-sense notion of a world of hard-and-fast objective reality.

Solipsism is thus located within the context of the interpretive and radical humanist paradigm as a logically tenable position, but one which is of little importance within the context of contemporary sociology.

Phenomenology

As we have already noted, the phenomenological movement is not altogether a coherent one, since it reflects a number of lines of development. Taking the work of Husserl as a point of departure, it branches off in a number of directions according to the perspective of its particular exponent. Writers such as Scheller, Heidegger, Schutz, Sartre and Merleau-Ponty have all made significant and distinctive contributions towards its overall development.[16]

We will discuss phenomenology here under two broad headings. First, we shall devote attention to what is known as 'transcendental' or 'pure' phenomenology, which is most often associated with the work of Husserl. Second, we will consider a derivative of this, 'existential' phenomenology, particularly as reflected in the work of Schutz.

Transcendental phenomenology

It will be recalled that Husserl was a mathematician and physicist who, early in his career, became concerned with what he regarded as the precarious foundations of logic and science. It was characteristic of the man that he should decide to investigate the source of these foundations. In so doing he embarked upon a life's work, throughout which he was preoccupied by the problem of foundations.

One of his earliest observations was that science was characterised by 'intentionality'. Despite the fact that the results of science were always approximate and imperfect, the scientist was guided by the intention of absolute objectivity. It was this aim of science, this idea of science rather than its results, that was important in distinguishing it as a discipline worthy of its name.

In his quest for the objective foundations of science, Husserl attempted to open up a new direction in the analysis of consciousness. Bringing a mathematical mind to the subject, he contented himself with the manipulation of ideal essences. Rather than bother with factual realities or the formulation of hypotheses, he addressed himself to the central question of meaning. He put reality aside (or in his term, 'in brackets') and sought to penetrate to the level of the phenomenon. In other words, he sought to practise phenomenology. As Thévenaz puts it,

> Phenomenology is never an investigation of external or internal facts. On the contrary, it silences experience provisionally, leaves the question of objective reality or of real content aside in order to turn its attention solely and simply on *the reality in consciousness*, on the objects insofar as they are intended by and in consciousness, in short on what Husserl calls ideal essences. By this we must not understand mere subjective representations (which would leave us on the plane of psychology) nor ideal *realities* (which would 'reify' or hypostasise unduly the data of consciousness and would put us on the level of metaphysics), but precisely the *'phenomena'* . . . The phenomenon here is that which manifests itself immediately in consciousness; it is grasped in an invitation that precedes any reflexion or any judgement. It has only to be allowed to show itself, to manifest itself: *the phenomenon is that which gives itself (Selbstgebung)*. The phenomenological method then, faced with the objects and the contents of knowledge, consists in neglecting what alone counts for philosophers and scientists, namely their value, their reality or unreality. It consists in describing them such as they give themselves, as pure and simple intentions (*visées*) of consciousness, as meanings, to render them visible and manifest as such. In this *Wesenschau*, the essence (*Wesen*) is neither ideal *reality* nor psychological reality, but ideal intention (*visée*), intentional object of consciousness, immanent to consciousness. (Thévenaz, 1962, pp. 43–4)

Such is the nature of the phenomenon which Husserl sought. In his quest for the source, for the foundations of logic and the sciences and eventually the whole of philosophy, Husserl began to develop his phenomenological analysis. In his search he quickly realised that phenomenological analysis had to penetrate way beyond superficial description of appearance or intuition. With Husserl, knowledge, which in ordinary pre-philosophical thought is the most natural thing in the world, assumes the status of a 'mystery'. The search was for the primary, absolute evidence which, like the phenomenon, was complete, clearly established and in need of nothing outside itself to give it form.

In this endeavour the method of *épeche*, to which we have already referred, was to play a central role, opening the way for the 'phenomenological reduction' and the exploration of a new and fundamental level of meaning — the transcendental field. In this transcendental philosophy Husserl attempts to grasp 'the world as phenomenon' — to grasp it not as an object, but as pure meaning. The fundamental, original and essential purpose of the reduction is to 'bring to light [the] essential intentional contact between consciousness and the world' (Thévenaz, 1962, p. 47).

The phenomenological reduction thus leads to a conjunction between pure consciousness and the world phenomenon. All the assumptions of everyday life are brushed aside in the pursuit of pure subjectivity, of transcendental consciousness, the intentionality of which is the source of all meaning. This notion of intentionality — the idea that consciousness always has an object that constitutes it — plays a crucial role in Husserl's philosophy. It denies the possibility of there being an independent reality of any kind. At the same time, reality is not constructed by consciousness; it is revealed to it through the act of intentionality. This pursuit of transcendental consciousness brought Husserl perilously close to solipsism. As the external everyday world was swept away in search of the transcendental, pure consciousness was left in splendid isolation, its intentionality the sole link with any semblance of a wider reality. It occupied an isolated and self-contained realm of its own. All else was a product of its intentional nature. Accordingly, there was no external means of validating its existence. The 'reef of solipsism' loomed near.

This was a problem which greatly concerned Husserl during his later years, and he fought hard to find a way out of this solipsist dilemma, particularly through the notion of 'intersubjectivity'. He sought 'to show how the transcendental ego constitutes other egos as equal partners in an intersubjective community, which in turn forms the foundations for the 'objective' (that is, the intersubjective) world. His arguments in this direction were not altogether convincing, given that the transcendental aspects of his philosophy were to be maintained intact, but, as we shall see, they laid important foundations for the development of 'existential phenomenology', particularly as developed by Shutz. Most of Husserl's followers were content to dwell on the lived-in world of experience.[17] They were not prepared to follow the road to transcendentalism and largely abandoned this aspect of Husserl's philosophy. As far as the interpretive paradigm is concerned, transcendental phenomenology has been the subject of very little further development. Occupying a position towards the subjectivist extreme of the paradigm, its main significance has been as a springboard, or at least a point of departure, for less subjectively orientated brands of phenomenology. We will discuss the most important of these in the next section.

Interestingly enough, Husserl's transcendental notions have been adopted to a certain extent by theorists operating within a perspective characteristic of the radical humanist paradigm. Transcendence, from their point of view, has been seen as indicating a potential for release from the bonds of everyday life. The work of Sartre, in particular, reflects the direct influence of Husserl, and we will return to a discussion of this in a later chapter.

Existential phenomenology

The existential wing of the phenomenological movement is most often associated with the work of Heidegger, Merleau-Ponty, Sartre and Schutz. They share a common concern for what Husserl called the 'life-world' (*Lebenswelt*), for the world of everyday experience as opposed to the realm of transcendental consciousness. However, apart from this concern with the 'life-world' and the way in which men exist within it, it is misleading to view their work in similar terms. Each develops a theoretical perspective which, whilst adhering to a roughly similar position in terms of the various strands of the subjective—objective dimension of our analytical scheme, addresses itself to quite different issues and problems.[18] We will confine our discussion of existential phenomenology here to the work of Schutz who, in his attempt to develop a 'phenomenology of the social world', brings the subject down from the realm of philosophical discourse to something approaching a sociological perspective.

The work of Alfred Schutz (1899–1959) can be characterised as a sustained effort to relate the idea of phenomenology to the problems of sociology. In essence, it seeks to link the perspectives of Weber and Husserl, drawing also upon the philosophy of Bergson.

Schutz commences his classic work *The Phenomenology of the Social World*, first published in 1932, by stating that it is based upon an intensive concern of many years' duration with the theoretical writings of Max Weber. Whilst convinced that Weber's approach was correct and that it provided 'a proper starting point for the philosophy of the social sciences', Schutz felt sure that it 'did not go deeply enough to lay the foundations on which alone many of the problems of the human sciences could be solved' (1967, pp. xxxi).

Driving down to these foundations, in the manner of Husserl, Schutz identified a number of ambiguities in Weber's position and subjected them to thorough philosophical analysis. While agreeing with Weber that the essential function of social science was to be *interpretive*, that is, to understand the subjective meaning of social action, he felt that Weber had failed to state the essential characteristics of 'understanding' (*verstehen*), 'subjective meaning' and 'action'. For Schutz, a thorough-going analysis of these concepts was essential in order to place the subject matter and methods of the social sciences upon a firm basis.

Schutz embarks upon a phenomenological analysis of meaning, searching for its origins in the 'stream of consciousness'. This notion, which he derives from Bergson, is crucial to his analysis, since it introduces the temporal dimension which underlies the concept of 'reflexivity'. Schutz argues that consciousness is fundamentally an unbroken stream of lived experiences which have no meaning in themselves. Meaning is dependent upon reflexivity – the process of turning back on oneself and looking at what has been going on. Meaning is attached to actions retrospectively; only the already-experienced is meaningful, not that which is in the process of being experienced.

Schutz also argues that this process of attributing meaning reflexively is dependent upon the actor's identifying the purpose or goal which he or she is supposedly seeking. This introduces the notion of being able to attribute meaning, in advance, to future experiences. The concept of meaningful action thus contains elements of both past and anticipated future; intrinsically it has a temporal dimension. Schutz's analysis of this 'constituting process in internal time consciousness' is a direct application of the 'phenomenological reduction' as described by Husserl. The natural attitude towards the 'world-given-to-me-as-being-there' is suspended in the manner of the *époche*, in an attempt to penetrate to the essence of consciousness and meaning. Whilst appropriate for the above purpose, Schutz specifically recognises that the analysis of meaning in everyday social life does not require the transcendental knowledge yielded by the phenomenological reduction. As he proceeds to the study of the social world, therefore, he abandons the strictly phenomenological method. He accepts the existence of the social world as presented in the natural attitude and focuses upon the problem of intersubjective understanding, 'by-passing a whole nest of problems' identified by Husserl in relation to the issue of transcendental subjectivity and intersubjectivity' (Schutz, 1967, p. 94).

Schutz's analysis of intersubjectivity is thus principally informed by a sociological as opposed to a phenomenological perspective. It reflects a predilection for the 'life-world' as opposed to that of transcendental philosophy. Basically, Schutz is concerned to throw light upon the way in which we come to know the lived experience of others. In this he makes a fundamental distinction 'between *the genuine understanding of the other person* and the abstract conceptualisation of his actions or thoughts as being of such and such a type' (1967, pp. xxv). Genuine understanding means the intentional grasping of the experience of the other, in a manner akin to looking into the other's stream of consciousness. It reflects the true comprehension of subjective meaning. The abstract conceptualisation does not refer so much to understanding, as to 'self-elucidation'; it is merely an ordering of one's own experience into categories. Genuine understanding is possible in face-to-face 'we-relations'; it depends upon direct exchange and interaction. As we pass from these situations of direct interaction to modes of indirect experience of others, we have to resort to more and more abstract conceptualisation.

For Schutz, the process of understanding the conduct of others can be understood as a process of *typification*, whereby the actor applies interpretive constructs akin to 'ideal types' to apprehend the meanings of what people do. These constructs are derived from the experience of everyday life and the stock of knowledge or common-sense understandings which comprise the natural attitude. It is through the use of typifications that we classify and organise our everyday reality. The typifications are learned through our biographical situation. They are handed to us according to our social context. Knowledge of everyday life is thus socially ordered. The notion of typification or ideal type is thus not a merely methodological device as envisaged by Weber, but an inherent feature of our everyday world.[19]

Schutz argues that the stock of knowledge which we use to typify the actions of others and understand the world around us varies from context to context. We live in a world of 'multiple realities', each of which is defined in terms of 'finite provinces of meaning'. The social actor shifts between these provinces of meaning in the course of his everyday life. As he shifts from the world of work to that of home and leisure or to the world of religious experience, different ground rules are brought into play. Whilst it is within the normal competence of the acting individual to shift from one sphere to another, to do so calls for a 'leap of consciousness' to overcome the differences between the different worlds.[20]

For Schutz, therefore, the problem of understanding the meaning structure of the world of everyday life was a central concern. 'To see this world in its massive complexity, to outline and explore its essential features, and to trace out its manifold relationships were the composite parts of his central task, the realization of a philosophy of mundane reality, or, in more formal language, of a phenomenology of the natural attitude' (Schutz, 1962, p. xxv). The central task of social science, according to Schutz, was to understand the social world from the point of view of those living within it, using constructs and explanations which are intelligible in terms of the common-sense interpretation of everyday life.[21]

Schutz thus attempts to link phenomenology and sociology in an analysis of the world of everyday affairs. His attempt, whilst generating many insights, is only partially successful. The substantive links with the transcendental philosophy of Husserl are at times very tenuous, particularly with regard to the issue of intersubjectivity. This notion is crucial to Schutz's analysis, yet extremely problematic within the context of transcendental phenomenology, for reasons which we have already discussed. The inner world of intentional consciousness and the outer manifestations of the world of everyday life are at times uneasy bedfellows. The phenomenological enterprise *per se* encounters serious difficulties in attempting to deal with any reality outside the individual's consciousness, and Shutz's work reflects this dilemma.

Judged from the standpoint of his other major intellectual point of departure – the theoretical work of Max Weber – Schutz's phenomenology of the social world must be considered a major advance in social theory. In essence, Schutz pursues the ontological assumptions implicit in Weber's methodology and develops an overall approach which reflects a consistent and coherent stance in terms of the four strands of the subjective—objective dimension of our analytical scheme. Schutz demonstrates that the notions of subjective meaning, understanding and social action have much wider ramifications than those reflected in Weber's work. In comparison with Schutz, Weber's location within the context of the functionalist as opposed to the interpretive paradigm becomes clearly evident.

Phenomenological Sociology

Both schools of thought identified in this category of interpretive theory occupy a similar position in relation to the two dimensions of our analytical scheme. We distinguish between them largely because they have developed from parallel but somewhat different phenomenological traditions. Ethnomethodology derives largely from the phenomenology of Schutz, and phenomenological symbolic interactionism from the work of G. H. Mead.

Ethnomethodology

Ethnomethodology is grounded in the detailed study of the world of everyday life. Essentially, it seeks 'to treat practical activities, practical circumstances, and practical sociological reasoning as topics of empirical study, and by paying to the most commonplace activities of daily life the attention usually accorded extraordinary events, seeks to learn about them as phenomena in their own right' (Garfinkel, 1967, p. 1). It is concerned to learn about the ways in which people order and make sense of their everyday activities and the ways in which they make them 'accountable' to others, in the sense of being 'observable and reportable'. Interactions between people in everyday life can be regarded as ongoing accomplishments, in which those involved draw upon various assumptions, conventions, practices and other types of resources available within their situation to sustain and shape their encounters in various ways. Ethnomethodology seeks to understand such accomplishments in their own terms. It seeks to understand them from within.

The term 'ethnomethodology' was invented by Harold Garfinkel as a result of his work on a 'jury project' (Garfinkel, 1968). The proceedings of a jury had been bugged. It was

Garfinkel's job to listen to the tapes, to talk to the jurors and to consider the broad question 'What makes them jurors?' Garfinkel and a colleague were interested in establishing 'how the jurors knew what they were doing in doing the work of jurors'. They recognised that the jurors, in going about their work, were adopting various methods for making their activities as jurors accountable to themselves and to others. They were engaged in a process of 'making sense' of the practice of jury work. They were concerned with such things as 'adequate accounts', 'adequate description' and 'adequate evidence'. They sought to avoid being 'common-sensical', they sought to act in the manner that they thought jurors should act. The term 'ethnomethodology' was coined to characterise the jurors' engagement in a methodology relating to a specific area of common-sense knowledge. They were engaged in a process which called upon them to use a specific set of practices for making sense of a particular social activity. However, ethnomethodology has come to mean many different things. As Garfinkel (1968) has noted, 'it has turned into a shibboleth', and he frankly disclaims any responsibility for what persons have come to make of ethnomethodology.[22] Many would not accept Garfinkel's disclaimer. His writings are unnecessarily obscure and convoluted and they stand in a somewhat paradoxical relationship to the fact that ethnomethodology is concered with understanding the everyday world of simple practical activities and the realm of common-sense knowledge.

The work of ethnomethodologists is very much concerned with identifying the 'taken for granted' assumptions which characterise any social situation and the ways in which the members involved, through the use of everyday practices, make their activities 'rationally accountable'. In this analysis the notions of 'indexicality' and 'reflexivity' play an important part. Everyday activities are seen as being ordered and rationally explicable within the context in which they occur. The way in which they are organised makes use of expressions and activities which are shared and not necessarily explicitly stated (indexicality); this depends upon the capacity to look back on what has gone on before (reflexivity). The social situation is viewed as a process of accountable action which is sustained by the efforts of the participants; the participants are seen as attempting to order their experience so as to sustain the everyday, common-sense suppositions which characterise the routine of everyday life.

Following Douglas (1970b), it is convenient to distinguish between two types of ethnomethodologists, linguistic and situational. The linguistic ethnomethodologists (for example, Cicourel, 1972; Schegloff and Sacks, 1973) focus upon the use of language and the ways in which conversations in everyday life are structured. Their analysis makes much of the unstated, 'taken for granted' meanings, the use of indexical expressions and the way in which conversations convey much more than is actually said. The situational ethnomethodologists (McHugh, 1968, for example) cast their view over a wider range of social activity and seek to understand the ways in which people negotiate the social contexts in which they find themselves. They are concerned to understand how people make sense of and order their environment. As part of their method ethnomethodologists may consciously disrupt or question the 'taken for granted' elements in everyday situations, in order to reveal the underlying processes at work.

Ethnomethodology is thus firmly committed to an understanding of the 'life-world'. Garfinkel acknowledges an intellectual debt to Husserl, Schutz and Parsons, and his work can perhaps be best understood as a particular type of response to Schutz's concern for analysing the natural attitude. As Giddens notes, Garfinkel

> is concerned with how the 'natural attitude' is *realised* as a phenomenon by actors in day to day life . . . This leads him away from phenomenology, with its Cartesian emphasis upon the (essential or existential) primacy of subjective experience, towards the study of 'situated actions' as 'publicly' interpreted forms. It is not hard to see that the direction of movement is toward Austin and toward the later Wittgenstein. For the notion of illocutionary acts, or as Wittgenstein says, 'that the words are also deeds', although serving descriptive rather than philosophical ends, fits fairly closely with Garfinkel's preoccupations. (Giddens, 1976, p. 36)

Giddens makes much of the convergence of interest in phenomenology and ordinary language philosophy (as expressed in the work of the later Wittgenstein and his followers) upon the everyday world, and we shall have more to say of this in the concluding section of this chapter.

Garfinkel's debt to Parsons is expressed through his concern for the problem of social order. Ethnomethodology is clearly geared to providing explanations of the ordered nature of the social world, and it is largely for this reason that, along with phenomenologists and symbolic interactionists, the ethnomethodologists have been labelled the 'new conservatives' in sociology (McNall and Johnson, 1975). However, the ethnomethodological approach to order differs significantly from that which characterises the Parsonian scheme and other schools of thought characteristic of the functionalist paradigm. The concern is not to explain any ordered structure or patterning of events or regularities in human behaviour; rather, it is to provide an explanation of the way in which individual actors appear to order their world through the use of various 'accounting' practices. The ethnomethodologists are interested in the way in which actors make evident and persuade each other that the events and activities in which they are involved are coherent and consistent. They are interested in understanding the methods which characterise this accounting process. From the ethnomethodological point of view, 'order' in human affairs does not exist independently of the accounting practices employed in its discovery.[23]

Many ethnomethodologists resist very strongly any attempt to link their work with the conventional problems and concerns of academic sociology. For them, every man is his own sociologist, committed to an understanding of his everyday life. In this connection, Garfinkel draws the distinction between 'lay' and 'professional' sociologists, the activities of both being open to ethnomethodological analysis. The sociology of the professional, like that of his lay equivalent, can be regarded as a particular type of accounting practice. As Giddens puts it, 'social science is a practical accomplishment like any other rationally accountable form of social activity, and can be studied as such' (Giddens, 1976, p. 39). Many ethnomethodologists specifically dissociate themselves from orthodox sociology as such, particularly from its orientation towards 'constructive analysis', and confine their efforts to studying the indexicality of everyday accounts and the ways in which they are made rationally accountable.

The substance of ethnomethodology thus largely comprises a set of specific techniques and approaches to be used in the study of what Garfinkel has described as the 'awesome indexicality' of everyday life. It is geared to empirical study, and the stress which its practitioners place upon the uniqueness of the situations encountered projects an essentially relativist stance. A commitment to the development of methodology and field-work has occupied first place in the interests of its adherents, so that related issues of ontology, epistemology and human nature have received less attention than they perhaps deserve.

Phenomenological symbolic interactionism

It will be recalled from our discussion in Chapter 4 that it is possible to distinguish two strains of symbolic interactionism –

behavioural and phenomenological. The latter is typified by its emphasis upon the emergent properties of interaction, through which individuals create their social world rather than merely reacting to it. Meaning is attributed to the environment, not derived from and imposed upon individual actors; action is built up instead of being a response or mere release mechanism. Both groups of interactionists normally acknowledge their principal intellectual debt to the work of G. H. Mead, though, as we have argued, they tend to interpret this in fundamentally different ways.

The differences between the phenomenological and the behavioural interactionists is not always as clear as it might be, since the former have often been attracted by positivist research methods which go against their basic theoretical orientation. As Douglas has noted, 'the general problem of the interactionist tradition of thought and research in sociology is that its practitioners have rarely seen clearly and consistently the fundamental theoretical and methodological differences between a positivistic (absolutist) sociology and a phenomenological or existential sociology' (Douglas, 1970, p. 18).

This confusion is also reflected in the debate over whether there can be a genuine synthesis between symbolic interactionism and ethnomethodology. Norman Denzin, a prominent symbolic interactionist, has argued that a synthesis is possible; Don Zimmerman and Lawrence Wieder, two prominent ethnomethodologists, have argued that it is not.[24] Interpreting interactionism from a phenomenological rather than a behavioural perspective, Denzin's case rests largely on the view that both symbolic interactionism and ethnomethodology cover largely the same ground. As he puts it,

> symbolic interactionism encompasses a large number of the problems and peculiarities now taken as the special province of ethnomethodology – namely, that the study of human conduct, within any type of social order, demands consideration of how interacting selves co-operate in the construction of a routine, and for the moment a taken-for-granted set of meanings necessary for joint action For the interactionist any social order emerges through the process of interaction in a situation where selves take the point of view of one another. The foundation of such orders is to be found in the meaning interacting selves bring to the objects and acts at hand. Meaning arises out of interaction, and not the other way around. The task of the interactionist is to discover how interacting selves come to agree upon certain meanings and definitions for co-ordinated action. The central role of the self in shaping such definitions is of paramount importance... It is

necessary to note only that such a conception of the interaction process demands a special view of empirical research ... a cardinal feature of interactionist research is the casting of the researcher's self into the position of those he is studying. (Douglas, 1970, pp. 295–6)

The ethnomethodologists claim that one of the primary ways in which they differ from this standpoint is that they have a fundamentally different view of the problem of social order and its analysis. Zimmerman and Wieder claim that whilst the interactionist treats the point of view of the actor as only one aspect of the problem of order, seeking to relate it to a wider context in terms of scientifically valid description and explanations, the ethnomethodologist limits his activities to the actor's world. He is not very interested in going beyond this. As they put it, 'the ethnomethodologist is *not* concerned with providing causal explanations of observably regular, patterned, repetitive actions by some kind of analysis of the actor's point of view. He is concerned with how members of society go about the task of *seeing*, *describing*, and *explaining* order in the world in which they live' (Douglas, 1970, pp. 287–9). The ethnomethodologist sees himself as being much more fully committed to the perspective of the actor than the interactionist is – there is a much greater commitment to studying the actor on his own ground. Denzin disputes that there is any radical difference between the two approaches on this point and the debate remains inconclusive.

For our purposes here it would seem that the similarities between the two approaches are of the utmost importance, since they clearly define the way in which both ethnomethodology and phenomenological symbolic interactionism differ from other schools of thought. Both follow the phenomenological tradition of attributing to social reality a very precarious ontological status. It is recognised that social reality comprises little more than a complex set of typifications which may be intersubjectively shared. The notion of the 'ideal type', which in Weber's approach to interpretive sociology is offered merely as a methodological tool, assumes ontological status within the context of phenomenological sociology. Phenomenological sociologists recognise that social reality is created and sustained through the use of typifications or 'ideal types', as individuals attempt to order and 'make sense' of the world in which they live. Linguistic ethnomethodologists attempt to focus upon this by understanding the way in which 'accounting practices' develop, and they emphasise language as the central medium through which people see and create their social world and through which intersubjectively shared meanings may arise. The 'situational ethnomethodologists', like the phenomenological symbolic interactionists, are more concerned to study the way in which social reality reflects a precarious balance of intersubjectively shared meanings, which are continually negotiated, sustained and changed through the everyday interaction of individual human beings. Social reality is for them either reaffirmed or created afresh in every social encounter.

The Underlying Unity of the Paradigm

Theorists of all schools of thought within the interpretive paradigm tend to share a common perspective, in that their primary concern is to understand the subjective experience of individuals. Their theories are constructed from the standpoint of the individual actor as opposed to the observer of action; they view social reality as an emergent process – as an extension of human consciousness and subjective experience. Insofar as a wider social environment is accorded ontological status, it is regarded as the creation and extension of the subjective experience of the individuals involved. Ontologically, theories characteristic of the interpretive paradigm are indisputably nominalist; with regard to human nature, they are essentially voluntarist.

All theories constructed in the context of the interpretive paradigm are anti-positivist. They reject the view that the world of human affairs can be studied in the manner of the natural sciences. In the context of the interpretive paradigm the central endeavour is to understand the subjective world of human experience. To retain the integrity of the phenomena under investigation, an attempt is made to get inside and to understand from within. The imposition of external form and structure is resisted, since this reflects the viewpoint of the observer as opposed to that of the actor directly involved. Ideographic rather than nomothetic methods of study are favoured from this point of view.

In these respects theories characteristic of the interpretive paradigm are significantly different from those of the functionalist paradigm. Though certain theorists within the latter have attempted to incorporate ideas and insights from the former, particularly in terms of method (for example, Weber and his use of the notion of *verstehen*), the two types of theory remain fundamentally distinct. The ontological assumptions of a truly interpretive theory do not permit a functionalist perspective; the two types of theories are based upon fundamentally different assumptions with regard to the ontological status of the social world.

At the same time there are points of similarity between interpretive and functionalist theories – similarities which become clearly evident when these theories are compared with their counterparts in the radical humanist and radical structuralist paradigms. Interpretive and functionalist theories reflect a common concern for the sociology of regulation. By and large, interpretive theories concentrate on the study of ways in which social reality is meaningfully constructed and ordered from the point of view of the actors directly involved. They present a perspective in which individual actors negotiate, regulate and live their lives within the context of the *status quo*. The fact that interpretive theories are cast in the mould of the sociology of regulation reflects the frame of reference of their proponents rather than basic ontological and methodological assumptions. As will be seen in Chapter 8, hermeneutics in the hands of Habermas and phenomenology in the hands of Sartre are directed towards quite different ends within the context of a sociology of radical change.

If one were required to draw a single line of division between the theories located within the context of the interpretive paradigm, perhaps the most significant would be that between the highly subjectivist orientation of solipsism and transcendental phenomenology on the one hand and existential phenomenology, phenomenological sociology and hermeneutics on the other. Whereas the former embark upon a journey into the realm of pure subjectivity and remain within the bounds of purely philosophical discourse, the latter are more concerned with the 'life-world' and are amenable to study from a more sociological perspective. Within the context of the latter it is worth noting a convergence of interest upon the role of language as a medium of practical social activity. Existential phenomenology, ethnomethodology and hermeneutics have features in common with the theory of language as developed in the work of the later Wittgenstein (1963) and his followers.[25] All of these areas of analysis emphasise the importance of meaning in context. As Wittgenstein puts it, 'an expression only has meaning in the flow of life.' In language, as in other areas of social activity, the process of communication is an ongoing accomplishment characterised by indexicality and reflexivity. All human activity takes much for granted, and what constitutes reality depends upon the rules which underlie what Wittgenstein calls 'forms of life'.

These notions have fundamental implications for our view of

science, since it follows that what poses as science is no more than a particular form of life or language game. Science is based on 'taken for granted' assumptions, and thus, like any other social practice, must be understood within a specific context. Traced to their source, all activities which pose as science can be traced to fundamental assumptions relating to everyday life and can in no way be regarded as generating knowledge with an 'objective', value-free status, as is sometimes claimed. What passes for scientific knowledge can be shown to be founded upon a set of unstated conventions, beliefs and assumptions, just as everyday, common-sense knowledge is. The difference between them lies largely in the nature of the rules and the community which recognises and subscribes to them. The knowledge in both cases is not so much 'objective' as shared.

This view has close parallels with the view of science articulated by Kuhn (1970) and the notion of paradigm. In essence, his work represents a theoretical perspective characteristic of the interpretive paradigm — a theory in the tradition of Schutz's analysis of multiple realities and Wittgenstein's 'forms of life'. Scientific knowledge here is in essence socially constructed and socially sustained; its significance and meaning can only be understood within its immediate social context.

This view of science is explicitly recognised in the work of phenomenologists and ethnomethodologists operating within the interpretive paradigm. It explains in large measure their indifference to the functionalist and radical structuralist paradigms, or the deep-seated scepticism with which they view the work of theorists operating within these contexts, and their vigorous efforts to construct social theories based upon a fundamentally different view of the role and nature of science.

Notes and References

1. Hughes identifies the generation of writers influential during the period 1890–1930 as follows: Freud (born 1856), Durkheim (1858), Mosca (1858), Bergson (1859), Meinecke (1862), Weber (1864), Troeltsch (1865), Croce (1866), Benda (1867), Pirandello (1867), Alain (1868), Gide (1869), Proust (1871), Peguy (1873), Jung (1875), Mann (1875), Michels (1876), Hesse (1877).

   To this list he adds Dilthey (1833), Gramsci (1891), Spengler (1880), Wittgenstein (1889) and Mannheim (1893).

He could well have added Simmel (1858) and Husserl (1859), who were also very much influenced by the German idealist tradition.

The responses of these writers to the problem of the 'subjective' has indeed been diverse. Durkheim, for example, found a solution consistent with a functional orientation; Sorel veered in the direction of Marxism and Freud into the realm of psychoanalysis. As Hughes notes, most of these theorists concerned themselves 'with the irrational only to exorcise it. By probing into it they sought ways to tame it, to canalise it for constructive human purposes' (Hughes, 1958, p. 36). For the most part they addressed the irrational from a standpoint characteristic of the sociology of regulation.

2. The contribution to the development of modern Western philosophy and social theory made by Wilhelm Dilthey is coming increasingly to be seen as of importance. He has made a considerable contribution to basic issues of epistemology and methodology, and his work has had a significant influence upon social theorists such as Weber, Husserl, Heidegger and others. The similarities between the methodological contributions of Dilthey and Weber are particularly striking. Unfortunately, the major part of Dilthey's work is still not available in English. For a sample of what is available so far, see Rickman (1976).

Dilthey was concerned to explore the epistemological problems of the cultural sciences, particularly history, and devise ways of generating objective knowledge that would meet the traditional requirements of science. For a clear discussion of his attempt, see Tuttle (1969). For a general discussion of his work and influence, see Hodges (1952) and Makkreel (1975).

3. For a further discussion of some of these issues, see Parsons (1949), vol. II, pp. 473–87 and Hughes (1958), pp. 183–200.

4. Weber's principal works on methodology can be found in Weber (1949).

5. To this definition it may well be useful to add a further comment on Weber's view of 'action': 'In "action" is included human behaviour when and insofar as the acting individual attaches a subjective meaning to it. Action in this sense may be either overt or purely inward or subjective; it may consist of positive intervention in a situation, or if deliberately refraining from such intervention, or passively acquiescing in the situation' (Weber, 1947, p. 88).

6. Hughes conveniently summarises the essential characteristics of the 'ideal type' construct in the following terms:

> An ideal type is formed by the one-sided *accentuation* of one or more points of view and by the synthesis of a great many diffuse, discrete, more or less present and occasionally absent *concrete individual* phenomena, which are arranged according to those one-sidedly emphasised viewpoints into a unified *analytical* construct. In its conceptual purity, this mental construct cannot be found empirically anywhere in reality. It is a *utopia* . . .
>
> It has the significance of a purely ideal *limiting* concept with which the real situation or action is *compared* and surveyed for the explication of certain of its significant components. Such concepts are constructs in terms of which we formulate relationships by the application of the category of objective possibility. By means of this category, the adequacy of our imagination, orientated and disciplined by reality, is judged. (Hughes, 1958, p. 312)

The notion of an 'ideal type' thus represents a heuristic which can be used as a means of analysis in many realms of scientific enquiry. Concepts such as bureaucracy, economic man and capitalism are examples of 'ideal types' – useful fictions against which the real world can be compared.

7. For a perspective on some of the issues involved here, see Runciman (1972), pp. 16–19 and Gerth and Mills (1948), pp. 55–61.

8. For a full discussion of the life and work of Husserl, see Natanson (1973b) and Spiegelberg (1965), vol. I, pp. 73–167.

Spiegelberg's analysis indicates quite clearly how Husserl's thought progresses in successive stages to an increasingly subjectivist position. Only after 1906 does Husserl's philosophy become that of a pure phenomenologist.

9. We have chosen to present the interpretive paradigm in terms of four broad categories of theory to reflect the key divisions from a sociological perspective, since this is what is central to our present task. At a philosophical level, it would perhaps be more appropriate to characterise it in terms of three broad categories, *solipsism*, *subjective idealism* (comprising phenomenology and phenomenological sociology) and *objective idealism* (comprising hermeneutics). These three categories of philosophical thought are discussed in the text.

10. For an analysis of the hermeneutic tradition, see, for example, Palmer (1969).

11. Unfortunately, most of Gadamer's work is not yet available in English. For a useful discussion of his work, see Giddens (1976).

12. Quoted in Giddens (1976), p. 57. As Giddens notes, there are remarkable parallels between Gadamer's hermeneutics and post-Wittgensteinian philosophy as developed by Winch in *The Idea of a Social Science* (1958). Both lines of enquiry, which appear to have developed independently of each other, arrive at similar views on the nature and significance of language in social life (Giddens, 1976, pp. 54–5).

13. For a comprehensive discussion of the phenomenological basis of solipsism and its variations, see Todd (1968).

14. Berkeley's own position can perhaps be more accurately described as that of an 'immaterialist' rather than a solipsist. He did not deny that there was an external world; he asserted that everything is relative to mind; see Berkeley (1962) (this work was originally published in the early eighteenth century).

15. In a similar vein of levity, it is also said that Berkeley, on a visit to the house of Dean Swift, was left standing on the doorstep on the pretext that if immaterialism was a tenable position, he would be able to walk through the door without its being opened for him.

16. For a full discussion of the phenomenological movement, including an analysis of the intellectual debt of Husserl to his teacher, Franz Bretano, and fellow pupil, Carl Stumpf, see Spiegelberg (1965), vols I and II. The essay by Thévenaz (1962) presents a very clear account of the development of the central notions. See also Husserl's own account of phenomenology in the *Encyclopædia Britannica*, 14th ed. (1929).

17. In his later writings Husserl also devoted increased attention to the idea of the *Lebenswelt* ('life-world'), in the hope that it would throw light on intentionality in action. This notion was taken up by Husserl's followers, in line with their increased interest in the lived-in world as opposed to the transcendental. We shall have more to say of this in the next section.

18. Heidegger interested himself primarily in the meaning of 'being'. He saw in phenomenology a means of establishing the categories of human existence for a 'fundamental ontology'. Towards this end he developed a 'hermeneutic

phenomenology' designed to interpret the ontological meanings of various human conditions (being in the world, anxiety, etc.).

For a comprehensive discussion of Heidegger's version of phenomenology, see Spiegelberg (1965), pp. 271–357 and Thévenaz (1962), pp. 53–67.

Merleau-Ponty has played a key role in the development of the phenomenological movement in France. For a discussion of his work, see Spiegelberg (1965), pp. 516–62. The work of Sartre will be discussed in Chapter 8.

19. For a full discussion of the role of typification in Schutz's analysis, see Schutz (1964), part I.

20. For a full discussion of multiple realities, see Schutz (1967), pp. 207–59.

21. For an overall perspective on Schutz's methodology, see Schutz (1967), pp. 3–47.

22. As will be clear from our discussion below, ethnomethodology has developed in a number of directions. For some useful reviews of the subject as a whole, see Douglas (1970b), Dreitzel (1970), Filmer et al (1972) and Giddens (1976).

23. For a discussion of an ethnomethodologist's view of the problem of order, see the article by Zimmerman and Wieder in Douglas (1970b), pp. 286–95.

24. The debate is presented in Douglas (1970b), pp. 259–84, 285–98; see also Meltzer *et al*. (1975).

25. It is important to note that the work of the early and later Wittgenstein is based upon fundamentally different ontological assumptions. Although we are unable to consider this at length here, it is interesting to note that Wittgenstein's early philosophy reflects assumptions consistent with the functionalist paradigm; the later philosophy reflects the assumptions of the interpretive paradigm. Wittgenstein, like a number of other social philosophers discussed here (for example, G. H. Mead, Husserl, Marx), embarked during his lifetime upon an intellectual journey which involved a change in basic paradigm.

7. The Interpretive Paradigm and the Study of Organisations

As will be clear from our discussion in the previous chapter, the intellectual history of the interpretive paradigm is as complex and conceptually as rich as that of the functionalist paradigm. The underlying assumptions of the interpretive paradigm with regard to the ontological status of the social world reject the utility of constructing a social science which focuses upon the analysis of 'structures'. It rejects any view which attributes to the social world a reality which is independent of the minds of men. It emphasises that the social world is no more than the subjective construction of individual human beings who, through the development and use of common language and the interactions of everyday life, may create and sustain a social world of intersubjectively shared meaning. The social world is thus of an essentially intangible nature and is in a continuous process of reaffirmation or change.

Such a view does not allow for the existence of 'organisations' in any hard and concrete sense. Whilst certain schools of thought accept the *concept* of organisation and its use as an 'accounting practice' by which people attempt to make sense of their world, they do not recognise organisations as such. From the standpoint of the interpretive paradigm, organisations simply do not exist.

Strictly speaking, therefore, the notion of there being a theory of organisations characteristic of the interpretive paradigm is somewhat contradictory. However, in recent years a number of theorists located within this paradigm have involved themselves in a debate about various aspects of organisational life. They have done so as sociologists concerned to demonstrate the validity of their point of view as against the prevailing orthodoxy characteristic of the functionalist paradigm. As will be apparent from our discussion in Chapter 5, most organisation theorists tend to treat their subject of study as a hard, concrete and tangible empirical phenomenon which exists 'out there' in the 'real world'. The interpretive sociologists are firmly opposed to such 'structural absolutism', arguing that social science should be based upon fundamentally different assumptions about the ontological status of the social world. In order to demonstrate this point, they have engaged in research designed to illustrate the fallacy of the functionalist standpoint. They have sought to show how the supposedly hard, concrete, tangible and 'real' aspects of organisational life are dependent upon the subjective constructions of individual human beings. In doing this they have produced a certain amount of literature which has considerable relevance for our analysis here, since it opens up a debate about the assumptions which underwrite the contemporary orthodoxy in organisation theory. This literature, however, is not without its problems, since in attempting to undermine the notions informing more orthodox functionalist approaches to the study of organisational life, the interpretive sociologists have often been drawn into a battle fought upon their opponents' ground. In adopting a reactive stance they often endorse, by implication, the validity of certain background assumptions which define the functionalist problematic. Consequently, their stance is often somewhat contradictory, and there tends to be a divergence between theoretical pronouncements and the assumptions reflected in empirical research.

In this chapter we hope to move some way towards clarifying the issues involved here. We shall review some of the literature and we shall attempt to evaluate it in terms of the assumptions upon which it is based. This literature is confined to the perspectives described in the previous chapter as ethnomethodology and phenomenological symbolic interactionism, though, as we have suggested, we do not wish to place too much emphasis upon the importance of this distinction.

Ethnomethodological Approaches to the Study of Organisational Activities

One of the earliest ethnomethodological critiques of functionalist organisation theory is found in Egon Bittner's article, 'The Concept of Organisation', first published in 1965. In this article Bittner argues that organisation theorists, who define organisations as 'stable associations of persons engaged in concerted activities directed to the attainment of specific objectives', tend to take the concept of organisation structure as unproblematic. He argues that this notion of structure represents no more than a common-sense assumption of certain actors within a given situation. To take this common-sense assumption at face value, and use it as a basis for organisational analysis, is thus fraught with difficulty. He argues, in effect, that the sociologist who uses such a concept as a 'resource' for explaining organisational activities is committing a fundamental error, and that such concepts should be the 'topic' rather than the tool of analysis. In the course of his argument Bittner illustrates his case in relation to the work of Selznick and Weber, and suggests that their theories are based upon a whole set of unstated presuppositions and theoretical shortcuts which build a protective mantle around the subject of study. The concept of bureaucracy, for example, builds upon background information that normally competent members of society take for granted as commonly known. In building upon this Bittner suggests that Weber is in collusion with those about whom he theorises. He summarises his views very forcefully in the following terms: 'If the theory of bureaucracy is a theory at all, it is a refined and purified version of the actor's theorising. To the extent that it is a refinement and purification of it, it is, by the same token, a corrupt and incomplete version of it; for it is certainly not warranted to reduce the terms of common-sense discourse to a lexicon of culturally coded significances to satisfy the requirements of theoretical postulations' (Bittner, 1974, p. 74).

In the place of this 'corrupt' and 'incomplete' version of the actor's theorising about organisational structures, Bittner suggests the study of organisation as a common-sense construct in which the 'methodologist' must be concerned with the procedures and considerations which actors invoke in the construction of their world. In the last part of his paper Bittner goes on to develop an explicitly ethnomethodological approach to the rational constructions subsumed under the concept of organisation, which reflects a programme of enquiry rather than a specific interest in producing a theory of organisations as such. In this Bittner assumes that the actor in an organisation is not a disinterested bystander but a toolsmith using the concept of organisation in a certain relatively specific way and for certain variable reasons. He suggests that organisational actors can, for example, use the concept of rational organisation as a 'gambit of compliance', in which certain rules of conduct are invoked simply by using the term. On the other hand, there is an 'open realm of free play' within and outside these rules which presents us with the opportunity 'to attain a grasp of the meaning of the rules as common-sense constructs from the perspective of those persons who promulgate and live with them'. Moreover, the concept of 'formal organisation' acts as a 'model of stylistic unity' and as a 'corroborative reference', two interrelated notions concerned with the regulation and discipline of behaviour in organisational contexts. Taken together with the 'gambit of compliance', they form three ways within organisations in which 'competent users' of the term 'formal organisation' utilise it as a mechanism for control. In these ways Bittner's analysis points towards an understanding of the manner in which the organisational world is constructed by the actors involved.

The main thrust of Bittner's article lies in its suggestion that the concept of organisation, and related issues such as structure, hierarchy and efficiency, are problematic social constructs. He argues that these constructs should be the *topic* of research in sociological analysis and should not be taken for granted. In subsequent work, however, Bittner and his followers have not always proved true to these requirements. His article 'The Police on Skid Row' (1967), for example, illustrates this very clearly.

Bittner's research with the police departments of two large urban areas used the accounting practices of the police officers as its analytical focus of attention. By centring attention on Skid Row, which is seen by the police as a special area, divorced from society at large, characterised by gratuitous violence, uncertainty in human behaviour and a shifting, uncommitted population of deviant misfits, Bittner is able to depict the policeman as the 'definer of the situation' *par excellence*. The 'peace-keeping' role adopted by the police on Skid Row allows them considerable freedom of action, relatively unconstrained by the judiciary and central authority, as a result of which they are free to define local people's behaviour, motivation and past actions in terms of *their* expectations only.

Bittner, nevertheless, is at pains to point out that Skid Row is unusual, in that the men who patrol it are not subject to 'any systems of external control'. Implicitly, then, and by the back door of his analysis, the notion of social and organisational structure appears on the stage. At one point in his analysis Bittner introduces the concept of 'structural determinants' but attempts to define them in a subjective way as 'the typical situations that policemen perceive as *demand conditions* for action without arrest'.[1] What he seems to be implying, here and throughout the article, is that structural factors at both social and organisational level tend to have less impact in the role performance of policemen on Skid Row than elsewhere. The article does not question the problematic nature of the concepts of 'external control', 'society in general', 'normalcy' and 'superiors'. Somewhat paradoxically, therefore, rather than the study of Skid Row representing an ethnomethodological refutation of the importance of structural factors, its very unusualness seems to underline the crucial impact of structure upon 'normal' everyday life. Bittner's research is of importance in demonstrating the role of accounting practices in the social construction of 'reality', but it is presented in such a way as to rekindle the probing reader's belief in the existence of 'structure' within the vast segment of society which is not Skid Row. Thus, whilst Bittner's theoretical article 'The Concept of Organisation' warns about the danger of 'collusion' or complicity within the subject under investigation, the empirical work of some two years later seems to fall into the self-same trap. The article's own schema of background assumptions is predicated upon a series of organisational and societal relationships which seem to be accepted unquestioningly.

This discrepancy between theoretical pronouncement and empirical research also characterises the work of Don Zimmerman and his associates. In certain articles Zimmerman adheres to a nominalist ontology characteristic of the interpretive paradigm, but in others he veers in a much more objectivist direction. In the article written with Wieder (1970), for example, the social world is regarded as the direct product of human consciousness. The authors specifically reject the notion that there exist intersubjectively shared meanings, norms and values to which the activities of individuals are orientated. Instead they account for the seeming presence of such phenomena by suggesting that human beings 'continuously rely on, and if pressed, insist upon, the capacities of others to find a presumptively shared sense in what they are saying' (Zimmerman and Wieder, 1970, p. 294). In other words, they emphasise that the social world is created through the accounting practices of individuals as they engage in the routine activities of everyday life. The nominalist ontology reflected in this point of view is perfectly consistent with the assumptions which characterise the interpretive paradigm.

In two articles presenting the results of empirical work Zimmerman takes a different line. We have in mind here 'The Practicalities of Rule Use' (1970a) and 'Record Keeping and the Intake Process in a Public Welfare Organisation' (1970b). Both pieces of work are based upon research at the offices of a State Bureau of Public Assistance, the first looking at the 'reception function', not so much in terms of the prescribed work, but from the point of view of the receptionists themselves. As a paper it examines certain aspects of the work activities of these bureaucratic actors, particularly their role in inducting applicants for public assistance into their organisational routine. Following Bittner, Zimmerman attacks the notion that a formal organisational structure is an unproblematic facticity, pointing out that 'the issue of what rules, policies, and goals mean for the bureaucratic actor upon the concrete occasion of their use (for example, to guide, to account for, or to justify action) must be treated as problematic' (Zimmerman, 1970a, p. 224). The piece shows quite clearly that individuals use the rules of the organisation to relate to their work and for reconciling organisational and individual requirements. For Zimmerman, it is the receptionist's interpretation which is crucial rather than the supposed fact that rules and regulations exist 'outside' the individuals involved in any fixed, unbending, objectively defined sense. The 'competent use' of a rule, which in itself can never be fully determinate of behaviour, lies behind the reproduction of a day-by-day, 'normal' state of affairs. However, Zimmerman clearly accepts the facticity of organisational structures and the existence of externally imposed rules. What he suggests as Bittner did before him, is that movement *within* this structure is possible. Ontologically, this stands in stark contrast to the theoretical article written with Wieder (1970). Although a marked measure of voluntarism is common to both articles, since human beings as 'competent rule users' are relatively free to create their own social world, the ontological foundations seem to differ between the theoretical and empirical works. In the former the social world is largely a product of consciousness; in the latter a vague disquieting ambience of 'structure', dark and threatening but not quite fully discernible, is felt to be the 'real' core of social reality.

A structural 'presence' is also evident in Zimmerman's other empirical piece on 'sensible intake work' (1970b). The social welfare caseworker, like the receptionist, is engaged in an ongoing process of interpretation of how much of a client's story is fiction and how much 'fact'. Documentation is crucial here, and the case record is of particular importance as an example of an attempt to *assemble* the world of a client, which is inherently rule-governed and made accountable through *post facto* reconstruction in a way reminiscent of Schutz's notion of reflexivity. These documented sets of 'facts' then assume a concrete facticity and immutability, and are seen as objective, detached and inherently reliable. For the caseworker the world is viewed as non-problematic, indeed as 'obvious', and the case records come to reflect this assumption. Zimmerman admits that external constraints are important. For example, he states that speed and verification are central to the caseworker's role, but the reader is left to infer that this is because of the caseworker's position within an organisational hierarchy with its own rules and disciplinary procedures. This acceptance of the ontological status of organisational structures is not consonant with the nominalist ontology characteristic of Zimmerman's more theoretical work.

The theory and research of both Bittner and Zimmerman is thus characterised by what may be usefully described as a form of *'ontological oscillation'*. Analytically, they stress a highly subjectivist stance which denies the existence of social structures and concrete social reality of any form. Yet the attempt to operationalise their ideas within an empirical context frequently leads them to admit a more realist form of ontology through the back door. Whilst this is unintended, it does pose great difficulties for students attempting to understand their work and to distinguish it from research typical, for example, of the action frame of reference and the interactionism characteristic of the functionalist paradigm. Yet this ontological oscillation is prevalent in all forms of phenomenological sociology which attempt to illustrate its basic propositions through the empirical study of situations drawn from everyday life.

It is characteristic, for example, of the work of David Silverman who, since his advocacy of the action frame of reference (Silverman, 1970), has produced work with a significantly different orientation. As we have argued in Chapter 5, Silverman, like many other theorists who have adopted the action frame of reference as a basis of analysis, has frequently drawn inspiration from the writings of more phenomenologically orientated theorists, particularly Schutz. However, following Weber, they have used the action framework as a tool for studying a relatively 'realist' social reality, largely ignoring the ontological implications which their framework reflects. As we have shown in Chapter 6, the true significance of phenomenological sociology rests in its recognition of the ontological status of typifications or 'ideal types' which comprise the core of social reality. In *The Theory of Organisations* (1970), Silverman recognises that reality is socially constructed, socially sustained and socially changed, yet he interprets this essentially as indicating the need for social theories to adopt a more voluntaristic theory of action and to avoid the reification of social phenomena. In other words, as we have argued at length in Chapter 5, Silverman (1970) adheres to a highly voluntaristic view of human nature but to an ontology, an epistemology and a methodology characteristic of the subjectivist region of the functionalist paradigm. *The Theory of Organisations* is addressed to organisation theorists who hold to a functionalist view of social reality; its main contribution lies in its advocacy of a particular methodology for studying *that* reality.

In his more recent work (Filmer *et al.*, 1972; Silverman, 1975a, 1975b; Silverman and Jones, 1973, 1976), Silverman has pursued the latent phenomenological issues which occupy a background role in *The Theory of Organisations* and has adopted a theoretical position firmly located within the context of the interpretive paradigm. A comparison of this body of work with *The Theory of Organisations* clearly illustrates the implications of a paradigm change. To organisation theorists located within the functionalist paradigm, Silverman's recent work usually appears confusing, if not unintelligible, and is largely dismissed as unhelpful, if not irrelevant. Yet from the standpoint of the interpretive paradigm, it contains many genuine insights and has contributed a great deal to the debate in contemporary circles interested in phenomenological sociology.

Silverman's recent work seeks to provide an ethnomethodological interpretation of various activities within the context of organisational situations.[2] The publication of *New Directions in Sociological Theory* (1972), written in conjunction with Filmer et al, marks an explicit move to an ontology characteristic of the interpretive paradigm. In this work Silverman and his colleagues seek to shift sociological perspectives away from the functionalist orthodoxy and towards more phenomenologically inspired approaches. Chapter 6 is of particular interest, since it partly concerns itself with the specific study of organisational activities. In it Silverman attacks functionalist organisation theory for its excessive belief in 'social facts' and, by drawing upon the work of Bittner (1965), Zimmerman (1970a) and Sudnow (1965), argues that organisational 'rules' are, in point of fact, the 'ongoing practical accomplishments' of organisational members. Silverman is at pains to reject the 'structural absolutism' of most sociological theorising, particularly for ignoring the 'processual relationship between subject and object in the social world, i.e. acknowledgement of the *intersubjective* character of social life' (Filmer *et al.*, 1972, p. 168). In this piece of work Silverman sees phenomenological sociology as concerned not so much with 'unique experience' as with the commonalty of 'raw materials', notably language, which underpin social experience as a whole. Silverman appears to accept that there is an intersubjectively shared reality which offers itself for investigation by the phenomenological sociologist.

In 'Getting In: The Managed Accomplishments of "Correct" Selection Outcomes' (Silverman and Jones, 1973), a shift of attention is evident, in that considerable emphasis is placed not so much upon the commonality of raw materials which underpin social experience, but upon the conflicting views of reality which characterise any given situation. The study presents a preliminary report of empirical research on staff selection interviews within a large organisation. It shows the manner in which the interview situation is built around verbal and non-verbal exchanges in which motives and personal qualities are attributed to others through the use of typifications, and how the interview can be seen as an accounting process influenced by the need for 'authoritative accounts' through which it can be made accountable to others. Silverman and Jones demonstrate how the interview situation is characterised by multiple realities, as people attempt to make sense of the situation. As they note, their theoretical focus is the idea that 'an account of any reality derives its rationality *not* from its direct correspondence with some objective world but from the ability of its hearers (readers) to make sense of the account in the context of the socially organised occasions of its use (and thereby *to treat it* as corresponding to an objective world)' (Silverman and Jones, 1973, pp. 63–4). This focus clearly reflects a nominalist ontology characteristic of the interpretive paradigm, with Silverman and Jones emphasising how reality is specific to particular social contexts. However, as with so many other phenomenological studies, the presence of structure in the form of hierarchical influence and 'scientific peer groups' lurks in the background as a force influencing the need for 'authoritative accounts' of events and the achievement of 'correct' selection outcomes.

In 'Accounts of Organisations' Silverman returns to a position approaching that reflected in his 1972 piece, with a critique of functionalist conceptions of organisation from an ethnomethodological standpoint. In this he stresses the need, for example, to understand organisational activities in terms of accounting practices and to understand bureaucracy as not 'in itself "an object" but a language-category which provides for the object-like qualities of an activity' (Silverman, 1975a, p. 296). Its ontological premises, whilst consistent with a position within the interpretive paradigm, are not as subjectivist as those reflected in 'Getting In' (Silverman and Jones, 1973).

Organisational Work (Silverman and Jones, 1976) bears witness to yet another change. This book presents the final report of their empirical work on the staff-selection process within an organisational situation and focuses upon the power and authority relations reflected in the language used in organisational contexts. Silverman and Jones report how a 'fresh look' at their interview tapes revealed that organisational members in their interaction and accounting procedures had 'lay' conceptualisations of a 'hierarchy'. Whilst this is seen as providing evidence in favour of the phenomenological construction and reconstruction of organisational structure (that people create structure through their accounting practices), Silverman and Jones argue that it is not 'to be construed as a solipsistic denial of the factual character of organisational structures', for their reality is 'undeniable' (Silverman and Jones, 1976, p. 20). Such an assertion on the ontological status of structures, which attributes to them an existence on their own terms, is quite out of keeping with the positions articulated in the earlier work referred to above and testifies to what appears to be a major change in theoretical orientation. Whilst Silverman and Jones do not deny the role which individuals play in the construction of their social world, they proceed to argue that the nature of accounting practices sustain 'our all too real technological/bureaucratic community', and that our speech and language of discourse tends to lock us into a relatively passive role as 'mere functionaries' within our present society. They illustrate their point of view through the evidence of their empirical research on interviews, demonstrating 'the grading of language' in which speech and written reports come to reflect the hierarchical nature of the context in which they are located. The hierarchical or grading element in the interview process, for example, is seen as being linked to 'the canons of rationality' in which there are (1) premises all can accept, (2) steps all can follow and (3) conclusions all must accept. These canons come to be used within organisations as legitimate devices for defining the 'seriousness' or authentication of community accounts. The parallels between this analysis and Habermas's theory of 'communicative distortion', which we discuss in the next chapter, is particularly striking, though the authors do not specifically acknowledge the link. They do, however, identify parallels with the work of Heidegger and Marx. Silverman and Jones argue that selection interviewing is a form of evaluation, and that this involves stratification within a society whose 'form of life' is seen, in essence, as a market in which language and speech constitute commodities. Both Heidegger and Marx are seen as having recognised this in their different ways. Grading and accounts of grading become, for Silverman and Jones, alienated labour, 'in which men are related to their mode of speech as to an alien object; in which they use speech to do things (like grading) but in using it are mastered by it since the form of life which makes that speech intelligible dehumanises human activities (makes them something)' (Silverman and Jones, 1976, p. 172). Alienated labour then forms a nexus with the hierarchical nature of our mundane existence and with the predominance of 'exchange value' as the standard of discourse within our society. Thus Silverman and Jones conclude that our present social structure requires a grading of language, which itself affirms 'market hierarchy and a separation of Being from Writing'. 'What,' they ask, 'might it be like to write no longer merely as a functionary?' (Silverman and Jones, 1976, p. 180).

In discovering the power and authority relationship within accounting practices, language and 'speech acts', Silverman and Jones are, in effect, articulating a perspective characteristic of the hermeneutic approach to critical theory within the radical humanist paradigm. As we have noted above, it has much in common with the work of Habermas and must be regarded as a major change in theoretical orientation. The ontological oscillation characteristic of the earlier work is resolved, perhaps unwittingly, through the recognition of a dimension of power and domination beneath the ongoing process through which social reality is created and sustained. This power dimension is able to account for the seeming presence of structural factors in the background of reports on empirical work, but it is not entirely consistent with the phenomenological sociology characteristic of the interpretive paradigm, since it implies that the social construction of reality is underwritten by a pervasive form of ideological domination. The essentially conservative orientation of interpretive sociology, with its concern for understanding how individuals create and impose order upon their world, is displaced along the regulation—radical change dimension of our analytical scheme by the radical humanist concern for understanding how individuals become trapped as 'mere functionaries' within the context of a social formation alien to the nature of their true being.

Phenomenological Symbolic Interactionism and the Study of Organisational Activities

The focus of interest of the phenomenological symbolic interactionist differs from that of the ethnomethodologist in the degree of attention devoted to the manner in which social reality is negotiated through interaction. Whereas the ethnomethodologist usually focuses upon the way in which individual actors account for and make sense of their world, the phenomenological symbolic interactionist focuses upon social contexts in which interacting individuals employ a variety of practices to create and sustain particular definitions of the world. They demonstrate how 'reality' and 'facts' are essentially social creations, negotiated through the interaction of various competing themes and definitions of reality. We will consider here, two studies which illustrate this approach.

David Sudnow in 'Normal Crimes' (1965), attempts to demonstrate the way in which criminal sentences in certain courts in the USA are negotiated through interaction between the District Attorney, the Public Prosecutor, the Public Defender and the defendant. Sudnow explains how, in an attempt to speed up progress through the courts and reduce the work load, the defendant may be persuaded to plead guilty in exchange for a reduced charge and sentence. This occurs in the context of a deal consisting of an offer from the District Attorney to alter the original charge. However, such an offer is shown to depend on whether the crime committed by the defendant fits one of the 'typifications' classified by the legal parties in their mental case-files as a 'normal crime'. The legal process, which is usually regarded as governed and bound by the nature of the penal code, is thus shown to operate through a process of interaction and negotiation mediated by the socially constructed realities adhered to by the parties involved. It thus demonstrates that the legal code and criminal statistics, which are commonly treated as hard 'social facts', are by no means reliable and clear-cut descriptions of particular social realities. The implication is that social reality is socially negotiated and socially sustained, even within the context of rule-bound and tightly controlled bureaucratic situations.

A similar perspective is evident in Joan Emerson's 'Behaviour in Private Places' (1970). In this article Emerson seeks to illustrate how a dominant definition of reality may be invaded by counter-realities which oppose or qualify the dominant definition in various ways. The gynaecological examination presents a situation in which different realities are precariously balanced. The situation is characterised by an impersonal, clinical and medical definition on the one hand, and a personal, intimate, sexual definition on the other. Emerson clearly demonstrates how the sexual aspect can unintentionally invade the clinical definition, so that the parties involved have continually to strive to define the situation as a 'gynaecological examination going right', a situation in which no one is embarrassed and no one is thinking in sexual terms. She demonstrates very clearly how this occurs, with the gynaecologist and nurse acting in concert to sustain the dominant definition through a particular kind of language and technique. When the dominant definition breaks down (through, for example, the patient blushing, or refusing to co-operate through modesty), a whole battery of interventions and techniques is brought into play to restore the balance. The reality of the gynaecological examination is shown to rest upon a complex and sustained series of negotiations between all the parties involved.

Emerson maintains that the precarious balance of competing realities found in the gynaecological examination represents but an extreme case illustrative of the ongoing process which characterises a wide range of situations in everyday life. It merely exaggerates the internally contradictory nature of definitions of reality which are found in everyday situations, at work, in social encounters, or whatever. The study emphasises how individuals have to involve themselves in a deliberate effort to maintain a balance between the conflicting themes reflected in any given social situation, and how the social reality which emerges is essentially negotiated by the actors directly involved.

As in the case of Sudnow's study, Emerson's work, whilst distinctly phenomenological in its basic orientation with regard to the socially created status of reality, does admit of a more concrete form of social organisation in the background. Reality in each case is constructed upon what appears to be a pre-set stage by actors who have already been allocated roles. In neither study is this background subjected to scrutiny; the focus is upon the ways in which the actors construct the scene in which they find themselves.

As in the case of the ethnomethodological studies considered earlier, certain ontological problems are reflected in this research. Later in this chapter we will consider the dilemma which phenomenological sociologists face in engaging upon empirical work of this kind. For the moment, however, we will turn to consider the implications which this type of phenomenologically orientated research, despite its problems, has for organisation theorists located within the functionalist paradigm.

The Phenomenological Challenge to Contemporary Organisation Theory

The challenge which phenomenological sociology presents to contemporary organisation theory is clearly of a very fundamental kind.[3] It suggests that the whole enterprise of 'organisation theory' is based upon very dubious foundations. The ontological assumptions which characterise the functionalist paradigm stand in fundamental opposition to those which underwrite the phenomenological perspective. For phenomenologists, organisations as tangible and relatively concrete phenomena simply do not exist; the social world is essentially processual and emerges from the intentional acts of human beings acting individually or in concert with one another. The social reality 'created' in the course of this process consists of little more than images of reality which can be understood in terms of a network of typifications. They do not comprise a solid definition; they gloss over complexity; the complex nature of social reality only emerges when individuals are forced, through the pressures of interaction with one another, or in attempting to make sense of their world, to dive deeper and deeper for new or modified typifications to account for and make sense of their situation. The complex and tangible nature of reality 'out there' is, from this point of view, a socially constructed phenomenon of dubious intersubjective status and as transient as the moment in which it is viewed.

Organisations, therefore, are seen, from the phenomenological perspective, as social constructs; an organisation stands as a concept which means different things to different people. As a universal concept, its intersubjective status is extremely dubious. Organisation theorists are seen as belonging to a small and self-sustaining community which believes that organisations exist in a relatively tangible ontological sense and theorises about them. From the phenomenological standpoint, organisation theorists theorise about concepts which have very little significance to people outside the community which practises organisation theory and the limited community which organisation theorists may attempt to serve.

For the phenomenologists, organisation theorists sustain their enterprise by colluding with those whom they attempt to serve, or, more appropriately, those to whom they feel they need to make their activities rationally accountable. It is for this reason that contemporary organisation theory is accused of having a managerial bias. It uses managerial concepts in order to construct its theories. These concepts are used as a 'resource', whereas, as Bittner (1965) suggests, from the phenomenological point of view they should provide the 'topic' of analysis.

The phenomenological challenge to contemporary organisation theory is total and complete, because the issue at dispute is that of ontology. It follows from this that *all* the concepts which the organisation theorist uses to construct his view of organisational reality are open to criticism. The concepts of organisation structure, job satisfaction, organisational climate, etc., are all reifications which are often confused with social reality. Should the organisation theorist claim that they are merely of heuristic value, then the question of 'ownership' arises, and the unwitting or conscious collusion which this implies. Much of the phenomenological research which we have considered in this chapter can be understood as an attempt to demonstrate to theorists located within the functionalist orthodoxy that they are over-concretising the social world. The studies which have demonstrated, for example, how individuals create the rules within an organisational context, negotiate the nature of 'crime' and hence, of criminal 'statistics', demonstrate that to view reality in terms of these rules, structures and statistics is to view the world in terms which are all too simple. The core of social reality lies in what Garfinkel (1967, p. 11) has described as 'the awesome indexicality' of everyday life. Reality does not exist on the surface of human affairs, offering itself for straightforward study as the functionalist organisation theorist so often assumes. Social reality lies deep within the network of typifications which individuals, if pressed, will summon to make sense of the situation in which they find themselves.

The implications of a phenomenological sociology true to the ontological assumptions of the interpretive paradigm are completely destructive as far as contemporary organisation theory is concerned. The phenomenological sociologist and the organisation theorist occupy different social realities to all intents and purposes; they live in different intellectual worlds. The contemporary organisation theorist cannot build his theories within the context of the interpretive paradigm.

What, then, can the contemporary organisation theorist learn from the phenomenologist? What can he incorporate within the bounds of the functionalist paradigm? It would seem that here there is some scope for integration — a potential which others have already tried to explore. It will be recalled from the previous chapter that the concern to integrate the perspectives of idealism and positivism was a preoccupation of many social theorists in the years of the late nineteenth and early twentieth centuries. It was one of the major problems to which Dilthey and Weber addressed themselves, for example, and, as we have suggested, social action theory and certain varieties of interactionism can be understood as the direct products of this concern. In many respects these schools of thought represent the functionalist reaction to the idealist view of social reality which underwrites the phenomenological perspective, and offer scope for further development within organisational theory. Silverman's book *The Theory of Organisations* (1970), for example, suggests one possible line of development.

Clearly, there is much more that can be done within the context of functionalism to explore the implications of studying a social reality which is far less clear-cut, certain and solid, and more processual, than has been envisaged in theory to date. There is more scope for recognising the role of individuals in interpreting and sustaining particular views of social reality than is generally recognised. There is scope for adopting an epistemology, a view of human nature and a methodology consonant with this revised view of the ontological status of the social world. In short, contemporary organisation theory can usefully assess and reappraise its basic orientation with regard to its assumptions on each of the four strands of the subjective—objective dimension of our analytical scheme.[4] Such action would represent a response which meets the phenomenological challenge upon the functionalist's own ground. As far as the phenomenologist is concerned, it would be an inadequate response. At heart, the basic challenge of phenomenology to functionalist theory is to respect the nature of the social world and, for the phenomenologist, this is just not possible within the bounds of the functionalist problematic.[5]

Phenomenological Approaches to the Study of Organisational Situations: Problems and Dilemmas

Adopting the standpoint of the phenomenological sociologist rather than that of the functionalist organisation theorist, what implications emerge from the discussion and analysis presented in earlier sections of this chapter? Clearly, there are many problems for the phenomenological sociologist concerned to study the nature of organisational situations, since he is often unwittingly led to recognise and acknowledge features within any given situation which, if pressed, he would be forced to deny. We have made much of this point in our discussion of the 'ontological oscillation' between theoretical and empirical work.

It would seem that many of these problems arise because the researchers concerned have not been sufficiently explicit about what they are attempting to demonstrate. Focusing upon the four elements of the subjective—objective dimension of our analytical scheme, it is unclear whether the empirical work of these theorists aims to illustrate a particular view of ontology, to demonstrate the superiority of a particular approach to epistemology and methodology, or merely to emphasise the voluntarism which they see as characterising human affairs. No doubt some of the studies attempt to achieve all these aims, though their success is questionable.

If the concern of the phenomenological sociologist is to tackle the problem of ontology, as his theoretical perspective requires, then it is important that he be explicit about this. It is important to emphasise that the reality which his work reflects is fundamentally different from that conceptualised by, for example, the functionalist theorist. Insofar as he confines himself to illustrating movement within organisational rules or against the background of a bureaucratic structure, as some of the studies discussed earlier have sought to do, then his work tends to affirm the basic existence of the reality upon which functionalist theory, for example, is based. The choice of unusual situations for research such as Skid Row, which are far removed from the realm of everyday life for the majority of people, also tends to reaffirm the concrete status of everyday reality in situations which are not Skid Row. If the phenomenologist is concerned to tackle the problem of ontology, it would seem that it is necessary to study situations in which people are typically regarded as having relatively little discretion in the way in which they mould their reality. Up to now phenomenological research has focused upon what the functionalist theorist would regard as high-discretion roles, such as those of the receptionist, district attorney, police officer, gynaecologist, etc. Phenomenological studies of what are usually seen as low-discretion situations (characteristic of the assembly line, for example) tend to be conspicuous by their absence.

A focus upon the ontological problems involved here would require the phenomenological sociologist to take a firm stand on the precise status of the concepts of organisation, hierarchy, bureaucratic rules, etc., and other background features inherent in much of the empirical work produced to date. It would clarify whether they actually intend to dispute the realist ontology which characterises the functionalist orthodoxy, or whether they are merely attempting to illustrate the complex and voluntaristic nature of human actions and the inadequacies of positivist epistemology and nomethetic methodology for developing an adequate understanding of this process. It would bring them face to face with the basic assumptions which underwrite the interpretive paradigm, since they would be obliged to be specific about the precise status of social reality and the form which it takes. As we noted in our discussion on the work of Silverman and his colleagues, the attempt to deal with a socially contructed and socially sustained reality which appears all too 'real' has introduced a new dimension into his work consonant with 'critical theory' within the radical humanist paradigm. The attempt to handle the seeming presence of pattern and structure reflected in the social construction of reality has led to a focus upon ideological issues intimately related to the regulation—radical change dimension of our analytical scheme. Phenomenological sociology characteristic of the interpretive paradigm is underwritten by the basic assumption that there is a tendency towards order in social affairs. Insofar as a part of this order is reflected in a pattern and structure which provides a context within which reality is created, it needs to be explained. It is precisely this concern which has led many social theorists who wish to continue to subscribe to a nominalist perspective characteristic of the idealist tradition to forge alternative frameworks.

As we shall find in the next chapter, this concern is very much reflected in the work of Hegel and in the problem of the dialectical relationship between subject and object worlds. It is also reflected in the work of the young Karl Marx, Jean-Paul Sartre and, more recently, Habermas. In their different ways they have sought to demonstrate that the socially created world can become all too real and provides a framework which constrains the actions and orientations of human beings, as if it had an existence on its own account. We do not wish to imply here that phenomenological sociology can *only* be further developed within the context of the radical humanist paradigm. Our intention is to pose the issues which arise if phenomenological sociologists acknowledge the seeming presence of structure which hangs in the background of their current work. By confronting the basic ontological problem which this involves, they will clarify the nature of their enterprise. For those who remain convinced that social reality is entirely the creation of autonomous human beings involved in the flow of everyday life, the problem will be to develop epistemologies and methodologies adequate for studying the nature of this world. For those for whom structure and pattern in social reality appear all too 'real', a consideration of the power dimension inherent in the ability of the individual to create his reality is likely to prove a major issue and, pursued to its logical end, will undoubtedly call for a major reorientation in theoretical perspective. It will call for a perspective which has much more in common with radical humanism than with the sociology of regulation which characterises the interpretive paradigm.

Notes and References

1. Silverman, in defence of Bittner's view, has suggested that he uses 'structural determinants' in a highly specific sense (Silverman in McKinlay, 1975, p. 282).
2. We shall not consider here Silverman's book *Reading Castaneda* (1975b), which seeks to provide an ethnomethodological analysis of Castaneda (1970) and thus does not focus upon practices within organisational contexts.
3. We shall confine our discussion here to the implications of phenomenology for theories characteristic of the functionalist paradigm. It is clear that there are also implications for theories located in the other paradigms. Unfortunately, it is beyond the scope of our present endeavour to address these here.
4. For a discussion of some of the epistemological and methodological implications of phenomenological sociology, see, for example, Blumer (1969), Cicourel (1964), Douglas (1970b). Many of their arguments are conveniently brought together in Mennell (1974).
5. We wish to emphasise here the point made in note 3 above. The nature of the concept of paradigm, as used here, necessarily implies that the legitimacy of the world view reflected in a particular paradigm is fundamentally opposed by the perspectives characteristic of the other three.

8. Radical Humanism

Origins and Intellectual Tradition

The intellectual origins of the radical humanist paradigm can be traced back to the tenets of German idealism and the Kantian notion that the ultimate reality of the universe is spiritual rather than material in nature. It thus derives from the same intellectual source as the interpretive paradigm, though the essentially subjectivist orientation which the two paradigms have in common are made to serve fundamentally different ends.

The interpretive and radical humanist paradigms are both founded upon the notion that the individual creates the world in which he lives. But, whereas the interpretive theorists are content to understand the nature of this process, the radical humanists subject it to critique, focusing upon what they regard as the essentially alienated state of man.

This critique proceeds along two avenues of discourse. One of these is associated with a 'subjective idealist' position, which derives from the same source as the philosophy of Husserl and other phenomenologists discussed in Chapter 6. Although the roots of the subjective idealist tradition can be traced back to the philosophy of Kant and earlier, it is in the work of Fichte (1762–1814) that it first receives its most explicit and coherent expression.[1] Fichte was a follower of Kant, and his brand of subjective idealism rested upon the assumption that individual consciousness is a continuously creative entity generating a perpetual stream of ideas, concepts and perspectives through which a world external to mind is created. From Fichte's point of view, any understanding of this created reality involved understanding the nature, structure and functioning of conscious mind. However, he was at pains to distinguish between this internal domain of consciousness and what was created by it and thus made external to it. In so doing he was able to steer clear of the solipsist perspective by recognising the existence of an external world, thus establishing a position some way between the immaterialism of Bishop Berkeley and the perspective of 'objective idealism' as, for example, reflected in the work of Hegel (1770–1831). For Fichte, the external world was to be understood in terms of the projection of individual consciousness. Fichte saw human beings as externalising their experiences into a form of reality which in turn is reflected back upon them, and through which they became conscious of themselves and their actions. As noted above, this perspective has had a widespread influence upon contemporary philosophy and social theory through the work of Husserl and other phenomenologists. Its influence upon the radical humanist paradigm is most clearly evident in the work of Sartre and his followers within the French existentialist movement. In essence, they have radicalised the phenomenological perspective which characterises the subjective idealist's position, viewing the individual as trapped within the mode of existence which he creates. Ontologically, they view the world as the product of individual consciousness; consciousness is seen as being projected onto the external through acts of intentionality, thereby creating it. The subjective idealists within radical humanism focus upon the pathology of intentionality, whereby, in creating the external world, man separates himself from his true 'Being'.

The second avenue of discourse within radical humanism is based upon the tradition of 'objective idealism', which received its earliest and most comprehensive expression in the work of Hegel.[2] The Hegelian system of thought rests upon his first and perhaps most significant work, *The Phenomenology of Mind*, which investigates the ontological status of human knowledge. In this book Hegel seeks to demonstrate how knowledge passes through a series of forms of consciousness until a state of 'absolute knowledge' is reached, wherein the individual is at one with the 'absolute spirit' which pervades the universe. For Hegel, the ultimate reality rests in 'spirit' (*Geist*). 'Absolute knowledge' rests upon the realisation that consciousness is 'spirit' and that the object of consciousness is nothing other than itself. Hegel presents human beings as living in a world characterised by a constant interplay between individual consciousness and its objectification in the external world. Consciousness and the external world are viewed as two sides of the same reality. They are locked in a dialectical relationship in which each defines and influences the other.[3] For Hegel, everything is its own opposite. The truth lies on both sides of every question in an antagonistic relationship to itself. As a method of analysis the dialectic stresses that there is a basic antagonism and conflict within both the natural and the social world which, when resolved, leads to a higher stage of development. This dialectical process is seen as a universal principle, which generates progress towards the state of 'absolute knowledge' in which the distinction between subject and object is overcome and human consciousness becomes aware of its location within 'absolute spirit'.

Hegel, like Fichte, saw individual consciousness as a focal point for the understanding of the nature of the social world. However, whereas in Fichte's brand of subjective idealism, the individual creates his world, in Hegel's brand of objective idealism, individual consciousness is subservient to an external pattern of universal reason which reflects the existence of a universal force or spirit above and beyond the individual. Human consciousness and human history, for Hegel, are to be understood in terms of the unfolding of the universal spirit which will lead with certainty to the perfect society. In his later years, Hegel increasingly saw the Prussia of his day as the embodiment of the 'absolute spirit', the perfect society in which the individual became subservient to the state.

Hegel's philosophy thus became wedded to a very conservative political creed, and has been subjected to a wide range of interpretation. Early on a deep cleavage of opinion arose between the perspectives of the so-called 'Right Hegelians', who more or less accepted Hegel's system of philosophy in its entirety, and the views of the 'Left' or 'Young Hegelians', who directed Hegel's system of thought to fundamentally different ends.

Prominent among the 'Young Hegelians' was the young Karl Marx (1818–1883), who in essence inverted the Hegelian system and united it with a critique of the society of his day.[4] In so doing he laid the basis for the development of a radical humanism in the objective idealist mould. Marx employed Hegel's historical perspective and dialectical method of analysis within the context of a philosophy which placed the individual rather than 'absolute spirit' at the centre of the stage. Marx, along with the other Young Hegelians, particularly Feuerbach,[5] argued that there was no absolute above man. They argued that religion and the State were the creations of man rather than reflections of any 'absolute spirit'. They emphasised that all objectifications encountered in the social world were humanly created and pointed the way to an emancipatory philosophy which stressed how individuals, through self-consciousness, could create and thus change the society in which they lived. Marx, in particular, started from the premise of the alienation of man. He saw the society of his day as dominating human experience; objectified social creations reflected back upon man as an alienating force, dominating his essential being and nature. This point of view is expressed most forcibly in *Economic and Philosophical Manuscripts* (1844), in which Marx demonstrated how the capitalist system of production lay at the heart of man's alienation.[6] Whereas for Hegel alienation was a necessary phenomenon on the path to self-realisation and 'absolute knowledge', for Marx it became a concept wedded to an attack upon the *status quo* and the shortcomings of the totality of capitalism.

In later work Marx moved away from the idealist perspective to one rooted in a more realist interpretation of the nature of the social world. In *The German Ideology* (1846), written with Engels, Marx sought to settle accounts with German idealism, and this work is often seen as defining the so-called 'epistemological break' in Marx's thought (Althusser, 1969). From the point of view of the analytical scheme presented here, it signifies Marx's break with radical humanism, and the beginning of a move towards radical structuralism. The perspectives characteristic of the latter paradigm, which are explored in Chapter 10, receive increasing attention in Marx's *Grundrisse* and *Capital*.

Despite these early origins, the radical humanist perspective remained dormant until the early 1920s, when Lukács, under the influence of neo-idealism, sought to re-emphasise the influence of Hegel upon Marx. The discovery of the lost *Economic and Philosophical Manuscripts* some ten years later reinforced, and in some ways legitimated, this interest, which found its expression in a radical humanist critical theory. The growth of critical theory, along with French existentialism, its subjective idealist counterpart, can largely be understood as the radical response to the renewal of interest in the idealist tradition which, as we have seen from Chapter 6, emerged at the turn of the twentieth century.

The Structure of the Paradigm

As will be apparent from the above discussion, the radical humanist paradigm comprises the subjective and objective idealist strains of thought, both of which have their origins in German idealism. These constitute the principal philosophical perspectives. In addition, it is possible to identify the shaping influence of solipsism and a category of anarchist thought which, though deriving largely from Hegelianism, must be regarded as having followed a different line in terms of detailed development. We may consider the work located within this paradigm under four broad headings: (a) solipsism; (b) French existentialism; (c) anarchistic individualism; (d) critical theory.

The broad interrelationships between these four categories of social theory are illustrated in Figure 3.3.

Solipsism characterises the most subjectivist region of the paradigm, just as it does within the interpretive paradigm. As we have argued, it represents a philosophical position without sociological equivalent, although some social theories, when taken to their logical extremes, run dangerously close to what Sartre (1969) has described as the 'reef of solipsism'. Since we considered this perspective in Chapter 6, we will not discuss it further here.

French existentialism occupies the middle range of the paradigm. It represents a perspective in the tradition of subjective idealism. Deriving largely from the work of Fichte and Husserl, it receives its clearest expression in the work of Sartre. This variety of existentialism has influenced literary interpretation and some psychiatry, as well as philosophy.

Anarchistic individualism, most usually associated with the thought of Max Stirner, occupies a position in the least subjectivist and most change-orientated region of the paradigm. It is a category of thought which few subscribe to, but it is worthy of consideration as an example of an extreme social theory which advocates radical change, focusing upon individual consciousness as the basic unit of analysis.

Critical theory represents the principal line of development in the objective idealist tradition and is located in the least subjectivist region of the radical humanist paradigm. Within critical theory we recognise three broad schools of thought based upon Lukácsian sociology, Gramsci's sociology and the work of the Frankfurt School. These differ considerably at a substantive level but are all predicated upon Marx's inversion of the Hegelian system of thought.

We begin our detailed consideration of these categories of thought with 'Critical Theory'.

Critical Theory

Critical theory represents a category of sociological thought built explicitly upon the work of the young Marx.[7] As a term it is often used as a synonym for the work of the Frankfurt School of social theorists, but we wish here to expand its usage to cover three interrelated yet discrete schools of thought. The Frankfurt School owes much to the work of Lukács, which, in turn, bears a remarkable similarity to that of Gramsci, so that these approaches have substantial areas of overlap. Critical theory is a brand of social philosophy which seeks to operate simultaneously at a philosophical, a theoretical and a practical level. It stands firmly in the idealist tradition of critique deriving from Kant's *Critique of Pure Reason*; its proponents seek to reveal society for what it is, to unmask its essence and mode of operation and to lay the foundations for human emancipation through deep-seated social change. It is an overtly political philosophy, in that it stresses the need to follow the logic of one's philosophical and sociological analysis with practical action of a radical kind. Lukács, Gramsci and the Frankfurt School, whilst sharing this overall aim, differ in the nature and methods of their specific critiques. We will examine each in turn.

Lukácsian sociology

In the early 1920s Georg Lukács (1885–1974) sought to develop a critical theory which offered an alternative to the orthodox Marxism of his day.[8] In essence, he was concerned to overhaul its socio-philosophical foundations, by emphasising and restoring the strong Hegelian influence which characterised Marx's work before the so-called 'epistemological break'. In particular, Lukács sought to develop a theory of revolution which laid strong emphasis upon the role of the proletariat and its class consciousness in the overthrow of capitalist society. For Lukács, as we shall see, the proletariat provided a solution to the epistemological, theoretical and practical issues facing Marxism in the 1920s.

Lukács's influence, like that of his one-time teacher Simmel, is dissipated and fragmented. Lukácsian sociology consists not so much of Lukácsians who are dogmatically faithful to his key texts, problems and conceptualisations, as of a widely constituted body of thought which uses, to a greater or lesser extent, Lukács's key notions. This influence has been felt internationally, so that in France Lukács's work has been developed by Lucien Goldmann, in Britain by Mészáros and in the USA by Alvin Gouldner, who has gone so far as to describe Lukács as 'the greatest Marxist theorist of the twentieth century' (Gouldner, 1976, p. x).

It is important to note, however, that Lukács' influence stems from his early work and that his later output is steadfastly ignored. In fact, Lukács is a thinker whose work can be located on at least three points on the subjective—objective dimension of our analytical scheme. He began his career in Hungary with the publication of a series of books connected with the theory of the novel, in which he acknowledges his position to be that of subjective idealism. Lukács had been attracted to subjective idealism under the influence of Dilthey's approach to the *Geisteswissenschaften* and Husserl's phenomenology through his studies at Berlin and later Heidelberg. At Heidelberg Lukács was introduced to Hegel's work and by 1923 had produced a collected series of essays entitled *History and Class Consciousness*. Based upon Hegelian objective idealism, this work represented an attempt to emphasise the humanist, more subjective aspects of Marxism some ten years before the rediscovery of Marx's *Economic and Philosophical Manuscripts* of 1844. The reaction against *History and Class Consciousness* within orthodox Marxism was such that Lukács was labelled an ultra-Leftist and a heretic insofar as Engels' interpretation of dialectical materialism was concerned.[9] As a result, he retracted his views on the link between Hegel and Marx and moved to a position of middle-of-the-road materialism. This was done, one might suggest without exaggeration, in order to survive in Stalinist Russia at a time when the life expectancy of heretical intellectuals was not high. In our terms, Lukács made a complete paradigmatic shift in the face of this threat. So total was his embrace of materialism, and so unexceptionable his treatment of it, that Lichtheim maintains that Lukács's writings in the thirties were 'the work of a man who had performed a kind of painless lobotomy upon himself, removed part of his brain and replaced it by slogans from the Moscow propagandists' (Lichtheim, 1970, pp. 83–4).

In the sixties, however, relations with the West were 'normalised' and Stalin's intellectual and political influence explicitly rejected. Lukács could assert again that *History and Class Consciousness*, although flawed, was a book he was prepared to discuss and see republished under his name. This book has had a quite crucial impact upon Marxism and is significant in that 'materialism' and the ideas of Engels play only a minor role. Lukács stresses the role of superstructural factors within society and their part in its transformation. Emphasis is placed upon consciousness, ideology, literature and art, which are seen not as epiphenomenal to the relations and means of production, but as quite central to any understanding of capitalism. Consciousness, in particular, is assigned key importance, for proleterian consciousness was crucial to both Lukács's philosophy and his political methodology.

Class consciousness was central for Lukács, because he saw it as the escape route from a fundamental problem associated with Hegel's notion of alienation. For Hegel, alienations occurred as a result of the objectification of 'ideas' in the external world which reasserted themselves within man's consciousness. The ability to move beyond alienation within this dialectical loop was provided by the existence of an 'identical subject – object' which is 'at one' with itself and not internally alienated. Hegel explained this through the notion of 'absolute spirit'; Lukács replaced this notion with that of the proletariat, which becomes an 'identical subject-object' not alienated within itself if and when it acquires true or 'imputed' consciousness of the reality of capitalism and of its ability to transform and overthrow it.[10] The class consciousness of the proletariat then both provides a philosophical solution to one of the Hegelian puzzles and represents the means whereby existing society can be overthrown. By this device Lukács seeks to evade some of the primary epistemological and practical problems facing Marxism.

The proletariat represents an identical subject-object not only in its ability to transcend alienation, but also in its position in the centre of the world historical stage, from which it can comprehend, more than any other group or class, the 'totality' of capitalist society.[11] Lukács's notion of 'totality' serves to unify *History and Class Consciousness*, but it is a difficult concept to comprehend. In a most general sense it refers to the Hegelian and Marxist view that everything must be grasped as a whole; the whole dominates the parts in an all-embracing sense. Marx used the notion of 'totality' to conceptualise the process of social change. 'Stages' in societal development represent specific 'totalities', so that each transformation of society replaces one totality by another. Capitalism is one such totality, quite distinct from feudalism or communism, and it is one in which objective and subjective elements are combined within a complex, dynamic, structured process which can only be comprehended holistically. This implies that one cannot understand any aspect of capitalism without first understanding capitalism itself in its entirety. As we have seen, for Lukács it is the proletariat which has the ability to comprehend society, to see the internal connections of the parts within it and the whole network of relationships in the total social structure. Once this totality is subjected to analysis it is unmasked and stands revealed to all men in the moments of history before its overthrow.

A central aspect of this notion of totality lies in the intimate connection, first postulated by Hegel, between objective and subjective dimensions within social reality, which are synthesised, according to Lukács, within the class consciousness of the proletariat. The process whereby these dimensions are made falsely discrete and differentiated, so that they are no longer seen as 'identical', Lukács calls 'reification'. This has clear links with both Hegelian and Marxist views of alienation, which revolve in different ways around the separation of objective and subjective factors. Arguably, 'reification' is one of the central concepts of *History and Class Consciousness*, for it provides the focus for Lukács's critique of the capitalist form of society. Reification, of course, refers to the fact that whilst men in their day-to-day productive activities create their social world, these activities and what results from them are seen as divorced from men, as independent, objectified 'things'. Whilst objectification of man-made artefacts is probably necessary and inevitable in all forms of social life, Lukács, like Marx, seeks to stress the political, constraining aspects of reification and the effective barrier it provides to the comprehension, by the working class, of the totality in which they live. Put simply, for Lukács alienation in the form of reification is something to be overcome, since it is the key to the release of the explosive energies of the proletariat, which is so necessary for the transformation and reconstruction of capitalist society.

In terms of our major analytical dimensions, Lukácsian sociology occupies a position on the least subjectivist wing of the radical humanist paradigm. Ontologically, it invokes the omnipresent dialectic, since social processes are seen to consist of the 'objective' acting upon the 'subjective' and of the 'subjective' acting in its turn upon the 'objective'. For Lukács, then, the ontological nature of the world is neither crudely nominalist nor crudely realist. Lukácsians invoke the dialectic to meet the need to synthesise objective and subjective factors within an integrated harmonious socio-philosophical approach. However, since revolutionary proletariats have rarely, if ever, succeeded, and since they have rarely understood the totality which is capitalism, the achievement of the 'identical subject – object' through the dialectic has remained an unfulfilled promise.[12]

Epistemologically, Lukács takes up an interesting position. He maintained that Marxism was a revolutionary methodology rather than a set of laws or truths. For Lukács, truth was always historically specific, relative to a given set of circumstances, so that one did not search for generalisations or the laws of motion of capitalism. For example, success within a revolution was not guaranteed by the immanent dynamics of the capitalist system; there was no law of nature or history which said that it *would* be so. Revolution depended upon the actions of the working class and the tactics developed by its leaders. Lukácsians, then, are not epistemological positivists seeking general laws of societal development. They are tacticians and methodologists of revolt and revolution stressing the scope of action open to the proletariat. They indicate the voluntarist aspects of life within capitalism, not the determinist ones, continually pointing to the freedom of choice in the type of class consciousness the proletariat accepts. Almost by an act of will, the 'actual' class consciousness of the vast majority of the proletariat could become 'true' class consciousness through an intellectual grasp of the totality of capitalism. Lukácsians seek to change the world; their epistemology and methodology blend to form a body of thought which seeks not general laws for future contemplation but practical methods for radically transforming society here and now.

Gramsci's sociology

The influence of Antonio Gramsci (1891 – 1937), an Italian Marxist theoretician and political activist, has been rapidly increasing in Western academic circles since the early 1960s, when English translations of his work started to become more readily available. His 'philosophy of praxis' represents not only a rigorous social theory, but also a political methodology for the working class. Gramsci's Marxism, like that of Lukács, presents a radical humanist critique of capitalism and also a methodology for achieving its overthrow. As Boggs has noted, 'the Marxism that emerges from the pages of Gramsci's *Prison Notebooks* can be defined as a *critical theory* that fuses elements of structure and consciousness, science and philosophy, subject and object – a conception which, however unsystematically formulated, is a marked advance upon what, until the 1920s, was the paradigm of orthodox Marxism' (Boggs, 1976, p. 32).

Gramsci's ideas, which developed independently of Lukács, are extremely similar to the Hungarian's. While studying at Turin, Gramsci became influenced by the Hegelianism of Benedetto

Croce, which stood opposed to orthodox Marxism. Gramsci believed that the Marxism of his day had lost its revolutionary zeal through a misguided incorporation of positivist notions and a crude almost mechanistic determinism which totally ignored the voluntarist, practical aspects of working-class radical potentialities.[13] He felt that what was needed was a truly dialectical theory which transcended the classical philosophical antinomies of voluntarism—determinism, idealism—materialism and the subjective—objective. Such a theory would constitute a 'philosophy of praxis' which would represent a total world view, in that it would transcend in itself, all previous philosophical dichotomies and the philosophies based upon only one element within them. As Gramsci put it, 'the philosophy of praxis is "sufficient unto itself"' in that it contains in itself all the fundamental elements needed to construct a total and integral conception of the world, a total philosophy and theory of natural science and not only that but everything that is needed to guide life to an integral practical organisation of society, that is, to become a total integral civilisation' (Gramsci, 1971, p. 406).

This 'philosophy of praxis', this truly 'critical theory', sought to introduce into orthodox Marxism comprehension of and sympathy for an understanding of 'superstructural' factors within capitalist societies. Gramsci believed that power and domination in capitalism rested not only with the materially located means of coercion and oppression, but also within men's consciousness, through 'ideological hegemony'.[14] The ruling class, it was maintained, always seeks to legitimate its power through the creation and perpetuation of a belief system which stresses the need for order, authority and discipline, and consciously attempts to emasculate protest and revolutionary potential. For Gramsci, it was precisely in the area of ideological hegemony in the schools, family and workshop that capitalism was most likely to develop and increase the unseen power of the ruling class, by attacking or infiltrating the consciousness of the individual worker. But this is the crucial weakness of ideological hegemony, too. For whilst hegemony creates alienation, the individual worker is still his own theorist, his own source of class consciousness, and is therefore the most able to resist the forces of hegemony. It is from such ideological resistance in the day-to-day life of workers that, for Gramsci, revolutionary struggle and victory would first come. Consciousness was not treated as being abstract and spiritual; it was a concrete force for a political end.

Gramsci's 'philosophy of praxis' stressed practical involvement in politics, and he, more than any of the other critical theorists, became engaged in revolutionary activity. He aimed to produce within Italian society a 'network of proletarian institutions', mainly factory councils, which were to be the foundations upon which the workers' State could be built. This activity of his declined in the years after 1920, as the factory occupations which had taken place were gradually ended. In 1926 Gramsci was imprisoned by the Fascists for his role in the Communist Party, and whilst in prison he wrote his *Prison Notebooks*, upon which his reputation stands today.

Gramsci's sociology is clearly orientated to action and radical change. More than any other critical theorist, Gramsci stresses the importance of 'praxis' – the unification of theory and practice. Whilst his conceptualisation of the critical problems within society differs from those of other critical theorists, his location in terms of the subjective—objective dimension of our analytical scheme is much the same. Like that of Lukács, Gramsci's approach to Marxism stresses the Hegelian influence. Reality does not exist on its own account in a strict materialist sense, but it exists in a historical relationship with the men who modify it. His position reflects an objective idealism in the tradition of critical theory and the work of the young Karl Marx.

The Frankfurt School

The Frankfurt School's claim on critical theory as its own property owes much to Horkheimer's famous essay of 1937 (reprinted in Horkheimer, 1972), which drew a distinction between traditional science and critical theory. In this, Horkheimer attempted to relate Marx's *Critique of Political Economy* to the German idealist tradition. Just as Marx attacked bourgeois political economy, so Horkheimer differentiated between the traditional approach to social science and the critical theory perspective. Whereas traditional science rested upon the distinction between the observer and his subject and the assumption of value freedom, critical theory emphasised the importance of the theorist's commitment to change.

The 'Frankfurt School' is now used as a generic title for a well-known group of German scholars who have shared, through their links with the Institute for Social Research, common academic and political interests over a number of decades and in a

number of places. Under the influence of members such as Horkheimer, Adorno, Benjamin, Fromm, Kirschheimer, Lowenthal,
Marcuse, Habermas and many others, critical theory has
developed in many directions.[15] Based upon the ontological and
epistemological foundations reflected in the theories of the 'Young
Hegelians' particularly Marx, these critical theorists have forged a
wide-ranging perspective which has consistently aimed to reveal
the nature of capitalist society for what it is. They have sought to
lay bare its underlying nature and set the basis for social change
through a revolution of consciousness. In this endeavour they
have subjected a wide range of social practice to critique in the
tradition of critical theory; they have provided thorough-going
Kulturkritik of the superstructure of capitalism. Positivist science,
modes of rationality, technology, the legal system, the family
unit, patterns of bureaucracy, language, art, music, literature,
the authoritarian personality and psychoanalysis have all been
subjected to critique from a radical humanist perspective. Thus
critical theory in the Frankfurt tradition embraces a polymathic
critical philosophy geared to emancipatory aims. As in the case of
Lukácsian sociology and that of Gramsci, it developed in reaction
to developments within orthodox Marxism, with its emphasis
upon historical determinism, and the general trend towards
totalitarianism in the USSR and Nazi Germany. It has also
developed in reaction to the positivist tradition in a more general
sense, particularly as reflected in the sociology of the functionalist
paradigm. In many respects, critical theory inverts the functionalist problematic, subjecting its tools and basic concepts to
thorough-going analysis. The antithetical stances of critical theory
and the functionalist paradigm are clearly illustrated, for example,
in the philosophical debates between Adorno and Popper,[16] and
the writings of the social theorists to be considered in this section
and the following chapter. In recent years critical theory has also
developed in opposition to trends in interpretive sociology and, as
we shall see, has sought to incorporate central notions in the
hermeneutic tradition within the bounds of its critical philosophy.

In contrast to the work of Lukács and Gramsci, critical theory in
the Frankfurt tradition places far less emphasis upon political
action. Its proponents tend to be theoreticians rather than activ-
ists, and with the passage of time, the School has moved increasingly towards philosophy and intellectual criticism rather than
revolutionary practice. Interestingly enough, after playing a relatively minor role from the 1930s to the early 1960s, it came into
increasing prominence in the wake of student revolution in France

and the counter-culture movement in the USA. Critical theory in the Frankfurt tradition provided the ideal intellectual counterpart to the 'revolution through consciousness' sought by the idealists of the early 1970s. Within the limited context of our present work it is impossible to provide a detailed overview and analysis of the work of the Frankfurt School as a whole. In the rest of this section, therefore, we will focus upon the ideas of Herbert Marcuse and Jürgen Habermas, two of the School's leading contemporary theorists, whose work may be regarded as illustrative of the critical theory perspective.

Marcuse has become well known for his scathing attack upon the 'one-dimensional' nature of modern technological society, particularly under capitalism. His work stands in the true Hegelian-Marxist tradition of critical theory, and represents a conscious attempt to present an emancipatory philosophy which stands against both the phenomenology and the sociological positivism characteristic of the sociology of regulation. For Marcuse, phenomenology is inadequate, in that it ignores the scope for, and influence of, human potentiality; positivism is also inadequate, because of its false assumptions with regard to value neutrality and its role as an instrument of control in the interests of the *status quo*. Marcuse's special contribution to critical theory lies in his attempt to incorporate the ideas and insights of Freud and Weber within the Hegelian-Marxist perspective characteristic of much of the radical humanist paradigm.[17] His critique is most forcibly expressed in two of his major works – *Eros and Civilisation* (1966; first published in 1955) and *One-Dimensional Man* (1964).

In *Eros and Civilisation* Marcuse, following Adorno and Fromm, seeks to develop the links between human personality and the totality in which it is located, taking the Freudian concepts of the 'pleasure principle' and the 'reality principle' as the starting points for analysis. In the Freudian perspective civilisation rests upon the repression of man's internal drives. The 'pleasure principle' by which these drives are allowed to follow an unconstrained search for satisfaction is seen as being subjugated in a civilised society by the 'reality principle', according to which men are prepared to postpone self-gratification in the interests of social order. Marcuse starts from the position that the 'reality principle' is a historically specific element. It is found of necessity only in eras of scarcity, which presuppose the need to master nature in order to survive. Marcuse maintains that scarcity is no longer a characteristic of modern, technologically advanced societies, since they are able to put an end to material shortages of all kinds. The need to repress instinctive desires in such a society is thus no longer so strong. However, it continues, and the level of repression we now find in the advanced industrial state is that of 'surplus repression' – constraint over and above that which is necessary to maintain civilisation. Surplus repression, perceived and retained within the psyche, and supporting the system of production, is seen by Marcuse as lying at the core of man's psychological domination by, and alienation within, the modern world. He sees human emancipation from this dominating social order as being brought about by ridding society of surplus repression, thus giving more emphasis to the 'pleasure principle' expressed through libidinal drives. The message of *Eros and Civilisation* is an optimistic one which views advanced technology as a force for liberation in its ability to eliminate material scarcity.

In *One-Dimenional Man* Marcuse moves to a more Weberian stance, though the direct links with Weberian sociology are not specifically acknowledged or developed to any degree.[18] It is a less optimistic book, in that the liberalising potential of Eros is seen as undermined by the 'one-dimensional' nature of technological societies, in which the centrifugal forces in human and social life are dominated by technology and a one-sided commitment to efficiency and material progress. Marcuse puts forward the thesis that

> technical progress, extended to a whole system of domination and co-ordination, creates forms of life (and of power) which appear to reconcile the forces opposing the system to defeat, or refute all protest in the name of the historical prospects of freedom from toil and domination. Contemporary society seems to be capable of containing social change – qualitative change which would establish essentially different institutions, a new direction of the productive process, new modes of human existence. This containment of social change is perhaps the most singular achievement of advanced industrial society. (Marcuse, 1964, p. 10)

Marcuse argues that modern society is essentially totalitarian, in that the technical apparatus of production and distribution imposes itself upon the whole society. Its products and the individuals it ostensibly serves are moulded to serve its own internal requirements. Technology is seen as a political force, a system of domination which evolves new, increasingly effective and 'more pleasant' means of social control and cohesion. It produces the 'one-dimensional' society, in which there is a flattening out of the difference and conflict between actuality and potentiality; in which alternatives appear to be increasingly unrealistic; in which the industrial system appears to have a logic of its own. Marcuse argues that affluence and the creation of false needs impedes the development of radical protest against the established order. Consciousness is seen as being moulded and controlled through the media. The welfare state and the 'warfare state' are seen as instruments for maintaining the level of consumption necessary for sustaining a 'happy' workforce. All are seen as part of the 'one-dimensional' nature of the totality of modern technological society, in which the logic of purposive rationality pervades modes of thought and the organisation of the material world. For Marcuse, it is the task of critical theory to investigate the roots of this 'totalitarian universe of technological rationality', and to examine their historical alternatives, as a means of revealing unused capacities for improving the lives of human beings.

Within the last few years the writings of Jürgen Habermas have attracted increasing attention as his major works (Habermas, 1970a and b, 1971a and b, 1972, 1974 and 1976) have become available in English translation. A leading exponent of contemporary critical theory, his work is impressive for its range and ability to utilise ideas and concepts drawn from a variety of perspectives in the service of a radical humanism. In essence, his work can be understood as a reaction against the shortcomings of interpretive sociology and sociological positivism. Habermas believes that the discourses of these two traditions are inadequate and that they reflect and serve the interests of those who use them. He distinguishes between the empirical/analytic sciences of a positivist orientation, which serve the interests of control; the historical/hermeneutic sciences of the phenomenological tradition, which aim at understanding meaning without influencing it; and the critical science perspective characteristic of the Frankfurt School, which aims both to understand the world *and* to change it (Habermas, 1972). The critical theory which he favours incorporates notions derived from Parsonian systems theory and its latter-day German equivalents; hermeneutics, as reflected, for example, in the work of Gadamer (1965); and various concepts drawn from psychoanalysis. These diverse perspectives are welded together into a critical theory which for Habermas must be emancipatory, dialectical (in transcending the philosophical antinomies of subject and object, observer and observed, fact and value), and hermeneutic in its endeavour to understand the socio-cultural world in which subjective meaning is located.

Habermas has attempted to shift the attention within Marxism away from a consideration of the economic structure of capitalism towards some of the key features of post-capitalist societies. Whereas Marcuse has created a similar shift in attention by pointing towards the Weberian minotaur of purposive or technical rationality, Habermas has stressed the structure of domination embedded within our language and everyday discourse. For Habermas, the structure of language, its nature and use, provide a key with which to unlock many insights into the fundamental mode of operation of different social formations.

Recent developments in linguistics and ordinary language philosophy demonstrate to Habermas's satisfaction that today the 'problem of language' has replaced the traditional 'problem of consciousness'. In order to deal with these developments, he has developed a theory of 'communicative competence', which borrows conceptualisations from hermeneutics in order to provide the link between the political macro-structure and speech acts within a context of symbolic interaction. Habermas develops the concept of an 'ideal speech situation', in which 'symbolic interaction' is possible since genuine consensus is arrived at between parties in communication and is recognised as a consensus without the operation of power. This 'ideal speech situation' is contrasted with one characterised by 'communicative distortion', in which a supposed consensus is arrived at through discourse within the context of an unequal power distribution.

Habermas illustrates the difference between these two situations through the concepts of 'work' and 'interaction'. These are seen as being fundamentally different categories of social life, with purposive rationality dominating the former, and symbolic interaction the latter. 'Work' is viewed by Habermas as the dominant form of social action within capitalist industrialised society. He sees this social form as based upon a purposive rationality which stresses the importance of goal attainment, defined in terms of means—ends relationships. The system develops technical rules to guide action and modes of thinking, and places stress upon the learning of skills and qualifications. Social life is compartmentalised and language is 'context-free'. The rationalisation of the system of action as a whole lies in the growth of productive forces and the extension of power of technical control. 'Work' is seen as a form of 'communicative distortion' characterised by asymmetrical choice in the use of speech acts which reflects an unequal power relationship.

'Interaction', on the other hand, is based on communicative

action between men in which shared norms develop and are reflected in an intersubjectively shared ordinary language. Implicitly, 'interaction' is seen as more typical of societies in the pre-capitalist era, with their low levels of specialisation and relatively undeveloped division of labour. 'Interaction' subsumes 'labour' as a cohesive and integral part of social life. Within this social form there are reciprocal expectations about behaviour, violations of which attract widely based social sanctions. The norms and values which govern social affairs are acquired through a process of role internalisation. The rationalisation of this system of action lies in 'emancipation', 'individuation' and the 'extension of communication free of domination' (Habermas, 1971b). 'Interaction' is seen as based upon 'ideal speech' situations in which man is emancipated from 'work' and domination. Habermas's vision is of a post-modern world based on 'interaction', with equal access to speech acts afforded to all and an equality of opportunity within discourse. As Schroyer (1971) has noted, to the extent that Habermas's version of critical theory is based upon the liberating potential of self-reflexive language, the new form of critical science which he advocates is essentially based upon a 'pathology of communication'.

Despite the emphasis placed upon language as a focus for social analysis, Habermas is also at pains to stress that the theory of communicative competence must be linked to the fundamental assumptions of historical materialism if it is to be adequate and effective. In his more recent works, however, in which he deals with the variety of crises which might affect modern society, the crucial area is seen as the legitimatory superstructure of the political system (Habermas, 1976). He argues that a permanent economic crisis is no longer likely within advanced capitalism because of the pervasive intervention of the State. Thus, Marx's analysis, with its dependence on class struggles and their relationship to economic crises, is implicitly seen as outdated. For Habermas, the key problem within advanced capitalism is the 'legitimation crisis'.[19] Therefore, whilst recognising the analytical importance of material production, his concern is primarily with 'superstructural' factors, which are normally seen within orthodox Marxism as epiphenomenal to any understanding of the economic foundations of society. The materialist and idealist strands within Habermas's work are always yoked in a relationship of great tension, and his theoretical orientation aims at their reconciliation.

Like Marcuse, Habermas has sought to update the Hegelian-Marxist critique of contemporary society and, in so doing, has drawn heavily upon developments taking place within the sociology of regulation for the purpose of analysis. Their work clearly demonstrates the way in which critical theory in the Frankfurt tradition inverts the concerns and problematic of regulative social theory, particularly that characteristic of the functionalist paradigm. The functionalist tends to accept the norm of purposive rationality, the logic of science, the positive functions of technology, and the neutrality of language, and uses them as building blocks in the construction of supposedly value-free social theories. The Frankfurt theorists concentrate upon demolishing this structure, indicating the essentially political and repressive nature of the whole enterprise. They seek to demonstrate the way in which science, ideology, technology, language and other aspects of the superstructure of modern capitalist social formations are to be understood in relation to the role which they play in sustaining and developing the system of power and domination which pervades the totality of this social form. Their function is to influence the consciousness of the people living within it, with a view to eventual emancipation and the pursuit of alternative forms of life.

The focus of critical theory upon the 'superstructural' aspects of capitalist society is highly significant, in that it reflects the attempt of theorists working within this tradition to move away from the 'economism' of orthodox Marxism and to elevate the Hegelian concern for the role of the dialectic in social affairs. It is through the dialectic that the objective and subjective aspects of social life are thought to be reconciled. The 'superstructure' of capitalist society is of key interest to the critical theorists, partly because it is the medium through which the consciousness of human beings is controlled and moulded to fit the requirements of the social formation as a whole. It thus lies at the interface between subjective and objective worlds. In early Hegelian-Marxist theory various elements of the superstructure, such as religion and the State were seen as the sources of human alienation. As Marx argued in his early writings, these 'intermediaries' which exist between man and his experience of the world 'mystify', projecting a spurious unity and order. He argued that they stood as seemingly independent and alienating forces, created by man, yet reflecting back upon him as independent presences. It was the task of the work of the youthful Marx to 'de-mystify' through critique, in the true idealist tradition.

The critical theorists reviewed in this section are all firmly located in this intellectual tradition, and their work is to be understood in similar terms. The relationship between key concepts such as 'totality', 'consciousness', 'alienation' and 'critique' which seem to permeate Marx's early work are not always spelt out and, indeed, do not always attract specific attention in the writings of critical theorists. We wish to close our discussion here by emphasising how crucial these four notions are to the perspective upon which critical theory is built, and we present Table 8.1 as a means of demonstrating some of the links which exist between the work of the writers which we have considered here.

Table 8.1

Critical theory: central concepts and orientations

Totality

The notion that any understanding of society must embrace in their entirety the objective and subjective worlds which characterise a given epoch. Totality embraces everything; it has no boundary. An understanding of this totality must precede an understanding of its elements, since the whole dominates the parts in an all-embracing sense.

Consciousness

The force which ultimately creates and sustains the social world. Consciousness is internally generated but influenced by the forms which it assumes through the process of objectification and the dialectic between subjective and objective worlds.

Alienation

The state in which, in certain totalities, a cognitive wedge is driven between man's consciousness and the objectified social world, so that man sees what are essentially the creations of his own consciousness in the form of a hard, dominating, external reality. This wedge is the wedge of alienation, which divorces man from his true self and hinders the fulfilment of his potentialities as a human being.

Table 8.1 (continued)

Critique
In their critique of contemporary society, critical theorists focus upon the forms and sources of alienation, which they see as inhibiting the possibilities of true human fulfilment. The various exponents of this perspective approach it in somewhat different ways, at varying levels of generality.

Lukács	focuses upon the concept of *reification*, which provided the socio-philosophical solution to the epistemological and practical problems facing Marxism in the 1920s.
Gramsci	focuses upon the notion of *ideological hegemony* as reflecting a belief system among the proletariat fostered by the ruling class. In his view, the belief system stressed the importance of *order*, *authority* and *discipline*, and was propagated through institutions such as the *family*, *school* and *workplace*.
Marcuse	through his notion of *one-dimensional man*, focuses attention upon the alienating characteristics which he sees as being embedded in the growth of *purposive rationality* within advanced industrial societies. In particular, he emphasises the alienating role of *technology*, *science* and *logic*. These supplement other forces identified in his earlier work relating to the excessive repression of *libido* and the maintenance of a happy work force through the creation of *affluence* and *false needs*.
Habermas	focuses upon the role which *language* plays as an alienating force in all aspects of social life. His theory of *communicative competence* seeks the common denominator in human interaction, whether verbal, sexual, productive or whatever, and seeks to show how in contemporary Western societies there is an element of *communicative distortion* which lies at the heart, and most basic level, of man's alienation.

Anarchistic Individualism

Like so many large-scale intellectual movements, anarchism is not so much a relatively unified, political and theoretical position as a clustering of perspectives. Anarchistic individualism represents one such perspective, advocating total individual freedom, untrammelled by any form of external or internal regulation.[20] Anarchistic individualism is a doctrine closely associated with Max Stirner, a German school-teacher, whose inversion of the Hegelian system of philosophy went far beyond that of Marx in its rejection of all social institutions and the notion of the 'absolute' in any form.[21] His position resembles that of the existentialists in some respects, since his notion of the ego comes close, as we shall see, to Sartre's concept of 'being-for-self'. Stirner emphasised the primacy of individual existence and totally rejected any search for universal laws governing social life. Far from sharing the Hobbesian vision of the cataclysmic 'war of all against all' as the crucial problem facing man, Stirner celebrates such a 'war' as the *solution* to man's problems. Only through a 'union of egoists' – men who pursue ruthlessly, without constraint, their own individual interests – can true release and human freedom be attained.

Stirner studied at Berlin under Hegel and became associated with the Left-Hegelians about the same time as Karl Marx. On the publication of his principal work, *The Ego and His Own* (1907), Stirner became branded as a fanatic and a dangerous revolutionary, not only by those committed to maintenance of the *status quo*, but also by his less violently disposed anarchist and socialist colleagues. His book focused upon what we might now term the forces of the *id* and argued that only by releasing these from all restraints and restrictions could true human freedom be attained. Human freedom, for Stirner, is freedom not for the human species but for the individual ego. The Hegelian concept of individual freedom within State control is totally overthrown in this perspective, which emphasises emancipation through the entire removal of the State and its trappings.

The State, in Stirner's eyes, was the greatest enemy of human freedom, since it represented a regulatory collectivity which, in de-emphasising the individual's happiness, stood for all he rejected. Its overthrow and demolition was envisaged not through revolution but through rebellion and insurrection. In *The Ego and His Own* Stirner suggests:

> Revolution and insurrection must not be looked upon as synonymous. The former consists in an overturning of conditions, of the established conditions or status, the State or society, and is accordingly a *political* or *social* act; the latter has indeed for its unavoidable consequence a transformation of circumstances, yet does not start from it, but from men's discontent with themselves, is not an armed rising, but a rising of individuals, a getting up, without regard to the arrangements that spring from it. (Woodcock, 1977, p. 167)

Stirner saw such a rebellion as being initiated by 'the union of egoists', not acting in concert in any organised way, but as individuals carrying out disruption of an ostensibly similar order. Anarchist individualism meant putting anarchist notions into practice immediately, without awaiting any societal transformations.

The core issue was the cognitive disposition of the individual, his attitude of mind, rather than structural constraints or any external ideological hegemony. Stirner's book is in the tradition of objective idealism and focuses upon the subjective dispositions within the individual as the starting point for any radical transformation of society, in which, indeed, the whole notion of society is itself threatened.

Anarchistic individualism has never made a great impact, although it enjoyed a brief revival with the artistic resurgence of interest in individualism of all kinds before World War I. There are few anarchists today who accept or adhere to Stirner's position, although Woodcock maintains that 'as late as the 1940s I encountered a group of anarchist working men in Glasgow for whom [Stirner's book] was still a belated gospel' (Woodcock, 1975, p. 91).

However, many of Stirner's ideas have been incorporated into the canons of 'mainstream' anarchism, and his emphasis upon 'cognitive liberation' and 'freedom for the ego' have been taken up by writers such as Murray Bookchin (1974). Although himself committed to the more objectivist 'anarchistic communism', Bookchin echoes some of Stirner's feelings when he emphasises the subjective aspects which link our understanding of society with the individual psyche. As he suggests, 'anarchists have probably given more attention to the subjective problems of revolution than any other revolutionary movement. Viewed from a broad historical perspective, anarchism is a libidinal upsurge of the people, a stirring of the social unconscious that reaches back, under many different names, to the earliest struggles of humanity against domination and authority' (Bookchin, 1974, p. 19).[22]

Stirner's work is a political document, designed as an exhortation to individuals of all classes to rebel. The nature of the rebellion envisaged, with its total commitment to the rejection of all existing social institutions, identifies anarchistic individualism as one of the most extreme theories of radical change that one is likely to encounter. Since there is scarcely any room for 'society' in such a conceptualisation, this brand of anarchism has come in for much criticism, particularly from Marxists. Anarchistic individualism's rejection of the 'sociological' category places it outside the Marxist concern for replacing one form of society with another through revolutionary means. For many Marxists, anarchism of this kind is seen as essentially reactionary. From our point of view here, it provides a good example of a philosophy of radical change emphasising the importance of subjectivist factors. Whilst not claiming many sociological adherents, it serves as an illustration of an extreme perspective within the radical humanist paradigm.

French Existentialism

French existentialism reflects a philosophical perspective firmly located in the subjective idealist tradition deriving from the work of Fichte and Husserl. In terms of our subjective—objective dimension, it occupies a position between solipsism and the objective idealism characteristic of critical theory. Phenomenology and existentialism are often seen as related schools of thought, and are sometimes considered identical.[23] In line with our distinction between the perspectives characteristic of the sociologies of regulation and radical change, we find it helpful to emphasise the distinction between them. Existential phenomenology characteristic of the work of Schutz, as discussed in Chapter 6, is quite different from the existentialism characteristic of the work of Sartre, to be discussed here. Whilst from a distance they may appear to focus upon similar areas of enquiry and to lend each other mutual support, their basic orientations are fundamentally distinct. Whilst the work of Schutz focuses upon the social construction of everyday life as a basis for understanding (almost as an end in itself), the existentialism of Sartre is concerned with the understanding of the pathology of such constructions, with a view to changing them. Existentialism differs from phenomenology in its vigorous humanism and its political commitment to the desirability of change in the existing social order.

However, it would be wrong to suggest that existentialist philosophers and social theorists comprise a coherent school of thought in the manner, for example, of the Frankfurt School. Rather, existentialism stands for a somewhat broad and amorphous movement, comprising theorists who acknowledge a common debt to Kierkegaard. Among these theorists Jean-Paul Sartre has emerged as by far the most important, and it is through a consideration of his work that we wish to characterise the essential orientation of French existentialism as an illustration of the existentialist movement as a whole.

It is the early writings of Jean-Paul Sartre which have established him as a leading exponent of the French existentialist mode of thought. Sartre's philosophical and literary works are extremely diverse and wide-ranging, and they testify to the direct influence of a number of social theorists including Hegel, Husserl, Kierkegaard, Lukács and Marx.[24] His existentialist views reflect a time when the influence of the first three of these theorists was in the ascendency and are expressed most forcibly in *Being and Nothingness*, first published in 1943, and *Existentialism and Humanism*, published just a few years later in 1948. In his later work Sartre moved to a philosophical position consonant with a Hegelianised form of Marxism, and the concepts emerging from his existentialist works are harnessed in a critique of society in the mould of a critical theory reflecting a more objective idealist view of the world. This is most evident, for example, in Sartre's *Critique of Dialectical Reason* (1976).

Sartre defines existentialism in the tradition of Kierkegaard as the conviction that 'existence comes before essence'; this belief implies that 'we must begin from the subjective' — that is, the individual located within existence is the fundamental concern of the philosophical enterprise. It precedes any emphasis of interest in the 'essences' of the 'real' world and in the make-up of external reality. The individual is actively involved in the creation of his world and not a mere observer or reflection of it. As Sartre puts it, we do not 'survey the world' but rather, 'are engaged' by it. Sartre, in the tradition of phenomenology, takes the consciousness of man as a starting point for his philosophical enquiry and weds it to humanism and a basic concern for human freedom. It is this theme which preoccupies his early work. For Sartre, existentialism is humanism, and he is concerned to demonstrate the way in which 'nothingness' and 'freedom' are essential aspects of the ontological relationship between subjective and objective worlds as experienced by individual human beings.

Before one can get to grips with Sartre's concept of 'nothingness' and its intimate relationship with 'freedom', it is essential first to understand his three concepts of 'modes of being', which have their origins, more or less, in Hegel's *Phenomenology*. Sartre identifies 'being-in-itself' (*en-soi*), the world of external reality or the stuff of which this real world is made up; 'being-for-self' (*pour-soi*) which denotes consciousness and the inner subjectivity of men; and 'being-for-others'. Sartre's problem, like that of so many idealist philosophers before him, is the nature of the relationship, if any, between *pour-soi* and *en-soi*, between consciousness and reality. His treatment of this central issue rests upon the idea that consciousness is always of *something* in the real world, so that the relationship between *pour-soi* and *en-soi* is that between the knower and the known. This relationship, however, depends upon a distance or gap between the real world and the consciousness of individual men, so that the separation between them is always evident. Such a vacancy Sartre calls 'nothingness', for herein lies the ability to conceptualise that which does not exist. 'Nothingness' allows men to think beyond the limitations of today and this place and to imagine non-objects, new forms of social life or any type of alternative reality in the future. 'Nothingness' represents freedom, therefore, in the sense that it is here that man has total freedom to dream and to hope. The measure of a man's freedom, then, is the degree to which he can conceive of non-objects and can look to potential actions rather than be constrained by the pre-existing actuality of the *en-soi*. For Sartre, individuals who retain the ability to conceive of 'nothingness' are free and unconstrained, their lives bounded only by what amounts to a voluntarist theory of action or, more precisely, interaction.

Sartre's position is interactive not so much in a sociological sense but in terms of man's consciousness, in a way faintly redolent of Mead's phenomenological concepts of the 'I' and 'me'. To myself, I am obviously *pour-soi* (a 'being-for-self'), since I am a conscious, sentient being. However, to other men, I am but a real, external, physically concrete object — a 'being-in-itself' (*en-soi*). This paradoxical relationship between human beings in social contexts creates the third category of being — 'being-for-others', which is the interface between different individuals' consciousness in which *en-soi* and *pour-soi* meet in day-to-day interaction.

It is from this analysis that Sartre's notion of 'bad faith' emerges. Sartre uses this concept to refer to situations in which self-imposed constraints are placed upon human freedom; in which men come to accept external constraints from outside their *pour-soi* and consequently reduce the 'nothingness' or gap in consciousness which forms the core of their humanity. To the extent that men accept a determining, outside interference, their internal ability to conceptualise 'nothingness' is reduced. Sartre illustrates this clearly by indicating the way in which men often become imprisoned by their roles. Instead of being 'free', we become what we are, just as an oak tree is an oak tree. A waiter is a waiter and a father is a father, incapable of being radically free and unable to escape at will from the roles which they play. Sartre maintains that to live in one's role is a form of self-deception. We know that as conscious individuals it is false to see ourselves from outside ourselves as objects, but this process is part of an attempt to escape from the problem of 'anguish'. As Sartre puts it, 'We flee from anguish by attempting to apprehend ourselves from without as an Other or as a *thing*'

(Sartre, 1966, p. 82). It is in the flight from 'anguish' that 'bad faith' appears. Sartre's most famous example of this is his consideration of the waiter in *Being and Nothingness*:

> Let us consider this waiter in the café. His movement is quick and forward, a little too precise, a little too rapid. He comes towards the patrons with a step a little too quick. He bends forward a little too eagerly; his voice, his eyes, express an interest a little too solicitous for the order of the customer. Finally there he returns, trying to imitate in his walk the inflexible stiffness of some kind of automaton while carrying his tray with the recklessness of a tightrope walker by putting in a perpetually unstable, perpetually broken equilibrium which he perpetually re-establishes by a light movement of the arm and hand. All his behaviour seems to us a game. He applies himself to chaining his movements as if they were mechanisms, the one regulating the other; his gestures and even his voice seem to be mechanisms; he gives himself the quickness and pitiless rapidity of things. He is playing, he is amusing himself. But what is he playing? We need not watch long before we can explain it: he is playing at *being* a waiter in a café. There is nothing there to surprise us. The game is a kind of marking out and investigation. The child plays with his body in order to explore it, to take inventory of it; the waiter in the café plays with his condition in order to *realise* it. This obligation is not different from that which is imposed on all tradesmen. Their condition is wholly one of ceremony. The public demands of them that they realise it as a ceremony; there is the dance of the grocer, of the tailor, of the auctioneer, by which they endeavour to persuade their clientele that they are nothing but a grocer, an auctioneer, a tailor. A grocer who dreams is offensive to the buyer, because such a grocer is not wholly grocer. Society demands that he limits himself to his function as a grocer, just as the soldier at attention makes himself into a soldier-thing with a direct regard which does not see at all, which is no longer meant to see, since it is the rule and not the interest of the moment which determines the point he must fix his eyes on (the sight 'fixed at ten paces'). There are indeed many precautions to imprison a man in what he is, as if he lived in perpetual fear that he might escape from it, that he might break away and suddenly elude his condition. (Sartre, 1966, pp. 101–2)

The waiter here is playing at a role in a way which implies a fundamental alienation from his true being. The concept of 'bad faith' which it is intended to illustrate has much in common with Marx's concept of alienation, in which individuals meekly accept their social situation to the detriment of their true human potentialities. No doubt, for Max Stirner, Sartre's 'bad faith' would succinctly describe the constraining phenomenon his 'union of egoists' would seek to overthrow.

Whilst he has attracted few really committed disciples, Sartre's influence has been widespread. His brand of existentialism has been important as far as certain developments in psychoanalytic theory are concerned, particularly through the work of R. D. Laing, and as a result of the influence of his novels and other literary work. However, the reaction to Sartre's work in general has been somewhat confused. His shift in intellectual position to a form of Hegelianised-Marxism, his writings and activities in connection with the magazine *Les Temps Modernes*, and his political activism, particularly since the events of 1968, have drawn criticism and indeed abuse from many sides. Despite all this, however, his contribution to the development of French existentialism is beyond dispute and stands as a major achievement in its harnessing of the phenomenological approach in the service of radical humanism.

The Underlying Unity of the Paradigm

The work of theorists located within the radical humanist paradigm is underwritten by a common concern for the freedom of human spirit. Radical humanists focus upon human consciousness within the context of the totality which characterises a particular social formation. There tends to be a concern with what may be described as the 'pathology of consciousness', by which men come to see themselves as trapped within a mode of social organisation which they both create and sustain in their everyday lives. Radical humanists are concerned with understanding the manner in which this occurs, with a view to setting human consciousness or spirit free and thus facilitating the growth and development of human potentialities.

Like theories characteristic of the interpretive paradigm, radical humanist approaches to the study of social affairs are rooted in a subjectivism which recognises the precarious ontological status of the social world. Whilst varying in their degree of subjectivism, the different schools of thought within the paradigm are at one in emphasising that reality is socially created and socially sustained. Thus their perspective stands in fundamental opposition to approaches characteristic of the radical structuralist and functionalist paradigms. This opposition is clearly reflected in the ontological and epistemological divides within Marxism and the rare, but generally hostile, exchanges between social theorists adhering to the radical humanist and functionalist traditions. The divisions between the latter two are compounded by the fact that the ontological and epistemological distinctions are wedded to fundamentally different conceptions of the nature of society. They are divided in terms of both the dimensions of our basic analytical scheme. According to the radical humanist, functionalist social theorists create and sustain a view of social reality which reinforces the *status quo* and which is to be understood as but one aspect of the network of ideological domination which pervades contemporary Western society. The functionalist usually dismisses radical humanists as Utopian radicals hell-bent upon fanning the flames of revolutionary consciousness, or as mindless existentialists who will not or cannot adjust to the world of everyday 'reality' and accept the inevitable march of 'progress'.

Many contemporary radical humanists have developed their critique of society with the functionalist perspective firmly in mind and, consequently, are able to attack it on many fronts. Thus, as we have seen, within critical theory specific attention has been paid to demonstrating the role of science, logic, rationality, technology, language and other aspects of the superstructure of capitalism as vehicles of cognitive domination, which, from the radical humanist perspective, act as alienating 'intermediaries' which present a barrier to the achievement of full humanness. In the tradition of the work of the young Marx, the radical humanists are concerned with the alienation of modern man. They start from the premise that man lives in a world which constrains rather than develops his full range of possibilities, and they are committed to providing an analysis and critique of the way in which this occurs. It is a critique which reflects a complete inversion of the functional problematic and the view of society which it represents.

It is the emphasis which is given to consciousness in general and alienation in particular which distinguishes the substance of the radical humanists' thought from that of the radical structuralists. Theorists in both these paradigms are committed to revolutionary changes in society but, as we shall see, the radical structuralists tend to place much more emphasis upon deep economic and political 'structures' in their analysis. As we shall see, within the context of the radical structuralist paradigm, the concepts of 'totality', 'structure', 'contradiction' and 'crisis' take over as unifying features from those of 'totality', 'consciousness', 'alienation' and 'critique', which can serve as a convenient shorthand for the common concerns not only of critical theory, but also of the essential orientation of the radical humanist paradigm in more general terms.

Notes and References

1. For a general discussion of Fichte's work, see the introduction to Fichte (1970).
2. For a discussion of the Hegelian system of thought, see Hegel (1931) and Kaufmann (1966).
3. For a discussion of the Hegelian use of 'dialectic', see Kaufmann (1966), pp. 167–75.
4. For a discussion of Marx's views at this time, see McLellan (1975 and 1976).
5. The influence of Feuerbach is of considerable importance and calls for much greater attention than it is possible to give here. For more extensive discussion, see Althusser (1969) and McLellan (1976).
6. For a further discussion of Marx's theory of alienation, see Avineri (1968), McLellan (1976), Mészáros (1970b) and Ollman (1971).
7. For a further discussion of critical theory, see, for example, Jay (1973), Connerton (1976) and O'Neill (1977).
8. As will become evident from our discussion in Chapter 10, orthodox Marxism in the 1920s was based upon an extreme interpretation of the radical structuralism characteristic of Marx's later work.
9. For a discussion of Engels' influence on the interpretation of Marx's work, see Chapter 10.
10. For a discussion of Lukács's concept of the dialectic, see the article by Mészáros in Parkinson (1970).
11. For a discussion of Lukács's use of 'totality', see Lukács (1971) and the article by Pascal in Parkinson (1970).
12. For a further discussion of this point in relation to the consciousness and action of the working class, see Mann (1971).
13. See, for example, Gramsci's attack on positivism in 'Critical Notes on an Attempt at Popular Sociology' in Gramsci (1971).
14. For a discussion of this important concept, see Gramsci (1971) and Boggs (1976).
15. Jay (1973) provides an excellent analysis of the role of these key figures in the development of the Frankfurt School and its work.

16. For a good discussion, see, for example, Frisby (1972). Interestingly enough, the work of both Popper and Adorno is directed against totalitarianism; their different responses reflect their different paradigmatic perspectives.

17. The possibility of a marriage between the ideas of Marx and Freud has received increasing attention in recent years. For a discussion of some of the issues involved, see Rieff (1959) and Brown (1973).

18. See, however, Marcuse (1968) and Habermas (1971b).

19. In *Legitimation Crisis* (1976), especially Part II, 'Crisis Tendencies in Advanced Capitalism', Habermas deals with four types of crisis, of which one is 'economic crisis' in the classic Marxist mould.

20. For a discussion of anarchism in general and 'anarchistic individualism' in particular, see Woodcock (1975 and 1977).

21. Woodcock comments upon this most extraordinary man in the following terms:

> STIRNER MAX, (1806–1856). Kaspar Schmidt was a German school-teacher, employed in a Berlin academy for young ladies, when he wrote his single important book *The Ego and His Own*. This extremely individualist anarchist was closely associated with the Radical Young Hegelians who clustered around Arnold Ruge and Bruno Bauer, and took the nom-de-plume of Max Stirner because of the loftiness of his brow (*stirn*). The victim of an unhappy marriage, he became in his later years a hack translator, and *The Ego and His Own*, which influenced Nietzsche, remains his only work of real significance. (Woodcock, 1977, p. 379)

22. Bookchin's paper 'Listen Marxist' (1974) also makes interesting reading in this respect, whether or not one is being directly addressed.

23. For a discussion of some important differences as well as links between the two schools of thought, see Lee and Mandelbaum (1971).

24. For a discussion of Sartre's life and work, see Murdoch (1967), Spiegelberg (1965), Warnock (1965) and Natanson (1973a).

9. Anti-Organisation Theory

In the previous chapter we described the nature of the radical humanist paradigm, tracing its broad line of development and the way in which its basic tenets are reflected in contemporary schools of thought. As a paradigm within the context of social theory as a whole it must have some relevance for the study of organisations, but as yet it is almost completely unexplored from this point of view.[1] We intend to argue here that if the implications of the radical humanist paradigm are developed in relation to the study of organisations, the result will be an *anti-organisation theory*. Since the radical humanist perspective stands in fundamental opposition to that of the functionalist paradigm, reflecting a complete inversion of assumptions about the nature of science and of society, anti-organisation theory will stand in fundamental opposition to contemporary organisation theory.

From any perspective characteristic of the radical humanist paradigm, organisations as middle-range phenomena have a very precarious ontological status. At best, they are allowed an existence as intersubjective, reified social constructs, by means of which individuals relate to the world in which they live. The perspectives of the various schools of thought within the paradigm vary quite significantly on this score; consequently, they have differential contributions to make to an anti-organisation theory.

The solipsist and existentialist perspectives reflect a form of 'subjective idealism' which does not allow for the existence of organisations outside the realm of *individual* consciousness. The intersubjective status of the concept of organisation is extremely problematic. Whilst Sartre's notion of 'bad faith' has a great deal to offer towards an understanding of the relationship between individuals and what are regarded as their occupational roles,[2] subjective idealist perspectives have a limited contribution to make to a theory of organisations as such. Within the context of objective idealism the scope is much greater, and we wish to argue here that it is within the bounds of critical theory that the radical humanist anti-organisation theory has the most scope for development.

Critical theory contributes to our anti-organisation theory in a number of ways. As will be clear from our analysis presented in the previous chapter, the critical theorist is concerned with four core concepts: *totality* – the notion that the social world must be understood in its entirety before one can comprehend its parts; *consciousness* – the force which ultimately creates and sustains the social world; *alienation* – the cognitive wedge between consciousness and totality and which divorces man from his true being; *critique* – the analysis of the sources and forms of alienation which inhibit the possibilities of true human fulfilment.

These concepts emphasise the central importance of the relationship between consciousness and totality, and reduce the status of organisations to middle-range reified social constructs which intervene between the consciousness of individual human beings and their appreciation of the nature of the totality in which they live. Organisations are examples of the 'intermediaries' which, from a radical humanist perspective, contribute to man's alienation from his true being. It is through the critique of such alienating 'intermediaries', which reflect and sustain particular modes of social life, that critical theory has sought to contribute its own particular brand of insight into our understanding of the relationship between man and society. Within the context of this critique, emphasis tends to be placed upon revealing the nature and significance of the 'spirit' or *mode of organisation* reflected in a particular totality; understanding this *mode of organisation* in terms of the principles which it reflects is given greater priority than detailed analysis of its specific empirical forms. Thus whilst organisations as reified social constructs lend themselves as a focus for critique, it is always within the context of the mode of organisation which they reflect.

The critical theory perspective thus suggests an approach to organisational analysis which is an *anti*-organisation theory on a number of counts. It is anti-organisation in that it views organisations as having a precarious ontological status. It is anti-organisation in that it stresses the importance of the *mode of organisation* reflecting a particular totality, rather than the importance of organisations as discrete middle-range units of analysis worthy of attention in their own right. It is anti-organisation in the sense that it views the reified social constructs labelled 'organisations' as alienating 'intermediaries' which serve to mystify human beings in their attempt to comprehend and appreciate the nature of the totality in which they live. The perspective constitutes an anti-organisation theory in that its presuppositions stand in fundamental opposition to those of functionalist organisation theory;

as we shall see, anti-organisation theory inverts the functionalist problematic on almost every count. It is also an anti-organisation theory in the sense that it views functionalist theory as itself serving to mystify our understanding of the significance of organisations within everyday life. Functionalist organisation theory, in focusing upon the exclusive study of middle-range reifications, is seen as perpetuating the divorce between human consciousness and totality. It is seen as an alienating 'intermediary'; as an objectification of mind which hinders man's appreciation of the totality in which he lives. Organisation theory is viewed, from the perspective of anti-organisation theory, as an alienating force, concerned with the wrong issues and the wrong problems, as an essentially conservative enterprise which underpins the present system of ideological domination within contemporary society.

In its present state of development, anti-organisation theory can be regarded as no more than embryonic in form, at best comprising a few isolated and fragmentary case studies and discussions which have approached the study of organisational activities from a perspective consonant with critical theory. We shall return to these in a later section of this chapter. As a means of illustrating the general issues with which anti-organisation theory would concern itself, we will review here a part of the burgeoning body of literature which seeks to provide a critique of contemporary culture. Whilst approaching this endeavour in a variety of ways, and often claiming no specific allegiance to an intellectual tradition of any kind, much of this literature stands firmly in the radical humanist mould. It echoes the concerns and issues which have occupied the thoughts and attention of many idealist social philosophers who have pondered upon the human condition. Much of this literature has surfaced as part of the general resurgence of interest in the subjective aspects of human existence reflected, for example, in the developments in existentialism, phenomenology and ethnomethodology which took place during the 1960s and 1970s. Its particular trademark is that it combines its interest in the subjective with a radical critique of contemporary society.

We have in mind here the work of writers such as Illich (1973) and Dickson (1974) on alternative technologies; Castaneda (1970) and Pirsig (1976) on alternative realities; Roszak (1969) and Reich (1972) on counter-cultures; and Meakin (1976) and Anthony (1977) on work as ideology. In different ways these works advocate alternative forms of culture or 'alternative realities' to those which predominate within advanced capitalist societies. They range over a variety of disciplines, assuming the form of novels or academic texts, and are increasingly found on the recommended reading lists of social science courses, as reflecting relevant and interesting points of view which do not quite fit the orthodoxy in the particular subject area. However, as we hope to demostrate in the next section, they have much in common with the perspective of critical theory, particularly as reflected in the writings of Marcuse (1964), Habermas (1971a and b) and Gouldner (1976). In the style of our nascent anti-organisation theory, these writings seek to foster and point the way towards alternative realities through a radical humanist critique of the *status quo*. In so doing, they identify many of the concerns and constituent elements which a more systematically stated anti-organisation theory might seek to embrace.

Towards Alternative Realities

Many contemporary writers have pointed to the need for alternative technologies as a means of creating and sustaining alternative cultural forms. David Dickson in *Alternative Technology and the Politics of Technical Change* (1974), for example, seeks to demonstrate the links between technology, politics and social control, particularly those reflected in the nature of advanced technology and capitalism. It is Dickson's general thesis that the problems associated with contemporary technology might be resolved through the design of an 'alterative technology' which 'would embrace the tools, machines and techniques necessary to reflect and maintain non-oppressive and non-manipulative modes of social production, and a non-exploitative relationship to the natural environment' (Dickson, 1974, p. 11). However, in contrast to functionalist theorists who argue in favour of alternative technologies as a means of creating alternative modes of social life, Dickson emphasises the necessity of creating political change as a basis for technological and social change. In his view, alternative technologies on any significant scale can only be developed within the framework of alternative societies. Alternative technologies do not of themselves create alternative societies. This is seen as essentially a political task. As he puts it, 'the struggle for emancipation from an apparently oppressive and manipulative technology coincides with the struggle for emancipation from oppressive political forces which accompany it. To argue that technological change is *per se* able to bring about a more desirable form of society is technological determinism carried to Utopian extremes' (Dickson, 1974, p. 13). Technology, for Dickson, operates both materially and symbolically to reinforce a particular form of social organisation and control. It is seen as functioning politically to promote, within capitalism, the interests of a dominant class, particularly through ideologies which stress technology's role within society as a natural, progressive, inevitable and essentially non-political force. For Dickson, contemporary technology is inextricably linked with the fundamental nature of the totality of capitalism, and its significance and influence can only be understood in these terms.

Ivan Illich, in his book *Tools for Conviviality* (1973), focuses upon a related theme, arguing that society is in need of a 'convivial reconstruction' to restore what the development of technology has destroyed. Illich sees social and institutional development as having passed through two watersheds. At one stage knowledge and technique were utilised in the solution of specific problems; at another, the success of technique was exploited to demonstrate the existence of problems and needs previously unrecognised. He presents technological progress, backed by the interests of institutional elites, as fostering demands for further technological progress, through which men become enslaved by the tools which were originally intended to serve their needs. Illich argues that the crisis which has been created can only be solved

> if we learn to invert the present deep structure of tools; if we give people tools that guarantee their right to work with high, independent efficiency, thus simultaneously eliminating the need for either slaves or masters and enhancing each person's range of freedom. People need new tools to work with rather than tools that 'work' for them. They need technology to make the most of the energy and imagination each has, rather than more well-programmed energy slaves. (Illich, 1973, p. 23)

Society, in Illich's view, needs to be reconstructed to facilitate 'conviviality' − autonomous and creative intercourse among persons and in their relations with their environment. The convivial society is characterised by technologies which 'serve politically interrelated individuals rather than managers', and by 'responsibly limited tools' (Illich, 1973, p. 12). Like Dickson, Illich points to the political dimension of technology, and calls for a political inversion of the 'managerial fascism' which characterises our present mode of organisation.

In *The Greening of America* (1972) Charles Reich calls for a change in contemporary society through a revolution in consciousness based upon the values and ideals of the counter-culture youth movement of the late 1960s. Reflecting the unbashed optimism of the period, Reich boldly claims:

> There is a revolution coming . . . It will originate with the individual and with culture, and it will change the political structure only as its final act. It will not require violence to succeed, and it cannot be successfully resisted by violence. It is now spreading with amazing rapidity, and already our laws, institutions and social structure are changing in consequence. It promises a higher reason, a more human community and a new liberated individual. Its ultimate creation will be a new and enduring wholeness and beauty – a renewed relationship of man to himself, to other men, to society, to nature and the land. (Reich, 1972, p. 11)

Reich's vision is similar in many ways to those of Dickson and Illich, in that it seeks a restoration of the non-material and spiritual elements of man's existence, and aims to confer on science and technology a background and supportive role. In contrast to their work, however, Reich places his faith in revolution through revelation, as opposed to critique and political action. His book may be seen as reflecting the aspirations rather than the analysis of the radical humanist perspective.

Theodore Roszak's book of essays, *The Making of a Counter Culture* (1969) reflects similar themes, which are specifically linked to a variety of analytical perspectives characteristic of the radical humanist paradigm. His central focus is the struggle between 'youth culture' and the 'technocracy' characteristic of contemporary industrial, bureaucratised society. He examines the way in which the technocracy seeks to define reality in terms of an objective form of consciousness in ways which appropriate the whole meaning of 'reason', 'reality', 'progress' and 'knowledge', and speculates upon the ways in which this enterprise can be overthrown as a means of restoring human values and potentialities to a central place. His vision is of a community of love and affection, supported by honourable and enjoyable labour, in which personal vision replaces objective knowledge and the scientific expert is deposed by someone akin to the Indian village *shaman*.

The question of access to an alternative reality is also explored by Carlos Castaneda in the *Teachings of Don Juan* (1970) and its sequels, which report Castaneda's attempt to investigate and understand the world of don Juan, a Yaqui Indian sorcerer or 'man of knowledge'. The book neatly counterposes alternative realities, and illustrates the impossibility of embracing 'non-ordinary' modes within the logic of the scientific ethos which dominates Western culture.

In Robert Pirsig's *Zen and the Art of Motor-Cycle Maintenance* (1976) similar themes are presented, but they are explored in a radically different way. Whereas in Castaneda's work the focus is upon the difference in world view of a Yaqui Indian and a Californian anthropology student trying to get his Ph.D., in Pirsig's novel it is upon the struggle between the competing world views which exist within the central character's own psyche. Pirsig describes the way in which 'romantic' and 'classical' forms of understanding compete for dominance in the protagonist's attempt to negotiate and define everyday 'reality'. Whilst apparently remote in its implications for an academic anti-organisation theory, Pirsig's work, like that of Castaneda, Roszak, Reich, Illich, Dickson and many others who have addressed similar themes, provides good illustrations of the essential concerns of the radical humanist ethos. The struggle is between competing realities and the means by which they can be achieved. The conflict, crudely put, is between the commonly accepted and all too 'real' dominant reality of the functionalist paradigm, and the aspirations and vision of the radical humanist paradigm. Understood in these terms, all the works considered above counterpose functionalist and radical humanist perspectives and, in their different ways, clearly illustrate the inversion of fundamental assumptions upon which the two paradigms are built and from which they derive their distinctive perspectives upon the social world. They illustrate very clearly, too, how the two paradigms define alternative realities.

Returning to literature more consciously located in an 'academic' frame of reference, in that its mode of presentation adheres to a more conventional 'scientific' format, we find similar themes expressed. Gouldner, for example, in *The Dialectic of Ideology and Technology* (1976) focuses upon ideology as a 'symbol system', and seeks to demonstrate the intimate relationship between ideology and technology as modes of social domination. His work draws heavily upon critical theory, particularly the work of Habermas. As will be apparent from our discussion in the previous chapter of Habermas's theory of 'communicative distortion', there are many links between his distinction between work and interaction and the ideas of the writers considered here. Gouldner, in the tradition of critical theory, talks of present-day 'technocratic consciousness' and its links with science, positivism and technology, and contrasts it with 'romanticism'. His call is for an overthrow of the technocratic mode of consciousness and the establishment of more humanly orientated forms of life.

The distinctions between work and interaction, and 'scientific/technological rationality' and 'romanticism', as modes of social life are also reflected in the recent writings of two British theorists who have investigated conceptions of work and its social context. Though approaching the issue from the perspectives of quite different disciplines and adopting different styles, their writings reflect strikingly similar themes. David Meakin in *Man and Work* (1976) approaches the subject from a literary perspective, focusing upon the literature and culture of industrial society. Peter Anthony in *The Ideology of Work* (1977) approaches the subject from the perspective of an industrial relations theorist, and traces the relationship between attitudes to work and technological process. Both writers seek to provide a radical critique of the nature of work in contemporary society, and of the possible alternatives: they favour the romantic ideals of writers such as John Ruskin and William Morris, who stress the creative possibilities typical, for example, of the craft ethic. Meakin calls for a new ideology in which the distinction between 'art' and 'work' is lost, and Anthony calls for an end to the 'ideology of work' and its replacement by an ideology in which 'pleasure' and 'use' are the two guiding principles.

Table.9.1 seeks to counterpose the main concepts which the writers reviewed here utilise to present the key dimensions of the alternative realities with which they are concerned. Clearly, there is a considerable convergence of interest in their work, which will become all the more apparent from a reading of the original texts. However, even from the necessarily abbreviated and somewhat superficial reviews presented here, clear themes characteristic of the radical humanist perspective are quite evident.

First, there tends to be an overriding concern with what Marcuse has described as the 'one-dimensional' nature of modern society. These various writers tend to present society as reflecting a form of totalitarianism based upon the all-pervasive influence and control of factors such as work, rationality, science and technology, which shape, channel and control men's consciousness. Their concern is to articulate the nature of this influence and control, and stress that this totalitarianism makes men oblivious to alternative modes of consciousness and existence. They are concerned to demonstrate that alternatives are available. Alternative realities, alternative cultures, alternative technologies, alternatives to work — these lie at the centre of their attention.

Table 9.1

Key dimensions of alternative realities

Author	Concept used to characterise the crucial aspect of reality within contemporary capitalist social formations	Concept used to characterise the crucial aspect of reality within non-alienated modes of being
Dickson	'Industrial capitalism'	'Alternative technology'
Illich	'Productivity'	'Conviviality'
Gouldner	'Technocratic consciousness'	'Romanticism'
Roszak	'Objective consciousness'	'Personal vision'
Reich	'Consciousness II'	'Consciousness III'
Pirsig	Classical mode of thought	Romantic mode of thought
Castaneda	Ordinary reality	Non-ordinary reality
Habermas	'Work'	'Interaction'
Anthony	'Work'	'Craft'
Meakin	'Work'	'Creativity'

Second, this literature tends to be characterised by a posture which is fundamentally opposed to positivist science. Science as viewed from the perspective of the functionalist paradigm is totally rejected; the idea of progress through science completely inverted. Functionalist science is seen as creating rather than solving societal problems. Such problems are viewed as being the result of the ideology of domination upon which positivist science is based. The radical humanist sees the scientific ethos which has been used to conquer man's environment as having dominated man himself. Man is seen as the prisoner of science and the calculative rationality which it reflects. Problems characteristic of, for example, the ecological crisis figure prominently in the analysis of the ills of modern society, to the otherthrow of which the radical humanist is deeply committed. In place of science-dominated Western society, they advocate a return to a situation in which man lives in harmony with nature, as opposed to controlling and exploiting nature. For this purpose they often look to philosophies of the past or to those characteristic of different cultures. Hence the interest in the Eastern way of life, for example, and the philosophy of Zen. The search is for a vision of a world uncontaminated by the ethos of science and the worship of 'progress'. In line with C. P. Snow's celebrated distinction between the scientific and literary modes of thinking, (the 'two cultures' which exist *within* advanced Western societies), the body of literature under discussion often looks to art, drama, literature and the cinema for its references. It is to this culture that they turn for the source of their problems, analysis and solutions. Put simply, their humanism is derived from and reflects the humanities.

A third major theme in this literature is reflected in its 'objective idealism'. It views man-made notions and artefacts as objectified products of human consciousness which, within industrial society, come to be seen as alienating forces which lie outside man's control. In line with the tradition of critical theory, it is the alienated state of man in modern society that is ultimately the focus of attention.

These three related themes clearly reflect the romanticism and idealism which lie at the roots of the radical humanist philosophy. Alternatives to the present are sought in the past: windmills not power stations, craftsmanship not work, Zen not instrumentality. In its idyllic view of the past, this literature has a great deal in common with the communist vision of the young Marx, according to which men 'do one thing today and another tomorrow . . . hunt in the morning, fish in the afternoon, rear cattle in the evening, criticise after dinner, just as I have a mind, without ever becoming hunter, fisherman, shepherd or critic' (Marx, 1965, pp. 44−5).

This idyllic and Utopian image of society is underwritten by the assumption that scarcity is no longer a problem. Indeed, the notion of scarcity is seen as part of the system of ideological domination within which man lives. It is the overthrow of the concept of scarcity that man's salvation is, in large part, seen to lie, enabling him to live in harmony with nature whilst avoiding the physical deprivations commonly associated with a return to previous modes of life. The abolition of the *concept* of scarcity is seen as an avenue leading to the attainment of man's release from the domination of existing modes of social life.

Towards an Anti-Organisation Theory

In addition to the general work discussed in the previous section, a small number of isolated papers and case studies have been produced which can best be understood as attempts to articulate elements of the radical humanist approach to the study of organisations. Here again, these works have found their way on to the reading lists of many courses in organisation analysis and, again, stand in somewhat anomalous relationship to much of contemporary theory. We have in mind work such as that produced by

Beynon on *Working for Ford* (1973), Clegg on *Power, Rule and Domination* (1975) and a paper produced by the People and Work team at the Open University (Esland et al, 1975). In addition, there are signs towards the end of *Organisational Work* by Silverman and Jones (1976) of a move towards a perspective consonant with critical theory. All this literature is British. No doubt comparable European and American studies also exist, though it has not attained a level of any prominence within the British context.

All these works are characteristic of the critical theory perspective and reflect many of the ideas articulated in other contexts by writers such as Marcuse and Habermas. The links, however, are often far from explicit, and it is quite clear that some of the writers have arrived at their respective positions by quite different routes. The People and Work team express their views in general terms, emphasising that sociology is in need of a critical perspective. They criticise the sociology of organisations as being too little concerned with the study of organisations within a societal context, and as being too coy in its treatment of alienation and deprivation. They seek to replace industrial sociology, occupational sociology and the sociology of organisations with a 'critical sociology of work'. Their aims in this respect are clearly illustrated in the following quotation:

> a critical sociology concerned with the question of contemporary forms of domination and alienation has to take on increasingly the enormously self-evident legitimacy of applied positivism and technologised control, just as workers who attempt to move from economism to conflict over control and authority within the enterprise have to be prepared, in their attack on managerial 'rights', to question the whole system of inter-connected legitimations and assumptions of which any particular 'right' is a part. The combination of rational planning with politically neutralised bureaucracies serving the goal of economic progress has done much to desensitise workers and sociology itself as a way of understanding contemporary society. It is important that the sociology of work regains... political and social awareness... and that work activity and experiences should be seen in the context of more comprehensive critiques of capitalist society and mass capitalist culture. (Esland et al, 1975, p. 32)

These concerns are clearly related to the perspective of critical theory. Their anti-positivism, their emphasis upon totality, alienation, domination and control, and their desire to develop a critique of capitalist culture, are all firmly set within the context of critical theory, with the focus upon 'work' as the central subject of analysis.[3]

The work of Beynon (1973), Clegg (1975) and Silverman and Jones (1976) focuses upon very specific issues, and in essence presents empirical case studies which can be interpreted as consonant with a critical theory, though the links with this are, again, undeveloped. Beynon in *Working for Ford* focuses upon the car workers' experience of factory work, and the 'factory-class consciousness' which arises along with their understanding of the work situation and the realisation that they are being exploited by the management. Clegg's *Power, Rule and Domination* presents an analysis of power relationships on a construction site, and argues that they can only be fully understood as part of the rules of the game laid down within the context of a wider 'form of life'. The ideas and analysis reflected here are firmly in line with the hermeneutic critique offered by Habermas and other critical theorists interested in the role of language in the construction of social life. Silverman and Jones's *Organisational Work* also moves in this direction, with their analysis of the hierarchical nature of the language of organisational life, which has much in common with Habermas's theory of 'communicative distortion'.

The development of a systematic critical theory of organisations calls for a clear and explicit statement of basic assumptions, priorities and concerns. Only against such a background can the significance of the above studies be fully appreciated and the ground rules laid for more systematic research within this area. Such a development calls for a movement away from the reactive stance to functionalism reflected in much of the literature which has been produced so far, and for an explicit statement of the anti-organisation theory which derives logically from the underlying tenets of the radical humanist paradigm. In order to facilitate this, Table 9.2 seeks to spell out some of the characteristics which an anti-organisation theory might assume, so that organisation theorists can begin to appreciate the substantive implications of critical theory and the way in which it is fundamentally opposed to the orthodox view of organisational reality. It is a perspective which challenges, at a most fundamental level, the very basis of the enterprise in which most contemporary organisation theorists are engaged. In order to illustrate the strength of this challenge, we seek to juxtapose elements of the defining characteristics of anti-organisation theory with those of organisation theory. Table 9.2 identifies sixteen issues on which these perspectives are fundamentally opposed. The list is not exhaustive, but it does go a long way towards delineating the precise ways in which the competing frameworks diverge, and serves to emphasise the basic coherence and breadth of anti-organisation theory as a perspective in its own right. Insofar as anti-organisation theory is launched in a reactive and partial sense, it almost certainly appears as an attack upon functionalism and as a negative and destructive force. However, it is clear that, viewed from a wider vantage point, it is coherent, integrated and self-sustaining, since it draws upon a fundamentally different intellectual tradition. Its existence is not predicated upon the functionalist perspective *per se*; it does not feed upon it in any way and can operate within an intellectual preserve which is entirely its own. If offers an alternative view of the reality of organisational life.

Table 9.2

Towards the definition of anti-organisation theory

		Organisation theory	*Anti-organisation theory*
1.	Paradigmatic location	Functionalism	Radical humanism
2.	Intellectual source of problems, metaphor and example	Science	The humanities
3.	Conceptual focus (level of analysis)	Organisations	Mode of social organisation
4.	Society conceptualised as:	System	Totality
5.	Focus of ontology	Structures	Consciousness
6.	Predominant socio-economic problem	Widespread lack of job satisfaction	Universal alienation
7.	Generic term for contemporary society	Industrial society; post-industrial society	Capitalism, One dimensional society; corporate state; managerial fascism, etc.
8.	Man's relationship to nature seen as:	Exploitative/ competitive	Harmonious
9.	Predominant means of production	Industrial, factory-based technology	Alternative technology (non-urban, small-scale, co-operative)

Table 9.2 (continued)

		Organisation theory	Anti-organisation theory
10.	Concern for maximisation of	Productivity	Human creativity
11.	Technology seen as a:	Positive or neutral force	Negative force
12.	Current status of production	Universal scarcity and shortages	Widespread economic surplus available within capitalism
13.	Predominant productive mode advocated	Work/labour	Craft
14.	Predominant mode of human cognition	Logic	Intuition
15.	Human behaviour in accord with	Purposive rationality	Value rationality
16.	Ethico-political stance	To understand: possibly to alter the system	To understand: certainly to induce a new totality

Stated in more specific terms, anti-organisation theory seeks to demonstrate the sources of *alienation* inherent within a *totality*, which converge in an organisational context. It provides a systematic critique, in the tradition of critical theory, by identifying the factors which impinge upon and dominate human *consciousness* in the form of seemingly objective social forces over which man appears to have no form of direct control. Among the factors worthy of critique, the following are usually accorded considerable importance:

1. The concept of *purposive rationality* as the dominant and most valued mode of cognition within organisational contexts.
2. *Rules and control systems* which monitor the exercise of rational action.
3. *Roles* which constrain and confine human activities within narrowly defined limits.
4. The *language* of organisational life which reflects a situation of 'communicative distortion'.

5. The *ideological mechanisms* through which the worker is habituated to accept the roles, rules and language of the work place.
6. The worship of *technology* as a liberating force.
7. *Reification*, such as the concepts of *work*, *leisure*, *scarcity* and *profitability*, which serve to mystify the relationship between workers and the world they live in.

Anti-organisation theory, through critique, seeks to unmask the alienations reflected in the organisational mode of life. It seeks to stress how such alienations are intimately linked with the nature of the totality in which they are located, and hence to point towards the desirability of alternative modes of reality and social life.

At the present time anti-organisation theory exists in an embryonic form. Our above analysis provides no more than the roughest of frameworks upon which future developments might be based. It seeks to move towards the definition of the range of territory over which the fully-fledged anti-organisation theorists might be expected to roam. The perspective as a whole can only be developed systematically against the intellectual background of the radical humanist paradigm. It is necessary, therefore, for the anti-organisation theorist to be thoroughly conversant with the German idealist tradition and the way in which it is reflected in the various schools of thought discussed in Chapter 8. It is not something which can be developed in isolation as a practical critique of contemporary organisation theory. The tenets of anti-organisation theory are set so fundamentally against the principles which underpin the functionalist paradigm that the writer, researcher or student who seeks to align himself with the former, must, if he is to be consistent with his underlying assumptions, end up by rejecting the latter. To embrace radical humanism involves the rejection of organisation theory as a naïve, misconceived and politically distasteful enterprise. It involves entering another paradigm, another intellectual world – indeed, an alternative reality.

Notes and References

1. At first sight the literature relevant to the field of organisation studies which advocates a radical form of humanism may seem truly extensive. However, as will be clear from our analysis of the functionalist paradigm, the word 'radical' is

much overused, in that many theorists who profess a radical point of view do little more than take a mildly deviant stand-point in relation to their immediate reference group. All the so-called neo-human relations theorists who advocate a humanist approach to the design of organisations, techno-logy, etc., do so from a perspective firmly grounded in the functionalist problematic. Their humanism represents a plea for reform rather than a well-founded and consistent theoret-ical perspective committed to an alternative view of society. For the most part, their perspective is grounded in a philos-ophy of social engineering and piecemeal reform within the problematic which defines the *status quo*. Once this seem-ingly 'radical' literature is placed on one side, the field is dramatically reduced in size. Even prominent 'radical' works such as those of Berger et al (1974), Ellul (1964) and Douglas (1970a) disappear from the sociology of radical change on this score.

Radical humanism, as defined here, refers to a well-grounded intellectual tradition whose basic problematic is described and defined in some detail in the previous chapter.
2. For a discussion of 'bad faith' and occupational roles, see Eldridge (1971), pp. 158–65.
3. In point of fact, the papers presented in Esland *et al.* (1975) range beyond the bounds of critical theory, and include papers characteristic of the functionalist and radical struc-turalist perspectives. The overall picture which they present is thus somewhat inconsistent in terms of underlying meta-theoretical perspectives.

10. Radical Structuralism

Origins and Intellectual Tradition

The radical structuralist paradigm is rooted in a materialist view of the natural and social world. It is based upon an ontology which emphasises the hard and concrete nature of the reality which exists outside the minds of men. The social world, like the natural world, is seen as having an independent existence. Its facticity is taken for granted; it is seen as being material rather than spiritual in nature. This 'realist' view of social reality is supplemented by an essentially positivist epistemology which is geared to discovering and understanding the patterns and regularities which characterise the social world. Little distinction is drawn between the assumptions, aims and methods of the natural and social sciences. The radical structuralist tends to see himself as engaged in 'science', and in this endeavour shares many points of similarity with the approach of the functionalist. However, for the radical structuralist, 'science' is made to serve fundamentally different ends.

Radical structuralism is aimed, first and foremost, at providing a critique of the *status quo* in social affairs. It is a perspective which is concerned not just to understand the world, but to change it. The underlying focus of interest tends to be upon the structures within society, and particularly the way in which they interrelate. Writers within the paradigm tend to view society as composed of elements which stand in contradiction to each other. They are interested in the effects of these contradictions, particularly with regard to the role which they play in creating economic and political crises. Radical structuralism is a view which focuses upon the essentially conflictual nature of social affairs and the fundamental process of change which this generates. Deep-seated conflict is viewed as the means by which man achieves emancipation from the structures of the social world in which he lives. It is a sociology of radical change but, in contrast to that of the radical humanist paradigm, one which tends to place relatively little direct emphasis upon the role and nature of man as an individual human being. However, common to both is the underlying aim of man's release from the various forms of domination which are seen as characterising contemporary industrial society.

The intellectual foundations of the radical structuralist paradigm were laid in the second half of the nineteenth century in the work of Karl Marx. As a theoretical perspective it has had a chequered history, in that Marx's work has been subjected to a wide range of interpretations, vulgarisations and misunderstandings. Nowhere is this better illustrated than in the term 'Marxism'. Whilst from within it represents a heterogeneous and widely differentiated body of social theory, from outside it is often identified as a narrow and polemical political creed. Analytically, there are many varieties of Marxism. As we have seen the work of the young Marx had a major impact upon certain developments within the radical humanist paradigm. In this chapter we intend to trace the effect which his later work has had upon the radical structuralist paradigm. As we shall see, the contemporary structure of Marxist thought within this paradigm is extremely complex, calling for careful analysis in terms of the two dimensions which define our analytical scheme. In essence, the radical structuralist paradigm constitutes a body of social theory as complex, conceptually rich and widely differentiated as any of the other three paradigms considered in this work.

As we have noted in our discussion of the radical humanist paradigm, in his early work Marx was principally involved in a reinterpretation of the Hegelian system of philosophy, inverting its central tenets to produce a radical critique of contemporary German society. With the publication of *The German Ideology* in 1846, however, a distinct move away from his earlier preoccupation with and commitment to Hegelian idealism can be detected. In particular, he sought to turn from the objective idealism which characterised his earlier work to a position reflecting a more materialist view of the social world. It represented the beginning of a general movement away from philosophical concerns to those of political economy, and an attempt to develop the outlines of a radical social theory capable of meeting contemporary positivism on its own ground. It signified a redirection of his overall thought which was to receive a fuller and more explicit treatment in later work such as the *Grundrisse*, and *Capital*, written in the late 1850s and early 1860s.[1] These works were produced after more than a decade of active but unsuccessful political involvement which embraced the 'Year of Revolutions' of 1848. In essence, they reflect Marx's attempt to obtain 'self-clarification' on the operation of the historical process and the economic structure of the capitalist mode of production. In terms of analysis, they place emphasis upon conceptualisations derived from political economy; the idealist concerns of his early work receive much less emphasis. Although there is considerable debate about the extent to which the Hegelian influence was to stay with Marx throughout his life, a claim is often made that his writings in the period after 1850 reflect a major epistemological break when compared with his earlier work. In terms of our analytical scheme, they involve a shift in perspective away from the radical humanist and towards the radical structuralist paradigm.

Given the wide range of interpretations which have been placed upon Marx's later work, it is extremely difficult to provide any authoritative, clear-cut statement of his precise perspective. Our plan in the rest of this section, therefore, will be to provide an overview of Marx's central concerns and then to proceed to discuss some of the widely different interpretations placed upon them. As we shall see, these interpretations have dictated in large measure the precise development of the radical structuralist paradigm.

At the most basic level, Marx's model of society, as expressed in his later work, consists of two elements – the 'superstructure' and the 'substructure'. The metaphor 'substructure' was used to refer to the economic base of society, in which production was given the central role. His analysis of this distinguished between (a) the 'mode of production' (capitalism, feudalism or communism); (b) the 'means of production' (technology, land, capital, labour); and (c) the 'relations of production' (producers and non-producers, owners and non-owners, the class system). Marx argued that within each mode of production there were particular associations between the 'means' and the 'relations' of production. The term 'superstructure' was used to denote other, non-economic factors within society, such as the state, religion, art, literature, etc. These were seen, 'in the last instance', as being determined by the nature of the substructure, though in turn influencing it to some degree.

Within the *Grundrisse* and *Capital* the notion of 'contradiction' was given a central role in Marx's analysis of the operation of society. As will become apparent later in the chapter, this notion has been interpreted in many ways.[2] Common to these interpretations is the idea that society contains within it elements which stand in antagonistic relationships one to another, and which generate conflicts which eventually lead to the breakdown of the mode of production and its related social configurations. Marx was primarily interested in the contradictions which exist within the substructure of society, and he placed considerable emphasis upon his notion of 'surplus value' as the concept upon which the contradiction between the means and relations of production was based.[3] His interpreters have also stressed the contradictions which exist between the substructure and superstructure, and within the superstructure itself. The notion of contradiction is central to Marx's explanation of social change and the way in which one form of society replaces another through crises produced by these contradictions. Marx saw these crises within a given mode of production as getting progressively worse and eventually leading to the cataclysmic crisis which would overthrow the society as a whole.

As we have noted, the focus of Marx's analysis is upon the political economy of capitalism. 'Structures', 'contradictions' and 'crises' take over from the concepts of 'consciousness', 'alienation' and 'critique' reflected in his earlier work. Whilst this marks a considerable change in orientation of analysis, which is consonant with Marx's more materialist view of the social world, a certain continuity within the Hegelian tradition is also evident.[4] The notion of contradiction is ultimately derived from the dialectic, and the concern for alienation also remains. In Marx's later work, however, it tends to be imbued with the terminology of political economy and becomes the 'fetishism of commodities', for within the capitalist system alienation is seen as intimately linked with the fact that man is treated as a commodity or resource to be bought and sold upon the labour market. Marx's overall change in orientation was aptly expressed by Lassalle, one of his contemporaries, who described him as 'a Hegel turned economist, a Ricardo turned socialist'. This description summarises succinctly the two developments which characterise the thought of his later years, in which he moved away from a radical idealism towards a radical interpretation of 'bourgeois', 'positivist' economics. It is this move which laid the essential foundations of the radical structuralist paradigm.

As we have noted, subsequent developments within the context of the radical structuralist paradigm have been largely based upon different interpretations placed upon Marx's later work. At least three distinct lines of development can be identified. One focuses upon Engels' interpretation of Marx and the subsequent development of a 'scientific socialism' in the Russian mould.[5] It is this line of development which is most often equated with 'Marxism' when evaluated from within a context outside the paradigm. A second line of development has focused upon an interpretation of the

Grundrisse and *Capital* as representing the essence of Marx's work; this has largely arisen as a response to the developments in critical theory discussed in our chapter on the radical humanist paradigm. The third line of development can be understood as the result of a confrontation between the various elements of the work of Marx and Weber. These three developments largely define the present structure of the radical structuralist paradigm, and it will be as well if we review them in general terms prior to more detailed discussion later in the chapter.

As we have seen, the direction of Marx's thought in his later years was towards a radical reinterpretation of political economy. Under the influence of Engels, particularly after Marx's death, this general trend was much intensified, leading to an eventual picture of Marxism as revealing the essential 'laws of motion' underlying the capitalist system. Under Engels' influence, the work of Marx was increasingly seen as presenting a total science of man's political, economic and social life, which contained within its system the laws of social evolution.[6] This interpretation, which sought to stress the links between the work of Darwin and Marx, was the one which predominated under Engels' influence after Marx's death. In Engels' hands, the dialectic between subjective and objective worlds was left further and further behind as a materialist view of history and of society was forged. As Engels himself notes in a discussion of dialectical materialism,

> dialectics reduced itself to the science of the general laws of motion, both of the external world and of human thought — two sorts of laws which are identical in substance, but differ in their expression insofar as the human mind can apply them consciously, while in nature, and also up to now for the most part in human history, these laws assert themselves unconsciously, in the form of external necessity, in the midst of an endless series of seeming accidents . . . (Engels in Marx and Engels, 1951, pp. 349–50)

It was precisely this type of rendering of the dialectic within 'dialectic materialism' which impressed the socialists and 'social democrats' of the late nineteenth century.[7] Within its intellectual sway, they became the instruments of historical necessity, hand-maidens of fate who held in their palms the truly superior philosophy cum science. The Russian, Plekhanov, adopted this perspective on Marx's work and thereafter set the ground rules for the study, analysis and interpretation of Marxism under Bolshevism. In many respects the tradition of Russian social theory over the last hundred or so years has, in large measure, been established by this Engels-Plekhanov dialogue.

The second line of development within the radical structuralist paradigm, somewhat paradoxically, originates from the work of Lenin. As we have seen, Marx's later work retained certain Hegelian features. This fact was recognised by Lenin who, shortly before his death, came to the conclusion that Marx, and especially *Capital*, could not be understood without a knowledge of Hegel. As Conquest (1972) reports, since Hegel had been ignored for some fifty years, Lenin concluded that no Marxist had yet understood Marx.

This line of reasoning was not developed within Russian social theory, but it was taken up in the 1960s by a group of Marxists who stood outside both the Hegelian and the Engelsian tradition. They tended to see Lenin as the Marxist theorist who came closest to tapping the essence of Marx's work.[8] Their interpretation of Hegel is a critical one, and in no sense can they be regarded as belonging to the Left Hegelian brand of theorising discussed in connection with the radical humanist paradigm. Rather they stand *between* the critical theory of radical humanism and the tradition of orthodox Russian Marxism. Marxist philosophers such as Della Volpe, Althusser and Colletti grew up in cultures dominated by neither German idealism nor sociological positivism and, as we shall see, were able to distance themselves from existing interpretations of Marx.

The third line of development focuses upon what may be described as 'radical Weberianism'. As is well known, Weber was, in certain aspects of his work, engaged in a dialogue with the 'ghost of Marx', and certain of his key concepts have been used as a means of exploring the interface between Marx and Weber. As we have sought to show in earlier chapters, Max Weber's influence has been felt in all of the four paradigms. Whether one points to his discussion of scientific rationality which pervades much of radical humanism, or his development of the notion of *verstehen* in the interpretive paradigm, or his work on bureaucracy which, though often misunderstood, dominates functionalist organisation theory, Weber cannot be ignored. Within radical structuralism, certain strands of his work which are consistent with the orientation of a sociology of radical change have been developed by a small group of European social scientists. In order to distinguish their reading of Weber from those more typical of functionalism, for example, we wish to use the term 'radical Weberianism'.

Weber's writings contain political and sociological elements welded together, sometimes under great strain and tension, within the context of one overall framework.⁹ For Weber, the central political question in a unified Germany was the issue of leadership. How was the newly created State to be governed? He accepted unquestioningly the 'rightness' of its existence and sought its continuing growth through a concern for the form of development of industrial capitalism and its emergent bourgeoisie. Weber was a sociologist of economic order interested in the social consequences of capitalism, with regard to which his views were somewhat ambivalent. His orientation to capitalism demarcates him quite clearly from the Marxists and the German romantic conservatives of his time. The former opposed the capitalist mode of production for its deleterious effects on the newly created working population; the latter, for its effects upon the established Junkers' aristocracy. Between these perspectives Weber advocated a capitalism containing a strong, intellectually refined bourgeoisie which would remain true to the superior German culture.

What is important for radical Weberianism, however, is not that Weber was primarily a sociologist of order and regulation, but that his ambivalent attitude to capitalism, and particularly to the place of bureaucracy within it, left open avenues for exploration which lead to a sociology of radical change. Weber saw bureaucracy as a reflection of the process of rationalisation which paralleled the development of capitalism; a process which invaded all aspects of social life, from politics to religion. As we have seen, Marcuse took this notion of rationality and used it critically as a cornerstone in his treatment of 'one-dimensional man'. Within radical structuralism theorists tend to be most interested in Weber's analysis of bureaucracy as an instrument of social domination, most forcibly expressed in the notion of the 'iron cage of bureaucracy'. For Weber, bureaucracy posed a threat to human freedom, making it increasingly more difficult for men to exercise control over their everyday lives. The threat of this 'iron cage' was seen as characterising societies of both a capitalist and a socialist nature. Under the latter Weber emphasised that the strength of bureaucracy was increased because in the capitalist mode there was at least an area for the free play of market forces. Under both systems, however, the growth of bureaucracy and the mode of purposive rationality which it reflects was viewed as a force detrimental to the interests of those subject to its control.

Thus, in the context of radical structuralism, radical Weberianism focuses upon bureaucracy, authority and power as the points of concentration for theoretical analysis as a means of understanding important aspects of social life under capitalism. Rarely, however, does it produce politically radical alternatives; as may be said of other schools of thought, it seeks to interpret critically rather than to change. Nevertheless, Weber did joust with the Marxian heritage and fought the battle on its ground, at least on occasion, and it is the product of this sort of confrontation which forms the kernel of contemporary 'radical Weberianism'. In essence, it seeks to emphasise the role of factors which do not receive extensive treatment within 'Marxism', and which portray man's domination and enslavement by the social structures in which he lives. This radical Weberianism comprises the third strand in the intellectual development of the radical structuralist paradigm.

The Structure of the Paradigm

The radical structuralist paradigm is thus a complex body of social theory which is the result of the fusion of a plurality of philosophical, political and sociological traditions. Any broad categorisation of its constituent schools of thought must do violence to this fact but, bearing this in mind, one can recognise the three very broad approaches discussed above. We describe them as (a) Russian social theory; (b) contemporary Mediterranean Marxism; and (c) conflict theory. Each of these occupies a distinctive position within the paradigm, as illustrated in Figure 3.3.

Russian Social Theory stands within the Engelsian tradition, having been introduced into pre-revolutionary thought by Plekhanov. It later developed into the *historical materialism* of Bukharin, and influenced, to a degree, Kropotkin's version of *anarchistic communism*. Although these approaches are politically divergent, they share a common set of meta-theoretical assumptions which are unquestionably positivistic and naturalistic. They are located in the most objectivist region of the paradigm.

Contemporary Mediterranean Marxism stands in the tradition of Marx's mature works, particularly *Capital*, and Lenin's reading of it. This set the tone for an approach which is of core importance at the present time. We recognise within it *Althusser's sociology* and *Colletti's sociology* which, whilst having close parallels with each other in terms of their rejection of both Hegelianised Marxism and orthodox Russian Marxism, again differ politically. To this extent they occupy different positions on the regulation—radical change dimension of our analytical scheme.

Conflict theory is the sociological expression of radical Weberianism and involves the utilisation of several Marxian concepts. We distinguish between *Rex's conflict theory* and *Dahrendorf's conflict theory*, although, here again, striking similarities appear, given a sufficiently broad perspective.

We will discuss each of these schools of thought in turn.

Russian Social Theory

We use this term in order to emphasise certain commonalities which exist between apparently distinct schools of thought in Russian intellectual history.[10] We seek to point to connections between the socio-philosophical approaches of the so-called 'orthodox Marxism' of Bukharin and the 'anarchistic communism' developed by Kropotkin. These bodies of thought have something in common in terms of their intellectual backgrounds and origins, despite the undisguised hostility between them. The orthodox Marxism propounded by Bukharin was virulently opposed to anarchism in all its forms, just as the followers of Kropotkin stood out against the political elitism and administrative centralisation then nascent in Bolshevism. Indeed, anarchistic communists went so far as to explode a bomb in a Bolshevik Party Committee meeting, killing twelve senior members and injuring Bukharin in the process. Such violent contempt, however, belies a similarity in meta-theoretical terms between the perspectives of these men. Both Kropotkin and Bukharin were familiar with the natural sciences, both used 'scientific' conceptualisations as the cornerstone of their systems in a thoroughly positivistic way, and both were committed to the revolutionary overthrow of the Tsarist government in particular and capitalism in general.

Although easy to overemphasise, their mutual 'objectivism' derived from Plekhanov and, dependent upon the 'naturalistic' assumptions of the scientific method, has remained, in some degree, typical of contemporary Russian social theory, which has much in common with functionalist social systems theory so far as the subjective—objective dimension of our analytical scheme is concerned. Indeed, Gouldner (1970) has made much of the current Soviet interest in functionalism, with which there are the ties of a common positivist epistemology,[11] and there has also been interest in the reverse direction. Nisbet (1976), for example, has sought to portray Kropotkin as an ecologist before his time.

We begin our analysis of Russian social theory with the work of Bukharin.

Bukharin's historical materialism

In the tradition of 'scientific socialism' developed by Engels and Plekhanov stands the work of Nikolai Bukharin (1888–1938), a one-time 'lieutenant of Lenin' who met his death at the hands of Stalin. Bukharin sought, in perhaps his best-known work, *Historical Materialism: A System of Sociology*, published in 1921, to provide a textbook in which Marxism was presented as sociology rather than political economy. The interest at this time in the sociological challenges to Marx from Weber and Pareto, for example, required a Marxist response, and Bukharin saw himself as fulfilling this role.

The son of a Moscow teacher turned bureaucrat, Bukharin joined the Bolshevik party at the age of 17 as part of its 'intelligentsia', though deeply committed to the life of a professional revolutionary.[12] Arrested for the second time in 1910, he was exiled to north Russia, from whence he escaped, returning to Moscow in 1917. Before his exile he had become one of the Party's leading · theorists, interested in developing Marxism through dialogue with theoretical developments in non-Marxist 'social science'. In exile in Europe and briefly in New York, his intellectual contribution was increasingly acknowledged, to the extent that, for some Bolsheviks, he outshone Lenin, with whom his relations were usually strained. After the Revolution, he became editor of the Party newspapers for ten years, during which time he produced both 'political' and 'theoretical' writings. Towards the end of the 1920s his differences with Stalin grew over the way forward for the USSR, particularly with regard to agricultural policy. Stalin's 'revolution from above', in which he took over total control of the reins of Soviet government, marked the beginning of the end for the more cautious and gradual policies advocated by Bukharin and his 'Rightist' colleagues. He was arrested in 1937 and brought before a court in the infamous Moscow 'show trials' by which he was convicted and sentenced to death. His reputation in Russia has, even to this day, never recovered from the effects of the Stalinist Purge.

In *Historical Materialism*, Bukharin claims that sociology is 'a method for history' and, even more controversially, that bourgeois sociology has something to offer Marxism. As he puts it, historical materialism itself 'is not political economy, nor is it history; it is the general theory of society and the laws of its evolution, i.e. sociology' (Bukharin, 1965, p. xv). It is, in effect, 'proletarian sociology.

Bukharin did not have much time for 'dialectics'. Lenin, just before his death, remarked of Bukharin that 'his theoretical views can only with very great doubt be regarded as fully Marxist, for there is something scholastic in them (he has never studied and I think, never fully understood dialectics)' (Cohen, 1974, p. 152). An economist by training, Bukharin felt more at home with the new physics of the twentieth century than with the German idealism in philosophy of the century before. 'Materialism', for him, stood against Hegelian metaphysics and for science and technology; as a consequence his book is based upon the mechanical analogy derived specifically and in unmodified form from physics. Rather than accept the thesis, antithesis and synthesis elements of the dialectic, Bukharin preferred to equate these with 'the condition of equilibrium; in the second place, disturbance of this equilibrium; in the third place, the re-establishment of equilibrium on a *new* basis' (Bukharin, 1965, pp. 74–5). His discussion at this point goes on to consider 'systems theory' from the Marxist perspective, viewing society as being in a state of unstable equilibrium because of imbalance with its environment. Balance with the environment is sought through the development of technology in which the relationship between the society and nature is regulated. Social change comes about through alterations in this balance, which leads to periods of revolutionary disequilibrium at times of crisis and its ultimate replacement by an equilibrium at a higher stage of development. In this way Bukharin sought to reject the biological analogy then prevalent in Western sociology, which saw social change as somehow pathological, but his Russian critics were quick to point out, as others were later to say of functionalism, that the notion of equilibrium, in whatever form, suggests harmony and co-operation as the primary modes of social organisation. Indeed, Bukharin admits such a bias when he maintains that without harmony 'society will not grow but decline'.

It is important to note, however, that this disturbance of equilibrium implicitly takes the form of a 'catastrophe' or 'cataclysmic crisis', through which social revolution is brought about. Bukharin's concept of a 'new equilibrium' implies a 'totality shift' of enormous proportions and not the evolutionary or morphogenic process envisaged by even the most change-orientated of functionalists. The equilibrium models are thus comparable only in name. In essence, Bukharin's model has more in common with the catastrophe than the mechanical analogy for the study of social change.

Clearly, then, Bukharin is a Marxist committed to the revolutionary overthrow of capitalism through violent conflict, but is convinced that in the end social harmony will prevail. A systems model of a crude but early type is seen as the best theoretical perspective through which to understand both this new socialist society and the laws of motion of pre-socialist societies. In a sense, then, Bukharin developed a kind of functionalism before it became established in the West, with a concomitant focus upon understanding social life in terms of long periods of relative stability. In his case, however, it was first necessary to transform existing Western societies through violent and sometimes bloody revolution. In this way the location of Bukharin's sociology within our analytical scheme parallels that of functionalism, but within the context of a sociology of radical change. Ontologically, Bukharin is firmly realist. In talking of idealism, Bukharin describes solipsism as 'this insane philosophy' which 'is contradicted by human experience at every step'. For 'when we eat, conduct the class struggle, put on our shoes, pluck flowers, write books, take a wife or husband, none of us ever thinks of doubting the existence of the external world i.e. the existence – let us say – of the food we eat, the shoes we wear, the women we marry' (Bukharin, 1965, p. 56). Here the reality of the world is accepted on a common-sense level. There is a total acceptance of the unproblematic nature of real objects like 'books' and 'class struggles', which are seen to have material, concrete existence outside human consciousness. Indeed, human consciousness is seen as wholly dependent upon economic production, for material production, and its means, the material productive forces, are the foundation of the existence of human society. Without it there cannot be a 'social consciousness'.

Epistemologically, Bulkarin adopts the positivism of the natural sciences as his model. Historical materialism is a 'scientific sociology' which explains the general laws of human evolution; it serves as a method for history. What Bukharin seeks, then, primarily through the notion of equilibrium, is to explain in a generalisable way the story of human development. The historical materialism of Marx and Engels provides a means whereby such general laws are attainable. Furthermore, these laws provide causal explanations. As he puts it, 'Both in nature and in society there exists objectively (i.e. regardless of whether we wish it or not, whether we are conscious of it or not) a law of nature that is causal in character' (Bukharin, 1965, p. 30). In this way Bukharin adopts a naturalistic positivism for his epistemological stance and the nomothetic methodology that it implies in the attainment and analysis of what he believes to be the constantly observable connection between phenomena.

Bukharin also devotes some time to a discussion of the free will—determinism debate. He discusses a number of examples drawn from everyday life, and goes on to suggest that

> A consideration of these examples has shown that under all conditions, both usual and unusual, both normal and abnormal, the will, the feeling, the actions of the individual man always have a definite cause: they are always conditioned ('determined'), defined. The doctrine of freedom of the will (indeterminism) is at bottom an alternated form of a semi-religious view which explains nothing at all, contradicts all the facts of life, and constitutes an obstacle to scientific development. The only correct point of view is that of determinism. (Bukharin, 1965, p. 37)

In his own words, therefore, Bukharin clearly places himself upon our analytical schema. He is a determinist, rejecting the notion of a creative free will and its role in social life. Adding to this his positivism and realism, *in toto* Bukharin occupies a position of extreme objectivism within the sociology of radical change. He delimits the objectivist wing of the radical structuralist paradigm, a position which many in the West now describe as 'vulgar Marxism'. It is a variety of Marxism, however, which owes more to Engels than to Marx; indeed, it takes Engels' reformulation of the work of Marx to its logical extreme. It is the variety of Marxism on which systems theorists have seized in their attempt to equate dialectical materialism and functionalism and pronounce that the order—conflict debate is now dead.[13]

Anarchistic communism

Anarchistic communism is most closely associated with Peter Kropotkin (1842–1921), a Russian prince at whose funeral in Moscow the Bolsheviks mourned.[14] After a time as a page in the Tsar's court, Kropotkin journeyed as a geographer and naturalist into Siberia, where he came into contact with several nomadic groups which were to influence his later theoretical work. After adopting the revolutionary cause and being forced into exile for forty years, he returned to Russia in 1917, only to become disillusioned with the Bolshevik Revolution before his death in 1921.

Kropotkin continually sought to put anarchistic communism on a firm philosophical and theoretical footing, which demarcates him from many of the more activist nihilists of the anarchist movement, who were anti-intellectuals almost to a man. At university, Kropotkin had studied mathematics and geography. The methodology and epistemology of the natural sciences were to form, throughout his life, the basis of his social philosophy. He described his own work in these terms in an early entry in the *Encyclopædia Britannica*:

> As one of the anarchist-communist direction Peter Kropotkin for many years endeavoured to develop the following ideas: to show the intimate, logical connection which exists between the modern philosophy of the natural sciences and anarchism; to put anarchism on a scientific basis by the study of the tendencies that are apparent now in society and may indicate its further evolution; and to work out the basis of anarchist ethics. As regards the substance of anarchism itself, it was Kropotkin's aim to prove that communism – at least partial – has more chances of being established than collectivism, especially in communes taking the lead, and that free or anarchist-communism is the only form of communism that has any chance of being accepted in civilised societies; communism and anarchy are therefore two terms of evolution which complete each other, the one rendering the other possible and acceptable. (Quoted in Bose, 1967, p. 262)

As a naturalist, the evolutionary theories of Darwin had a profound effect upon him, but he argued vehemently against the notions of Herbert Spencer, whose concepts of the survival of the fittest Kropotkin saw as implying that competition and conflict were endemic to all animal species, including man. Rather, he pointed to the widespread existence of 'mutual aid' in human societies not characterised by the capitalist mode of production. For, as Avrich notes,

> His own observations indicated that, in the process of natural selection, spontaneous co-operation among animals was far more important than ferocious competition, and that 'those animals which acquire habits of mutual aid are undoubtedly the fittest' to survive. By no means did Kropotkin deny the existence of struggle within the animal kingdom, but he was confident that mutual dependence played a much larger role – indeed, mutual aid was 'the chief factor of progressive evolution'. (Avrich, 1967, p. 30)

His belief in 'mutual aid' had been inspired by his experiences in Siberia, where small-scale tribal groups of nomads lived according to 'anarchist' principles. Kropotkin's experiences in these years convinced him that the natural attitude of man was one of co-operation and solidarity, and that the principle of hierarchy was a recent 'pathological' development in man's history. The centralising tendencies of the Russian State, which was undergoing a late transition to capitalism, were the first objects of his attention, but his forty years in exile in Western Europe convinced him that capitalism, wherever it was found, represented an aberration in man's evolution. Anarchistic communism stood, for Kropotkin, in direct opposition to the wage system of capitalism, the supercession of which depended upon violent mass revolution. Once the wage system had been overthrown, a new society would be set up, based upon communes which would be self-governing, decentralised, almost self-sufficient units. He did not see this vision as Utopian but as the only possible solution to the problems of capitalism, the State and bureaucracy. The overthrow of capitalism brought about through economic crisis would be a bloody affair and, although less disposed towards violence and terrorism than many others, Kropotkin did believe in 'propaganda of the deed' and thought it quite legitimate to engage in political assassination. After 1917 he came to see the Bolshevik's version of Marxism as a new form of human enslavement, one form of centralisation having been replaced by another, thereby preventing the *return* which he sought to a form of society based upon mutual aid in which conflict was minimised.

In Kropotkin's publications,[15] one is able to see quite plainly the objectivist stance which he derived from the wholesale incorporation of natural science methods and assumptions. He describes his orientation as follows:

> I gradually began to realise that anarchism represents more than a mere mode of action and a mere conception of a free society; that it is part of a philosophy, natural and social, which must be developed in a quite different way from the meta-physical or dialectical methods which have been employed in sciences dealing with men. I saw it must be treated by the same methods as natural sciences . . . on the solid basis of induction applied to human institutions. (Kropotkin, in Woodcock, 1975, P. 184)

Kropotkin is representative of that stream of Russian social theory which sees no distinction between the natural and social sciences and believes that the 'laws of nature' serve as models for the study of society. Also typical of Russian sociological thought at this time is his firm commitment to radical change, though his vision of this differs quite substantially from that of his contemporaries.

The social theory of the USSR before 1925, therefore, was rooted in an equation of the social sciences with the natural sciences. The influence of Darwinism, and the intimate relationship which was seen to exist between man and nature, created variants of an evolutionary theory in which capitalism was regarded as a 'genetic' monstrosity, the dispatch of which would herald a new era of social life in which harmony and understanding would prevail. The perspective of theorists such as Bukharin and Kropotkin differs from that of positivist social theorists located in the functionalist paradigm, in that the analogy which they use to characterise the process by which this will be brought about is that of catastrophe and revolution. It is this crucial feature of their work which locates it within the bounds of the sociology of radical change as opposed to the sociology of regulation.

Contemporary Mediterranean Marxism

Within this brand of theorising we recognise two separate schools, which, although distinctive in their approaches to many substantive issues, are based upon a set of common meta-theoretical assumptions. These are the sociologies of Althusser and Colletti. Whilst both theoreticians stand in the mainstream of contemporary Western Marxist thought, they adopt perspectives consciously distinct from the Hegelianised Marxism of Lukács, Gramsci and the Frankfurt School on one hand, and the orthodox Marxism of Plekhanov and Bukharin on the other.[16] They seek to temper what they see as the extreme objectivism of 'vulgar' Marxism and the subjectivism of critical theory by adopting an intermediate position.

Althusser and Colletti, in spite of their intellectual proximity, or perhaps because of it, have conducted a rather fierce academic battle in which both participants have had their noses bloodied.[17] This internal conflict notwithstanding, there is a close interrelationship in their work in terms of their theoretical stance, although there are many who believe that Althusser is far and away the more creative thinker. He has built a system; Colletti seeks to destroy those of other people.[18] Whilst we do not wish to denigrate the role of essayist and critic, we believe that Althusser's conceptualisations have more scope for development than those of Colletti.

We have chosen the epithet 'Mediterranean Marxism' to emphasise not merely the origins of both men, but the fact that their theoretical stance is located outside the north European idealist tradition and is, at most, peripheral to the Anglo-French positivist tradition. It is a hallmark of Althusser's and Colletti's perspective that the extremes of both these broad currents of thought are rejected in favour of an 'intermediate' position which, although unmistakably objectivist, is familiar with, and not totally unsympathetic to, German idealism. We begin our analysis with the recognition that we cannot do justice to the quite marked differences in detail between the perspectives of Althusser and Colletti, but this is a task which they themselves are not slow to address. For us, their broad similarities are of more interest at this point, although some attention will be paid to differences between them in terms of the regulation—radical change dimension of our analytical scheme. We begin our analysis with a consideration of the work of Louis Althusser.

Althusserian sociology

Louis Althusser is one of the world's most influential contemporary Marxist philosophers, and he has attracted a great deal of attention from not only radical sociologists, but writers in many disciplines. An Algerian by birth, Althusser fought in World War II and was taken prisoner by the Germans in 1940. He returned to Paris in 1945, studied under the philosopher Bachelard and has remained there to teach ever since. He is a member of the Communist Party and has explicit political views which are often described as Stalinist.[19] Whilst his work is extremely complicated, sometimes contradictory and, indeed, still in the process of being developed, it is possible to identify certain conceptualisations which have been the subject of much discussion and critical assessment. Althusser uses the notion of a circle to describe parts of his work, and in any analysis it is often very difficult to know where to begin. However, Althusser's work can be interpreted as a reaction against the Hegelianised Marxism of Lukács, Gramsci and the Frankfurt School, and represents an attempt to develop a more sophisticated riposte to it in the tradition of 'orthodox' materialism. Crucial here is Althusser's notion of the 'epistemological break' in Marx's work, which delimits the early 'philosophical' work from the more mature 'scientific' analyses of *Capital* and the later writings.[20] The early work is seen as completely distinct from the texts upon which Althusser wishes to focus, for he rejects the notion of Marx as a 'theoretical humanist'. Althusser maintains that for the mature Marx, humanism represented nothing more than an ideology, since it assumed both a fixed human nature and a crucial role for subjective factors in the historical process. Neither is a correct assumption, according to Althusser, whose reading of Marx's *Capital* supposedly demonstrates that the notion of 'dialectic' therein, represents a 'process without a subject'.[21] Marx was seen as transforming the Hegelian 'dialectic' by removing the limitations within it created by both an emphasis on man's consciousness and a dependence upon a belief in the historical necessity of man's progress through ever-developing stages. Put crudely, for Althusser and his Marx, men do not make history; it is made by particular configurations of structures which arise at given points in time. Althusser, then, stands against and between the 'subjective humanism' of the Hegelian Marxists and the thesis of historical inevitability proposed by Engels and Bukharin. For him, the dialectic leads neither to subjectivism nor to historicism.

Althusser's 'structuralism'[22] depends upon an understanding of the 'totality', *not* just as an assembly of parts to be only understood as a whole, but as something shaping and present within *each* part. The parts reflect the totality; not the totality the parts. Of these parts, Althusser recognises four 'practices' — the economic, the political, the ideological and the theoretical (scientific). Although, in the final analysis, the economic 'practice' is seen as the most important, at given historical 'conjunctures' each of the 'practices' has relative independence, despite the possible domination of one 'practice' (though not necessarily the economic) over the others. Althusser calls such a concept a 'structure in dominance'.[23] Any particular historical event, therefore, represents the complex interrelationship between 'practices', which are linked through the idea of 'overdetermination', defined rather obscurely by Callinicos as 'the idea of a structure whose complexity, the mutual distinctness and interdependence of its elements, is expressed through the way in which the economy displaces the dominant role within the structure to a particular instance, organising the other instances in terms of this structure in dominance' (Callinicos, 1976, p. 51).[24] In Althusser's view, then, superstructural elements can be as important as, if not more important than, those of the economic substructure. At the most basic level this implies a multi-causal theory of history, since economic factors are not seen as determinate in all instances. As social development consists of a series of historical events, the configurations of particular 'over-determinations' create in given societies quite different social forms. This is the famous 'law of uneven development', which rejects, of course, any concept of historical necessity or prede-termination in the social process (Althusser, 1969, p. 249).

Social change, for Althusser, depends upon the type and extent of 'contradictions' in the social formation. Some contradictions are antagonistic and their 'explosive' interrelationships will pro-duce, in the long run, sweeping societal transformations at times of great crisis. Other contradictions are non-antagonistic and play a less important role in social change. The motor force of history, then, is found in the interrelationship of particular contradictions at a given point in time which surface as perceptible socio-economic crises.[25]

The logic of this position, politically, has not been obscured as far as Althusser's critics are concerned. If revolution is to be achieved in this perspective, it depends upon particular conjunc-tions of contradictions and overdetermination. The role of the political activist is thereby de-emphasised.[26] For what can the revolutionary hope to do to bring about radical social change, if this is determined ultimately by deep, hidden structures? Althusser's philosophy, then, is open to the charge of his non-structuralist critics of 'quietism' and to the accusation that it implies a rejection of 'praxis'. Regis Debray, a one-time student of Althusser's, thus commented on his mentor's separation of 'thought' from 'reality' and '"the operation of society" from "the operation of knowledge". In other words, all we had to do to become good theoreticians was to be lazy bastards' (Callinicos, 1976, p. 60). Althusser's claim that philosophy is 'the class struggle in theory' certainly permits armchair theorising, and it is relatively easy for cynics to point to the popularity of Althusserianism amongst the academic Marxists of Europe as an indication of this.

Ontologically, Althusser assumes a real, concrete world exter-nal to the individual and his consciousness of it. This real world, in Althusser's theory, may be thought to consist of 'structures' which together, in the 'totality', represent given 'social formations'. These conceptualisations, however, according to Althusser's epis-temology, are not necessarily based upon any correspondence with the real world. Indeed, as Callinicos has suggested, Althusser argues that 'there exists the sharpest possible separation between the real object, that is, the reality which the theory seeks to explain, and the thought-object, the theoretical system which makes up a science' (Callinicos, 1976, p. 32). The idea that a theory should mirror or fit exactly the reality it purports to explain Althusser terms 'empiricism', and he is fundamentally opposed to it. The separation of the real from the theoretical which this implies leads inexorably to the tendency of armchair theorising, which requires no empirical work, whether 'research' or political activism, since theory needs no anchors in the real external world. Althusser's version of anti-empiricism, however, does not preclude positivism in the sense of the search for universal causal laws. It does, in fact, explicitly seek to provide a causal analysis, but one which, in recognising the variety of overdeterminations and the 'law' of uneven development, does not pursue the production of uni-causal explanations of, say, social change. The social reality, which we as men can only perceive as surface bubbles upon a deep, hidden and mysterious pool, is seen as contingent upon a variety of structural interrelationships and must be analysed in terms of conjunctures – specific historical events. The logic of Althusser's position, in effect, calls for a case-study method of analysing particular 'conjunctures', each of which is unique, for only in this way can our knowledge of history be developed.

Althusser rejects the perspective of economic determinism found, for example, in Plekhanov and Bukharin, and its more extreme form, economic predeterminism – the unfolding of the inexorable laws of capitalist development which inevitably leads to its overthrow. He still maintains a determinist position, however, in that humanism, which for him emphasises subjective and voluntarist notions, is ruled completely out of court. Man's actions and historical events are determined fundamentally by the social formations in which they are located. Individuals, according to this view, are not 'subjects' but agents within the mode of production, and are correspondingly moulded by the forces acting upon the economic 'practice'.

As for Althusser's position on our subjective—objective dimension, his philosophical sophistication makes for an interesting configuration upon the four analytical strands. Ontologically, he is a realist, but the real world can only be understood through theory, which need not be located or rooted in reality at all. Epistemologically, in seeking 'scientific' knowledge outside ideology, he is a positivist, though not of an extreme kind, since he totally rejects empiricism. Methodologically, Althusser's position emphasises the case-study method of analysis for any given historical 'conjuncture', whilst his view of human nature is fundamentally determinist. His overall position within the radical structuralist paradigm is that of a 'mild' or tempered objectivist. He has sought, and in large measure achieved, a compromise between the orthodox Marxism of the Russian State and the Hegelianised Marxism of the West.

Colletti's sociology

The work of Lucio Colletti reflects a development in Italian Marxism which is more notable for its wide-ranging and trenchant criticism than its development of any socio-philosophical system. A student of Della Volpe,[27] Colletti joined the Italian Communist Party in 1950 and has been concerned both with the role of the Italian working class in revolutionary activity in a 'post-Fascist' society, and with sketching the outlines for a 'scientific' Marxism. Unlike Althusser, he became disaffected with developments in the internal politics of Russia and her satellites, and in 1956 he left the Party. Colletti's work, which he calls 'sociology',[28] consists primarily of detailed attacks upon variants of Hegelianised Marxism, particularly that of the Frankfurt School, and upon orthodox Marxism represented in the main by Engels and Plekhanov (Colletti, 1972). On the face of it, he seeks not to reconcile these perspectives within an overall synthesis, but to recognise that Marx's work reflects two faces, that of the philosopher and that of the scientist. The unifying link between these is found in the notion of 'opposition', which in Marx is seen to have two distinct meanings. First, there is the meaning of the *real* opposition of 'things', which have no synthesis and hence no dialectic relationship. As Marx put it, 'Real extremes cannot be mediated, precisely because they are real extremes. Nor do they have any need for mediation, for their natures are totally opposed. They have nothing in common with each other, they have no need for one another, they do not complement one another' (Colletti, 1975, p. 6). For Colletti, this view of 'opposition', which is found predominantly in *science*, must be contrasted with that of dialectical opposition, which, of course, derives from Hegel and refers to the opposition of abstractions, concepts or ideas which can be synthesised in a 'higher' reconciliation. This is the *philosophical* view of opposition. 'Opposition' in the 'science' of Marxism is equated with the notion of *'contradiction'*, which is regarded as inadequately emphasised by the Hegelianised brands of thought. On the other hand, 'alienation' represents 'opposition' in the philosophical conceptualisations of Marxism, and this is underemphasised by orthodox Marxism. So in Colletti's words, 'The theory of alienation and the theory of contradiction are now seen as a single theory', different elements of which tend to be ignored by competing versions of Marxist thought (Colletti, 1975, p. 27). Significantly, Colletti makes no attempt at the periodisation of Marx's work. He specifically maintains that the notion of 'alienation' represents a theme running throughout the writings of Marx, even in the pieces dealing with abstract political economy. Thus, for Colletti, there are two parallel strands in Marx, not two distinct phases of intellectual activity. His criticism of Marcuse, for example, and of Plekhanov is rooted in this basic assertion. He polarises Marxism on the basis of the relative emphasis put upon either the philosophical strand of 'alienation' or the scientific strand of 'contradiction'. His 'solution' to such polarisation is found in the recognition of its existence, and he is content to

> confine myself for the moment to registering this fact. I do not attribute any conclusive significance to it. The social sciences have not yet found a true foundation of their own. Hence I do not know whether the existence of these two aspects is fatal or advantageous. What is not at issue is the fact that our task now is to find out whether and how they can be reconciled. It is one we must take seriously. It is not to be solved by verbal subterfuge. (Colletti, 1975, p. 29)

Whilst a skilled and knowledgeable critic, Colletti has added little to the conceptual armoury of Marxism, but his position is one which has attracted many followers. Without developing a 'system' in any coherent or rigorous way, Colletti provides a refuge in the interstices provided by, or left between, the dominant Marxist traditions. It is a refuge characterised by the following set of meta-theoretical assumptions. Ontologically, Colletti assumes the real existence of the external world. As he puts it, 'Progress, then, consists in restoring and re-establishing these 'facts', these *real processes*, eluded and transcended by metaphysics and opposing the hypostatis that conceals them. Their objective existence, is in short, the indispensable premiss for any kind of scientific enquiry' (Colletti, 1972, p. 5). Whilst he rejects an extreme realism, and asserts that 'materialism', the philosophical position he subscribes to, necessarily involves a consideration of man as a 'knowing subject', Colletti nevertheless sees the nature of the social world in what is fundamentally a realist way.[29] Epistemologically, Colletti is a positivist in the tradition of Della Volpe. He sees Marxism as a 'science' which, though not overcommitted to empiricism, is based upon the method of hypothesis testing in the search for underlying causal laws. When it comes to a choice of orientation over epistemology, Colletti comes down firmly on the positivist side. In talking of Husserl and Sartre (*inter alia*) Colletti proclaims, for example, that 'Against the dangers of this spiritualist idealism, I personally would prefer to incur the opposite risks of neo-positivism' (Colletti, 1974, p. 20). Methodologically, however, Colletti tends to be anti-historicist and does not seek a method of providing laws valid for all societies at all points in time. He believes that Marx was concerned primarily with capitalism, and that Marxian theory is aimed in this direction and nowhere else. With regard to human nature, Colletti assumes a tempered determinism, for whilst he accepts that someone of Gramsci's stature could contribute to change in a capitalist society ('his research on Italian society was a real preparation for transforming it'), Colletti nevertheless stresses the objective facticity of capitalism's structure and the great problems involved in its supercession.

All in all, Colletti stands within the radical structuralist paradigm in a fairly objectivist position. Faced with the self-imposed choice of a Hegelian Marxism or an orthodox Marxism, Colletti seems to reject the former while certainly not fully embracing the latter. For Colletti, it seems that Lenin is the Marxist thinker who is least incorrect.

In terms of the regulation—radical change dimension of our analytical scheme, Colletti occupies an interesting position, and one which is differentiated from that of Althusser. By continuing to adhere to the 'philosophical' concept of 'alienation', Colletti emphasises the importance of potentiality in man's development and the way in which this is constrained by capitalism. The overthrow of this form of social organisation is not seen as depending solely upon violence. The Stalinist tradition, against which Colletti particularly reacts, believed that 'it was only violence that was the real hallmark of a revolution: everything else – the transformation of the nature of power, the establishment of socialist democracy – was of no importance' (Colletti, 1974, p. 22). In place of this Colletti seeks to emphasise that revolution and violence are by no means interchangeable concepts and that in the last resort there could even be non-violent revolution. Nevertheless, revolutionary activity by the working class is seen as the main solution to the social problems posed by capitalism. For Colletti, it is not sufficient for academics to develop good theory, for, as he puts it, 'Marxism is not a phenomenon comparable to existentialism, phenomenology or neo-positivism. Once it becomes so, it is finished.' Marxism, for Colletti, involves revolutionary political practice – a strategy for radical social change which has an intimate connection with the 'life of the workers' movement.

There are thus clear differences between Colletti and Althusser. Colletti has attempted to link the philosophy in Marx's work to Kant's *Critique of Pure Reason* and his politics to those of Rousseau. For Althusser, Spinoza is the intellectual antecedent of Marx. Furthermore, as Perry Anderson has observed, 'their two accounts of the development of Marxism since the 1920s are incompatible, since Althusser's categories explicitly include Colletti in the Hegelian tradition he repudiated, while Colletti's logic assigns Althusser to the Hegelian heritage he denounced' (Anderson, 1976, p. 70). Nevertheless, as we have sought to show, *both* writers retain elements of Hegelianism within an objectivist framework. Colletti seeks, through the lifeline of 'alienation', to maintain links with the Hegelianised Marxism which he wishes to distance himself from, whilst for Althusser the association with Hegelianism is supported by the notions of 'totality' and 'dialectic'. The similarity of their intermediate stance in terms of the subjective—objective dimension of our analytical scheme provides the rationale for their consideration here as distinct but related exponents of what we have called contemporary Mediterranean Marxism.

Conflict Theory

As we have noted, conflict theory is a product of 'radical Weberianism'. Weber's conceptualisations, although not necessarily specifically intended as rejoinders to those of Marx, have been used in precisely such a way. For whereas Marx talks of 'class', Weber speaks of 'class, status' and 'party'; Marx of 'the means of production', Weber of 'the means of administration'; Marx of the 'dialectic', Weber of 'explanation at the level of cause and meaning', and so on. Such distinctions, although obviously very important, in fact delineate different approaches to the same intellectual terrain, namely, the problems of social relations within a capitalist society.[30] Both Marx and Weber saw that capitalism represented a new mode of societal organisation, certainly different from feudalism (in many ways superior to it), but nevertheless beset by its own forms of repression, oppression and human bondage. However, Weber did not see capitalism as the social mode in which such tendencies reached their apogee. His concern for the forms of domination characteristic of a whole range of societies emphasised the role of power in social life throughout history, not just within capitalism. The rich conceptualisations of 'status' and 'party' sought to encompass the plurality of forms of social stratification throughout historical development, and not just the glaring inequalities of the class structure under pre-World War I capitalism. Weber's emphasis on bureaucratisation within capitalism was, again, rooted in history. Although he saw the hierarchical principle, when wedded to purposive rationality, as the basis for the workers' exploitation and alienation under capitalism, he found elements of the bureaucratic mode of domination in many places and at many points in time.

The radical Weberians of today make much of Weber's conceptual armoury for the analysis of contemporary society. For in Weber's notion of the 'iron cage of bureaucracy', in his elaboration of the complexity of modern social stratification, in his emphasis upon power and authority, they find rich and productive insight. In line with Marxists, they conceive of capitalism, or its latter-day transmutations, as beset by gross economic inequalities and by vast discrepancies in power, both of which mean that social life must inevitably rest upon domination and conflict. For them, the interests of the power holders are so clearly distinct from the interests of the relatively powerless that deep-seated, irreconcilable conflict is viewed as the natural and the only permanent feature of social life. Radical Weberians share Weber's pessimism; they see no end to such inequalities. Marxism is seen as Utopian if it expects an end to the principle of hierarchy and imbalance of power. Social revolution, for these writers as it was for Weber, is often more dangerous than the retention of the *status quo*. Thus, the essence of the radical Weberians' position consists of a trenchant criticism of capitalism but without any associated commitment to its transcendence by another form of social organisation. It is the strength and nature of their critique and arguments in the first half of this configuration, at its interface with contemporary Marxism, that identifies their work as part of the sociology of radical change. In the following pages we will consider the conflict theory of Ralf Dahrendorf and John Rex as representative of this school of social thought.

We have already given a certain amount of attention to Dahrendorf's work in Chapter 2, where we argued that his distinction between the integration and coercion theories of society parallels that drawn here between the sociology of regulation and the sociology of radical change. Dahrendorf's coercion or conflict theory is developed in *Class and Class Conflict in Industrial Society* (1959) as a part of a critique of Marx's work, 'in the light of historical changes and sociological insights'. Dahrendorf argues that Marx's basic analysis is faulty, in that his historical predictions have not borne fruit,[31] and seeks to revamp his conceptual schema with sociological insights drawn primarily from Weber. Dahrendorf's conflict theory aims at explaining the relative absence of order within industrial society and reflects one of the central theses of his study: that 'the differential distribution of authority' within society 'invariably becomes the determining factor of systemic social conflicts of a type that is germane to class conflicts in the traditional (Marxian) sense' (Dahrendorf, 1959, p. 165). His analysis focuses upon the way in which conflict groups are generated by the authority relations in what he describes as 'imperatively co-ordinated associations'. These are defined as those forms of organisation, institution or aggregate in which authority plays the key role in the day-to-day running of affairs. It is Dahrendorf's thesis that within such imperatively co-ordinated associations there exists an authority relationship in which a clear line, at least in theory, can be drawn between those who participate in the exercise of authority in given associations and those who are subject to the authoritative commands of others. Dahrendorf thus sets up a two-'class' model of contemporary social structures, based upon Weber's notion of hierarchical authority but dichotomised in a manner reminiscent of Marx's thesis of polarisation. He sees the basic conflict groups of society as rooted in this differentiation of authority, for different positions involve, or at least imply, the different interests of the respective role incumbents. Such interests may be perceived, recognised and acted upon by an aggregate of persons in a common position in the authority structure, in which case interests become manifest and the aggregate becomes a 'group for itself'. If these interests remain latent, however, then one is dealing merely with a 'quasi-group'. It is the 'group for itself', the 'interest group' which, for Dahrendorf, is the true conflict group, having a structure, a form of organisation, a programme or goal and a personnel of members. Such interest groups become the motive force behind societal change, creating transformations of the social structure with varying degrees of effect, ranging from revolution to small-scale political reform. Violent class struggle is thus presented as but one extreme point on a more general scale of social conflict.

As a summary of his position, Dahrendorf presents a 'theory of social classes and class conflict', of which the following is an edited version.[32]

1. The heuristic purpose of the approach proposed in the study is the explanation of structure changes in terms of group conflict. This purpose is, therefore, neither purely descriptive nor related to problems of integration and coherence in or of society.
2. In order to do justice to this heuristic purpose, it is necessary to visualise society in terms of the coercion theory of social structure, i.e., change and conflict have to be assumed as ubiquitous, all elements of social structure have to be related to instability and change, and unity and coherence have to be understood as resulting from coercion and constraint.
3. The formation of conflict groups of the class type follows a pattern that can be described in terms of a model involving the following partly analytical, partly hypothetical steps:
4. In any imperatively co-ordinated association two, and only two, aggregates of positions may be distinguished: positions of domination and positions of subjection.
5. Each of these aggregates is characterised by common latent interests; the collectivities of individuals corresponding to them constitute quasi-groups.
6. Latent interests are articulated into manifest interests; and the quasi-groups become the recruiting fields of organised interest groups of the class type.
7. Once the formation of conflict groups of the class type is complete, they stand, within given associations, in a relation of group conflict (class conflict).
8. Group conflict of the class type effects structure changes in the associations in which it occurs.
9. The radicalness of structure change co-varies with the intensity of class conflict.
10. The suddenness of structure change co-varies with the violence of class conflict.

Dahrendorf's analysis is thus firmly rooted in Weberian conceptualisations. Rather than seeing class conflict as a product of capitalism, he sees it almost as ubiquitous in any hierarchically organised society. His focus upon power, and particularly authority, borrows from Weber rather than from Marx. However, by concentrating upon social change, radical conflict and the role of coercion in social life, and by attacking what he sees as the basic 'one-sided' assumptions of functionalism, Dahrendorf adopts a stance consonant with the sociology of radical change.

Dahrendorf's conflict theory has many points of similarity with that developed by John Rex in his book *Key Problems in Sociological Theory* (1961), though Rex is also more committed to revamping sociological theory in terms of its assumptions in relation to the subjective—objective dimension of our analytical scheme. Whereas Dahrendorf is content to wed his conflict analysis to an approach which is firmly committed to the sociological positivist tradition, Rex starts from the assertion that both positivism and empiricism are inadequate. In their place he advocates a model based upon the Weberian action frame of reference which, as will be clear from our discussion in previous chapters, stands at an intermediate position between positivism and idealism. Rex's conflict theory thus follows Weber on *two* counts rather than just one: in terms of both concepts *and* methods. Rex's action theory specifically recognises that the ends which actors pursue may be 'random ends' from the point of view of the social system within which they are located and, indeed, in conflict with it. As a result, he argues that, 'if there is an actual conflict of ends, the behaviour of actors towards one another may not be determined by shared norms but by the success which each has in compelling the other to act in accordance with his interests. Power then becomes a crucial variable in the study of social systems' (Rex, 1961, p. 112).

In Rex's scheme we have a conflict theory characteristic of the sociology of radical change, based upon the action frame of reference. He summarises the main characteristics of his model in the following terms:

1. Instead of being organised around a consensus of values, social systems may be thought of as involving conflict situations at central points. Such conflict situations may lie anywhere between the extremes of peaceful bargaining in the market place and open violence.
2. The existence of such a situation tends to produce not a unitary but a *plural society*, in which there are two or more classes, each of which provides a relatively self-contained social system for its members. The activities of the members take on sociological meaning and must be explained by reference to the group's interests in the conflict situation. Relations between groups are defined at first solely in terms of the conflict situation.
3. In most cases the conflict situation will be marked by an unequal balance of power so that one of the classes emerges as the ruling class. Such a class will continually seek to gain recognition of the legitimacy of its position among the members of the subject class and the leaders of the subject class will seek to deny this claim

and to organise activities which demonstrate that it is denied (e.g. passive resistance).

4. The power situation as between the ruling and subject classes may change as a result of changes in a number of variable factors which increase the possibility of successful resistance or actual revolution by the subject class. Amongst these variable factors are leadership, the strength of the members' aspirations, their capacity for organisation, their possession of the means of violence, their numbers and their role in the social system proposed by the ruling class.

5. In the case of a dramatic change in the balance of power the subject class may suddenly find itself in a situation in which it cannot merely impose its will on the former ruling class, but can actually destroy the basis of that class's existence. New divisions within the revolutionary class may open up, but these may be of an entirely different kind to those which existed in the previous conflict situation.

6. The social institutions and culture of the subject class are geared to, and explicable in terms of, the class's interest in the conflict situation. So far as its long-term aims are concerned, these tend to be expressed in vague and Utopian forms. When the subject class comes to power its actual practices will still have to be worked out. But it is likely that they will be justified and even affected by the morality of conflict and by pre-revolutionary charters and utopias.

7. A change in the balance of power might lead not to complete revolution, but to compromise and reform. In this case new institutions might arise which are not related simply to the prosecution of the conflict, but are recognised as legitimate by both sides. Such a truce situation might in favourable circumstances give rise to a new unitary social order over a long period, in which limited property rights and limited political power are regarded as legitimately held by particular individuals. But such situations are inherently unstable because any weakening of the countervailing power of the formerly subject class would lead the former ruling class to resume its old ways and the maintenance of this power could easily encourage the subject class to push right on to the revolutionary alternative. (Rex, 1961, pp. 129–30)

The conflict theories of both Dahrendorf and Rex, whilst differing in terms of the subjective—objective dimension of our analytical scheme, both emphasise that central attention must be devoted to the structure of power and authority in any analysis of contemporary society. They both draw upon the concept of class as an analytical tool and recognise the conflict between interest groups as the motor force of social change. Their theories radicalise the strains and tensions which, as will be apparent from our discussion in Chapter 4, characterise functionalist theory. In particular, they start from the premise that society is characterised by divergent interests rather than the functional unity presumed in the organismic model. They adopt a model which stresses that society is 'factional' rather than organismic in nature, and in this respect can be seen as developing a line of enquiry which logically emerges from Merton's concept of 'dysfunction'. As we suggested in our discussion on conflict functionalism in Chapter 4, this notion lays the basis for a truly radical critique of society, since, as noted by Gouldner (1959), it opens the door to 'functional autonomy' and hence 'contradiction' as a basic system characteristic. Dahrendorf and Rex stop some way short of developing the full implications of this possibility, which would lead them much closer to various forms of Marxist analysis and a greater and more specific emphasis upon the notions of 'contradiction' and 'catastrophe'.

Interestingly enough, the spirit of this critique of the conflict theory of Dahrendorf and Rex has been captured by Lockwood, who approaches their work from a slightly different perspective. In his well-known article 'Social Integration and System Integration' (1964), he takes Dahrendorf and Rex to task for focusing their attention upon 'social integration' rather than 'system integration'. Linking this basic distinction with Marxist theory, he contends that the propensity to class antagonism is a reflection of the degree of 'social integration' and can be affected by superstructural factors which influence the degree of 'identification', 'communication', etc., whereas the dynamics of class antagonisms are fundamentally related to contradictions within the economic system. In Marxist theory emphasis is explicitly placed upon these 'contradictions' or problems of 'system integration', whereas in the work of the conflict theorists emphasis is placed upon the analysis and problems of 'social integration'. Lockwood believes that whilst these two features are interrelated they are both analytically separate and distinguishable, and that at any point in time different combinations of 'social integration' and 'system integration' may prevail (Lockwood, 1964, pp. 249–50). In essence, Lockwood seeks to explain the possibility of social order within a system characterised by fundamental contradictions in its basic structure. In this and other ways his position is quite similar to that of Althusser.

The interface between the work of Marx and of Weber appears as an intellectual terrain calling for a great deal more attention than it has received up to now. It seems possible, for example, to clarify many of the points at issue between radical Weberians or conflict theorists and their Marxist critics by recognising that the intellectual traditions upon which they draw approach the study of contemporary social formations from different *perspectives*, using different analytical *constructs* and, as a result, they stress in the course of their analysis the importance of different *elements* of the totality which characterises a particular social formation. Let us examine these points in a little more detail. The radical Weberians, following Weber, approach the study of contemporary society from a *perspective* concerned with explaining the degree and nature of 'social integration'. The Marxist theorists approach the study from a perspective concerned to explain why the social system is in the process of change and disintegration. This is the distinction which Lockwood (1964) has drawn between the concern for 'social integration' as opposed to 'system integration', or perhaps more appropriately, 'disintegration'. These different perspectives favour different analytical *constructs*. Thus, the radical Weberians favour 'power', whereas the Marxist theorists favour 'contradiction'. A focus upon power allows the radical Weberian to explain how society is integrated through coercion or the domination of particular interest groups. A focus upon contradiction allows the Marxist theorist to explain social change in terms of the antagonistic relationship between system elements striving to achieve autonomy from the dominating forces which weld them together. As a result, the radical Weberians and Marxists tend to stress the importance of different *elements* of the social formation. The radical Weberians within the radical structuralist paradigm tend to focus upon the 'superstructure', where the conflict of interests between different power groups are most evident. Thus there is often a primary concern for the role of the State and the political, legal, administrative and ideological apparatus through which the dominant interest groups secure their position within society. The Marxist theorist focuses his interest, first and foremost, upon the forces operating within the 'substructure' or economic base of society.[33] Although many Marxist theorists have concerned themselves with the nature of the relationship between substructure and superstructure and the relative autonomy of the latter (Althusser and Balibar, 1970; Cutler et al, 1977), they are at one in recognising an analysis of the economic substructure as central to an understanding of the contradictions which act as the generators of social change and disintegration.

Stated in this somewhat bald and oversimplified way, some of the distinctions and similarities between the views of the radical Weberian and the various types of Marxist thought become easier to see. For the most part their respective problematics have been quite distinct. The radical Weberians have tended to focus upon the relationships between *social integration* and *power* as manifested in the *superstructure* of the social formation. Marxist theorists, have tended to focus upon the relationships between *system disintegration*, *contradiction*, and *substructure/superstructure* relationships.

The increasing attention which has recently been devoted to the nature of the relationships between substructure and superstructure could usefully be extended to embrace the interrelationships between the other elements which distinguish radical Weberian and Marxist thought. The relationships between the concepts of contradiction and power, and social integration and system disintegration, also seem worthy of attention. It seems clear, for example, that the concepts of contradiction and power are connected in some form of dialectical relationship in which the form of one presupposes the form of the other. Power can be seen, for example, as the manifestation of 'contradictory' relationships between elements within the social formation as a whole. Similarly, as Lockwood has argued, there is a balance and a relationship between 'social integration' and the state of 'system disintegration'. Further developments in sociological theory within the radical structuralist paradigm thus might well focus upon the complex network of relationships and concepts which characterise theories seeking to explore the relationship between the contributions of Marx and Weber.

This discussion perhaps serves to illustrate the similarities and distinctions between the perspective of the radical Weberian conflict theorists and Marxists such as Althusser, and their respective locations within the bounds of the radical structuralist paradigm. As will be clear from Figure 3.3, conflict theory, in its attempt to explore the interface between Marx and Weber (albeit in a very limited way), can be regarded as characteristic of a sociology of radical change located on the boundary of the radical structuralist paradigm.

The Underlying Unity of the Paradigm

Theories within the radical structuralist paradigm are thus based upon relatively objectivist assumptions with regard to the nature of social science, and are geared to providing a radical critique of contemporary society. They do so by focusing upon the in-built forces which they see as creating basic and deep-seated pressures for social change. With the possible exception of conflict theory, they present theories of social change in which revolution, often bloody, plays a central part. The paradigm reflects a sociology of radical change in which the idyllic vision of non-violent revolution through consciousness, such as that envisaged by many radical humanists, is left far behind. From the standpoint of radical structuralism, change in society almost inevitably involves a transformation of structures which, even given favourable circumstances, do not fall or change of their own accord. Structures are seen as being changed, first and foremost, through economic or political crises, which generate conflicts of such intensity that the *status quo* is necessarily disrupted or torn apart and replaced by radically different social forms.

All schools of thought within the paradigm are predicated, in varying degrees, upon four central notions. First, there is a general acceptance of the notion of *totality*. All theories within the radical structuralist paradigm, like those of the radical humanist paradigm, address themselves to the understanding of total social formations. Second, there is the notion of *structure*. The focus, in contrast to that of the radical humanist paradigm, is upon the configurations of social relationships which characterise different totalities and which exist independently of men's consciousness of them. Structures are treated as hard and concrete facticities, which are relatively persistent and enduring. Social reality for the radical structuralist is not necessarily created and recreated in everyday interaction, as, for example, many interpretive theorists would claim. Reality exists independently of any reaffirmation which takes place in everyday life.

The third notion is that of *contradiction*. Structures, whilst seen as persistent and relatively enduring, are also seen as posed in contradictory and antagonistic relationships one to another. The notion of contradiction, like that of alienation within the radical humanist paradigm, has both a symbolic and a substantive aspect. It is symbolic in the sense that it stands for the radical structuralists' hope and belief that capitalist social formations contain within them the seeds of their own decay. In substantive terms, the notion of contradiction varies in definition and use within the context of this overall symbolic umbrella. Some of the fundamental contradictions which have been recognised are those between the relations of production and the means of production; between exchange value and surplus value; between the increasing socialisation of the forces of production and the narrowing basis of their ownership; between capital and labour; between the increasing anarchy of market and centralisation of production. Different theorists tend to select and emphasise different contradictions, and with varying degrees of explicitness. Where Bukharin's historical materialism is concerned, for example, the notion of contradiction pervades his work in implicit fashion, in terms of a basic incompatibility between any given technology and the basis of man's relationship to nature. In Althusser's sociology the notion of contradiction is more explicit, and also more varied. He identifies many forms of contradiction which, in certain configurations, act as the motor force behind revolutionary social change. Within the context of conflict theory, the treatment of contradiction is more implicit and, indeed, more superficial. For example, attention is devoted principally to the analysis of class conflict as the surface manifestation of a more deep-seated structural imbalance embedded in the nature of contemporary industrial society.

The fourth notion central to schools of thought belonging to the radical structuralist paradigm is that of *crisis*. All theories within the paradigm view change as a process involving structural dislocation of an extreme form. The typical pattern is that in which contradictions within a given totality reach a point at which they can no longer be contained. The ensuing crisis, political, economic, and the like, is viewed as the point of transformation from one totality to another, in which one set of structures is replaced by another of a fundamentally different kind.

The underlying unity and distinctive nature of the paradigm becomes clearly evident when compared with its functionalist neighbour. Despite sharing an approach to the study of social reality, which emphasises how society is ontologically prior to man and can be understood through positivist epistemology, the orientation of radical structuralism is towards fundamentally different ends. As we have seen, the emphasis in radical structuralism is upon contradiction and crisis. These factors receive no attention within the functionalist paradigm; they are essentially alien to this perspective, since its fundamental aim is to account for the persistence and survival of existing social forms. Functionalism is concerned with evolutionary as opposed to catastrophic change. Even the most change-orientated schools of thought within the context of the functionalist paradigm are markedly different from, and conservative in orientation when compared with, their immediate neighbours within radical structuralism.

Notes and References

1. In the *Grundrisse*, Marx provides the 'outlines' or foundations of the critique of political economy which was to occupy the remainder of his life's work. These 'outlines' were primarily in note form and probably never intended for publication. Though written in the late 1850s, they were not published until 1939, and they have only recently been translated from the original German and published in English for the first time.

   The three volumes of *Capital* – Marx's major work – elaborate but a small part of the schema put forward in the *Grundrisse*. Marx died with the vast proportion of his work incomplete.

2. See, for example, Godelier (1972). He maintains that in *Capital* there are two central notions of 'contradiction', and a variety of contexts in which they are used. As he puts it,

   > First of all there is the contradiction between workers and capitalists. Then there are the economic 'crises' in which contradictions appear between production and consumption, between the conditions of production of value and surplus value and the conditions of their realisation, and basically between production forces and relations of production. Finally there are the contradictions between capitalism and small peasant or artisan property, capitalism and socialism, etc. This simple list reveals differences of nature and importance among these contradictions, of which some are internal to the system, and others exist between the system and other systems. They must therefore be analysed theoretically. (Godelier, 1972, p. 350).

   In this 'theoretical analysis' Godelier posits that Marx sees some contradictions as 'specific' to capitalism, created by it and reproduced continually within it. *Within* such a structure these are internal contradictions 'antagonistic' to social stability and likely therefore to be central to the violent overthrow of the capitalist mode of production. Such an antagonistic contradiction is evident to sociologists, etc., in the class struggle. More important, however, says Godelier, there is a contradiction *between* structures recognised within *Capital*. This is the contradiction between the increasing socialisation of the forces of production (that is, their widening societal impact) and the narrowing basis of ownership. Thus in the long term there are more and more producers:

fewer and fewer of the bourgeoisie. However, this contradiction is not originally present within capitalism; it only comes about at a certain stage in the development of the capitalist productive mode, when its 'positive' liberating element has dried up and large-scale industry replaces the small-scale production typical of early capitalism.

3. The concept of 'surplus value' and its link with the economic structure of capitalism is by no means an easy one to grasp and it has been the subject of much debate within economics. Whilst surplus value is clearly defined as the extra value a capitalist has control of after he has paid wages to the worker – that is, the terrain upon which industrial relations and particularly wage bargaining is fought – it is unclear how 'surplus value' relates to the tendency within capitalism for 'the rate of profits to fall'. In other words, there is an opacity about the status of the concepts and nature of the relationship between 'surplus value', the 'fundamental contradictions' within capitalism and the 'economic crises' to which these inevitably lead. Contemporary Marxist political economy is replete with new identifications of *the* fundamental contradiction and discussions of the empirical evidence or lack of it, for the falling rate of profit. The arguments are beyond the scope of this exposition, but what is important is that one recognises that, for Marx, 'surplus value' and the 'exploitation' which it reflects lies at the heart of the contradictions which blight capitalism. The central empirical reflection of these contradictions (between the relations of production and means of production, between exchange value and surplus value, between capital and labour, between the measure of labour time and the use of labour time, etc.) is the tendency for the rate of profits to fall. As this happens, and the deeply rooted antagonistic contradictions work to the surface, the final, cataclysmic economic crisis occurs. Surplus value, then, represents the economic conceptualisation central to Marxian analysis which provides the link between deep-seated structural contradictions and their reflection in economic cataclysms for which revolution becomes the only possible solution.

4. For the view that the move from an emphasis on 'alienation' to 'surplus value' indicates a *continuity* within Marx in the study of the 'dialectics of labour', see *From Alienation to Surplus Value* (Walton and Gamble, 1972).

5. McLellan describes this movement succinctly as follows:

Towards the end of his life Marx moved nearer to the positivism then so fashionable in intellectual circles. This tendency, begun in *Anti-Dühring* and continued by Engels in his *Ludwig Feuerbach* and *Dialectics of Nature*, reached its apogee in Soviet textbooks on dialectical materialism. It was this trend which presented Marxism as a philosophical world-view or *Weltanschauung* consisting of objective laws and particularly laws of the dialectical movement of matter taken in a metaphysical sense as the basic constituent of reality. This was obviously very different from the 'unity of theory and practice' as exemplified in, for instance, the *Theses on Feuerbach*. This preference for the model of the natural sciences had always been with Engels, though not with Marx, who had, for example, a much more reserved attitude to Darwinism. (McLellan, 1976, p. 423)

6. In *Anti-Dühring*, a personal attack upon a German socialist (for which, incidentally, Engels had received Marx's approval for publication) Engels set the scene for the movement towards positivistic 'scientific socialism'. He painted a picture of Marx's ideas as representative of a totally comprehensive frame of reference which provided the laws of motion for a causally determined process in which socialism would inevitably replace capitalism. Furthermore, such a view replaced philosophy itself.

   At Marx's graveside, Engels explicitly compared the work of Darwin in the natural sciences with that of Marx in the social sciences.

7. It is important to emphasise that Marx himself did not use the terms 'historical materialism' or 'dialectical materialism', and that there has been much debate about what exactly they mean.

8. See, for example, Colletti (1972) and Althusser (1971).

9. For a discussion of the relationship between Weber's political and sociological views, see Giddens (1972b).

10. Plekhanov stands as the founding father of contemporary Russian social theory. For a selection of his work, see Plekhanov (1974) in which his stance within the Engelsian tradition is described thus:

   Plekhanov was an ardent defender of materialist dialectics, which he skilfully applied to social life, correctly considering it as an achievement of Marxist philosophic thought. He saw in it the great and the new which, combined with the masterly discovery of the materialist conception of history, distinguishes Marx's materialism from the teachings of materialists before him.

Plekhanov brings out the various aspects of materialist dialectics and brilliantly expounds the theory of development, the correlation between evolution and revolution, leaps, etc. In this connection he shows the opposition between Marx's dialectical method and Hegel's, and considers the role of Hegel's idealist philosophy as one of the theoretical sources of Marxism. (Plekhanov, 1974, p. 49)

The work of both Bukharin and Kropotkin discussed here owes a great deal to Plekhanov.

11. See, for example, Gouldner (1970), 'Functionalism goes East', in Gouldner, *The Coming Crisis of Western Sociology*, op. cit., pp. 455–58.
12. For a detailed study of Bukharin's biography, see Cohen (1974).
13. See, for example, van den Berghe (1969) and the discussion in Chapter 2 of this book.
14. There are several very readable biographical accounts of Kropotkin and his work. See, for example, Woodcock (1975), pp. 171–206; Avrich (1967), pp. 26–32; Bose (1967), pp. 257–98.
15. For a comprehensive list of Kropotkin's publications, see Bose (1967), pp. 261–2.
16. Perry Anderson in *Considerations on Western Marxism* (1976) tends to view Althusser and Colletti in the same light as Lukács, Gramsci, Marcuse, etc., as part of 'Western Marxism'. In using the term 'contemporary Mediterranean Marxism' we seek obviously to differentiate this type of theorising from other varieties of Marxism in Western Europe which stand, for us, in a different paradigm. Interestingly, 'Mediterranean Marxism' is relatively popular in Britain.
17. See, for example, Colletti (1974).
18. See, for example, Anderson (1976), p. 46.
19. For a further discussion of Althusser's background and approach to Marxism, see Callinicos (1976).
20. For a discussion of the 'epistemological break', see Althusser (1969). This notion is taken from Bachelard.
21. In addition to Althusser (1969), see also Althusser and Balibar (1970).
22. For a comparison of Althusser's structuralism with that of Lévi-Strauss, see Glucksmann (1974).
23. For a useful glossary of Althusser's terminology, see Althusser (1969), pp. 248–57.

24. The obscurity is also present in Althusser. The concept of 'overdetermination' is taken in modified form from Freud.

25. For a further discussion of this, see Althusser (1969), pp. 88–116.

26. For a discussion, see, for example, Shaw (1975).

27. Della Volpe (1897–1968) was a Marxist philosopher who sought to provide a much more positive interpretation of Marxism than those of Lùkács and Gramsci.

28. See, for example, the essay 'Marxism as a Sociology' in Colletti (1972).

29. See, for example, Colletti (1974), p. 12.

30. For a discussion of the commonality of interest between Marx, Weber and Durkheim, see Giddens (1971).

31. In particular, Dahrendorf argues that the crisis of capitalism, based upon increasing immiseration of the proletariat, increasing polarisation between proletariat and bourgeoisie and increasing homogeneity within the two classes has been 'proved' empirically untenable at every turn (Dahrendorf, 1959, pp. 36–71).

32. This is taken from Dahrendorf (1959), pp. 237–40. The list of thirty-nine assumptions presented by Dahrendorf has been reduced here, largely by removing those which are purely definitional.

    It is interesting to note that in his conceptualisation Dahrendorf draws upon Merton's distinction between 'manifest' and 'latent' functions, developing the radical implications which these suggest.

33. 'Marxist' is used here as a shorthand for Marxist theorists located within the radical structuralist paradigm. The focus of interests of 'Marxists' within the radical humanist paradigm is, of course, quite different.

11. Radical Organisation Theory

In recent years a number of social theorists have sought to approach the study of organisations from a perspective characteristic of the radical structuralist paradigm. For the most part they have attempted to do this by providing a critique of the problems inherent in the functionalist approach. As in the case of the interpretive and radical humanist paradigms, the radical structuralist approach to the study of organisations has developed in a reactive mould. The critique which has evolved has been wide-ranging, far from coherent and, at times, highly polemical. Functionalist theorists in general, and organisation theorists in particular, have been accused of being the mere servants of the capitalist system; of being mindlessly empiricist; of neglecting the historical dimensions of their subject; of ignoring the whole body of social thought reflected in the works of Marx; of underplaying the importance of class relationships in contemporary society; of ignoring the importance of the State; and of adopting analytical models which are generally orientated towards the preservation of the *status quo*, as opposed to accounting for the phenomena of ongoing social change. Not all theorists who have attempted to provide a critique of functionalism in this way are located within the radical structuralist paradigm. Indeed, as will be apparent from our discussion of functionalist sociology, many functionalists have criticised their colleagues on some of these grounds, in order to forge a more radical perspective *within* the context of the functionalist paradigm. Again, radical structuralists have not always provided a critique upon all the above grounds. Typically, one or more has been given the focus of attention. The critique of functionalism has been launched from a variety of perspectives and with a variety of objectives in mind.

We wish to argue here that behind the radical structuralist critique of functionalism lies a latent and only partially developed approach to the study of organisations. Whilst not altogether coherent, it is united on certain themes. As an attempt at the articulation of some of these, Table 11.1 presents a sample of twelve points on which functionalist theory has been criticised and counterposes these with the assumptions which implicitly underlie the radical structuralist critique. In criticising functionalism, the radical structuralists imply that they hold an alternative point of view. Whilst this is not always systematically developed or clearly articulated, it does underwrite their criticism, and it is as well that it be spelt out. The twelve points thus go some way towards presenting the overall flavour of the wide-ranging nature of the radical structuralist critique.

Table 11.1

The unity of the radical structuralist attack upon organisation theory

Points of criticism directed against organisation theory	By implication this would suggest the following guidelines for a radical organisation theory
1. Organisation theory is locked into an acceptance of managerially defined problems.	Instead of 'having their eyes turned downward and their palms upward', organisation theorists should 'study the structure of social oppression and bring this knowledge and the power that it conveys to the powerless and exploited social majority'.[1]
2. Organisation theorists consciously or *unconsciously* play an active and concrete role in man's degradation within the work place.	Organisation theorists should seek to carry out 'action-research' which has discontinuous revolutionary change as its objective. Theory and practice should be unified into a seamless, intellectual activity of which the theorist is well aware.[2]
3. It ignores the contribution of Marx.	Detailed and extensive knowledge of the work of the mature Marx is a *sine qua non* for any radical organisation theory.
4. It neglects the analysis of class relations.	The concept of class should form an integral part of any coherent radical organisation theory.
5. It is based upon a very narrow and misleading interpretation of Weber.	Weber should be read in more depth and with greater understanding. Most functionalist organisation theorists completely misrepresent his views on bureaucracy, and misuse his concept of the 'ideal type'.
6. It neglects the role of the State.	Organisational analysis depends upon a theory of the state which is still in need of detailed articulation.

Table 11.1 (continued)

Points of criticism directed against organisation theory	By implication this would suggest the following guidelines for a radical organisation theory
7. It is ahistorical.	Radical organisation theory should have a historical dimension. In order to understand organisations today, there is a need to comprehend them as they have been in the past, and indeed, to understand how and why they developed in the first place.
8. It is 'static', i.e., it assumes a tendency to equilibrium, a societal consensus and organic unity.	Organisation theory should be dynamic – it should conceive of society as a process which develops through the interplay of contradictory forces, which can result in major upheavals and irregular patterns of change.
9. It is basically empiricist, i.e. concerned with methodology above all.	Instead of beginning with an emphasis upon the rigour of observation and 'experimental' technique, radical organisation theory should seek to assert the primacy of a coherent theoretical perspective which is not necessarily subject to the tyranny of data.
10. It is anti-theoretical.	Suspicion of 'theory' in conventional analysis should be inverted, so that radical organisation theory must celebrate the development of large-scale, politically relevant theoretical perspectives.
11. It is basically unaware of the crucial importance of macro-societal factors 'external' to the organisation.	Radical organisation theory must start from the basic assumption that organisations cannot be understood without a *prior* analysis of the social processes and structures in which organisations are thought to exist.
12. Its recurrent attempts to provide a general theory suggest the possibility and desirability of a synthesis when in fact, this is unattainable.	Conventional organisation theory and its radical counterpart are mutually exclusive. No synthesis is possible because their 'problematics' are incompatible. Radical organisation theory cannot, nor should it, seek to incorporate its functionalist adversary.

The significance of this critique, however, can only be fully understood, developed and refined against the background of the intellectual tradition of radical structuralism as a whole. Elements of the critique are usually based upon elements of this perspective. As will be apparent from our discussion in the previous chapter, radical structuralism presents a diverse and complex body of thought. However, there does appear to be a measure of coherence among its constituent elements, and these provide useful guidelines by which to chart the general direction in which the overall thrust of radical structuralism takes us as far as the study of organisations is concerned.

We concluded our previous chapter by suggesting that the core concepts of 'totality', 'structure', 'contradiction' and 'crisis' were in large measure unifying themes. Transferred to the realm of the study of organisations, they assume significance in the following ways. The notion of totality implies that it is crucial to study total social formations as a means of understanding the elements of a social system. It implies that an understanding of the nature of the whole must precede any understanding of constituent parts. 'Totality' thus implies that organisations can only be understood in terms of their place within a total context, in terms of the wider social formation within which they exist and which they reflect. The significance of the nature and form of organisations only becomes fully apparent when viewed from this all-embracing point of view.

From the radical structuralist standpoint, the totality can be characterised in terms of its basic structural formation. Structures are treated as hard and concrete facticities which are relatively persistent and enduring, and which exist independently of men's consciousness of them. From this point of view, organisations are structural facticities, but they represent only part of the wider structural facticity which constitutes the totality. Organisations are thus structural elements of a wider structure which they reflect and from which they derive their existence and true significance. The organisation is, in this sense, a partial reflection of totality.

The notion of contradiction is of relevance to the study of organisations since, from the radical structuralist view, it is at the point of production that many of the contradictions within society come to the fore. Organisations, particularly economic organisations, are viewed as the stage upon which the deep-seated cleavages within the social formation as a whole are most visible. It is in the workshop and factory, for example, that the contradictions between the relations and the means of production, capital and labour, the measure of and use of labour time, and the fundamental problem of overproduction, are seen as working themselves out. It is in the empirical facets of this organisational life that contradictions are seen as taking their most visible form. Not all radical structuralists address themselves to the study of these contradictions in a direct and specific fashion. As we noted in the previous chapter, there is a division between the so-called radical Weberians and the Marxian structuralists on this score. The former are most concerned with the ways in which contradictions surface at the level of empirical reality through the interplay of power relationships and the conflicts which ensue. Their interest in contradictions is thus of an indirect as opposed to a direct nature, and the concepts which they use and the approach which they adopt reflect this very clearly.

The radical structuralist notion of crisis, involving the view that macro-social change is characterised by structural contradiction and dislocation of an extreme form, has significance for organisations, in that as structures they are necessarily involved in this process of dislocation. If there is a change in totality, there is of necessity a change in organisational forms. The significance of changes in the structure of organisations can thus be seen in terms of the changes occurring in the totality as a whole. Organisations monitor and reflect the movement of totality from one crisis to another. The study of organisations in crisis, therefore, is of particular interest to the radical structuralist, as reflecting the processes which contribute to and characterise totality shifts. Crises of ownership and control, factory occupations, Wall Street crashes and large-scale redundancies are of particular significance from the radical structuralist point of view, not as problems to be solved, but as episodes yielding considerable insights insofar as the understanding of the nature of the social formation is concerned.

The notions of 'totality', 'structure', 'contradiction' and 'crisis' thus provide core concepts from which a radical organisation theory characteristic of the radical structuralist paradigm can be forged. Taken together, these core concepts, along with the implications which underlie the radical structuralist critique of functionalism, provide clear indications of the form such a radical theory of organisations might take. Up to now it has remained largely embryonic, its various elements scattered around a truly diverse body of literature. As a means of establishing the basis for a fuller understanding and further development of the perspective as a whole, it seems necessary to move towards a much more systematic statement. This is our aim in this chapter. In the following sections we intend to explore some of the relevant literature in this area, and we will attempt to specify some of the key issues of debate.

As will become clear, it is not possible to say that there is but one approach to the study of organisations from a radical structuralist perspective. As in the case of the functionalist paradigm, different views can be put forward according to the nature of the assumptions made in relation to each of the two dimensions of our analytical scheme. In our previous chapter we demonstrated the existence of a number of distinct schools of thought within the radical structuralist paradigm. Of these, the two described as conflict theory and contemporary Mediterranean Marxism appear to underwrite and be most closely connected with radical organisation theory at the present time. There may also be literature addressed to the study of organisations from the standpoint of what we have called Russian social theory, though of this we are unaware.

Before discussing the radical organisation theories akin to conflict theory and contemporary Mediterranean Marxism, some further remarks are in order. First, the organisation theorists who adopt the conflict theory perspective may shun association with the sociological school of thought which we have described under that name. Although linked with that perspective, they have developed their ideas somewhat independently and within the context of different disciplines. What they have in common, however, is a commitment to the radical Weberianism which we have described as characterising conflict theory at a sociological level. For this reason, and in order to avoid unnecessary confusion, we shall discuss their contribution to a radical theory of organisations under the heading radical Weberianism. Second, the contribution to a radical theory of organisations from the Marxist viewpoint, whilst sharing many points in common with Althusserian structuralism, is not necessarily derived from it, and would not always claim an allegiance to that perspective as a whole. The work of Baran and Sweezy (1968) (which we shall consider later), for example, was developed in parallel with that of Althusser. We shall thus use the term 'Marxian structuralist' to characterise this brand of radical organisation theory. Third, as we have argued earlier, and as all radical theorists would accept, it is not possible to develop a theory of organisations independent of a theory of the totality of which they are part. The literature which is relevant to the development of radical organisation theory is diverse and contains many works which approach the problem of totality rather than organisations as such. At first sight, therefore, their relevance to the study of organisations may seem somewhat remote.

Radical Weberian Approaches to a Radical Organisation Theory

The general flavour of the radical Weberian approach to the study of organisations is perhaps best captured in the notion of 'corporatism', a term which has come to stand for the development of the seamless web of bureaucratic institutions which exist in modern society as appendages of (and subservient to) the State.[3] The State is regarded as being at the centre of an octopus-like structure, whose bureaucratic tentacles stretch out and invade all areas of social activity. The radical Weberians tend to be interested in the relationship between the State and this general process of bureaucratisation, and they are particularly concerned to understand the ways in which the State apparatus dominates the wider social structure within which it exists. The radical Weberians are interested in 'power' relationships and draw many of their ideas and conceptualisations from the realm of political science.

The radical Weberian contribution to a radical theory of organisations, therefore, can be elicited from literature which focuses upon a theory of the totality, in which the State is accorded a central role. Its implications for organisations as such, whether State-related or not, have to be culled from this wider background. Although considerable emphasis is placed upon the analysis of bureaucracy, it only represents one part of a wider analysis geared to obtaining an understanding of the social formation as a whole. A radical theory of organisations from this point of view, therefore, only has significance when developed and interpreted against this wider background.

We will commence our review of relevant literature with Ralph Miliband's book *The State in Capitalist Society* (1973). At first sight the assertion that Miliband, a leading intellectual of the New Left and co-editor of the *Socialist Register*, has an affiliation with radical Weberianism might seem to be stretching the imagination too far. However, it will be remembered that we maintained in the previous chapter that radical Weberianism explores that intellectual terrain in which the interests of Marx and Weber may be thought to coincide. Just as Rex and Dahrendorf attempt to infuse Marxian notions with a potent draught of Weberianism, so too does Miliband in his consideration of the role of the State within the advanced capitalist societies. Since Marx himself never managed to complete a systematic study of the State, Miliband sets himself the task of providing a Marxist political analysis which can confront democratic pluralism on its own ground. Whilst pluralism assumes a competitive, fragmented and diffuse power structure, Miliband seeks to demonstrate that this view 'is in all essentials wrong' and 'constitutes a profound obfuscation' of social reality (Miliband, 1973, p. 6).

Whilst Miliband believes that today we still live within authentically capitalist societies, there have been many changes since Marx himself wrote of capitalism. Miliband regards advanced capitalism as all but synonymous with the giant form of enterprise found throughout the industrialised West. The 'economic base' of advanced capitalism is seen as constituted in large measure by these ubiquitous corporations, and the political arrangements of the industrialised nations as taking on a fundamentally similar form. Within these societies, social stratification presents a differentiated appearance but, says Miliband, although there is a plurality of competing elites within such social structures, taken together these form a 'dominant economic class, possessed of a high degree of cohesion and solidarity' (Miliband, 1973, p. 45). The State's relationship with such a dominant class is the focus of the book, but for Miliband the notion of the State is a complex and problematic one. In fact, it turns out that the State consists of the bureaucracies (the 'institutions') whose interrelationships shape the form of the State system; these are 'the government, the administration, the military and the police, the judicial branch, sub-central government and parliamentary assemblies' (Miliband, 1973, p. 50). Miliband goes on to argue that the governments of the advanced capitalist societies act positively and with good will towards business and propertied interests (that is, the corporations) and, furthermore, that the other bureaucracies which together form the State can normally be counted upon to support the dominant economic interests. Of course, says Miliband, perturbations within this integrated structure occur, primarily through competition between organised interest groups, but these are superficial and incidental to the underlying structure of domination. This domination also occurs 'at the level of meaning' and Miliband considers the process of legitimation of the existing power structure through, for example, political propaganda, the media of mass communications and the universities, each acting as a source of political socialisation. In his final chapter Miliband considers the future, in terms of both the dangers of conservative authoritarianism and the immense obstacles to the creation of a truly 'socialist' society. He concludes, following Marx, that only within the latter will the State be converted 'from an organ superimposed upon society into one completely subordinated to it'.

It should be clear from this brief exposition of Miliband's book that he adopts a position much closer to radical Weberianism than to Althusserian structuralism, a fact revealed quite clearly by Poulantzas (1969) in his famous critique of *The State in Capitalist Society*.[4] Whilst one cannot maintain that Miliband's ideas are at one with those of Dahrendorf and Rex, there are at this level more similarities between them than differences. For example, like these conflict theorists, Miliband recognises the existence of a lacuna in Marxist thought; he discusses the notion of power as his central unifying concept; he admits a complicated form of social stratification within capitalism; his position permits a concern for explanation 'at the level of meaning' and, last but not least, the notion of bureaucracy underpins much of his analysis. Of course, Miliband's references to Weber are few and then mostly hostile, but this does not and should not mask the essential fact that his underlying theoretical position is akin to that of radical Weberianism.

As far as the development of a radical theory of organisation is concerned, Miliband's analysis emphasises the importance of obtaining an understanding of the theory of the State as a precursor to a theory of organisations. From this point of view, the latter cannot be adequately developed before the former. To understand the operations of the police force, the judiciary and local government, as well as industrial organisations, it is imperative to see them as parts of the State apparatus and to attempt to understand the processes of mutual interrelationship which link them together. The radical Weberian perspective emphasises that organisations cannot be understood as isolated enterprises; their meaning and significance derive from their location within the context of the wider social framework, and their activities only become fully intelligible with this reference point in mind.

Other ideas with a radical Weberian flavour emerge from a close reading of Eldridge and Crombie's book *A Sociology of Organisations* (1974). In essence, the book can be seen as comprising three parts.[5] The first deals with the literature on organisation theory and is underpinned by a concern to elucidate a range of sociological approaches and interests. This concern follows from Eldridge and Crombie's attack upon organisation theory for its '*ad hoc*' nature and its attempts to create a 'general theory' when there is no hope of such a unifying conceptual framework. Thus, rather than imply conceptual homogeneity, they draw upon organisational analysis from both the functionalist and radical structuralist traditions in an effort to demonstrate the heterogeneity of approaches to the sociology of organisations. In the second part of the book Eldridge and Crombie consider the contributions of Spencer, Durkheim, Weber and Marx through their respective treatments of the 'organisational phenomenon'. It is important to note, however, that the incorporation of Spencer and Marx at this point is achieved through a conceptual leap of imagination, since the authors make no clear-cut distinction between organisations as empirical facticities and the 'mode of social organisation'.[6] This allows an important link to be made between the levels of analysis of society and organisation, but, at the cost of a certain amount of confusion.[7] It is only in the third part of Eldridge and Crombie's work that radical Weberianism becomes evident, as they become involved in a discussion of the links between organisation and society provided by the notion of power. Their analysis draws heavily upon the literature and concepts of political science. They discuss in some detail totalitarianism, with particular reference to Nazi Germany; Michels's 'iron law of oligarchy' is also considered, and a final section of their work is devoted to a 'critique of pluralism', in which Miliband's analysis plays a central part. Their attitude to Miliband, however, is somewhat ambivalent, for they seem to sympathise with the analysis contained within *The State in Capitalist Society* but are doubtful about the 'solutions' and prophecies which it advocates. Eldridge and Crombie's book thus reflects various elements of the radical Weberian perspective, though they must be sifted from the contents of their work as a whole.

A third example of a nascent radical Weberianism is to be found in Nicos Mouzelis's introduction to the 1975 edition of *Organisation and Bureaucracy*. Whilst the original edition of this book focuses primarily upon the tradition of functionalist organisation theory and presents a well articulated account of the development of organisational analysis within this paradigm, the new introduction to the 1975 edition reflects a considerable change in theoretical orientation. Here Mouzelis seeks to point to some of the ways in which organisation theory might fruitfully develop, and in so doing adopts a position in many ways characteristic of radical Weberianism. After discussing various aspects of the problem of reification in social analysis, Mouzelis turns to the work of Althusser as a means of providing a critique of what he sees as the excessive empiricism and atheoretical nature of much contemporary organisation theory. Whilst suggesting that Althusser's perspective has much to offer organisation theory, he does not develop its implications to any marked degree. Instead, he turns to emphasising the need for a more historically based approach to the study of organisations, which Althusser does not provide, and proceeds to illustrate what he has in mind through a discussion of the development of State bureaucracies. This discussion draws heavily upon the work of Weber, and elaborates upon the class relations and power struggles which have characterised the emergence and development of the process of bureaucratisation in Western Europe. Mouzelis demonstrates very clearly the way in which bureaucracies have developed their power base and have achieved a high degree of autonomy within society, to the extent that they now stand not so much as 'a neutral tool at the service of the people and its legitimate leaders', but as 'the real master' (Mouzelis, 1975, p. xxxiv). His analysis reflects many of the concerns of radical Weberianism. The concern for the power structure within society, the place of the State bureaucracy within it, and the possibility of bureaucracy's domination of its intended masters, are central to his perspective. Mouzelis thus points the way towards a radical organisation theory based upon an historical analysis which pays central attention to the nature of organisations within the context of the power structure of society as a whole. Within this framework, the nature and role of the State apparatus would qualify for special attention.

In their paper 'Organisation and Protection' (1977) McCullough and Shannon address a number of the issues referred to above, and place particular emphasis upon relationships between organisations and the State. They maintain that within organisation theory the predominant conceptualisation of the relationship between organisations and the State is one of dissociation, in which organisations and the State are viewed as 'separable, rational, self-conscious and self-determining entities' (McCullough and Shannon, 1977, p. 72). In practice, they argue, the relationship is quite different from this, with the State extending 'protection' to organisations which lie within the scope of influence – and that, historically, this is the role which the State has always performed. In line with this argument, they see the multi-national corporations of today not so much as phenomena which stand in opposition to the sovereignty of nation states, but as phenomena which are to be understood as part and parcel of the development which has led to the nation state in its present form; as components of the same repressive system of world division of labour based upon exploitation. McCullough and Shannon adopt a historical perspective for much of their analysis, and they present evidence concerning the role of the State in the growth of the East India Company, for example, and other State—organisation relationships, as a means of illustrating the 'hegemonic' nature (as against the liberal, pluralistic or countervailing nature) of governmental and industrial organisations. In their view the State and organisations have, internationally and historically, formed an integrated bureaucratic framework which represents a structure of domination in which power rests with a small fraction of the population. However, the integration of this institutional framework is not immutable, nor does it carry a life-long guarantee, and they point to the contemporary situation in Northern Ireland as an illustration. The inability of the State there to offer protection to organisations and its lack of a monopoly of force have, it is argued, entirely disrupted the normal pattern of organisational life, since the present administrative, military and legal apparatuses are in a condition of disintegration (McCullough and Shannon, 1977, p. 83). Such a crisis offers an opportunity, they suggest, to examine the relationships between organisations and the State which protects them, in a way unknown to contemporary organisation theory.

The essence of the radical Weberian perspective which emerges from this brief review of relevant literature is that organisations must be studied as elements within the political structure of society as a whole. This necessarily involves an analysis of power relationships, particularly in relation to the role of the State, which stands as the dominant institutional structure offering itself for analysis. Organisations cannot be understood in isolation. Their significance arises from their location within the network of power relations which influence societal processes. From the radical Weberian standpoint it is this issue of power which stands at the centre of the analytical stage. The theory of power which underwrites this perspective is in stark contrast to the pluralist theory discussed in earlier chapters. It is a theory of power which stresses the integral as opposed to the intercursive nature of this phenomenon. The central role accorded to power as a variable of analysis redirects the organisation theorist's attention towards issues such as the process of bureaucratisation itself, the increasing concentration of the means of administration in the hands of bureaucrats, and the rapid development of State intervention in almost every area of social activity. The macro-orientation of radical Weberianism points the way towards the development of macro-theories of organisational process which stand in stark contrast to the middle-range theorising reflected in the work of the majority of organisation theorists located within the functionalist paradigm. We shall return to some of these issues later in the chapter.

Marxian Structuralist Approaches to a Radical Organisation Theory

Those theorists who approach the study of organisations from this perspective tend to place the problems inherent in monopoly capitalism at their centre of analysis. Whereas the radical Weberians are most concerned with the role of the State within an essentially political network of bureaucratic power relationships, the Marxian structuralists focus upon the economic structure of society, which they see as the key determinant of the power relationships to which the radical Weberians address their attention. For the Marxian structuralists, therefore, political economy provides the most useful intellectual reference point and source of conceptualisations. They are primarily concerned with the analysis of the economic structures of capitalist society, and they draw upon Marx's *Capital* and the notion of 'contradiction' as central elements in their perspective. The modern corporation is of interest as an empirical reflection of the underlying structure of monopoly capitalism; it is studied as a means of throwing light upon the nature of this underlying structure rather than as an entity in its own right. As in the case of the radical Weberian perspective, organisations only have significance in relation to the totality in which they are located.

This concern for totality is clearly apparent in the first work which we consider in our review of literature in this area: Baran and Sweezy's *Monopoly Capital*. They begin by quoting Hegel's dictum 'the truth is the whole', and stress the need to understand the social order as a totality rather than 'as a collection of small truths about various parts and aspects of society' (Baran and Sweezy, 1968, p. 16). Although Marxism is seen to provide the starting point, *Capital* itself is seen as a limited document because of its failure to appreciate the contemporary importance of monopoly rather than competition within the capitalist market place. The authors give Lenin full recognition for his understanding of the importance of monopolies to the growth of capitalistic imperialism, and it is to the analysis of the large-scale monopoly corporation that Baran and Sweezy direct their attention. They suggest that 'the typical economic unit in the capitalist world is not the small firm producing a negligible fraction of a homogenous output for an anonymous market but a large-scale enterprise producing a significant share of the output of an industry, or even several industries, and able to control its prices, the volume of its production and the types and amounts of its investments' (Baran and Sweezy, 1968, p. 19). They argue that any model of the economy within advanced capitalist societies cannot afford to ignore this central point. The book is seen as a 'scientific' sketch on the American economic and political order, in which 'the generation and absorption of the surplus' produced under monopoly capitalism is given primary consideration, since it is seen as the link between the economic substructure and the political, cultural and ideological superstructure of society. The economic base is regarded as consisting largely of giant corporations which act as engines for the accumulation of capital and the maximisation of profits. Such is their monopoly position that corporations, by controlling price and cost policies, creat a tendency for the amount of surplus to rise. This surplus is seen as being consumed, wasted or invested in an effort to ensure that it is absorbed by the capitalist system without being distributed among the populace. Thus imperialism, militarism, the sales effort, government spending and research and development are all seen as ways of consuming the surplus and postponing the inevitable crisis of overproduction. Baran and Sweezy then go on to ask how this consumption of surplus has affected the quality of life within a monopoly capitalist society. Using measures of divorce rates, housing conditions, juvenile delinquency and so on, they conclude that it represents an 'irrational system'. Monopoly capitalism is seen as irrational, because it has at its heart a fundamental contradiction; whilst the actual processes of production are becoming more thoroughly rationalised, more controlled and better understood, the system as a whole retains an undiminished elementality – that is, men may seek to understand it but, like the wind or tides, it remains beyond their control. Baran and Sweezy, in essence, argue that the deep structures of monopoly capitalism are not amenable to empirical knowledge if one uses an 'ideology' of bourgeois economics. They argue that only with a 'scientific' recognition that it is these economic structures and their interrelationships which are the key to social injustice, and that no alterations to their superstructural manifestation can fundamentally affect them, will social revolution be possible in America.[8] Baran and Sweezy argue that the crisis produced by the profound economic contradictions inherent in monopoly capital have already produced, and will continue to produce, revolutionary wars which have as their goal decolonisation from 'this intolerable social order'.

We have here an analysis which draws upon the tradition of Marxist political economy in order to arrive at an understanding of the essential structure of capitalist society. The monopolist corporation is given central attention, and the authors demonstrate that in terms of wealth and control of economic resources, it is often more powerful than the state within which it is located. Baran and Sweezy have stimulated much interest in the analysis of multi-national corporations, and it is at this level that their work is perhaps of most relevance to the development of a radical organisation theory. Their use of the concept of economic surplus as a basic analytical tool presents organisations in a light which is quite different from that which arises from the notion of the purposive, goal-orientated rationality which dominates functionalist organisation theory. From Baran and Sweezy's standpoint the significance of the monopolistic corporation is ultimately related to the position which it occupies within the fundamental economic base of society; its activities − research and development, production, marketing, etc. − are to be understood in terms of the role which they play in the generation and use of the economic surplus necessary to sustain the structure of the capitalist system. Baran and Sweezy demonstrate the relevance of the concept of surplus to an analysis of organisations. It provides an important concept linking organisations to the totality and offers the radical organisation theorist a powerful tool with which to forge a view of organisations in fundamental opposition to that evident in the functionalist perspective.

The relevance of Baran and Sweezy's perspective for the study of organisations has been taken up by Harry Braverman in a book entitled *Labor and Monopoly Capital* (1974). In essence Braverman attempts to 'fill in the gaps' left by *Monopoly Capital* by applying Baran and Sweezy's approach to a study of the labour process, and, in particular, he is concerned with the de-skilling of work, which he sees as an integral part of organisational reality in the Western world. The book presents a study of the development of the capitalist mode of production during the past hundred years or so, and uses as its starting point the first volume of Marx's *Capital*, the obvious core of any Marxist analysis of the labour process. Braverman rejects any assertion that Marx was a 'technological determinist' and points out that, for Marx, it was technology itself which was determined by the social form in which it was placed. Thus Braverman focuses upon the labour process as it reflects the relations of production in terms of the class system; he is interested not so much in 'consciousness' or working-class activities as in how the labour process is dominated and shaped by the accumulation of capital. Following an historical analysis of the development of both labour and management, Braverman turns to a consideration of various schools of management theory and their role as reflected in the development of the capitalist mode of production.

First, he turns his attention to 'scientific management'. Taylorism for him is not a 'science of work', nor is it the 'best way' to do work 'in general'; it is, on the contrary, 'a science of the management of others' work' and represents an answer to the problem of how best to control 'alienated' labour. The followers of Mayo, in a continuation of this line of argument, are presented as the 'maintenance crew' for the human machinery created by Taylor's 'scientific management'. Today Taylor's successors inhabit work design and work study departments, while the Mayoites are to be found upstairs in the personnel office. These tendencies, initiated by Taylor, have ensured that 'as craft declined, the worker would sink to the level of general and undifferentiated labour power, adaptable to a large range of simple tasks, while as science grew, it would be concentrated in the hands of management' (Braverman, 1974, p. 121). Braverman elaborates on these processes in some detail, giving historical examples drawn from throughout the capitalist world. He attaches particular importance to the scientific-technical revolution and the development of machinery which offers to management the opportunity to do by wholly mechanical means that which it had previously attempted to do by organisational and disciplinary means. Machinery, then, can only be seen as part of the control system of the organisation and hence as a reflection of the capitalist mode of production. Under capitalism the socio-technical system, of whatever kind, represents for Braverman a 'modern', 'scientific', 'dehumanised prison of labour'.

Having looked at what stands as contemporary management theory in this highly critical way, Braverman addresses himself to the question of the form which monopoly capitalism takes. Following Baran and Sweezy, he maintains that monopoly capitalism consists primarily of monopolistic organisations. However, for him, these are more *consumers of surplus labour* than producers of surplus value. The existence of the modern giant corporation is seen as having three consequences of key importance for the occupational structure of the advanced capitalist societies: 'the first is to do with marketing, the second with the structure of management and the third with the function of social co-ordination now exercised by the Corporation' (Braverman, 1974, p. 265). All of these are seen as serving to consume surplus labour. Since the market is the prime area of organisational uncertainty, marketing is necessary in order to control this threat to profitability. Similarly, the growth of an army of clerical workers aids the control and administration of the corporation, while reducing the level of surplus labour. Finally, and most important, the development of the internal co-ordination of the organisation is seen as necessary because of the lack of *overall* social co-ordination. The complexity of the division of labour under capitalism is regarded as requiring an immense amount of social control, which lies beyond the capabilities of the public functions of the total society. The *internal* planning of such corporations becomes, in effect, *social* planning to fill in the existing large gaps in social control left by the State.

Despite these three primary ways of consuming surplus labour, Braverman argues that *all* surplus labour cannot be absorbed by capitalism, so that one inevitably finds, as Marx described, a reserve army of the working class. It is among this reserve army that poverty and degradation are at their highest levels. In addition, Braverman argues, even among the ranks of the employed, poverty and degradation are essential features of labour under monopoly capitalism.

Braverman's work can be regarded primarily as a critique of the ways in which labour develops under monopoly capitalism. His analysis, in effect, attempts to fill in the interstices of Baran and Sweezy's work, and he accepts their basic theoretical position almost without cavil. What is interesting for our present purposes is the form taken by Braverman's attack upon many of the contemporary schools within management theory, an attack which is predicated upon an analysis of advanced capitalism in terms of its basic economic structure, using conceptualisations derived from Marx's *Capital*. With the aid of detailed examples, Braverman carefully links the developments of these schools with changes in the societal means and relations of production. In essence, he portrays management theory as a superstructural manifestation of the workings of the economic base of capitalist societies. He implies that 'as a branch of management science', it 'views all things through the eyes of the bourgeoisie'. To Braverman, however, scientific management, human relations, the socio-technical approach, the quality of working life debate and so on, all *reflect*, in their own ways, the development of the labour process within monopoly capitalism. Moreover, they become an important motive force in this process in their own right.[9] Thus, not only do theories of organisation and management describe and legitimate the labour process within advanced capitalism; through their intervention, they actively and in a concrete way ensure its survival and continued good health.

This is a view with a pedigree which has been further described and elaborated by V. L. Allen in his book *Social Analysis: A Marxist Critique and Alternative* (1975). Allen begins by giving a biographical account of his own intellectual development up to the point where he could see no alternative to the complete rejection of conventional sociological theory. This rejection is seen as the only possible reaction to a sociology which assumes that social reality is basically a 'static' phenomenon characterised by consensus, a tendency to equilibrium and an organic unity. Allen argues that it is in the attempts of sociological theorists to analyse organisations that this 'static' sociology is most readily visible. His first attack is upon the 'dogma of empiricism' which characterises much of organisational analysis. The organisational empiricists are seen as being anti-theory, in that they rely almost exclusively upon a number of seemingly disparate, data-packed, problem-centred studies, which seek description rather than causal analysis. If this trend continues, Allen maintains, the studies of the empiricists will end up as wholly irrelevant exercises in mathematical methods. Allen's second target is the theoreticians who have addressed themselves to the study of organisations. His criticism here is that they employ static models which view organisations primarily as self-equilibrating mechanisms. Theories of classical management, human relations, Weber, March and Simon (1958), and Etzioni (1961), are all found wanting in this respect, though Allen recognises that some attempt has been made by the latter to modify equilibrium analysis by introducing some consideration of 'movement' and conflict.

In opposition to these views, Allen offers a 'dynamic' sociology which is directly concerned with 'movement' and underpinned by the assumptions and methodology of dialectical materialism. Such a sociology, he suggests, would concern itself with the ongoing dynamic processes which affect social situations and would employ dialectical materialism in the analysis of their causes. A sociology of movement implies that organisations are causally related to their past states as well as to the hidden and observable features of their environments, with which there is a perpetual process of interaction and absorption. In line with such a view, Allen suggests that we should be concerned with the following questions:

First, what properties do organisations have in common with their environments? Second, in what way are organisations distinguished from both their environments in general and other arrangements of social relationships in particular? Third, what is the meaning of organisational autonomy in this context? And, lastly, what is the source of movement in organisations and the mechanism through which it passes? (Allen, 1975, p. 184)

Allen suggests that the answers to these questions present a theoretical perspective and approach to the study of organisations which is both distinct from, and preferable to, that presented by more statically orientated systems analysis.

Allen maintains that his perspective does not seek to provide a middle-range theory of organisations, but rather a dynamic *general* theory capable of analysing middle-range situations. In this task he uses as a building block the concept of structure. He asserts that economic factors are the 'primary' determinants of social behaviour but non-economic factors have a degree of autonomy. After giving some consideration to recent writings on structuralism, particularly those of Piaget, Boudon and the Marxist structuralists, he concludes that 'every situation possesses a structure and superstructure', the former ultimately determining the latter in an historical context. Allen then proceeds to equate the notions of structure and superstructure with the respective notions of 'environmental variables' and organisation, in a way which is arguably the source of much confusion.[10]

In considering the components of the superstructure, Allen posits that analytically it consists of three elements: skills, power and ideology (Allen, 1975, pp. 213–47). Organisational environments are seen as consisting of these same elements, which are entangled empirically but occupy distinct 'causal positions'. He later examines trade unions as organisations in terms of their interface and interrelationships with these three elements, particularly the dominant ideology of capitalist society.

In his final chapter Allen moves towards a form of dialectical materialism, treating the concept of dialectic as representative of a 'process between variables in real social situations', in which the totality is crucial. For Allen, the totality of capitalism is shot through with contradictions, some of which are 'primary', some 'internal' and some 'secondary'. Business organisations, for example, are seen as subject to crises of overproduction, which are a superstructural manifestation of the prime contradiction within the capitalist mode of production – the fact that production capacity often exceeds the proletariat's capacity for consumption because of its condition of poverty. The effect of the surfacing of a primary contradiction within the superstructure, says Allen, is akin to that of a pebble dropped into a pond. Waves of movement spread out from the source, producing a variety of effects within the totality. For Allen, the extent of a totality can be gauged by the spread of the repercussions (Allen, 1975, pp. 268–71). It is this form of analysis which Allen views as offering the potential for his 'dynamic' approach to social analysis. It is a perspective which emphasises the importance of looking at actual empirical situations, identifying structures and superstructures, and identifying the contradictions and their repercussions. Allen sees it as an approach which throws light on the process of change, 'but without ever allowing the process to be timed, the climax to be anticipated, and its parts named' (Allen, 1975, p. 292).

In this way Allen seeks to develop the rudiments of a radical organisation theory based upon a Marxian structuralist analysis. However, much of Allen's discussion is cast in a reactive mould, and great emphasis is placed upon providing a critique of functionalist theory. In certain respects Allen can be regarded as having been trapped by this preoccupation with functionalism, to the extent that he seeks to incorporate the distinction between organisation and environment in a way which is arguably counterproductive with respect to the development of a fully developed and self-sustaining Marxist theory of organisations. Despite these limitations, however, Allen's work stands as one of the most significant and systematic attempts at the construction of a radical organisation theory.

Allen's concerns have a relatively well developed pedigree as far as the literature on industrial relations is concerned. Allen has long been an advocate of a 'radical' or Marxist view of industrial relations in opposition to the functionalist perspective which dominates this area of study. Other writers, such as Goldthorpe (1974), Hyman (1975), Hyman and Fryer (1975), Hyman and Brough (1975) and Wood (1976), have also been concerned to provide a Marxist critique of functionalist industrial relations theory, in terms which stress the importance of developing a theory of the totality of capitalism before one can begin to understand contemporary industrial relations. In varying degrees these writers address themselves to the political economy of capitalism, directing attention to inequalities inside and outside the work place, the problems of trade union organisation within such a mode of production and the possibilities for sweeping social change. As yet, however, these authors, collectively and individually, have not yet produced a well developed radical industrial relations theory which stands on its own. For the most part they have contented themselves with providing a critique of the functionalist orthodoxy and consequently have been locked into a reactive stance.

Towards the Further Development of Radical Organisation Theory

Our review of literature in the two previous sections of this chapter has suggested that it is possible at the present time to identify two relatively distinct approaches to the study of organisations from within the radical structuralist paradigm. The radical Weberian and Marxian structuralist perspectives tend to draw upon relatively distinct intellectual traditions and focus upon different areas of interest. In defining the relationship between these two approaches it is convenient to recognise at least five points of difference, as illustrated in Table 11.2. In the rest of the chapter we seek to discuss the significance of these differences, as a means of clarifying the foundations upon which further developments in radical organisation theory might be based.

Table 11.2

Some differences in emphasis between Marxian structuralist and radical Weberian approaches to radical organisation theory

The Marxian structuralist approaches to a radical organisation theory tend *to stress:*	*The radical Weberian approaches to a radical organisation theory* tend *to stress:*
1. Political economy	1. Political science
2. Economic structures	2. Political administrative structures
3. Monopoly capitalism	3. Corporatism
4. Contradiction	4. Power
5. The catastrophe analogy	5. The factional analogy

The Marxian structuralist approaches to a radical organisation theory, in looking to the work of the mature Marx as a source of inspiration, found their analytical framework upon the tenets of Marxian political economy. They focus upon the economic substructure of society as the centrepiece of analysis, particularly as it is reflected in the structure of monopoly capitalism. The notion of contradiction is emphasised as providing the principal means of explaining the process of ongoing structural change, generating periodic crises which will eventually lead to the complete transformation of the totality of capitalism. Insofar as an emphasis is placed upon crisis and social change upon a macro-scale, these theorists implicitly draw upon the catastrophe analogy as a means of modelling the socio-economic system, though the use of the factional analogy is often consistent with this point of view.

The radical Weberian approaches to a radical organisation theory, in looking to Weber as the primary source of inspiration, base their analytical framework upon conceptualisations drawn from political science. They tend to focus upon political and administrative structures rather than the economic substructures of society, and are principally concerned with 'corporatism' as opposed to monopoly capitalism. They address themselves particularly to the structure and development of the State apparatus within the power structure of society as a whole, and to the way in which the 'means of administration' come to fall under the control of fewer and fewer hands. Specific attention is devoted not so much to the *direct* analysis of contradictions as to the analysis of power relationships within the superstructure of society. Consequently, the factional as opposed to the catastrophic analogy is favoured as a basis for analysing basic social processes. Society is generally seen as dichotomised in terms of the factional interests of a relatively cohesive dominant class which controls the basic operation of society on the one hand, and the groups which tend to be subject to that control on the other; society is characterised by conflicts of interest and power struggles, which provide the motor force for major social change.

The Marxian structuralist and radical Weberian approaches to a radical organisation theory stand at the present time as relatively distinct approaches sharing a commitment to the meta-theoretical assumptions which characterise the radical structuralist paradigm. Whether they will follow separate lines of development in the future remains to be seen. They doubtless contribute their own special brand of insight to an understanding of organisations within contemporary society, though, as we argue below, it also seems that some measure of synthesis is possible. Insofar as they develop along separate lines, they may be expected to adopt the key conceptualisations and modes of analysis characteristic of the respective schools of thought from which they derive. as discussed in

Chapter 10. A great number of issues relevant to the development of Marxian structuralist and radical Weberian approaches to a radical organisation theory have already been thoroughly explored, and there is scope for adapting and welding them to a specific concern for the study of organisations.

As far as Marxian radical organisation theory is concerned, the field is wide open, since Marx himself did not specifically address the problem of organisations, and Marxist theorists up to now have largely disregarded this middle-range level of analysis.[11] Yet it would seem that a theory of organisations built around the notion of contradiction and specifically modelled upon some variation of the factional or catastrophic systems models would have a great deal to contribute to an understanding of the processes of organisational change, and to its significance within the context of the totality which characterises the contemporary social formation of advanced capitalism. Such a perspective would carry Gouldner's (1959) analysis of the notion of 'functional autonomy' to its logical conclusion, with a focus upon the contradictory relationships which exist within organisational contexts. It could also usefully draw upon work outside the Marxist tradition which has interested itself in the catastrophic or schismatic tendencies of various types of system. René Thom's recent work on catastrophe theory in the context of mathematical modelling, for example, may have much to contribute in terms of insight, if not formal technique (Thom, 1975).[12] Within the field of anthropology the outstanding work of Gregory Bateson (1973) and Marshall Sahlins (1974) constitute other sources of inspiration and analytical method. Bateson's notion of 'schismogenesis', and the analyses of both these theorists of the factional tendencies which exist within primitive societies, open the way to similar forms of analysis of the social formations within the considerably more complex structure of contemporary society.

As far as a radical Weberian organisation theory is concerned, it would seem that there is much scope for the development of models based upon the factional analogy, with a key focus upon the nature of power relationships within the structure of society as a whole. As will be evident from our discussion of the work of theorists already located in this tradition, the view of power which emerges stands in stark contrast to the unitary and pluralist perspectives characteristic of the functionalist paradigm. Indeed, the radical Weberian approach to the study of societies diverges from the unitary and pluralist views in terms of its assumptions with regard to interests, conflict and power, and the key features of this essentially 'radical' view can usefully be counterposed with those presented in Table 5.1 in the following terms:

Table 11.3

The radical Weberian view of interests, conflict and power

	The radical view:
Interests	Places emphasis upon the dichotomous nature and mutual opposition of interests in terms of broad socio-economic divisions of the 'class' type within social formations as a whole, which are also reflected in organisations in the middle range of analysis.
Conflict	Regards conflict as an ubiquitous and disruptive motor force propelling changes in society in general and organisations in particular. It is recognised that conflict may be a suppressed feature of a social system, not always evident at the level of empirical 'reality'.
Power	Regards power as an integral, unequally distributed, zero-sum phenomenon, associated with a general process of social control. Society in general and organisations in particular are seen as being under the control of ruling interest groups which exercise their power through various forms of ideological manipulation, as well as the more visible forms of authority relations.

The radical Weberian approach to a radical organisation theory thus offers a mode of analysis which, in focusing upon the totality of contemporary social formations, allows one to transcend the insights which emerge from an exclusive pre-occupation with the middle-range level of analysis characteristic of functionalist organisation theory. It is a perspective which emphasises the integral rather than the intercursive nature of power, interests and conflict within the context of society as a whole. Whether the radical Weberian view of power which, as suggested in the previous chapter, is largely confined to the superstructural aspects of capitalism, is adequate as an all-embracing perspective is open to question. It begs many questions in relation to the role and relative importance of the economic substructure and superstructure of society. It is important to emphasise the deep structural elements in the analysis of social power (what Lukes (1974) has described as the 'third dimension'), in addition to the view of power which emerges from the analysis of superstructural factors on their own account. The radical Weberian view clearly has a special contribution to make towards a radical organisation theory which attempts to locate and evaluate the significance of organisations, both public and private, within the context of the power structure of contemporary society as a whole.

The question of the relationship between substructural and superstructural factors within contemporary society conveniently leads to the issue of whether or not radical organisation theory might also develop through a further synthesis of the Marxian structuralist and radical Weberian perspectives. As we concluded in our discussion of conflict theory in Chapter 10, such a development seems quite a logical and attractive one, since the radical Weberians and Marxian structuralists tend to approach the study of social formations from different *perspectives*, which lead to the use of different analytical *constructs* with emphasis upon different *elements* of the total social formation. As we have suggested, each of these three factors can be regarded as being in a dialectical relationship both internally and in relation to one another. The respective concerns for social integration and system disintegration, power and contradiction, superstructure and substructure, presuppose an attitude to, and a definition of, the others. Radical organisation theorists might thus usefully focus upon organisations as elements within a totality which express a certain relationship between power and contradiction, and between substructural and superstructural factors, and which throw light upon the balance between social integration and system disintegration within the totality as a whole.

A systematically developed radical organisation theory characteristic of the radical structuralist paradigm, which follows any of the three lines presented above, is likely to offer many new insights with regard to our understanding of organisations in society. It is likely that it will offer new perspectives on processes of organisational control; the dynamics of organisational change; the relationship between substructural and superstructural elements of organisation; new typologies for understanding the role and significance of different organisations within the wider social formation; and other insights which emerge from the radical structuralist perspective as a whole. All three lines of development will seek to build upon the core concepts of totality, structure, contradiction, power and crisis, and will recognise that a theory of organisations consonant with radical structuralism would involve not so much the development of a radical theory of organisations as such, as a radical theory of society in which organisations are accorded a central role.

Notes and References

1. These quotes from M. Nicholaus are quoted in Horowitz (1971). They appear in a paper advocating a radical sociology but would also seem germane to a radical organisation theory.
2. For a discussion of this, see Willener (1971).
3. For a discussion of corporatism, see Pahl and Winkler (1974), Winkler (1975 and 1976).
4. The substance of Poulantzas' criticism is that (1) Miliband accepts the 'bourgeois problematic' and confronts their analysis at the level of concrete empirical reality (that is, he adopts an empiricist approach, according to Althusser's definition of that term); (2) his analysis is couched in inter-personal 'subjective' terms and not in terms of structures (that is, Miliband seeks explanation at the level of meaning as well as that of cause); (3) Miliband does not provide a political alternative; he is 'too discrete'. This form of criticism is precisely what one would expect, given the different assumptions and paradigmatic location of Althusserian sociology and conflict theory, as discussed in the previous chapter. See, however, Miliband's reply to this critique; both are reprinted in Urry and Wakeford (1973), pp. 291–314.
5. The book is published in a series of textbooks which stress exposition rather than the advocacy of a particular tradition. The radical Weberianism within the book is thus buried beneath the exposition of a variety of different perspectives. The three parts which we identify here are not specifically recognised in the text. The first part consists of pp. 1–124; the second, pp. 125–49, the third, pp. 150–204.
6. This conflation of two distinct meanings of 'organisation' follows from their definition of the term derived from Weber. They expand on this point as follows:

> We note in anticipation that the concept of organisation is certainly not a synonym for bureaucracy. Whereas we have seen that Caplow, Parsons and Etzioni define organisation as a kind of

social system and MacIver and Page as a kind of social group, for Weber it is treated as a kind of social relationship. This is the term employed to denote the existence of a probability that between two or more persons there is a meaningful course of social action. By pointing to the significance of an individual's social behaviour, Weber is wanting to avoid the reification of a collective concept like organisation, state, church and so on. (Eldridge and Crombie, 1974, p. 27)

7. Eldridge and Crombie's notion of the 'organisational phenomenon' only serves to mask two distinctive problematics. The first focuses upon organisations as middle-range, empirical facticities, which are seen as networks of social relationships forming, through their interdependencies, concrete structures. The second problematic lies not with organisations but with principles of organisation. Thus Spencer asked what rules or types of organising principle underpinned a whole range of social formations from the military to the industrial. Marx, on the other hand, was concerned to ask what forms of organising principle the proletariat should adopt in its revolutionary struggle.

Clearly, these two problematics may have in common the term 'organisation' but little else. Whilst it would be myopic to assert that these two aspects were completely independent (particularly when one looks at bureaucracy both as a mode of organisation and as a concrete structural form), they are not the same by any means. Any theoretical perspective which takes 'organisation' to mean only a principle of interrelatedness and ignores organisations in their empirical concreteness cannot claim, with any justification, to be an organisation theory true to the traditional concerns for 'real' structures which are at the core of radical structuralism. Looking further afield, John Eldridge's radical Weberianism is more evident in some of his other work. See, for example, his 'Industrial Relations and Industrial Capitalism' in Esland *et al.* (1975) pp. 306–24, 'Industrial Conflict: Some Problems of Theory and Method' in Child (1973) and 'Sociological Imagination and Industrial Life' in Warner (1973). In all of these, the last few pages are particularly important for their radical Weberian flavour.

8. Baran and Sweezy elaborate on their notion of 'scientific understanding' in the following terms:

Scientific understanding proceeds by way of constructing and analysing 'models' of the segments or aspects of reality under study. The purpose of these models is not to give a mirror image of reality, nor to include all its elements in their exact sizes and proportions, but rather to single out and make available for intensive investigation those elements which are decisive. We abstract from non-essentials, we blot out the unimportant, we magnify in order to improve the range and accuracy of our observation. A model is, and must be, unrealistic in the sense in which the word is most commonly used. Nevertheless, and in a sense paradoxically, if it is a good model it provides the key to understanding reality. (Baran and Sweezy, 1968, p. 27)

This approach has much in common with the perspective advocated by Althusser. However, their approach has been subjected to criticism. Gamble and Walton (1976), for example, have suggested that in focusing primarily upon the change in markets of monopoly capitalism, 'Baran and Sweezy focus attention on the level of appearances only', and therefore, by implication, ignore 'the real laws of motion of capitalism' rooted in production (1976, p. 108). Gamble and Walton also debate Baran and Sweezy's analysis of the rise in 'surplus' (1976, pp. 108–10). On a separate point, it is interesting to note that Baran and Sweezy spend some time discussing the role of the State, but in classic Marxist fashion they see it as but a superstructural feature of monopoly capitalism.

9. For example, it seems that, for Braverman, Taylorism represents the 'bringing to life', the concretisation of Marx's concept of abstract labour. Taylorism, in this way, becomes simultaneously an inevitable *part* of capitalism's development and a stimulus to it (Braverman, 1974, pp. 181, 315).

10. For example, it is possible to consider certain types of organisation as being located within the substructure as opposed to the superstructure of society. Allen appears to wish to retain the distinction between organisation and environment within the context of a Marxist analysis, though at the cost of a significant degree of theoretical clarity and consistency, as far as Marxist analysis is concerned.

11. Marx did not address himself to the study of organisations because, apart from the State, large-scale organisations comprised but a small element of the social formation of his day. Marxist analysts since then have expressed more interest in modes of organisation than in organisations as middle-range phenomena.

12. For a very useful and readable discussion of catastrophe theory, see Zeeman (1976).

Part III

Conclusions

12. Future Directions: Theory and Research

In the previous chapters we have sought to provide an overview of our four paradigms in relation to the literature on social theory and the study of organisations. Each of the paradigms draws upon a long, complex and conceptually rich intellectual tradition, which generates its own particular brand of insight. Each of the paradigms has been treated on its own terms. We have sought to explore from within and to draw out the full implications of each for the study of organisations. Using our analytical scheme, destructive critique would have been a simple task. By assuming a posture in a rival paradigm, it would have been possible to demolish the contribution of any individual text or theoretical perspective, by providing a comprehensive critique in terms of its underlying assumptions. Using the dimensions of our analytical scheme, we could have attacked work located iń any given paradigm from each of the three other paradigms simply by locating ourselves in turn within their respective problematics. We could then have moved inside the given paradigm and provided a critique from within, evaluating it in terms of the consistency of its assumptions from the point of view of its own problematic. Many of the critical treatises in our general area of study attempt to do precisely these things. They evaluate in detail from within, or in terms of fundamentals from a given point outside which reflects their own paradigmatic location. Whilst there may be much to recommend the all-embracing style of critique which our analytical scheme suggests, particularly where the intention is to investigate a single work in depth, or in student essay writing, seminar sessions, and academic papers, it has little to offer here. The task of academic demolition is simply all too easy. We have consciously sought to adopt a constructive stance, to build rather than to demolish. We have sought to show what each of the paradigms has to offer, given an opportunity to speak for itself.

Treatment of the paradigms in these terms emphasises both their coherence and their distinctive natures. Viewing social theory and the literature on organisational analysis from the perspective of the functionalist paradigm, one has the impression that there is a dominant orthodoxy which is surrounded by critical perspectives, each of which seeks to adopt some form of 'radical' stance. Such a view is unduly narrow; it assumes that the perspectives are satellites which take their principal point of reference from the orthodoxy itself. It assumes that their aim and function is critique and the exposure of the limitations reflected in the orthodoxy. They tend to be regarded as 'points of view', which need to be considered and, if possible, rebuffed or incorporated within the context of the dominant orthodoxy. Such a view favours fusion and incorporation as the natural line of intellectual development. We have illustrated, in relation to the historical development of the functionalist paradigm, how various elements of idealism and Marxist theory have been incorporated in this way. Whilst strengthening the functionalist perspective, the fusion has not by any means done full justice to the respective problematics from which these elements derive. Indeed, it has been at the cost of their complete emasculation and a misunderstanding of their very nature.

Stepping outside the functionalist paradigm, we have had an opportunity to become more aware of the nature of the broad intellectual traditions at work. We have seen how at the level of social theory each of the paradigms, drawing upon a separate intellectual source, is in essence distinct, internally coherent and self-sustaining. At the level of organisation studies this distinctiveness tends to be less clear-cut, partly because theorists operating here have adopted a reactive stance with regard to the functionalist orthodoxy. Whilst deriving inspiration from alternative problematics, they have often been drawn into critique on the functionalists' ground, thus giving an impression of their satellite-like status. Our analysis of these approaches to the study of organisations has indicated that, in essence, they are linked with a completely different intellectual tradition. As we have argued, they seek to move towards alternative theories of organisations. Consequently, they should be seen as embryonic rather than fully-fledged theoretical perspectives. They represent partial and sometimes confused attempts to grasp an alternative point of view. Their reactive stance has often prevented them from realising the full potential which their paradigmatic location offers.

In our analysis of these theories of organisation outside the functionalist paradigm we have consciously and systematically attempted to relate them to their wider problematic. In so doing it has been possible to anticipate certain lines of development. The paradigm in which they are located defines the nature of the issues in which they are interested and the lines of enquiry which they may fruitfully pursue. We have been able to suggest, for example, that the radical humanist paradigm offers a nascent anti-organisation theory and to sketch out the form it might be expected to take. We have shown that the radical structuralist paradigm generates at least two strains of a radical organisation theory and, again, have attempted to identify some of the key issues relevant to future developments in this area. Our analysis of the interpretive paradigm has confronted the basic ontological problems which organisations as phenomena present. We have sought to show that from certain perspectives within this paradigm organisations are not permitted an existence on their own account, and that no theory of organisations as such is possible. From another standpoint within the interpretive paradigm we have sought to show that there is room for theorising and research in relation to the *concept* of organisation and the part it plays in the accounting practices within the context of everyday life.

Looking to the future from locations outside the functionalist paradigm, therefore, at least three broad lines of development offer themselves for exploration. The radical humanist, the radical structuralist and the interpretive paradigms all offer themselves virtually as virgin territory insofar as studies of organisations are concerned. Whilst each already contains an element of creative and insightful work in this area, the work is very fragmentary and not altogether coherent. Accordingly, it does not provide the ideal starting point nor offer an altogether firm foundation for subsequent work. Theorists who wish to develop ideas in these areas cannot afford to take a short cut. There is a real need for them to ground their perspective in the philosophical traditions from which it derives; to start from first principles; to have the philosophical and sociological concerns by which the paradigm is defined at the forefront of their analysis; to develop a systematic and coherent perspective within the guidelines which each paradigm offers, rather than taking the tenets of a competing paradigm as critical points of reference. Each paradigm needs to be developed in its own terms.

In essence, what we are advocating in relation to developments within these paradigms amounts to a form of isolationism. We firmly believe that each of the paradigms can only establish itself at the level of organisational analysis if it is true to itself. Contrary to the widely held belief that synthesis and mediation between paradigms is what is required, we argue that the real need is for paradigmatic closure. In order to avoid emasculation and incorporation within the functionalist problematic, the paradigms need to provide a basis for their self-preservation by developing on their own account. Insofar as they take functionalism as their reference point, it is unlikely that they will develop far beyond their present embryonic state – they will not develop coherent alternatives to the functionalist point of view. This conclusion is firmly in line with the perspective we have adopted throughout this work in suggesting that the paradigms reflect four alternative realities. They stand as four mutually exclusive ways of seeing the world. One of the major conclusions prompted by our journey through the realms of social theory, therefore, is that organisation theorists face a wide range of choices with regard to the nature of the assumptions which underwrite their point of view. For those who wish to leave the functionalist orthodoxy behind, many avenues offer themselves for exploration.

For those who feel inclined to remain within the functionalist paradigm, our analysis raises a number of important issues. The first of these relates to the ontological status of their subject of investigation, and the second, to the nature of the models which are used as bases of analysis. These two issues derive directly from the nature of the two dimensions which we have used to define our analytical scheme.

The ontological status of organisations is a question worthy of investigation. Organisation theorists frequently treat the existence of organisations in a hard, concrete sense as taken for granted. They assume there are real phenomena which can be measured through the nomothetic methods which dominate empirical research in this area. From their point of view, our journey into phenomenology and solipsism may seem a journey into the absurd and extreme. However, having made that journey, the position adopted by highly objectivist social scientists appears equally absurd and extreme. The notion that one can measure an organisation as an empirical facticity is as extreme as the notion that organisations do not exist. It is awareness of these extremes that underwrites the importance of examining the ontological status of our subject of study. Many intermediate perspectives offer themselves for consideration. As our discussion of the action frame of reference has demonstrated, there is room for a questioning of assumptions with regard to ontology within the bounds of the functionalist paradigm.

The implications of this issue can perhaps be most forcefully expressed by suggesting that there is a need for organisation theorists to adopt *methods* of study which are true to the nature of the phenomena which they are attempting to investigate. Our review of the dominant orthodoxy within organisation theory has shown that a large proportion of empirical research is based upon highly objectivist assumptions. The tendency in much empirical research has been for methodologies to dominate other assumptions in relation to the ontological, epistemological and human nature strands of our analytical scheme. The wholesale incorporation of methods and techniques taken directly from the natural sciences needs to be severely questioned. The problem of developing *methods* appropriate to the nature of the phenomena to be studied remains one of the most pressing issues within the whole realm of social science research.

Putting aside the problems of ontology, methodology and other issues related to social science debate, what model of society should organisation theorists use to underwrite their analysis? As we have argued, this is the second crucial issue facing theorists who wish to understand the nature of the social world. In the past organisation theorists have almost automatically based their work upon analogies which treat organisations either as mechanical or as organismic systems. Since the emergence of open systems theory as the dominant framework for organisational analysis, the choice of an organismic analogy has been almost automatic. As we have sought to show, the choice of this model is often implicit rather than explicit, since organisation theorists, like many other social scientists, have mistakenly equated open systems theory with the use of the organismic analogy. Whilst the organismic analogy provides an illustration of an open system, the two are by no means synonymous. Our discussion in Chapter 4, for example, identified three other types of open systems models – the morphogenic, the factional and the catastrophic. These three models reflect quite different assumptions about the nature of the social world. The morphogenic model emphasises 'structure elaboration' as a basic feature of social process. The factional model emphasises that system parts strive for autonomy rather than functional unity, and that the system has a tendency to split up and divide. The catastrophic model emphasises the possibility of small incremental changes in system inputs, leading to dramatic changes in the state of the system as a whole. In extreme cases the change produced replaces one state of affairs with a completely new one. The choice facing the organisation theorist and other social scientists lies essentially in the question of which of these models seem to present the most 'accurate' view of the social reality which he is attempting to study. Do groups and organisations have a set of needs and a functional unity binding constituent parts together in the interests of survival, as the organismic analogy would have us believe? Do groups and organisations have an inherent tendency to split up and divide as constituent parties attempt to preserve their autonomy, as the factional analogy would have us believe? The former places emphasis upon system integration as a key group and organisational attribute. The latter places emphasis upon system division as a key characteristic; it emphasises decentralisation and dispersion as opposed to centralisation and unity. Clearly, the simple polarisation of just these two models underlies the range and importance of the choices open to the social scientist in his decision concerning the analytical tools which he is to employ in his studies. The upshot of our argument is that social scientists need to be more conscious of the problem of being 'true' — even in their own terms — to the very nature of the phenomena under investigation.

The question relating to choice of analogy brings us back to the issue of paradigms. As we have argued in earlier chapters, the factional and catastrophic models emphasise and reflect an underlying view of society characteristic of the radical structuralist as opposed to the functionalist paradigm. Whilst functionalists may be able to incorporate and use these models within the framework of their analysis, taken to their logical conclusion the two models belong to a quite different reality. They stress how social formations have inbuilt tendencies towards radical change rather than the maintenance of a regulated order. Social analyses which attempt to be true to this perspective as a guiding principle find themselves confronted by the analysis of totalities in these terms. They are thus deflected from the problematic of organisations and groups towards an understanding of the organising principles which underlie the totality within which these organisations and groups may be located. The analysis of particular elements of society, in terms of their particular factional or catastrophic tendencies, is replaced by a concern for the study of these tendencies within the whole social formation, the basic characteristics of which elements such as organisations and groups merely reflect. In the hands of the radical structuralist, the use of factional and catastrophic analogies is located within quite a different analytical enterprise.

Our attempt to explore social theory in terms of four paradigms and their constituent schools of thought raises at least one further issue of some importance which we wish to address here. This concerns the question of the level of analysis adopted for the study of organisations. For the most part this is a concern of relevance to the functionalist paradigm, where the work of psychologists, organisation theorists, sociologists and industrial relations theorists are all offered as different ways of studying the same organisational reality. The differences between their respective approaches produces an impression of a wide range and diversity of point of view. It is our contention that this diversity is more apparent than real, since the different theorists often adopt identical postures in relation to their view of the social world. Not only are they usually located within the same paradigm, but they occupy similar perspectives within it. The emphasis upon the differences between theories relating to the individual, the group, the organisation and society has tended to mask much more important points of commonality. Multi-disciplinary teams, therefore, do not always give an all-round view, as is sometimes thought. Theories which seek to incorporate different levels of analysis do not always give the all-round view which is sometimes sought. They may merely serve to strengthen and reinforce an approach which is, in essence, very narrowly founded. This is an issue which has considerable relevance for the organisation of research activities within social science as a whole. Multi-disciplinary research teams, panels of advisers, grant-awarding bodies and university departments are growing in both numbers and importance, a development which is helping to broaden what are seen as the limited perspectives which have characterised the past. The nature of our four paradigms, however, clearly illustrates that the problem of obtaining an all-round perspective is much more far-reaching than this.

The path to the future is wide open. It is clear that the choices available to organisational analysts are extremely wide. Our journey through social theory has given a glimpse of its complexity and diversity, and has revealed the relatively narrow piece of ground which organisation theorists, along with many other groups of social scientists, have thus far tilled. It has become clear that the foundations of the subject are extremely narrow, and that for the most part organisation theorists are not always entirely aware of the traditions to which they belong. The subject is frequently viewed as having a short history. This appears to be a mistaken view. The ideas which it has utilised can be traced back to the broader intellectual traditions which have underwritten social science in the widest of terms. It is time that organisation theory became fully aware of its pedigree. It is time for it to think more consciously about the social philosophy upon which it is based. In short, it is time that it became more fully aware of its relationship to the 'big issues'. Only by grounding itself firmly in a knowledge of its past and of the alternative avenues for development can it realise its full potential in the years ahead.

Bibliography

ALLEN, V.L. (1975), *Social Analysis: A Marxist Critique and Alternative*. London and New York: Longman.

ALTHUSSER, L. (1969), *For Marx*. Harmondsworth: Penguin.

ALTHUSSER, L. (1971), *Lenin and Philosophy and Other Essays*. London: New Left Books.

ALTHUSSER, L. and BALIBAR, E. (1970), *Reading Capital*. London: New Left Books.

ANDERSON, P. (1976), *Considerations on Western Marxism*. London: New Left Books.

ANGELL, J.R. (1902), *The Relations of Structural and Functional Psychology to Philosophy*. Chicago: The Decennial Publications III, University of Chicago.

ANGYAL, A. (1941), *Foundations for a Science of Personality*. Cambridge, Mass.: Harvard University Press.

ANTHONY, P.D. (1977), *The Ideology of Work*. London: Tavistock.

ARGYRIS, C. (1952), *The Impact of Budgets upon People*. New York: Controllership Foundation.

ARGYRIS, C. (1957), *Personality and Organisation*. New York: Harper and Row.

ARGYRIS, C. (1964), *Integrating the Individual and the Organisation*. New York: Wiley.

ARON, R. (1965), *Main Currents in Sociological Thought — 1*. London: Weidenfeld and Nicholson.

ARON, R. (1968), *Main Currents in Sociological Thought — 2*. London: Weidenfeld and Nicolson.

AVINERI, S. (1968), *The Social and Political Thought of Karl Marx*. London: Cambridge University Press.

AVRICH, P. (1967), *The Russian Anarchists*. Princeton, N.J.: Princeton University Press.

BARAN, P. and SWEEZY, P. (1968), *Monopoly Capital*. Harmondsworth: Penguin.

BARNARD, C. (1938), *The Functions of the Executive*. Cambridge, Mass.: Harvard University Press.

BATESON, G. (1973), *Steps To An Ecology of Mind*. St. Albans: Paladin.

BAUMAN, Z. (1977), *Towards a Critical Sociology*. London: Routledge and Kegan Paul.

BEAUVOIR, SIMONE DE, (1963), *The Prime of Life*. London: Deutsch.

BELL, D. (1962), *The End of Ideology*. New York, London: Collier MacMillan.

BELL, G.D., ed. (1967), *Organisations and Human Behaviour*. Englewood Cliffs, N.J.: Prentice-Hall.

BENNIS, W. (1966), *Changing Organisations*. New York: McGraw Hill.

BENTON, T. (1977), *Philosophical Foundations of the Three Sociologies*. London: Routledge and Kegan Paul.

BERGER, P.L., ed. (1974), *The Human Shape of Work*. London and New York: Macmillan.

BERGER, P.L., BERGER, B. and KELLNER, H. (1974), *The Homeless Mind*. Harmondsworth: Penguin.

BERGER, P.L. and LUCKMANN, T. (1966), *The Social Construction of Reality*. New York: Doubleday.

BERGER, P.L. and PULLBERG, S. (1966), 'Reification and the Sociological Critique of Consciousness', *New Left Review*, 35, pp. 56–71.

BERKELEY, G. (1962), *The Principles of Human Knowledge and Three Dialogues Between Hylas and Philonous*. London: Collins.

BEYNON, H. (1973), *Working for Ford*. Harmondsworth: Penguin/Allen Lane.

BITTNER, E. (1965), 'The Concept of Organisation', in R. Turner, *Ethnomethodology*, op. cit.

BITTNER, E. (1967), 'The Police on Skid Row – a Study of Peace Keeping', *American Sociological Review*, 32 (5), pp. 699–715.

BLACK, M., ed. (1961), *The Social Theories of Talcott Parsons*. Englewood Cliffs, N.J.: Prentice-Hall.

BLACKBURN, R., ed. (1972), *Ideology in Social Science*. London: Fontana/Collins.

BLAKE, R.R. and MOUTON, J.S. (1964), *The Managerial Grid*. Houston, Texas: Gulf Publishing Company.

BLAU, P.M. (1955), *The Dynamics of Bureaucracy*. Chicago: University of Chicago Press.

BLAU, P.M. (1964), *Exchange and Power in Social Life*. New York: John Wiley.

BLAU, P.M. (1974), *On the Nature of Organisations*. New York: John Wiley.

BLAU, P.M. and SCHOENHERR, R.A. (1971), *The Structure of Organisations*. New York: Basic Books.

BLUM, M.L. and NAYLOR, J.C. (1968), *Industrial Psychology*. New York: Harper and Row.

BLUMER, H. (1962), 'Society as Symbolic Interaction', in A. Rose, *Human Behaviour and Social Processes*, op. cit.

BLUMER, H. (1966), 'Sociological Implications of the Thought of George Herbert Mead', *American Journal of Sociology*, 71 (5), pp. 535–48.

BLUMER, H. (1969), *Symbolic Interactionism: Perspective and Method*. Englewood Cliffs, N.J.: Prentice-Hall.

BOGGS, C. (1976), *Gramsci's Marxism*. London: Pluto.

BOOKCHIN, M. (1974), 'Listen Marxist', in *Post-Scarcity Anarchism*. London: Wildwood House, pp. 171–220.

BOOKCHIN, M. (1974), *Post-Scarcity Anarchism*. London: Wildwood House.

BOSE, A. (1967), *A History of Anarchism*. Calcutta: The World Press Private.

BOSWELL, J. (1953), *Life of Johnson*. London: Oxford University Press.

BOTTOMORE, T. (1975), *Marxist Sociology*. London: Macmillan.

BOTTOMORE, T. and RUBEL, M. (1963), *Karl Marx: Selected Writings in Sociology and Social Philosophy*. Harmondsworth: Penguin.

BOWEY, A. (1976), *The Sociology of Organisations*. London: Hodder and Stoughton.

BRAMSON, L. (1961), *The Political Content of Sociology*. Princeton, N.J.: Princeton University Press.

BRAVERMAN, H. (1974), *Labor and Monopoly Capital*. New York and London: Monthly Review Press.

BROWN, B. (1973), *Marx, Freud and the Critique of Everyday Life*. New York: Monthly Review Press.

BUCKLEY, W. (1967), *Sociology and Modern Systems Theory*. Englewood Cliffs, N.J.: Prentice-Hall.

BUKHARIN, N. (1965), *Historical Materialism: A System of Sociology*. New York: Russell and Russell. (First published 1925.)

BURNS, T. and BURNS, E., eds. (1976), *The Sociology of Drama and Literature*. Harmondsworth: Penguin.

BURNS, T. and STALKER, G.M. (1961), *The Management of Innovation*. London: Tavistock Publications.

CALLINICOS, A. (1976), *Althusser's Marxism*. London: Pluto Press.

CAREY, A. (1967), 'The Hawthorne Studies: A Radical Criticism', *American Sociological Review*, 32 (3), pp. 403–16.

CARTWRIGHT, D. and ZANDER, A. (1968), *Group Dynamics: Research and Theory* (3rd edn). New York: Harper and Row.

CASTANEDA, C. (1970), *The Teachings of Don Juan: A Yacqui Way of Knowledge*. Harmondsworth: Penguin.
CHADWICK-JONES, J.K. (1976), *Social Exchange Theory*. London: Academic Press.
CHILD, J. (1972), 'Organisational Structure, Environment and Performance: The Role of Strategic Choice', *Sociology*, 6 (1), pp. 1–22.
CHILD, J., ed. (1973), *Man and Organisation*. London: George Allen and Unwin.
CHOMSKY, N. (1959), 'Review of Skinner's "Verbal Behaviour"', *Language*, 35, (1), pp. 26–58.
CICOUREL, A.V. (1964), *Method and Measurement in Sociology*. Glencoe, Ill.: Free Press.
CICOUREL, A.V. (1972), *Cognitive Sociology: Language and Meaning in Social Interaction*. Harmondsworth: Penguin.
CLEGG, S. (1975), *Power, Rule and Domination*. London: Routledge and Kegan Paul.
CLEGG, S. and DUNKERLEY, D. (1977), *Critical Issues in Organisations*. London: Routledge and Kegan Paul.
CLINARD, M.B. (1964), *Anomie and Deviant Behaviour*. Glencoe, Ill.: Free Press.
COHEN, P.S. (1968), *Modern Social Theory*. London: Heinemann.
COHEN, S.F. (1974), *Bukharin and the Bolshevik Revolution*. London: Wildwood House.
COLFAX, J.D. and ROACH, J.L., eds. (1971), *Radical Sociology*. New York: Basic Books.
COLLETTI, L. (1972), *From Rousseau to Lenin*. London: New Left Books.
COLLETTI, L. (1974), 'A Political and Philosophical Interview', *New Left Review*, 86, pp. 3–28.
COLLETTI, L. (1975), 'Marxism and the Dialectic', *New Left Review*, 93, pp. 3–29.
COMTE, AUGUSTE (1853), *The Positivist Philosophy*, Vol. I (freely trans. by H. Martineau). London: Chapman.
CONNERTON, P., ed. (1976), *Critical Sociology*. Harmondsworth: Penguin.
CONQUEST, R. (1972), *Lenin*. London: Fontana/Collins.
COOPER, R. (1976), 'The Open Field', *Human Relations*, 29 (11), pp. 999–1017.
COOPER, W.W., LEAVITT, H.J. and SHELLEY, M.W., eds. (1964), *New Perspectives in Organisation Research*. New York: John Wiley.

COOPER, W.W., LEAVITT, H.J. and SHELLEY, M.W. (1964), 'Administrative Rationality, Social Setting, and Organisational Development', in Cooper et al, *New Perspectives in Organisation Research*, op. cit.

CORNFORTH, M. (1955), *Science Versus Idealism*. London: Lawrence and Wishart.

COSER, L.A. (1956), *The Functions of Social Conflict*. London: Routledge and Kegan Paul.

COSER, L.A. (1965), *Georg Simmel*. Englewood Cliffs, N.J.: Prentice-Hall.

COSER, L.A. (1967), *Continuities in the Study of Social Conflict*. Glencoe, Ill.: Free Press.

COSER, L.A. and ROSENBERG, B., eds (1969), *Sociological Theory* (3rd edn). New York and London: Macmillan.

CROZIER, M. (1964), *The Bureaucratic Phenomenon*. London: Tavistock Publications.

CUTLER, J., HINDESS, B., HIRST, P. and HUSSAIN, A. (1977), *Marx's Capital and Capitalism Today*, Vol. I. London: Routledge and Kegan Paul.

CYERT, R.M. and MARCH, J.G. (1963), *A Behavioural Theory of the Firm*. Englewood Cliffs, N.J.: Prentice-Hall.

DAHL, R. (1957), 'The Concept of Power', *Behavioural Science*, 2, pp. 201–15.

DAHRENDORF, R. (1959), *Class and Class Conflict in Industrial Society*. London: Routledge and Kegan Paul.

DALTON, M. (1959), *Men Who Manage*. New York: John Wiley.

DAVIS, F. (1967), 'The Cab-Driver and His Fare: Relationship', in G.D. Bell, *Organisations and Human Behaviour*, op. cit.

DAVIS, K. (1959), 'The Myth of Functional Analysis as a Special Method in Sociology and Anthropology', *American Sociological Review*, 24 (6), pp. 757–73.

DAVIS, L.E. and CHERNS, A.B., eds. (1975), *The Quality of Working Life*, Vols I and II. New York: Free Press.

DAVIS, L.E. and Taylor, J.C., eds (1972), *Design of Jobs*. Harmondsworth: Penguin.

DAWE, A. (1970), 'The Two Sociologies', *British Journal of Sociology*, 21, pp. 207–18.

DECHERT, C.R. (1965), 'The Development of Cybernetics', *The American Behavioural Scientist*, 8, pp. 15–20.

DEMERATH, N.J. (1966), 'Synecdoche and Structural Functionalism', *Social Forces*, 44 (3), pp. 390–401.

DENZIN, N.K. (1970), 'Symbolic Interactionism and Ethnomethodology', in J.D. Douglas, *Understanding Everyday Life*, op. cit.

DICKSON, D. (1974), *Alternative Technology and the Politics of Technical Change*. London: Fontana.

DILL, W.R. (1958), 'Environment as an Influence on Managerial Autonomy', in *Administrative Science Quarterly*, 2, pp. 409–43.

DILTHEY, W. (1976), *Selected Writings* (ed. H.P. Rickman). London: Cambridge University Press.

DOUGLAS, J.D. (1967), *The Social Meanings of Suicide*. Princeton, N.J.: Princeton University Press.

DOUGLAS, J.D., ed. (1970a), *Freedom and Tyranny in a Technological Society*. New York: Alfred Knopf.

DOUGLAS, J.D., ed. (1970b), *Understanding Everyday Life*. Chicago: Aldine Publishing; London: Routledge and Kegan Paul.

DREITZEL, H.P., ed. (1970), *Recent Sociology, No. 2*. New York: Macmillan.

DUBIN, R. (1956), 'Industrial Workers' Worlds: A Study of Central Life Interests of Industrial Workers', *Social Problems*, 3, pp. 131–42.

DUNLOP, J.T. (1958), *Industrial Relations Systems*. New York: Holt, Rinehart and Winston.

DUNNETTE, M.D. (1976), *Handbook of Industrial and Organizational Psychology*. Chicago: Rand McNally.

DURKHEIM, E. (1938), *The Rules of Sociological Method*. Glencoe, Ill.: Free Press.

DURKHEIM, E. (1947), *The Division of Labour in Society* (trans. G. Simpson). Glencoe, Ill.: Free Press.

DURKHEIM, E. (1951), *Suicide* (trans. J.A. Spalding and G. Simpson). Glencoe, Ill.: Free Press.

EASTON, D. (1953), *The Political System*. New York: Alfred Knopf.

ELDRIDGE, J.E.T. (1971), *Sociology and Industrial Life*. London: Nelson.

ELDRIDGE, J.E.T. and CROMBIE, A.D. (1974), *A Sociology of Organisations*. London: George Allen and Unwin.

ELLUL, J. (1964), *The Technological Society*. New York: Vintage Books.

EMERSON, J. (1970), 'Behaviour in Private Places', in H.P. Dreitzel, *Recent Sociology, No. 2*, op. cit.

EMERSON, R.M. (1962), 'Power-Dependence Relations', *American Sociological Review*, 27 (1), pp. 31–40.

EMERY, F.E. and TRIST, E.L. (1965), 'The Causal Texture of Organisational Environments', *Human Relations*, 18 (1), pp. 21–32.

EMERY, F.E. and TRIST, E.L. (1972), *Towards a Social Ecology*, Harmondsworth: Penguin.

ESLAND, G., SALAMAN, G. and SPEAKMAN, M.A., eds. (1975), *People and Work*. Edinburgh: Holmes McDougall (in association with the Open University Press).

ETZIONI, A. (1961), *A Comparative Analysis of Complex Organisations*. Glencoe, Ill.: Free Press.

EVANS-PITCHARD, E.E. (1954), *Social Anthropology*. London: Oxford University Press.

FARIS, R.E.L., ed. (1964), *Handbook of Modern Sociology*. Chicago: Rand McNally.

FARIS, R.E.L. (1967), *Chicago Sociology*. Chicago: University of Chicago Press.

FAYOL, H. (1949), *General and Industrial Management* (trans. C. Storr). London: Pitman.

FEYERABEND, P. (1972), *Against Method*. London: New Left Books.

FICHTE, J.F. (1970), *Science of Knowledge* (with first and second introductions; eds. P. Heath and J. Lachs). New York: Century Philosophy Sourcebooks.

FIEDLER, F.E. (1967), *A Theory of Leadership Effectiveness*. London and New York: McGraw Hill.

FILMER, P., PHILLIPSON, M., SILVERMAN, D. and WALSH, D. (1972), *New Directions in Sociological Theory*. London and New York: Collier Macmillan.

FINCH, H.A. (1949), *Max Weber on the Methodology of Social Sciences*. Glencoe, Ill.: Free Press.

FOX, A. (1966), 'Industrial Sociology and Industrial Relations', *Research Paper 3, Royal Commission on Trade Unions and Employers' Associations*, London: HMSO.

FOX, A. (1973), 'Industrial Relations: A Social Critique of Pluralist Ideology', in J. Child, *Man and Organisation*, op. cit.

FOX, A. (1974a), *Beyond Contract: Work, Power and Trust Relations*. London: Faber and Faber.

FOX, A. (1974b), *Man Mismanagement*. London: Hutchinson.

FRASER, R., ed. (1968), *Work*, Vols I and II. Harmondsworth: Penguin.

FRENCH, J.R.P. and RAVEN, B. (1968), 'The Bases of Social Power', in D. Cartwright and A. Zander, *Group Dynamics*, op. cit.

FRIEDRICHS, R.W. (1970), *A Sociology of Sociology*. New York: Free Press.

FRISBY, D. (1972), 'The Popper-Adorno Controversy: The Methodological Dispute in German Sociology', *Philosophy of The Social Sciences*, 2, pp. 105–19.

FRISBY, D. (1974), 'The Frankfurt School: Critical Theory and Positivism', in J. Rex, ed., *Approaches to Sociology*, op. cit.

GADAMER, H.G. (1965), *Wahrheit und Method*, Tubingen: J.C.B. Mohr, (English copyright: Sheed and Ward, London, 1975).

GAMBLE, A. and WALTON, P. (1976), *Capitalism in Crisis*. London: Macmillan.

GARFINKEL, H. (1967), *Studies in Ethnomethodology*. Englewood Cliffs, N.J.: Prentice-Hall.

GARFINKEL, H. (1968), 'The Origins of the Term Ethnomethodology', *Proceedings of the Purdue Symposium on Ethnomethodology*, Institute monograph No. 1, Institute for the Study of Social Change, Purdue University; reproduced in R. Turner, ed., *Ethnomethodology*, op. cit.

GAUS, J.M. (1936), *The Frontiers of Public Administration*. Chicago: University of Chicago Press.

GAUS, J.M. (1936), 'A Theory of Organisation in Public Administration', *The Frontiers of Public Administration*, op. cit.

GERTH, H.H. and MILLS, C. WRIGHT, eds. (1948), *From Max Weber*. London: Routledge and Kegan Paul.

GIDDENS, A. (1971), *Capitalism and Modern Social Theory*. London: Cambridge University Press.

GIDDENS, A. (1972a), 'Elites in The British Class Structure', *Sociological Review*, 20 (3), pp. 345–72.

GIDDENS, A. (1972b), *Politics and Sociology in the Thought of Max Weber*. London: Macmillan.

GIDDENS, A. (1974), *Positivism and Sociology*. London: Heinemann.

GIDDENS, A. (1976), *New Rules of Sociological Method*. London: Hutchinson.

GLUCKSMANN, M. (1974), *Structuralist Analysis in Contemporary Social Thought*. London: Routledge and Kegan Paul.

GODELIER, M. (1972), 'Structure and Contradiction in *Capital*,' in R. Blackburn, ed., *Ideology in Social Science*, op. cit.

GOFFMAN, E. (1959), *The Presentation of Self in Everyday Life*. New York: Doubleday.

GOFFMAN, E. (1961), *Asylums*. New York; Doubleday.

GOFFMAN, E. (1963), *Behaviour in Public Places*. Glencoe, Ill.: Free Press.

GOFFMAN, E. (1967), *Interaction Ritual*. New York: Doubleday.

GOLD, R.L. (1964), 'In the Basement – The Apartment Building Janitor', in P.L. Berger, ed., *The Human Shape of Work*, op. cit.

GOLDMANN, L. (1969), *The Human Sciences and Philosophy*. London: Cape.

GOLDTHORPE, J.H., LOCKWOOD, D., BECHHOFER, F. and PLATT, J. (1968), *The Affluent Worker: Industrial Attitudes and Behaviour*. London: Cambridge University Press.

GOLDTHORPE, J.H. (1974), 'Industrial Relations in Great Britain: A Critique of Reformism', *Politics and Society*, 4 (3), pp. 419–52.

GOLDTHORPE, J.H. (1974), 'Social Inequality and Social Integration in Modern Britain', in D. Wedderburn, ed., *Poverty, Inequality and Class Structure*, op. cit.

GOULDNER, A.W. (1954a), *Patterns of Industrial Bureaucracy*. Glencoe, Ill.: Free Press.

GOULDNER, A.W. (1954b), *Wildcat Strike*. New York: Antioch Press.

GOULDNER, A.W. (1959), 'Reciprocity and Autonomy in Functional Theory', in A.W. Gouldner, *For Sociology*, op. cit.

GOULDNER, A.W. (1969), 'The Unemployed Self', in R. Fraser, ed., *Work*, op. cit.

GOULDNER, A.W. (1970), *The Coming Crisis of Western Sociology*. London: Heinemann.

GOULDNER, A.W. (1973), *For Sociology*. Harmondsworth: Allen Lane.

GOULDNER, A.W. (1973), 'Anti-Minotaur: The Myth of a Value Free Sociology', in A.W. Gouldner, *For Sociology*, op. cit.

GOULDNER, A.W. (1976), *The Dialectic of Ideology and Technology*. London and New York: Macmillan.

GRAMSCI, A. (1971), *Selections From the Prison Notebooks of Antonio Gramsci* (eds. Quinton Hoare and Geoffrey Nowell-Smith). London: Lawrence and Wishart.

GROSS, N.M., WARD, S. and McEACHERN, W.A. (1958), *Explorations in Role Analysis: Studies of the School Superintendent Role*. New York: John Wiley.

HABERMAS, J. (1970a), 'On Systematically Distorted Communications', *Inquiry*, 13, pp. 205–18.

HABERMAS, J. (1970b), 'Towards a Theory of Communicative Competence', *Inquiry*, 13, pp. 360–75.

HABERMAS, J. (1971a), *Towards a Rational Society*. London: Heinemann.

HABERMAS, J. (1971b), 'Technology and Science as Ideology', in J. Habermas, *Towards a Rational Society*, op. cit.

HABERMAS, J. (1972), *Knowledge and Human Interests*. London: Heinemann.

HABERMAS, J. (1974), *Theory and Practice*. London: Heinemann.

HABERMAS, J. (1976), *Legitimation Crisis*. London: Heinemann.

HAGE, J. and AIKEN, M. (1967), 'Relationship of Centralisation to Other Structural Properties', *Administrative Science Quarterly*, 12, pp. 72–92.

HALL, R.H., (1972), *Organisations: Structure and Process*. Englewood Cliffs, N.J.: Prentice-Hall.

HARVEY, D. (1973), *Social Justice and the City*. London: Edward Arnold.

HEGEL, G. (1931), *The Phenomenology of Mind*. London: George Allen and Unwin.

HERZBERG, F., MAUSNER, B. and SNYDERMAN, B. (1959), *The Motivation to Work*. New York: John Wiley.

HICKSON, D.J., PUGH, D.S. and PHEYSEY, D.C. (1969), 'Operations Technology and Organisation Structure: An Empirical Reappraisal', *Administrative Science Quarterly*, 14, pp. 378–97.

HICKSON, D.J., HININGS, C.R., LEE, C.A., SCHNECK, R.E. and PENNINGS, J.M. (1971). 'A Strategic Contingencies Theory of Intra-Organisational Power', *Administrative Science Quarterly*, 16, pp. 216–29.

HINDESS, B. (1975), *The Use of Official Statistics in Sociology: A Critique of Positivism and Ethnomethodology*. London: Macmillan.

HODGES, H.A. (1952), *The Philosophy of Wilhelm Dilthey*. London: Routledge and Kegan Paul.

HOMANS, G.C. (1950), *The Human Group*. New York: Harcourt, Brace and World.

HOMANS, G.C. (1958), 'Human Behaviour as Exchange', *American Journal of Sociology*, 63 (6), pp. 597–606.

HOMANS, G.C. (1961), *Social Behaviour: Its Elementary Forms*. New York: Harcourt Brace and World.

HOMANS, G.C. (1964a), 'Contemporary Theory in Sociology', in R.E.L. Faris, ed., *Handbook of Modern Sociology*, op. cit.

HOMANS, G.C. (1964b), 'Bringing Men Back In', *American Sociological Review*, 29 (5), pp. 309–18.

HOMANS, G.C. and CURTIS, C.P. (1934), *An Introduction to Pareto, His Sociology*. New York: Alfred Knopf.

HOPPOCK, R. (1935), *Job Satisfaction*. New York: Harper.

HORKHEIMER, M. (1972), *Critical Theory: Selected Essays*. New York: Herder.

HOROWITZ, D., ed. (1971), *Radical Sociology: An Introduction*. New York: Harper and Row.

HORTON, J. (1964), 'The Dehumanisation of Anomie and Alienation', *British Journal of Sociology*, 15 (4), pp. 283–300.

HUGHES, E. (1958), *Men and Their Work*. Glencoe, Ill.: Free Press.

HUGHES, H. STUART (1958), *Consciousness and Society*. New York: Alfred Knopf.

HUSSERL, E. (1929), Entry on 'Phenomenology', in *Encyclopædia Brittannica*, 14th edn.

HYMAN, H.H. and SINGER, E. (1968), *Readings in Reference Group Theory and Research*. New York: Free Press.

HYMAN, R. (1975), *Industrial Relations: A Marxist Introduction*. London: Macmillan.

HYMAN, R. and BROUGH, I. (1975), *Social Values and Industrial Relations*. Oxford: Blackwell.

HYMAN, R. and FRYER, R. (1975), 'Trade Unions: Sociology and Political Economy', in J. McKinlay, ed., *Processing People: Cases in Organisational Behaviour*, op. cit.

ILLICH, I. (1973), *Tools for Conviviality*. London: Fontana/Collins.

JAQUES, E. (1951), *The Changing Culture of a Factory*. London: Tavistock.

JAQUES, E. (1962), *Measurement of Responsibility*. London: Tavistock Publications.

JAMES, W. (1890), *Principles of Psychology*, London: Macmillan.

JARVIE, I.E. (1964), *The Revolution in Anthropology*. London: Routledge and Kegan Paul.

JAY, M. (1973), *The Dialectical Imagination*. London: Heinemann.

KAHN, R.L. and BOULDING, E., eds. (1964), *Power and Conflict in Organisations*. London: Tavistock Publications.

KAST, F.E. and ROSENWEIG, J.E. (1973), *Contingency Views of Organisation and Management*. Chicago: Science Research Associates.

KATZ, D. and KAHN, R.L. (1966), *The Social Psychology of Organisations*. New York: John Wiley.

KAUFMANN, W. (1966), *Hegel*. London: Weidenfeld and Nicolson.

KEAT, R. and URRY, J. (1975), *Social Theory as Science*. London: Routledge and Kegan Paul.

KELLEY, H.H. (1968), 'Two Functions of Reference Groups', in H.H. Hyman and E. Singer, *Readings in Reference Group Theory*, op. cit.

KERR, C., DUNLOP, J.T., HARBISON, F.H. and MYERS, C.A. (1964), *Industrialism and Industrial Man* (2nd edn). London: Oxford University Press.

KOLAKOWSKI, L. (1972), *Positivist Philosophy*. Harmondsworth: Penguin.

KUHN, T.S. (1970), *The Structure of Scientific Revolution* (2nd edn). Chicago: University of Chicago Press.

LAING, R.D. (1967), *The Politics of Experience*. New York: Ballantine.

LANDSBERGER, H.A. (1958), *Hawthorne Revisited*. Ithaca, N.Y.: Cornell University Press.

LANDY, F.J. and TRUMBO, D.A. (1976), *Pyschology of Work Behaviour*. New York: Dorsey Press.

LAWRENCE, P.R. and LORSCH, J.W. (1967), *Organization and Environment*. Cambridge, Mass.: Harvard Graduate School of Business Administration.

LEE, E. and MANDELBAUM, M., eds. (1971), *Phenomenology and Existentialism*. New York: John Hopkins.

LEVI, A.W. (1967), 'Existentialism and the Alienation of Man', in E. Lee and M. Mandelbaum, eds., *Phenomenology and Existentialism*, op. cit.

LEWIN, K., LIPPITT, R. and WHITE, R.K. (1939), 'Patterns of Aggressive Behaviour in Experimentally Created Social Climates', *Journal of Social Psychology*, 10, pp. 271–99.

LICHTHEIM, G. (1967), *Marxism: An Historical and Critical Study*. London: Routledge and Kegan Paul.

LICHTHEIM, G. (1970), *Lukács*. London: Fontana/Collins.

LIKERT, R. (1961), *New Patterns of Management*. New York: McGraw Hill.

LIKERT, R. (1967), *The Human Organisation*. New York: McGraw Hill.

LOCKE, E.A. (1975), 'Personnel Attitudes and Motivation', *Annual Review of Psychology*, pp. 457–79.

LOCKWOOD, D. (1956), 'Some Remarks on "The Social System"', *British Journal of Sociology*, 7, pp. 134–43.

LOCKWOOD, D. (1964), 'Social Integration and System Integration', in G.K. Zollschan and W. Hirsch, eds., *Explorations in Social Change*, op cit.

LORSCH, J.W. and LAWRENCE, P.R. (1970), *Studies in Organisation Design*. Homewood, Ill.: Irwin.

LORSCH, J.W. and MORSE, J.J. (1974), *Organisations and Their Members: A Contingency Approach*. New York: Harper and Row.

LUKÁCS, G. (1971), *History and Class Consciousness*. London: Merlin. (First published 1923).

LUKES, S. (1973), *Emile Durkheim: His Life and Work*. Harmondsworth: Allen Lane.

LUKES, S. (1974), *Power: A Radical View*. London: Macmillan.

LUPTON, T. (1963), *On the Shop Floor*. Oxford: Pergamon Press.

LUPTON, T. (1971), *Management and the Social Sciences* (2nd edn). Harmondsworth: Penguin.

McCULLOUGH, A. and SHANNON, M. (1977), 'Organisation and Protection', in S. Clegg and D. Dunkerley, eds., *Critical Issues in Organisations*, op. cit.

McGREGOR, D. (1960), *The Human Side of Enterprise*. New York: McGraw Hill.

McHUGH, P. (1968), *Defining the Situation*. Indianapolis: Bobbs-Merrill.

MacINTYRE, A. (1970), *Marcuse*. London: Fontana/Collins.

McKINLAY, J.B., ed., (1975), *Processing People: Cases in Organisational Behaviour*. London and New York: Holt, Rinehart and Winston.

McLELLAN, D., ed. (1973), *Marx's Grundrisse*. St. Albans: Paladin.

McLELLAN, D. (1975), *Marx*. London: Fontana/Collins.

McLELLAN, D. (1976), *Karl Marx: His Life and Thought*. St. Albans: Paladin.

McNALL, S.G. and JOHNSON, J.C.M. (1975), 'The New Conservatives: Ethnomethodologists, Phenomenologists, and Symbolic Interactionists', *The Insurgent Sociologist*, 5 (4), pp. 49–65.

MAKKREEL, R.A. (1975), *Dilthey – Philosopher of the Human Studies*. Princeton, N.J.: Princeton University Press.

MANN, M. (1971), *Class Consciousness and Action Among the Western Working Class*. London: Macmillan.

MANIS, J.G. and MELTZER, B.N. (1967), *Symbolic Interaction*. Boston: Allyn and Bacon.

MARCH, J.G. (1965), *Handbook of Organizations*. Chicago: Rand McNally.

MARCH, J.G. and SIMON, H.A. (1958), *Organisations*. New York: John Wiley.

MARCUSE, H. (1954), *Reason and Revolution* (rev. edn 1964). New York: Humanities Press.

MARCUSE, H. (1964), *One-Dimensional Man*. London: Routledge and Kegan Paul.

MARCUSE, H. (1966), *Eros and Civilisation*. Boston: Beacon.

MARCUSE, H. (1968), *Negations: Essays in Critical Theory*. London: Heinemann.

MARCUSE, H. (1968), 'Industrialisation and Capitalism in the Work of Max Weber', *Negations: Essays in Critical Theory*, op. cit.

MARX, K. and ENGELS, F. (1968), *Selected Works*, London: Lawrence and Wishart Ltd.

MARX, K. and ENGELS, F. (1965), *The German Ideology*. London: Lawrence and Wishart. (First published 1846.)

MARX, K. (1973), *Grundrisse: Foundations of the Critique of Political Economy* (trans. M. Nicolaus). Harmondsworth: Penguin. (First published Moscow, 1939–41.)

MARX, K. (1975), *Early Writings* (trans. R. Livingstone and G. Benton). Harmondsworth: Penguin. (This contains *Economic and Philosophical Manuscripts*, 1844.)

MARX, K. (1976), *Capital: A Critique of Political Economy*, Vols 1–III, (trans. B. Fowkes). Harmondsworth: Penguin. (Vol. I first published 1867, Vol. II, 1885, Vol. III, 1894.)

MARTINS, H. (1974), 'Time and Theory in Sociology', in J. Rex, ed., *Approaches to Sociology*, op. cit.

MASLOW, A. (1943), 'A Theory of Human Motivation', *Psychological Reivew*, 50, pp. 370–96.

MASSIE, J.L. (1965), 'Management Theory', in J.G. March, ed., *Handbook of Organizations*, op. cit.

MAUSS, M. (1954), *The Gift*. Glencoe, Ill.: Free Press.

MAYO, E. (1933), *The Human Problems of an Industrial Civilisation*. New York: Macmillan.

MAYO, E. (1949), *The Social Problems of an Industrial Civilisation*. London: Routledge and Kegan Paul.

MAYS, W. (1975), 'Phenomenology and Marxism', in E. Pivčecić, ed., *Phenomenological and Philosophical Understanding*, op. cit.

MEAD, G.H. (1932a), *Movements of Thought in the Nineteenth Century* (ed. M.N. Moore). Chicago: University of Chicago Press.

MEAD, G.H. (1932b), *The Philosophy of the Present* (ed. A.E. Murphy). Chicago: Open Court Publishing.

MEAD, G.H. (1934), *Mind, Self and Society* (ed. Charles Morris). Chicago: University of Chicago Press.

MEAD, G.H. (1938), *The Philosophy of the Act* (ed. Charles Morris). Chicago: University of Chicago Press.

MEAD, G.H. (1956), *The Social Psychology of George Herbert Mead* (ed. Anselm M. Strauss). Chicago: University of Chicago Press (Phoenix Books).

MEAKIN, D. (1976), *Man and Work: Literature and Culture in Industrial Society*. London: Methuen.

MELTZER, B. and PETRAS, J. (1973), 'Theoretical and Ideological Variations in Contemporary Interactionism', *Catalyst*. 7, pp. 1–8.

MELTZER, B.M., PETRAS, J. and REYNOLDS, L. (1975), *Symbolic Interactionism: Genesis, Varieties and Criticism*. London: Routledge and Kegan Paul.

MENNELL, S. (1974), *Sociological Theory: Uses and Unities*. London: Nelson.

MERTON, R.K. (1948), 'Manifest and Latent Functions', in R.K. Merton, *Social Theory and Social Structure*, op. cit.

MERTON, R.K. (1968), *Social Theory and Social Structure*. New York: Free Press (enlarged edn).

MESZÁROS, I. (1970a), 'Lukács' Concept of Dialectic', in G.H.R. Parkinson, ed., *George Lukács: The Man, His Work and His Ideas*, op. cit.

MESZÁROS, I. (1970b), *Marx's Theory of Alienation*, London: Merlin.

MESZÁROS, I. (1971), *Aspects of History and Class Consciousness*. London: Routledge and Kegan Paul.

MICHELS, R. (1949), *Political Parties*. Glencoe, Ill.: Free Press.

MILIBAND, R. (1973), *The State in Capitalist Society*. London: Quartet.

MILLER, D.L. (1973), *George Herbert Mead: Self, Language and the World*. Houston, Texas: University of Texas Press.

MILLER, E.J. and RICE, A.K. (1967), *Systems of Organisation*. London: Tavistock Publications.

MILLS, C. WRIGHT (1959), *The Sociological Imagination*. London: Oxford University Press.

MINER, J.B. and DACHLER, H.P. (1973), 'Personnel Attitudes and Motivation', *Annual Review of Psychology*, 24, pp. 379–402.

MOUZELIS, N. (1975), *Organisation and Bureaucracy* (2nd edn). London: Routledge and Kegan Paul.

MURDOCH, I. (1967), *Sartre*. London: Fontana.

MYERS, C.S. (1924), *Industrial Psychology in Great Britain*. London: Cape.

NATANSON, M. (1966), *Essays in Phenomenology*. The Hague: Martinus Nijhoff.

NATANSON, M. (1973a), *A Critique of Jean-Paul Sartre's Ontology*. The Hague: Martinus Nijhoff. (First published 1951.)

NATANSON, M. (1973b), *Edmund Husserl: Philosopher of Infinite Tasks*. Evanston: Northwestern University Press.

NATANSON, M. (1973c), *The Social Dynamics of George H. Mead*. The Hague: Martinus Nijhoff. (First published 1956.)

NELL, E. (1972), 'Economics: The Revival of Political Economy', in R. Blackburn, ed., *Ideology in Social Science*, op. cit.

NEWCOMB, T.M. (1950), *Social Psychology*. New York: Dryden Press.

NEWCOMB, T.M. (1953), 'An Approach to the Study of Communicative Acts', *Psychological Review*, 60, pp. 393–404.

NISBET, R.A. (1967), *The Sociological Tradition*. London: Heinemann.

NISBET, R.A. (1969), *Social Change and History*. London: Oxford University Press.

NISBET, R. (1976), *The Social Philosophers*, St. Albans: Paladin.

OLLMAN, B. (1971), *Alienation: Marx's Critique of Man in Capitalist Society*. London: Cambridge University Press.

OLSEN, M., ed. (1970), *Power in Society*. London: Macmillan.

O'NEILL, J., ed. (1977), *On Critical Theory*. London: Heinemann.

OSBORN, R.N. (1974), 'Environment and Organisational Effectiveness', *Administrative Science Quarterly*, 19, pp. 231–46.

PAHL, R.E. and WINKLER, J. (1974), 'The Coming Corporatism', *New Society*, 30 (627), pp. 72–6.

PALMER, R.E. (1969), *Hermeneutics*. Evanston: Northwestern University Press.

PARETO, V. (1934), *An Introduction to Pareto, His Sociology* (eds. G.C. Homans and C.P. Curtis). New York: Alfred Knopf.

PARETO, V. (1935), *The Mind and Society*, (trans. Andrew Bongiorno and Arthur Livingstone), 4 vols. New York: Harcourt, Brace, Jovanovich.

PARK, R.E., and BURGESS, E.W. (1921), *Introduction to the Science of Sociology*. Chicago: University of Chicago Press.

PARKIN, F. (1973), *Class, Inequality and Political Order*. St. Albans: Paladin.

PARKINSON, G.H.R., ed. (1970), *Georg Lukács: The Man, His Work, His Ideas*. London: Weidenfeld and Nicolson.

PARSONS, T. (1949), *The Structure of Social Action*. Glencoe, Ill.: Free Press.

PARSONS, T. and SHILS, E.A., eds. (1951), *Towards a General Theory of Action*. Cambridge, Mass.: Harvard University Press.

PARSONS, T. (1951), *The Social System*. London: Tavistock; Glencoe, Ill.: Free Press.

PARSONS, T. (1959), *Economy and Society*. London: Routledge and Kegan Paul.

PARSONS, T. (1963), 'On the Concept of Political Power', *Proceedings of the American Philosophical Society*, 107, pp. 232–62.

PASSMORE, J.A. (1966), *A Hundred Years of Philosophy* (2nd edn). London: Duckworth.

PERROW, C. (1967), 'A Framework for the Comparative Analysis of Organisations', *American Sociological Review*, 32 (2), pp. 194–208.

PERROW, C. (1972), *Complex Organisations: A Critical Essay*. New York: Scott, Foresman and Co.

PETTIGREW, A.M. (1973), *The Politics of Organisational Decision Making*. London: Tavistock Publications.

PIRSIG, R.M. (1976), *Zen and the Art of Motorcycle Maintenance*. London: Corgi.

PIVČECIĆ, E., ed. (1975), *Phenomenological and Philosophical Understanding*. London: Routledge and Kegan Paul.

PIZZORNO, A., ed. (1971), *Political Sociology*. Harmondsworth: Penguin.

PLEKHANOV, G. (1974), *Selected Philosophical Works: Vol. I*. Moscow: Progress.

POPPER, K. (1963), *Conjectures and Refutations: The Growth of Scientific Knowledge*. London: Routledge and Kegan Paul.

POULANTZAS, N. (1969), 'The Problem of the Capitalist State', *New Left Review*, 58, pp. 67–78.

PUGH, D.S. (1966), 'Modern Organisation Theory: A Psychological and Sociological Study', *Psychological Bulletin*, 66 (21), pp. 235–51.

PUGH, D.S. and HICKSON, D.J. (1976), *Organisational Structure in Its Context*. Farnborough: Saxon House and Lexington Books.

PUGH, D.S. and HININGS, C.R., eds. (1976), *Organisational Structure, Extensions and Replications: The Aston Programme II*. Farnborough: Saxon House.

QUINN, R.E. (1977), 'Coping with Cupid: The Formation, Impact and Management of Romantic Relationship in Organisations', *Administrative Science Quarterly*, 22, pp. 30–45.

RADCLIFFE-BROWN, A. (1952), *Structure and Function in Primitive Society*. London: Cohen and West.

RAVETZ, J.R. (1972), *Scientific Knowledge and Its Social Problems*. Harmondsworth: Penguin.
REICH, C.A. (1972), *The Greening of America*. Harmondsworth: Penguin.
Report of the Royal Commission on Trade Unions and Employers' Associations. London: HMSO, Cmnd. 3623.
REYNOLDS, L.T. and MELTZER, B. (1973), 'Origins of Divergent Methodological Stances in Symbolic Interaction', *Sociological Quarterly*, 14 spring, pp. 189–99.
REX, J. (1961), *Key Problems in Sociological Theory*. London: Routledge and Kegan Paul.
REX, J. (1974), *Approaches to Sociology*. London: Routledge and Kegan Paul.
RICE, A.K. (1958), *Productivity and Social Organisation: The Ahmedebad Experiment*. London: Tavistock Publications.
RICE, A.K. (1963), *The Enterprise and its Environment*. London: Tavistock Publications.
RICKMAN, H.P. (1976), *Dilthey: Selected Writings*. London: Cambridge University Press.
RIEFF, P. (1959), *Freud: The Mind Of the Moralist*. London: Gollancz.
ROBERTSON, R. (1974), 'Towards the Identification of the Major Axes of Sociological Analysis', in J. Rex, ed., *Approaches to Sociology*, op. cit.
ROCHER, G. (1974), *Talcott Parsons and American Sociology* (trans. B. and S. Mennell). London: Nelson.
ROETHLISBERGER, F.J. and DICKSON, W.J. (1939), *Management and the Worker*. Cambridge, Mass.: Harvard University Press.
ROSE, A. (1962), *Human Behaviour and Social Processes*. London: Routledge and Kegan Paul.
ROSE, M. (1975), *Industrial Behaviour: Theoretical Development Since Taylor*. Harmondsworth: Allen Lane.
ROSZAK, T. (1969), *The Making of a Counter Culture*. New York: Doubleday and Co.
ROY, D. (1960), 'Banana Time: Job Satisfaction and Informal Interactions', *Human Organisation*, 18 (2), pp. 156–68.
RUNCIMAN, W.G. (1972), *A Critique of Max Weber's Philosophy of Social Science*. London: Cambridge University Press.
RUSSETT, C.E. (1966), *The Concept of Equilibrium in American Sociological Thought*. New Haven: Yale University Press.
SAHLINS, M. (1974), *Stone Age Economics*. London: Tavistock Publications.

SALAMAN, G. and THOMPSON, K., eds. (1973), *People and Organisations*. London: Longman.

SARTRE, J.-P. (1948), *Existentialism and Humanism* (trans. P. Mairet). London: Methuen.

SARTRE, J.-P. (1966), *Being and Nothingness*. New York: Washington Square Press.

SARTRE, J.-P. (1974), *Between Existentialism and Marxism*. London: Pantheon.

SARTRE, J.-P. (1976), *Critique of Dialectical Reason*, vol. I. London: New Left Books.

SAYLES, L.R. (1958), *Behaviour of Industrial Work Groups: Prediction and Control*. New York: John Wiley.

SCHEGLOFF, E.A. and SACKS, H. (1973), 'Opening Up Closings', *Semiotica*, 8 (4), pp. 289–327.

SCHEIN, E. (1970), *Organisational Psychology* (2nd edn). Englewood Cliffs, N.J.: Prentice-Hall.

SCHROYER, TRENT. (1971), 'A Re-Conceptualisation of Critical Theory', in J.D. Colfax and J.L. Roach, eds., *Radical Sociology*, op. cit.

SCHUTZ, A. (1967), *Collected Papers I: The Problem of Social Reality*. (2nd edn). The Hague: Martinus Nijhoff.

SCHUTZ, A. (1964), *Collected Papers II: Studies in Social Theory*. The Hague: Martinus Nijhoff.

SCHUTZ, A. (1966), *Collected Papers III: Studies in Phenomenological Philosophy*. The Hague: Martinus Nijhoff.

SCHUTZ, A. (1967), *The Phenomenology of the Social World* (trans. G. Walsh and F. Lehnert). Evanston: Northwestern University Press.

SCHUTZ, A. and LUCKMANN, T. (1974), *The Structures of the Life World*, London: Heinemann.

SCOTT, J.F. (1963), 'The Changing Foundations of the Parsonian Action Scheme', *American Sociological Review*, 28 (5), pp. 116–35.

SELZNICK, P. (1943), 'An Approach to a Theory of Bureaucracy', *American Sociological Review*, 8 (1), pp. 47–54.

SELZNICK, P. (1948), 'Foundations of the Theory of Organisations', *American Sociological Review*, 13 (1), pp. 25–35.

SELZNICK, P. (1949, 1966), *T.V.A. and The Grass Roots*. 1949 edn, Berkeley, Calif.: University of California Press; 1966 edn, New York: Harper and Row.

SELZNICK, P. (1957), *Leadership in Administration*. New York: Harper and Row.

SHAW, M. (1974), 'The Theory of the State and Politics: A Central Paradox of Marxism', *Economy and Society*, 3 (4), pp. 429–50.
SHAW, M. (1975), *Marxism and Social Science*. London: Pluto.
SILVERMAN, D. (1970), *The Theory of Organisations*. London: Heinemann.
SILVERMAN, D. (1975a), 'Accounts of Organisations – Organisational Structures and the Accounting Process', in J.B. McKinlay, *Processing People: Cases In Organisational Behaviour*, op. cit.
SILVERMAN, D. (1975b), *Reading Castaneda*. London: Routledge and Kegan Paul.
SILVERMAN, D. and JONES, J. (1973), 'Getting In: The Managed Accomplishments of "Correct" Selection Outcomes', in J. Child, ed., *Man and Organisation*, op. cit.
SILVERMAN, D. and JONES, J. (1976), *Organisational Work: The Language of Grading/The Grading of Language*. London and New York: Collier/Macmillan.
SIMMEL, G. (1919), *Nachgelassenes Tagebuch*, Logos VII.
SIMMEL, G. (1936), *The Metropolis and Mental Life*. Chicago: University of Chicago.
SIMMEL, G. (1950), 'The Sociology of Georg Simmel', in K.H. Wolff, *The Sociology of Georg Simmel*, op. cit.
SIMMEL, G. (1955), *Conflict and the Web of Group Affiliations* (trans. K.H. Wolff and R. Bendix). Glencoe, Ill.: Free Press.
SIMON, H.A. (1957), *Administrative Behaviour: A Study of Decision Making Processes in Administrative Organisation* (2nd edn). New York: Collier/Macmillan.
SIMON, H. (1964), 'On the Concept of Organisational Goal', *Administrative Science Quarterly*, 9 (1), pp. 1–22.
SKINNER, B.F. (1953), *Science and Human Behaviour*. New York and London: Macmillan.
SKINNER, B.F. (1957), *Verbal Behaviour*. New York: Appleton-Century-Crofts.
SKINNER, B.F. (1972), *Beyond Freedom and Dignity*. New York: Alfred Knopf.
SNOW, C.P. (1959), *The Two Cultures and the Scientific Revolution*. London: Cambridge University Press.
SPENCER, H. (1873), *The Study of Sociology*. London: Kegan Paul and Tench.
SPIEGELBERG, H. (1965), *The Phenomenological Movement*, vols. I and II. The Hague: Martinus Nijhoff.
STIRNER, M. (1907), *The Ego and His Own*. New York: Libertarian Book Club.

STRYKER, S. (1957). 'Role-taking Accuracy and Adjustment', *Sociometry*, 20, pp. 286–96.

STOUFFER, S.A. (1949), *The American Soldier*. Princeton, N.J.: Princeton University Press.

STRASSER, H. (1976), *The Normative Structure of Sociology*. London: Routledge and Kegan Paul.

STRAUSS, A.L. (1964), *G.H. Mead: On Social Psychology*. Chicago: University of Chicago Press.

SUDNOW, D. (1965), 'Normal Crimes: Sociological Features of the Penal Code in a Public Defender Office', *Social Problems*, 12 (3), pp. 255–76.

SUDNOW, D. (1972), *Studies in Social Interaction*. New York: Free Press.

TANNENBAUM, A.S. (1968), *Control in Organisations*. New York: McGraw Hill.

TAYLOR, F.W. (1947), *Scientific Management*. London and New York: Harper.

TERREBERRY, S. (1968), 'The Evolution of Organisational Environments', *Administrative Science Quarterly*, 12 (4), pp. 590–613.

THÉVENAZ, P. (1962), *What is Phenomenology?* New York: Quadrangle.

THOM, R. (1975), *Structural Stability and Morphogenesis*. New York: Benjamin.

THOMAS, W.I. (1971), 'The Definition of The Situation', in L.A. Coser and B. Rosenberg, *Sociological Theory*, op. cit.

THOMPSON, J.D. (1967), *Organisations in Action*. New York: McGraw Hill.

THORNS, D. (1976), *New Directions in Sociology*. Toronto: Rowmann and Littlefield.

TODD, W. (1968), *Analytical Solipsism*. The Hague: Martinus Nijhoff.

TRIST, E.L. and BAMFORTH, K.W. (1951), 'Some Social and Psychological Consequences of the Longwall Method of Coal-Getting', *Human Relations*, 4 (1), pp. 3–38.

TRIST, E.L., HIGGIN, G.W., MURRAY, H. and POLLOCK, A.B. (1963), *Organisational Choice*. London: Tavistock Publications.

TURNER, A.N. and LAWRENCE, P.R. (1965), *Industrial Jobs and the Worker*. Cambridge, Mass.: Harvard University Press.

TURNER, B.A. (1971), *Exploring the Industrial Subculture*. London: Macmillan.

TURNER, R., ed. (1974), *Ethnomethodology*. Harmondsworth: Penguin.
TUTTLE, H.N. (1969), *Wilheim Dilthey's Philosophy of Historical Understanding*. Leiden: E.J. Brill.
UDY, S. (1959), *Organisation of Work: A Comparative Analysis of Production Among Non-Industrial Peoples*. New Haven: H.R.A.F. Press.
URRY, J. and WAKEFORD, J., eds. (1973), *Power In Britain*. London: Heinemann.
VAN DEN BERGHE, P.L. (1969), 'Dialectic and Functionalism: Towards a Theoretic Synthesis', in W.L. Wallace, ed., *Sociological Theory*, op. cit.
VICKERS, G. (1966), *The Art of Judgement*. London: Chapman and Hall.
VON BERTALANFFY, L. (1950), 'The Theory of Open Systems in Physics and Biology', *Science*, 3.
VON BERTALANFFY, L. (1956), 'General System Theory', *General Systems*, 1, pp. 1–10.
VROOM, V.H. (1964), *Work and Motivation*. New York: John Wiley.
VROOM, V.H. and DECI, E.L. (1970), *Management and Motivation*. Harmondsworth: Penguin.
VROOM, V.H. (1976), 'Leadership', in M.D. Dunnette, ed., *Handbook of Industrial and Organizational Psychology*, op. cit.
WALKER, J. and GUEST, R.H. (1952), *The Man on the Assembly Line*. Cambridge, Mass.: Harvard University Press.
WALLACE, W.L. (1969), *Sociological Theory*. London: Heinemann.
WALTON, P. and GAMBLE, A. (1972), *From Alienation to Surplus Value*. London: Sheed and Ward.
WALSH, D. (1972), 'Varieties of Positivism', in Filmer et al., *New Directions in Sociological Theory*, op. cit.
WARNER, M., ed. (1973), *The Sociology of the Work Place*. London: George Allen and Unwin.
WARNER, W.L. and LOW, J.O. (1947), *The Social System of the Modern Factory*. New Haven: Yale University Press.
WARNOCK, M. (1965), *The Philosophy of Sartre*. London: Hutchinson.
WARR, P.B., ed. (1971), *Psychology at Work*. Harmondsworth: Penguin.
WEBER, M. (1947), *The Theory of Social and Economic Organisation* (trans. A. Henderson and T. Parsons). Glencoe, Ill.: Free Press.

WEBER, M. (1949), *The Methodology of the Social Sciences*. Glencoe, Ill.: Free Press.

WEDDERBURN, D. ed. (1974), *Poverty, Inequality and Class Structure*. London: Cambridge University Press.

WEIR, M., ed. (1976), *Job Satisfaction*. London: Fontana.

WHEELER, S., ed. (1970), *On Record*. New York: Russell Sage.

WHITEHEAD, A.N. (1925), *Science and the Modern World*. London: Macmillan.

WHITEHEAD, T.N. (1938), *The Industrial Worker*. London: Oxford University Press.

WHYTE, W.F. (1948), *Human Relations in the Restaurant Industry*. New York: McGraw Hill.

WHYTE, W.F. (1955), *Money and Motivation*. New York: Harper and Row.

WHYTE, W.F. (1969), *Organisational Behaviour: Theory and Application*. Homewood, Ill.: Irwin-Dorsey.

WILLENER, A. (1971), *The Action Image of Society*. London: Tavistock Publications.

WILLIAMS, R. (1976), 'Symbolic Interaction: The Fusion of Theory and Research', in D. Thorns, ed., *New Directions in Sociology*, op. cit.

WINCH, P. (1958), *The Idea of a Social Science*. London: Routledge and Kegan Paul.

WINKLER, J.T. (1975), 'Law, State and Economy: The Industry Act 1975 in Context', *British Journal of Law and Society* Vol. II, pp. 103–28.

WINKLER, J.T. (1976), 'Corporatism', *European Journal of Sociology*, Vol. 17, No. 1, pp. 100–36.

WISDOM, J.O. (1956), 'The Hypothesis of Cybernetics', *General Systems*, 1, pp. 111–22.

WITTGENSTEIN, L. (1963), *Philosophical Investigations*. Oxford: Blackwell.

WOLFF, K. H. (1950), *The Sociology of Georg Simmel*. Glencoe, Ill.: Free Press.

WOOD, S. (1976), 'The Radicalisation of Industrial Relations Theory', *Personnel Review*, 5 (3), pp. 52–7.

WOOD, S. and ELLIOT, R. (1977), 'A Critical Evaluation of Fox's "Radicalisation" of Industrial Relations Theory', *Sociology*, 11 (1), pp. 105–25.

WOOD, S. and KELLY, J. 'Towards a Critical Management Science', *Journal of Management Studies* (forthcoming).

WOODCOCK, G. (1975), *Anarchism*. Harmondsworth: Penguin.

WOODCOCK, G. (1977), *The Anarchist Reader*. London: Fontana/Collins.

WOODWARD, J. (1958), *Management and Technology*. London: HMSO.

WOODWARD, J. (1965), *Industrial Organisation, Theory and Practice*. London: Oxford University Press.

WOODWARD, J. (1972), *Industrial Organisation: Behaviour and Control*. London: Oxford University Press.

WRONG, D.H. (1968), 'Some Problems in Defining Social Power', *American Journal of Sociology*, 3 (4), pp. 673–81.

ZALD, M.N., ed. (1970), *Power in Organisations*. Vanderbilt: Vanderbilt University Press.

ZEEMAN, E.C. (1976), 'Catastrophe Theory', *Scientific American*, 234 (4), pp. 65–83.

ZIMMERMAN, D.H. (1970a), 'The Practicalities of Rule Use', in J.D. Douglas, ed., *Understanding Everyday Life*, op. cit.

ZIMMERMAN, D.H. (1970b), 'Record Keeping and the Intake Process in a Public Welfare Organisation', in S. Wheeler, ed., *On Record*, op. cit.

ZIMMERMAN, D.H. and POLLNER, M. (1970), 'The Everyday World as a Phenomenon', in J.D. Douglas, ed., *Understanding Everyday Life*, op. cit.

ZIMMERMAN, D.H. and WIEDER, D.L. (1970), 'Ethnomethodology and the Problem of Order', in J.D. Douglas, ed., *Understanding Everyday Life*, op. cit.

ZOLLSCHAN, G.K. and HIRSCH, W., eds. (1964), *Explorations in Social Change*. London: Routledge and Kegan Paul.

Subject Index

Name Index